REDWOOD WRITING PROJECT
Evaluating Writing

Evaluating Writing

The Role of Teachers' Knowledge about Text, Learning, and Culture

Edited by

Charles R. Cooper
University of California–San Diego

Lee Odell
Rensselaer Polytechnic Institute

National Council of Teachers of English
1111 W. Kenyon Road, Urbana, Illinois 61801-1096

Prepress: City Desktop Productions

Interior Design: Doug Burnett
Cover Design: Carlton Bruett

NCTE Stock Number: 16256-3050

Library of Congress Cataloging-in-Publication Data

Evaluating writing : the role of teachers' knowledge about text, learning, and
   culture / edited by Charles R. Cooper, Lee Odell.
      p.   cm.
   Includes bibliographical references.
   ISBN 0-8141-1625-6
   1. English language—Rhetoric—Study and teaching. 2. English language—
Composition and exercises. 3. English language—Rhetoric—Ability testing.
4. Report writing—Evaluation. 5. School prose—Evaluation. I. Cooper,
Charles Raymond, 1934–   . II. Odell, Lee, 1940–   .
PE1404.E93 1998
428′.007—dc21   98-37174
                                                                            CIP

Contents

v

Introduction: Evaluating Student Writing—What Can We Do, and What Should We Do?

Charles R. Cooper
University of California–San Diego

Lee Odell
Rensselaer Polytechnic Institute

When it comes to the evaluation of student writing, we school and college English teachers often find ourselves right at the center of a controversy. From one perspective come arguments in favor of evaluation, even for more frequent and more rigorous evaluation. Many parents tell us they have a right to know exactly how their children are doing, whether they are measuring up, whether they are on track for admission to college and a successful career. School administrators and citizens groups contend that schools must be "accountable," that there must be some form of public evidence—most often a score on a state or local assessment—that will indicate whether we are doing our jobs, especially the job of helping students meet "world-class standards." Faculty in other departments complain to us about their students' writing. And our own experience as learners and as teachers leads us to think that we have some sort of responsibility to help our students see where they are doing well and where their writing needs improvement.

From other perspectives come doubts about whether we should, or even can, evaluate students' writing. Both research and practical experience demonstrate that people often disagree radically about the quality of a particular piece of writing. What one person sees as an outstanding piece of work, someone else may consider mediocre or even unacceptable. Consequently, critics are often justified in arguing that our judgments may reflect only idiosyncratic values that we impose arbitrarily and unfairly on students, especially students who come from backgrounds different from our own. Other critics may argue that evaluation can distract us from the business of teaching and may even be unnecessary.

So here we stand—in our classrooms, with our students—beset by arguments that seem as contradictory as they are compelling. What can we do? What should we do? Every essay in this book is intended to speak to these questions and to help all of us take part in this ongoing debate. These essays represent a variety of approaches to evaluation. But underlying all of them are some common beliefs about what is fundamentally important to our work as writing teachers. Specifically, these articles assume that we need to:

- distinguish between *evaluation* and *grading*;
- develop our ability to describe students' writing;
- connect teaching and evaluation; and
- continually reexamine the assumptions and practices that guide our evaluation of student writing.

Distinguishing between Evaluation and Grading

People routinely talk as though evaluation and grading mean essentially the same thing. They do not. A grade or numerical ranking represents simply a final judgment about how well or poorly one has written a particular piece of writing. Evaluation, by contrast, can happen at any point in the writing process, and it specifically addresses all the issues that a grade or numerical score cannot. *Evaluation* may entail looking not only at students' final drafts, but also at their notes or early drafts. Evaluation requires us to answer all the hard questions that students should ask but often do not know, or dare, to ask: What, specifically, seems strong about my work? What is not so strong? What might I do to make some progress, either in revising this draft or in working on a comparable assignment in the future?

Describing Students' Writing

To answer these difficult questions, we have to be able to describe students' work. In part, this means that we have to get better at identifying specific passages in a text and explaining how we react to those passages. This work is important for helping students to understand how readers respond to their texts. But it is not enough. Even when students understand how readers are responding, they still need to understand the craft of writing. They—and we—need language that will let them understand what is going on in their texts, what they have done that is influencing the ways readers are responding.

The problem is that we have inherited a lot of evaluative language simply that is not very descriptive or useful. Consider, for example, familiar terms like "logical/illogical," "well-thought-out/superficial," or "reasonable/unreasonable." Such terms may capture perfectly our reaction to a particular piece of writing. And if we have been well trained in holistic scoring, we might be able to apply them in ways with which other readers will agree. But if we say to a student that his or her writing seems illogical, what have we told this student? Do we mean that a particular statement is inconsistent with something he or she has said elsewhere? That the student is not considering the consequences of what he or she is proposing? That a claim is not based on reliable information? That the student has said something that we happen not to believe? Further, what might this student do to become more logical?

Fortunately, we have access to language that is much more precise and descriptive and, thus, much more useful to both students and teachers. Most of the chapters in this book will introduce this language and suggest ways in which we (and our students) might use it in helping students to grow as writers. In Part I, Charles Cooper shows us some ways to identify how successfully students are using the resources available in different genres, and Phyllis Ryder and her colleagues discuss what we might say to students about how well they are meeting the needs of their audiences. Lee Odell explains how we might describe students' thinking, William Strong provides ways to talk about the variety and effectiveness of students' sentence structures, Martha Kolln shows how we can make sense of breakdowns in cohesion and coherence, and Sandra Murphy shows us ways of assessing writing portfolios.

Part II presents ways we might describe and learn from writing in other disciplines: Richard Millman discusses assessment in mathematics, Denise Levine in science, Richard Beach in literature, and Kathy Medina in social studies. Further, Part III helps us to recognize and understand the distinctive qualities of writing done by particular groups of students: Arnetha Ball discusses the language patterns that show up in the writing of some African American students, Guanjun Cai focuses on the writing of Asian American students, and Guadalupe Valdés and Patricia Sanders describe distinctive characteristics of writing done by Hispanic American students. To complete this volume, Part IV presents four different essays on issues tied to assessment of writing: Chris Anson expresses his concern that teachers become more reflective about how they respond to writing; Sandra Murphy and Mary Ann Smith advocate a major role for students in the evaluation of their writing portfolios; and Fran Claggett and Roxanne Mountford, in their respective essays, focus on specific issues tied to large-scale assessment of writing.

Connecting Teaching and Evaluation

Inevitably, there will be times when we, as teachers or as writers, will want to put evaluation as far out of our minds as we can. Writers sometimes need simply to plunge in, writing as fast and as much as possible, forcing themselves to suspend judgment on what they are producing. Nevertheless, there are ways in which the evaluation of writing and the teaching of writing are so closely interconnected that we cannot think of one without thinking of the other. The most important interconnection— and sometimes the most difficult to acknowledge—is that our values and value judgments permeate almost every act we perform as teachers. If we choose to do a lesson on, say, showing vs. telling, we are implying that, in at least some instances, writing that shows is better than writing that tells. We may not talk of grades, we may not explicitly use the words *good*, *better*, or *best*, but we do praise students when their personal or *observational* writing becomes more concrete, vivid, and memorable. The question, then, is not whether we can separate teaching and evaluating, but rather, whether the value judgments that get made—by us or by our students—will help them to become better writers.

Giving students this help involves another connection between evaluation and teaching: planning our classes so that students have time for in-process reflection on their writing. Maybe we ask them to get reactions from their peers, or maybe we ask them to talk with us (or write to us) about where their writing seems to be effective and what they are going to do to make it even more effective. Whatever strategy we use, we have to plan our teaching so that some sort of evaluation— not grading, but *evaluation*, an assessment of strengths and weaknesses in a piece of writing—occurs before a final draft is written.

To provide this evaluation, we will have to make yet another connection between evaluation and teaching. In addition to allowing class time for students to assess their own or each other's work, we will also need to devote class time to showing them how to do this sort of work effectively. As Karen Spear has pointed out, we cannot just assume that students will automatically know how to talk productively about their own or their classmates' writing. They may focus exclusively on editorial/proofreading matters, or they may offer highly arbitrary advice that ignores the purposes the writer is trying to accomplish in his or her writing. If students are to learn how to respond helpfully to a written text, especially if they are to help a writer assess a text's strengths and weaknesses, we'll have to spend class time teaching them how to do this. Specifically, we will have to work with them to develop an understanding of particular writing assignments so that their efforts at working in peer-response groups, assessing their own work, and revising their drafts can be more focused and productive.

There is at least one more connection between teaching and evaluation, the difficult and unsettling connection between what we do in our classrooms and what students are expected to do in large-scale assessment programs at the local, state, or national level. At worst, this connection may involve so much "teaching to the test" that teachers ignore students' needs and even replace serious instruction in writing with mindless drill or work on sterile "test prep" materials. These assessment programs may seem to loom so large that they become the tail that wags the dog. But let us be candid on two points.

First, bad, large-scale assessments can be truly bad, especially those that consist principally of short-answer, "objective" questions. These can only trivialize writing instruction and subvert the efforts of good writing teachers. Many of the best assessment programs, however, are well informed by good instructional practice. They may, as does the California writing assessment, ask students to write in different genres to different audiences; they may, as in the English Language Arts New Standards Reference Exam, allow students to read, discuss ideas, write a draft, and get peer feedback before writing a revised draft; or they may, as with the English Language Arts New Standards Portfolio System, involve students in the process of evaluation, asking them to write self-assessments and to select the pieces which will go into their portfolios for evaluation.

The second point on which we must be candid is this: In far too many cases, the dog badly needs to be wagged. In, perhaps, the majority of American classrooms, students rarely write anything longer than a paragraph. And in far too many, students write only five-paragraph "themes" for a single audience (usually the teacher) and for a single purpose (displaying knowledge). Or they do only informal journal writing, never producing extended, revised, public texts. If large-scale assessment accomplishes nothing else, it will do everyone an enormous favor by helping to change instructional practices in these classrooms.

In one way or another, most of the essays in this book try to help us make the connection between teaching and evaluation. All of the chapters that emphasize describing written texts suggest a vocabulary that teachers and students can come to share.

Examining Assumptions and Practices

During the past twenty years or so, our profession has learned a lot about assessment. We have learned how to design better assignments, whether for our own classes or for large-scale assessments. We have, for example, become better at thinking through the demands of our assignments, and we have become much more careful about seeing that students are writing to a specific audience for a specific purpose. But whatever we have accomplished thus far, we still have more to learn.

When we put together a collection on this topic two decades ago—*Evaluating Writing: Describing, Measuring, Judging* (1977)—our work as teachers and evaluators was more difficult and, at the same time, much easier than it is now. The difficulty came chiefly from the fact that our profession had produced little information about evaluating students' writing. Confronted with stacks of student papers, we seemed to be pretty much on our own. We had no disciplinary body of knowledge to guide our actions or to help justify our decisions. Most of our training as teachers focused on how to teach literature, not how to assess what our students were doing as they tried to learn to read and write. This fact, however, also made life appear to be simpler: lacking information, we could just proceed on intuition and on the (often tacit) assumptions we had inherited from our own teachers. We could do unto others as we had been done unto without having to think too much about the matter.

The problem was (and in too many cases, still is) that we were working from what has been called a "practical stylist" rhetoric. This rhetoric focused mainly on matters of style and correctness; it had nothing to say about the problems writers and evaluators encounter when writing is done for different audiences and different purposes, and it had very little to say about the processes by which writers explore their ideas and experiences in order to figure out what they want to say.

In contrast to our predecessors, we now have access to a lot of information—about, for example, how written language differs from talk or conversation and how dialect, register, and genre interact. We also know, for example, a good bit about how writers move through the composing process, how language and organization may vary according to a writer's audience and purpose, how writing is viewed by different cultural and ethnic groups, and how writers can make their sentences "flow." To help us place our own assignments and expectations in context, we know a great deal more about writing in the community, on the job, and in the various academic disciplines. We know that writing makes a powerful contribution to learning in all disciplines, and we now know how that happens.

With increased information, however, also comes increased responsibility. It is no longer enough, for example, to tell students that their writing seems "disorganized" or that their sentences seem "choppy." We now know how to help students organize their writing in different writing situations, some calling for narrative, some for categorization of information, and still others requiring step-by-step logical argument. Further, we are now able (and obliged) to show students how their texts can be made more cohesive or how their sentences can do more powerful work.

We can no longer approach all writing with one set of criteria, assuming that one size fits all. It may be that, ultimately, we value some highly general qualities, such as "organization" or "quality of ideas." But we now know that the strategies that make for good organization in a personal experience narrative may differ from the strategies that make a good report of information or a good persuasive letter. And we need to help students understand what those differences are, both by the way we teach and the way we evaluate their writing.

The contributors to the current volume hope that it will advance our understanding of evaluation, especially as it relates to teaching. But we also hope that as we teach and evaluate, we will continue to learn, not only about our students and their texts, but also about what we hope to teach and what we value.

As with the first volume, this one began at an NCTE Annual Convention during an all-day, preconvention workshop. We thank the NCTE Assembly for Research, who sponsored that workshop. We also thank Michael Greer, NCTE's Director of Acquisitions, who worked closely with us during a three-day, weekend review of penultimate drafts of all the chapters.

1 Describing Texts

For nearly thirty years, writing teachers in schools and colleges have been working out the implications of several, fundamentally important insights about the teaching of writing:

- That writing a text is a process that unfolds over time through a sequence of stages—invention or prewriting, drafting, revising, editing, reflecting on what has been accomplished; that these stages are recursive, for example, with invention continuing during revising; and that these stages present different possibilities and problems for writers.
- That writing instruction need not be fragmented into units or sentences, and then paragraphs, and then, finally, real writing; that we should ask students for authentic multiparagraph writing and then help them with their sentences and paragraphs within the context of that writing.
- That writing assignments should be given and writing projects defined within a full social (or communicative) situation so that students will understand their purposes and readers, whether the situation requires convincing other students to take action to resolve a school or community problem, explaining unfamiliar information to readers who may have a need to know it, or convincing a teacher that something has been learned.
- That writing is different from talk and must be learned attentively, consciously.
- That talk does play an important role in learning to write, through discussions of assignments, models, and criteria and through collaboration among students and between students and their teachers, as in conferences or peer workshops over work-in-progress.

1

- That writing is both free and constrained—both highly creative in that the next sentence is always a surprise and also highly conventional in that all writers work with a limited, describable syntactic repertoire and a set of culturally determined, widely recognized genres; that the conventions act as constraints but also as heuristics, making possible certain kinds of creative work at both the sentence and text levels, especially for developing writers.

- That self-reflection or self-evaluation in writing enables students to consolidate and remember longer what they have learned about writing.

These insights have transformed our thinking about literacy, and all of the authors in *Evaluating Writing* strive to organize instruction and evaluate students' writing in light of them. Not a list from which to choose two or three particular viewpoints, this collection is, rather, an interrelated set of principles that demand a lot of writing teachers by way of knowledge and practice.

The set of insights that now guides the work of knowledgable teachers has, we believe, one limitation: It no more than implies the importance of teachers' knowledge about written texts, knowledge that seems as important to us as knowledge about planning and sequencing activities for a writing assignment. All of our planning and effort leads toward the moment when a student hands us a draft or revison or portfolio. At that moment the question becomes what we can say about that text that will be most helpful to the student. We believe knowledge about texts to be the next frontier in our efforts to improve literacy.

The authors in Part I aim to expand our repertoire of strategies for describing students' texts. Each chapter includes students' texts and demonstrations of what might be said about them.

What *can* be said on the basis of our knowledge about texts will, we believe, help us to provide more helpful answers to the familiar questions we all ask continually about our students' writing: Where does this draft seem strong or weak, full of potential or full of holes? What kind of thinking about the subject is going on in this draft? What other kinds of thinking would help this student realize her purpose? What resources for this writing situation does the student need to learn more about? How can this student better anticipate readers' questions? How can these awkward sentences be strengthened? How can this section be made to flow so that readers will not be diverted and lose momentum? What can this portfolio tell me about this student's work and achievement in my class?

These are the kinds of questions the contributors will address in Part I. In these essays, the contributors' answers will be grounded not only in theory and research, but also in years of classroom experience, from middle school through college. And in all cases, the contributors assume that if we are to link instruction and evaluation, we must have ways to describe students' work, ways to help them look at their texts and to see what they are doing well and what they might begin doing, stop doing, or do differently.

Lee Odell, in Chapter 1, addresses ways we might assess the thinking reflected in students' work, while avoiding the trap of valuing thoughts that agree with our own and devaluing thinking we happen to disagree with. He argues that "important elements of the thinking process are conscious, knowable, and teachable" and demonstrates that "the thinking process leaves fingerprints all over a finished text." Pointing out that we should expect different kinds of thinking in different writing situations, Odell analyzes the thinking in an argument, a personal narrative, and an interpretation of literature.

Charles Cooper, in Chapter 2, offers a current definition of "genre" and outlines several influential classifications of genres (or types) of writing. His aim is to show that genres are not arbitrary forms, but social processes and cultural productions without which communication would be impossible. Relying on high school seniors' texts, he demonstrates how genre knowledge might inform our responses to four different kinds of texts valued in secondary school English programs: writing that takes a position, reflects on experience, narrates a remembered event, or interprets a literary text. After describing the unique characteristics of each of these genres, Cooper outlines genre-specific criteria that teachers and students might use to evaluate student essays. Cooper concludes by outlining one way to integrate evaluation into a genre assignment, giving students a major role as evaluators.

In Chapter 3, Phyllis Ryder, Elizabeth Vander Lei, and Duane Roen sample the vast amount of knowledge that has accumulated from classical times to the present about the role of audience (or readers) in writing. Focusing on various kinds of writer-audience relationships, they demonstrate how writers invoke audiences through various kinds of "moves" in their writing and how teachers can help them do so more effectively. These moves are textual—specific cues and information the writer includes in order to connect with readers and hold their interest. To illustrate how writers invoke audiences through various textual moves, the authors rely on excerpts from junior high, high school, and college students' essays. They explain how knowledge of audience relationships might influence how we give essay assignments, assign and respond to journal writing, set out assignments for co-authored essays, help students plan audience roles in workshops, and guide students in audience choices for academic writing.

William Strong, in Chapter 4, relies on James Moffett's growth sequences for syntax to "identify specific features of syntax that can be viewed developmentally, either when evaluating writing or when coaching students to expand their repertoires of sentence-level moves." Relying on texts written by students in grades 6, 11, and 12, Strong demonstrates the reality of syntactic development through a close look at the sentence options students choose. He explains how a developmental view of syntax helps us recognize when a student may be on a "syntactic threshold," that is, ready to risk new syntactic options which may lead temporarily to errors. He closes his introduction to syntax by demonstrating how genres like reportage, argument, and interpretation invite quite different kinds of sentences. Strong's aim is twofold: to trace syntactic development and to introduce the kinds of knowledge about syntax that writing teachers need in order to observe and encourage this development.

In Chapter 5, Martha Kolln introduces perhaps the least familiar area of knowledge about texts included in Part I—the system of cohesion that holds texts together from sentence to sentence, a system that contributes to the perceived coherence of a text. Much about cohesion is familiar to English teachers—pronoun reference, conjunctions, repetition of key words—but Kolln focuses on three aspects of sentence cohesion that remain invisible in school and college grammar handbooks: the ordering of sentence information known and new to readers, the control of sentence rhythm to throw stress on certain information, and the principle of end focus. Relying on excerpts from college students' writing, Kolln demonstrates that this unfamiliar and perhaps seemingly esoteric knowledge about written texts helps us to explain certain intuitions we frequently have about student writing that seems entirely correct but is nevertheless occasionally hard to follow or slightly out of focus.

Both Strong and Kolln are concerned not with correctness—as important as the conventions of usage and mechanics may be for students' writing development—but with clarity, readability, and style. For example, since readers remember primarily the gist of a text, writers can, through careful arrangement of known and new information in their sentences, keep in readers' view the main ideas from which readers create meaning. In this—and other—ways, writers guide readers to understand what is important in written texts. Strong and Kolln implicitly argue that syntactic fluency and cohesion offer goals for instruction that enable us to raise our expectations for students.

To close Part I, Sandra Murphy, in Chapter 6, proposes that we conceive a portfolio of student writing as a text itself and suggests that we evaluate this text on "dimensions of performance and learning derived from curriculum standards." These dimensions might include breadth and versatility of students' writing, quality of self-reflection, technical competence, and processes used in creating text. Knowledge about written texts offered in other Part I chapters would, as Murphy points out, contribute in important ways to readers' evaluation of "breadth" and "technical competence" in her proposed dimensional-scoring scheme. Dimensional scoring, of course, depends on curriculum standards like those promulgated in 1995 by the National Council of Teachers of English, which focus on processes and activities rather than grade-level standards of achievement in various kinds of writing. The controversy surrounding the NCTE standards suggests that the debate over curriculum standards in English—and hence over evaluating students' writing achievement—will be with us for some time. In the meantime, teachers, who are accountable every day to individual students and their parents, may want to experiment with dimensional evaluations of end-of-course portfolios. These could be supplemented with careful descriptions of one or more individual texts in order to show what a student has learned to do in particular writing situations.

The Part I authors provide only an introduction to various ways of describing texts. Each chapter concludes, however, with suggested further reading. If we succeed in convincing you that learning more about written texts will make you a better writing teacher, then we encourage you to begin the demanding but rewarding work of mastering this domain of knowledge. It need not be a solitary effort. College writing workshops in various genres—autobiography, argument, reportage, prose fiction, poetry, nature writing, family history and geneology—may be available. Inservice programs focusing on describing student texts in several genres might be arranged. Informal study groups with colleagues may be possible. And do not overlook what can be learned about text by writing different kinds of texts on your own or with your students.

As you read the chapters in Part I, you will notice that the authors do not necessarily advocate that you systematically teach thinking taxonomies, genre theory, syntactic categories, cohesion analysis, or dimensional scoring to your students. While the authors do occasionally refer to classroom materials and to activities they or others have developed, they seek primarily to convince you that current knowledge about written texts will make you a more confident, helpful writing teacher. Your understanding of students and your experience in the classroom will guide you in translating this knowledge into language, guidelines, or activities appropriate for your students. For example, you might want to plan whole-class demonstrations and activities—many are available for use or adaptation—or you might decide to use your text knowledge primarily when you confer with individual students or respond in writing to drafts to be revised.

1 Assessing Thinking: Glimpsing a Mind at Work

Lee Odell
Rensselaer Polytechnic Institute

When we assess students' writing, there's a good chance that, sooner or later, we will begin to talk about the thinking reflected in that writing. Sometimes we comment on the extent to which a text reflects "depth of thought" (Tierney, Carter, and Desai 1991, 98) or whether a writer's statements seem reasonable or logical or well considered. Other discussions may involve somewhat different terminology, with people commenting on whether a piece of writing seems sensitive, creative, or perceptive. In these latter discussions, we may not be concerned with logic or critical thinking, but we are still assuming that a text reflects a mind at work, a writer wondering about things, trying to make sense of feelings or perceptions, trying to imagine what *might* be.

This concern with a mind at work seems especially appropriate if we see writing as an act of discovery, an act of constructing meaning. In order to construct meaning, one has to be able to explore, imagine, analyze, speculate, observe—in short, to think. If this ability to think is essential for effective writing, an assessment of a student's writing should give us some insight into the thinking reflected in that writing.

But how is this possible? How can we assess thinking by looking at a written text? After all, thinking is a process, a series of actions taken over time. What can a product tell us about this process? Furthermore, what will count as evidence of thinking? How can we avoid the trap of equating "good thinking" with writing that just happens to agree with our biases or preconceptions? And what do we mean by *thinking*, anyway?

This last question may seem especially difficult, for there are limits to what we can know or say about thinking. The process is complex, it happens quickly, and it often entails imaginative leaps that are difficult to explain and impossible to predict. Moreover, no finished text can reflect all the thinking processes that went into creating that text. Nonetheless, our situation as teachers and as evaluators is not hopeless.

For one thing, important elements of the thinking process are conscious, knowable, and teachable. These elements consist of strategies, actions people can take to gather and reflect on information and to stimulate the creative process. Further, it's possible to find some evidence of these strategies reflected in a completed product. In effect, the thinking process leaves fingerprints all over a finished text.

As we learn to recognize strategies reflected in a completed text, we can talk more confidently about why that text seems (or doesn't seem) thoughtful, perceptive, sensitive, etc. And in so doing, we can solve some additional problems that often give us trouble as both teachers and evaluators. That is, we can improve our ability to (1) explain our value judgments; (2) look past surface errors to see the strengths of writing by nonmainstream students; and (3) integrate the assessment of writing and the assessment of students' interpretation of literary texts.

Understanding Thinking

When we start asking what we mean by *thinking,* we quickly encounter an unusual problem: It's not that we have too few potential answers to our question; if anything, we can find too many. We can draw on work from such diverse fields as cognitive psychology, philosophy, reading, and rhetoric, each discipline presenting its own perspective, sometimes overlapping with others, sometimes diverging, sometimes proceding as if no other discipline had anything to say about the matter. At the risk of oversimplifying, here's a synthesis of this work, an effort to sketch out the broad outlines of what people do when they think. (A more detailed discussion appears in Odell 1993.)

One key element of the thinking process entails what cognitive psychologists refer to as *dissonance*—a sense that things just don't add up, that our understanding is incomplete, that something is incongruous. We may be able to articulate a fairly specific question, problem, irony, conflict, etc. Or maybe we just feel some sort of undefined itch, some sense that things aren't quite right or that we'd like to try something new, if for no better reason than we wonder if we could actually do it.

As we engage in the thinking process, we have to recognize that we can't pay attention to everything that's going on. Common sense, not to mention theory and research, tells us that to understand anything, we have to be able to *select,* to pay attention to some things, deemphasize others, and completely ignore others. As we do this, we also have to *encode,* or represent, whatever we've selected. We may do this in a variety of ways—with visual images, music, or numbers, for example, as well as written or spoken language. Whatever medium we choose, we have to find some way to represent to ourselves and others what we are thinking, feeling, observing, remembering, reading.

In doing all this, we may engage—probably simultaneously—in several other processes: *drawing on prior knowledge,* trying to see how a present experience relates to what we already know; *seeing relationships,* asking, in effect, how one thing causes another, how things are similar or different, how something interacts with its physical or social setting; and *considering different perspectives,* perhaps trying to empathize with another person or asking how someone else's perceptions or interpretations might differ from our own.

This synthesis of work on thinking leads to a series of questions that can help us (and our students) gain some insight into how they are currently constructing meaning about a particular topic and what they might continue doing (or do differently) in the future (for an elaboration of these questions, see Appendix A):

> *Dissonance:* What sort of problems, ambiguities, ironies, questions, uncertainties, or conflicts do students mention (or overlook)?
>
> *Selecting:* What kinds of information (observations, "facts," personal experiences, feelings, memories) do students include in or exclude from their writing?
>
> *Encoding/Representing:* What sort of language do students use to articulate their ideas (feelings, perceptions, memories)?
>
> *Drawing on Prior Knowledge:* Do students explicitly refer to things they already know in order to understand something new?
>
> *Seeing Relationships:* What kinds of relationships (cause-effect, time, if . . . then, similarity, difference) do students mention in their writing?
>
> *Considering Different Perspectives:* To what extent do students try to consider ways in which other people might perceive, interpret, or respond to a given idea, fact, or experience?

These sets of questions won't tell us everything students thought or did during the composing process. Moreover, they do not constitute a checklist which can be applied indiscriminately in all situations. Sometimes it makes sense to focus on one or two questions; sometimes it helps to consider several or all of them. But in either case, these questions can help us see how a student text, or, indeed, any text, reflects a mind at work. That is, they can help us recognize students' use of strategies that are essential to making sense of what they read, feel, observe, or remember. They will give us a way to explain what we mean when we say that a text seems well thought out, sensitive, imaginative, and so forth.

Further, as I hope the next section of this chapter will illustrate, these questions can help us to assess very different types of student writing: personal experience narratives, for example, as well as persuasive letters and interpretations of literature. This is not to ignore important differences between various types of writing (see Cooper, this volume; Odell 1981). A personal experience narrative intended for a close friend may require a writer to select details or consider questions that may not be equally appropriate for a persuasive text intended for an unsympathetic audience. In writing a biology laboratory report, students might not draw on the same kinds of prior knowledge they would need in writing, for example, a history essay. But whatever the type of discourse and whatever the academic subject, both teachers and students need to consider the kinds of details students have selected, the kinds of questions they have asked, the kinds of relationships they have considered, and so on. As we consider such matters, both we and our students can begin to see how they might create or revise a text so that it helps them achieve a particular goal for a particular audience.

Looking at Students' Texts

In examining student texts, we inevitably run into a basic fact of human perception: What we see in a text is not simply a matter of observing what's "really there" and immediately apparent to anyone who can read English. What we see is heavily influenced not only by our values, past experiences, and expectations, but also by the language we use in talking about those texts. The questions suggested in the preceding section can't change this situation, but they do provide us with means to solve problems we often face in evaluating writing, particularly the three areas of concern mentioned earlier in this essay.

Articulating Value Judgments

Whether or not we choose to assign grades, we continually find ourselves making value judgments about students' work, remarking on whether a given piece of writing seems perceptive, imaginative, thoughtful, or engaging. Where we run into trouble is in trying to articulate these value judgments, especially when we try to explain to students why one piece of writing is better than another or why one piece of writing meets a certain standard and another does not.

This problem can be especially difficult when papers seem, in many respects, comparable. Here, for example, are excerpts from two essays in which, as part of a statewide writing assessment, students were to influence a school board's decision on whether to install metal detectors in the local high school. Although students were free to argue pro or con on this issue, both of the following writers opposed the installation of metal detectors. And both writers base their arguments, in part, on the likelihood that the metal detectors would cause students substantial delays in entering and leaving the school building. Despite these similarities, the students' papers reflect differences in thinking, differences that seem likely to make one argument more persuasive than the other.

The first student begins the essay by arguing that the money for metal detectors could be better spent on educational materials and supplies. The student then goes on to argue that

> I also feel that the metal detectors will cause much confusion before and after school when large masses of people want to enter the school (as well as be on time for class) and exit the building. Of course with every product (especially with one such as this) there will be many defects. Defects such as false alarms. There are many students who wear braces on their teeth, this may cause a false alarm. Things such as jewlry [*sic*], belt buckles, and zippers can cause false alarms. We can imagine all the confusion that can arise from a false alarm. A visitor to the school can be guilty of causing a false alarm, and thus, leaving the school in an uproar. The metal detectors will also slow down the students' speed when leaving the building in the event of a fire alarm or even a real fire. (*Writing Collection* 1993, G-25)

The second student begins by asserting that the presence of metal detectors would reinforce the student's view that "our school is like a prison" and that the use of such devices would be a "violation of our personal rights." The writer continues thus

> Next, just think how long it will take to check every person in the school. Encluding [*sic*] teachers and staff. We would have to lengthen our school day so that this could be done, and that's not fair. Our days are long enough without having to stand in line to go through a metal detector every morning. And what if it is accidentally triggered by someone's belt buckle or something similar. It takes even more time to check that person. No one wants to spend time to be searched, and waiting in line to be searched. (*Writing Collection* 1993, G-20)

Despite the similarities between these two excerpts, there are substantial differences in the thinking each reflects. Probably the most important difference is that the first student appears to have adopted the perspective of his or her readers, a group of adults who are likely to value orderliness and safety, not to mention the reaction of visitors to the school. The second student seems to be taking essentially a student's perspective, arguing on the basis of what is "fair" or convenient to a student.

This fundamental difference in thinking is echoed in all the other thinking strategies reflected in the two students' work. Consider the way these students encode their arguments. Both students use words and phrases that have emotional connotations. But the first student uses terms (*confusion, uproar*) that are likely to resonate with the values of an audience concerned with safety and good order. By contrast, terms used by the second student (*prison, violation of rights, not fair*) reflect the values of an aggrieved student.

A similar pattern appears in these students' efforts to see relationships and select details in support of their arguments. Both students describe hypothetical cause-effect relationships in which metal detectors register false alarms and create delays in entering and leaving the school building. But these hypothetical scenarios differ greatly in their plausibility. The first student selects a range of details that illustrates convincingly the probability of false alarms. Granted, it may seem unlikely that braces on someone's teeth would set off an alarm, but the other items mentioned (belt buckles, jewelry, zippers) should ring true for school board members who have waited in airport security lines where an alarm has been set off by some small, seemingly innocuous item. In selecting these details, the first student seems to have considered the matter more carefully than does the second student in that writer's general reference to "someone's belt buckle or something similar."

In all of this analysis, of course, I have been making some assumptions about what school board members are likely to need or value. These assumptions seem justified by my own experience, but I might be wrong about the specific school board that the second student had in mind. Maybe that school board contained members who are especially concerned about students' personal reactions and feelings. Maybe school board members were already aware of potential problems with metal detectors and therefore didn't need much elaboration as to what might set off false alarms. In such a case, the second student may have a considerably better argument than I have suggested. For purposes of a large-scale assessment, I have to rely on my best guess about the audience that the student is to address. But for purposes of working with a student in my own classroom, the preceding analysis would be just one part of an ongoing conversation with the student.

This conversation would begin well before the student writes a draft, back at a point where we negotiate some understanding of the values, needs, and knowledge of a particular audience, or even farther back where we discuss the importance of understanding the perspective of the audience for a given text. Given a common understanding of audience, it's possible for me—or for members of a peer-response group—to tell the student whether he or she seems to have described an appropriate cause-effect relationship or has selected compelling details. And it's also possible for the student to respond to criticism by saying something like "Yeah, I did select details X, Y, and Z, but what you're forgetting about the audience is . . ." or, "Yeah, that cause-effect relationship is not so hot. But what about these other scenarios over here on page 2? Don't they make good sense?" In effect, then, having a common way to talk about thinking can help open up the assessment process, making it more accessible and less mysterious to students, thereby enabling them not only to challenge the assessments of others, but also to make more informed assessments of their own work, assessments which they can use in revising a text or working on subsequent texts.

Looking Past Surface Errors

Increasingly, teachers at all grade levels find themselves working with nonmainstream students, many of whom are not native speakers of English or who come from homes where standard English is not spoken. Often, these students represent an extreme version of a familiar problem: Without denying the need for students to master the conventions of Standard Written English, how do we look past "errors" in order to assess a student's rhetorical or communicative ability? Consider, for example, the following narrative written by a middle school student:

When We Were Alone

It was a dark evening. My aunt Joaquina called from Mexico, Almost crying. She called my mom to tell her that my grandpa was very sick. My dad set down with me on a chair by the porch of my house. All of us were very sad. He said. "come here and sit down with me. You know your aunt Joaquina called from Mexico. Because your grandpa is very sick maybe he's all ready to died" He put his head dow. I kind of get like in shock for a while. I just couldn't believe it. My mom was fixing up to go. My dad went to our neighbors house. My dad went to tell them what was happening in our house and call to America Airlines to see which airplane was ready to go. They say at 11:00'o clock was going to go a airline to Mexico. My mom said that she was very scared when she was at the airport at Mexico because she was all by her self. My mom got to Juventino Rosas at 4:30 a. m. in the morning she said that my grandpa was already dead.

We were worried by my mom. That knight we slept at 11:00'o clock the first night that my mom was not with us I felt like an orphan because I didn't have my mom. Those days were terrible for me. My dad use to left to work and [take] all of my brothers and me to school. After school one of my aunts use to pick us up. She left us in our house when I open the door of my house, it was all alone from the inside without my mom when she was here she use to be always doing something. Alot of people use to envite me to there house, in my same neighborhood to go eat with them, but I never went instead of that I got mad, because I use to think that they were treating me like some kind of invalid. I didn't like that at all.

All of the people were getting ready for Christmas. But I was very sad we didn't know what to do. A good friend of my mom invite us to her house to pass Chrismas with them. We went over to her house my friend was there too. We were singing Chistmas songs we were happy but at the same time I was very sad because this was our first Chistmas with out my mom. But know that I'm with my mom again, I've been thinking how alot of children feel with out there moms. Now I always give thanks to god that I have all of my family complete.

Obviously, this personal experience essay contains errors in syntax, usage, and spelling. But the piece is also a sensitive, powerful narrative that shows the student using many of the meaning-making strategies described in this chapter. Much of the power of this piece comes from the way she encodes her experience. Throughout, this student's language reflects the perspective of someone who is young and, in some respects, naive. She refers to *my mom, my dad, my grandpa* instead of using the more formal terms (*mother, father, grandfather*) that older writers sometimes use when they are discussing their families with nonfamily members. Further, she uses familiar phrases in ways that don't quite fit the current context. She refers to her mother "fixing up to go," a phrase which, in the part of the country where she lives, is usually used in more pleasant contexts—getting ready to go on a date, out to dinner, to church. And finally, when she notes that her father calls to see "which airplane was ready to go," her language suggests a certain lack of understanding of the way things work in the world outside her family.

As we've seen in the previous section of this chapter, a limited, personal perspective can cause problems for a writer. But in this case, such a perspective serves to heighten a fundamental dissonance, the tension between the mystery and profundity of the subject (the death of a loved one, the separation from a family member) and the limited resources that a young person (or, indeed, any of us) can draw upon in trying to deal with such a subject.

Throughout the narrative, this writer also mentions a number of other dissonances. She mentions conflicts between what people hope or intend to do and what they actually accomplish. For instance, neighbors invite the writer to supper, presumably to cheer her up, but the invitation makes her angry since she feels that the neighbors are treating her like an "invalid." And she mentions several conflicts between what people routinely experience or expect and what is actually true in this situation. Usually, for example, the writer feels the presence of her mother in the house "always doing something," but now the house seems "all alone from the inside." Normally, singing Christmas carols with a friend's family would be a joyful occasion, but in this instance, the joy others take in the season only serves to heighten her feeling of sadness.

These dissonances are heightened by the writer's awareness of several different kinds of relationships. For one thing, she makes several comparisons, noting that she felt as though she was "in shock" when she first received the news of her grandfather, and mentioning later that she felt "like an orphan" and that friends were treating her "like some kind of invalid." These comparisons are not literally accurate—she is not deprived of parents and family; her friends, presumably, do not consider her disabled. But these comparisons strongly convey her sense of loss and isolation.

She also implies a relationship between feelings and physical settings. The effect of the bad news about her grandfather is intensified by the melancholy scene in which she hears it—a dark evening, her father, head down, seated alone on the porch of her house, separated from the warmth and companionship usually found within the house. Her sadness is heightened not only by the "alone"-ness of her own house, but also, ironically, by the carol singing at a neighbor's house. And finally, this student seems aware of the importance of time relationships. The call from Mexico comes after dark, a time when bad news always seems worse; her mother's plane leaves at 11 p.m., an hour that heightens a reader's sense of how the family routine has been disrupted; her grandfather's death occurs at a time of year when family seems especially important.

It may very well be that this student is a naturally gifted storyteller. Or perhaps she is simply recounting a story that is often told and discussed within her family. Whatever the case, the thinking reflected in this narrative represents a considerable accomplishment, one that should be instructive not only to her classmates but to writers of other age or supposed ability levels, especially those who simply recount events, never exploring how people feel or why they react as they do. At the very least we should help her and her classmates see some of the things she's done that make this piece so powerful, things that she and they might consider trying when they write their next personal experience narrative. If we attend only to her mastery of conventions, we will miss seeing this accomplishment and, consequently, diminish our ability to work with this writer or her classmates.

Integrating Writing and the Study of Literature

At the college level, there is some debate (see, for example, Tate 1993 and Lindemann 1993) as to whether the study of literature has a place in a composition class, especially a college-level course specifically designated as a "writing" class. There is, however, little disagreement about one point: The process of writing and the process of interpreting literature are both meaning-making activities. An interpretation is not something readers find prepackaged for them on the page they are decoding. It is, rather, something they arrive at through a process of reflection and intuition, a process that is guided in part by strategies discussed throughout this chapter. To reiterate a caution mentioned earlier: No written product can give us access to all the thinking processes a writer or reader has gone through. But a written interpretation of a literary text can reflect meaning-making strategies that are as important for students' reading as they are for their writing.

Consider, for example, the following excerpts from an essay, an unrevised first draft, written under the time pressures of a statewide writing assessment. The writer, a high school student, is interpreting the short story "Father and I." As these excerpts will make clear, the story consists of an adult narrator's reflection on childhood experiences that caused him to question the omnipotence and omniscience of his father.

> When children are young, they experience events only inside their own little world. They don't know of the world outside their own. Their world is filled with security and trust, where the people in their live (parents) are their idols. These idols can do no wrong, and are knowledgeable about everything. But at this young, tender age, their security is fragile and on the brink of destruction. This security is broken when they realize they realize tat there is a world outside their own. Added to which, their idolization of the people in their lives is also broken. This experience is best described in the story <u>Father and I</u>.
>
> This story accurately portrays the emotions of a child losing his haven. The confusion of this child as he comes to know the real world. But in order to describe the utter destruction of his world, it must be told of his world before his realization.
>
> As father and son first start their walk, the son's faith and unbreakable trust is profoundly present. To him, his father was the boss and indeed a special person. ". . . people were not allowed to go as a rule, but Father worked on the railway and so he had a right to." (pg. 1) This backs up the sons faith in his father. He feels previgiled because he was allowed to go where it was forbidden,

because his father worked there. This gives the son a sense of pride and importance.

. . . This faith is broken when a train passes which the father didn't know was coming. And when his father didn't recognize the conductor. This destroys the child's unshakable trust in his father.

The child is at utter loss when he discovers his father doesn't know everything. Because of this, he also starts to feel insecure about the fact that his father will protect him. ". . . it was the anguish that was to come, the unknown he wouldn't be able to protect me against." (pg. 5)

The child has realized his father isn't godlike and cannot protect him from everything. When this happens to a child, their confusion goes even beyond their once belief in their idols. This might help children mature, but they lose with them an innocence that can never be found again.

Fundamental to this essay/interpretation is this student's prior knowledge of the disillusionment and anxiety (i.e., the dissonances) that arise when children first recognize the limitations of their parents. By drawing on this prior knowledge, this student is able to appreciate the central conflict in the story.

This awareness of dissonance seems to govern much of the thinking reflected elsewhere in the essay. For one thing, the writer selects from the story only those details that help the reader appreciate the conflict that the narrator feels. For example, to emphasize the dissonance occasioned by the narrator's loss of innocence, the student carefully selects details that illustrate the narrator's initial faith in his father. The student mentions, for example, the narrator's comment that "Father worked on the railway and so he had a right to [go where others were forbidden to go]." The writer then goes on to explain how this quote reflects the narrator's sense of his father's uniqueness.

Further, this student elaborates on the dissonance in the story by selecting different types of information. In addition to including details about what happened in the story, the student also includes information about how characters felt ("'it was the anguish that was to come'") and how they viewed other characters ("To him, his father was the boss . . ."). This selection of details helps the writer avoid the tendency—especially evident in the writing of unsophisticated readers—merely to summarize the events of a given story.

The writer's awareness of the central conflict in the story also seems to govern the kinds of relationships the writer sees. The writer begins by suggesting a contrast between the way children and adults see the world, noting that children "experience events only inside their own little world" and pointing out that children "don't know of the world outside their own." To illustrate the narrator's initial esteem for his father, the student also points out a contrast between the limitations other people had to accept and his father's right to go where "people were not allowed to go as a rule." The writer also notes the change that takes place within the narrator, his movement from one emotional state (complete faith in his father) to another (confusion and anxiety). To describe this change, the student makes a number of statements that suggest time and/or cause-effect relationships: "When children are young, they experience . . ."; "As father and son first start their walk, the son's faith . . . is profoundly present"; the son feels privileged "because he was allowed to go . . ."; and the son's "faith is broken when a train passes which the father didn't know was coming." In noting all of these relationships, the writer is not simply recounting the events of the story, but, rather, is indicating the ways those events affect the central character.

This attention to the significance of events makes the student appear to be a more sophisticated reader than someone who merely summarizes the events of a story. Perhaps, however, the quality of this student's interpretation is determined by the nature of the story the student is reading. Certainly, it would be hard for any reader to avoid talking about the significance of what happens in this particular story. Thus, this one essay gives no basis for claiming that this student can use these same thinking strategies in interpreting other literary texts, but we can claim that this essay does reflect some powerful meaning-making strategies. And if we were to discuss this essay with the student and the student's classmates, we should be able to help them see how the strategies reflected in this essay might be useful in writing about other texts.

Implications for Teaching

Implicit in this chapter—and, indeed, throughout this volume—is the belief that assessment must serve not only to rank or grade students, but also to give us information we can use in our teaching. If we can get some insight into the way students are thinking in a particular situation, we may be able to help them see what they want to continue to do or do differently in other situations. This possibility, of course, is based on a further assumption: Thinking is something that people learn to do, and we can help them get better at it—not by giving them a steady diet of drills or exercises that claim to teach people to think, not by having them do the mental equivalent of push-ups—but, rather, by using what we already know about teaching writing.

To that end, we may want to design "mini-lessons" that illustrate a particular thinking strategy, or we may want to get students to analyze the thinking reflected in a piece of published writing. Fundamentally, however, we will help students to think better by asking them to look closely at their work—or a classmate's or ours—and to consider some of the questions described earlier in this chapter. For example, we might put a piece of writing—a journal entry, an early draft, a finished draft—on the overhead and raise questions such as the following:

What kinds of details has this writer selected?

Are there kinds of details that seem significantly missing?

What questions (problems, conflicts, dissonances) does the writer seem to have considered?

Can you think of other questions the writer might consider?

Has this writer considered different perspectives?

Is it necessary to consider different perspectives in this case?

It's always possible, of course, that our questions can take on a pseudo-Socratic tone, strongly implying the answer we want students to give. But it's equally possible that we can ask our questions honestly, posing them because they reflect our curiosity, our need to figure something out. When we do so, our natural tendency to talk about thinking can lead to a dialogue, one in which we and our students get a glimpse of each other's mind at work. And, in the process, both we and our students can continue to grow as writers and thinkers.

For Further Reading

Two of the best books on this topic are Richard Young, Alton Becker, and Kenneth Pike's *Rhetoric: Discovery and Change* (1970) and Robert Sternberg's *Intelligence Applied* (1986). For a relatively recent survey of work in this area, see Young's essay "Recent Developments in Rhetorical Invention" (1987). Sternberg, in Chapter 1 of *Intelligence Applied*, gives a concise, readable history of work in this area. Peter Elbow's discussion of the "doubting game" and the "believing game," in *Writing without Teachers* (1973), provides an excellent explanation of key elements of the thinking process. A more detailed discussion of the thinking processes described in this chapter appears in my essays "Strategy and Surprise" (1993) and "Measuring Changes" (1977). For a philosopher's approach to this topic, see Richard Paul's survey of the "dispositions" and "abilities" that comprise critical thinking (cited in Marzano et al. 1988, 19–21).

Works Cited

Elbow, Peter. 1973. *Writing without Teachers*. New York: Oxford University Press.

Lindemann, Erika. 1993. "Freshman Composition: No Place for Literature." *College English* 55: 311–16.

Marzano, Robert J., Ronald S. Brandt, Carolyn Sue Hodges, Beau Fly Jones, Barbara J. Presseisen, Stuart C. Rankin, and Charles Suhor. 1988. *Dimensions of Thinking: A Framework for Curriculum and Instruction*. Alexandria, VA: Association for Supervision and Curriculum Development.

Murray, Donald M. 1987. *Write to Learn*. 2nd ed. New York: Holt, Rinehart, and Winston.

Odell, Lee. 1977. "Measuring Changes in Intellectual Processes as One Dimension of Growth in Writing." In *Evaluating Writing: Describing, Measuring, Judging*, ed. Charles R. Cooper and Lee Odell, 107–32. Urbana, IL: National Council of Teachers of English.

———. 1981. "Defining and Assessing Competence in Writing." In *The Nature and Measurement of Competency in English*, ed. Charles R. Cooper, 95–136. Urbana, IL: National Council of Teachers of English.

———. 1993. "Strategy and Surprise in the Making of Meaning." In *Theory and Practice in the Teaching of Writing: Rethinking the Discipline*, ed. Lee Odell, 213–43. Carbondale: Southern Illinois University Press.

Sternberg, Robert J. 1986. *Intelligence Applied: Understanding and Increasing Your Intellectual Skills*. San Diego: Harcourt Brace Jovanovich.

Tate, Gary. 1993. "A Place for Literature in Freshman Composition." *College English* 55: 317–21.

Tierney, Robert J., Mark A. Carter, and Laura E. Desai. 1991. *Portfolio Assessment in the Reading-Writing Classroom*. Norwood, MA: Christopher-Gordon.

Writing Collection Elaboration Handout for Persuasive Writing. 1993. Austin: Texas Education Agency.

Young, Richard. 1987. "Recent Developments in Rhetorical Invention." In *Teaching Composition: 10 Bibliographical Essays*, ed. Gary Tate, 1–43. Fort Worth: Texas Christian University Press.

Young, Richard E., Alton L. Becker, and Kenneth L. Pike. 1970. *Rhetoric: Discovery and Change*. New York: Harcourt, Brace & World.

Appendix A: Additional Questions for Assessing Thinking

Dissonance

Do students, for example, point out things that surprise or puzzle them? Do they pose questions? Do they ever indicate that they are confused, uncertain, or ambivalent about something they have experienced? Do they comment on ways in which two strongly held beliefs (ideas, values) are inconsistent with each other? Do they notice ways in which people's actions seem inconsistent with their words? Do they mention ways in which something conflicts with what they had expected or would have preferred?

Selecting

For example, when students respond to literature or write personal experience narratives, do they focus solely on the events that happened, or do they include information about people's thoughts, feelings, and motivations? When they describe, do they look for details that will "show, not tell"? When they try to write persuasively or informatively, do they include the kind of information that is likely to be appropriate given the knowledge, needs, or values of their intended readers?

Encoding

When students discuss personal events, do they use relatively abstract, generalized terms, or do they use language that reflects the personal significance of those events? When students try to think through complicated issues, do they use highly emotional language that might limit their ability to see the complexity of a situation? Do they ever come up with metaphors that let them take a fresh look at the subject they are considering? Do they choose words whose connotations are appropriate for their subject matter, audience, and purpose?

Drawing on Prior Knowledge

When they read a complicated piece of literature, do students comment on how this piece relates to other texts they have read or movies they have seen? When they encounter a difficult problem, do they use what they know from comparable problems or from prior schoolwork in order to solve it? When they are introduced to new concepts in their courses, do students consider ways in which those concepts apply to their personal experience or ways in which they are or are not compatible with what they've learned previously?

Seeing Relationships

Do students, for instance, note when and why things happen? Do they create hypothetical scenarios, speculating about how one thing might cause or lead up to another? Do they make distinctions, noticing ways in which something is different from something else? Do they classify or note similarities? Do they comment on how things change? Do they notice ways in which a person or object fits into his/her/its physical surroundings?

Considering Different Perspectives

Do students, for example, consider good news as well as bad, pro as well as con? Do they try to adopt another's perspective, trying to imagine how, say, a character in a story might respond to a particular situation? Do they try to think of different conclusions that might be drawn from a particular set of data? Do they put themselves in their reader's place, trying to understand the knowledge, values, or needs with which that reader approaches their writing? When they disagree with someone, do they consider ways in which that person's views might possibly make sense?

2 What We Know about Genres, and How It Can Help Us Assign and Evaluate Writing

Charles R. Cooper
University of California–San Diego

Years ago, when I gave writing assignments as a young high school teacher, my students and I suffered a severe limitation: My two-part categorization of "writing." I did not always rely on the same two categories, but I always had two in mind. Sometimes they were expository and personal, sometimes expository and creative, sometimes formal and informal, and sometimes writing about literature and writing about everything else. I must have picked up these distinctions in my college English courses and brought them to my teaching, where they became the basis for my course planning, assignment giving, and evaluation of students' writing.

Our grammar and composition handbook (Warriner 1957) supported my abstract and limited categories of written texts. There was exposition, which included the essay of opinion and the one-paragraph factual report, the latter defined as "rather formal expository writing." And there was narration, which included assignments in personal narrative, process narration, and description. Then there were chapters on the research paper and letter writing (social and business). I understand now that my handbook was relying clumsily on a nineteenth-century classification scheme—with categories for narration, description, exposition, and argument—that still influences many school and college writing textbooks.

Fortunately, by the late 1960s, important new knowledge became available that began to change our understanding of writing. From these important beginnings, a vast literature has emerged, defining a new specialty we usually call "composition studies." An important part of this literature concerns genres and their teaching and learning. Knowledge about genres—about written discourse, our primary subject as English teachers—gave me new ways of thinking about my students' struggles with writing. It changed the way I helped students shape their own projects. It changed the way I gave assignments and evaluated students' works-in-progress. Because knowledge about genres also changed my ideas about the relation of reading to writing, it changed the way I organized my courses.

In this chapter I want to present some of what we know about genres and identify helpful resources. I'll begin by defining "genre" and then present four familiar genres, illustrated by high school students' essays. My purpose is to demonstrate that if we understand the unique characteristics of these genres (and others we might want to assign), then we can give more productive assignments and evaluate students' writing more insightfully. I'll then report on important work in classifying genres and speculate about how these classifications lead to various developmental assignment sequences. I'll conclude by detailing a model for integrating evaluation into a genre assignment.

A Definition of "Genre"

"Genre" is a familiar concept to English teachers. We speak of the novel as a genre, and the short story. Poetry joins the list, but we also refer to the genres of poetry—haiku, epic, lyric, sonnet, and others. Our students may learn these distinctions. A friend or neighbor might say, "I'm reading more autobiography than fiction now" or "My favorite reading is historical romances." In a general way, we and our students and friends understand "genre" to mean a type or category of text. Practioners, researchers, and teachers of other arts also rely on this understanding of genre. For example, television studies rely on genres like police shows, detective shows, situation comedies, made-for-TV movies, talk shows, TV churches, docudramas, and others (Rose 1985). Film studies rely on genres like horror, musical, war, crime, women's, epic, film noir, western, animal, high school, and others (Reed 1989).

Joseph W. Reed, who teaches movies, culture, and literature at Wesleyan University, writes about studies of film genres: "Any movie in genre study is as important as any other. Some are more interesting, certainly some produce better results when studied than others, but there is democracy in genre" (1989, 7). Like studies of television and movies, recent genre studies of written texts are broad and inclusive, democratically embracing texts of all kinds. As we will see, this important new research enlarges the possible scope of our work as writing teachers by suggesting genres we may want to bring into our courses. It also refines our present work by introducing us to significant subgenres within familiar genres, for example, problem-solution within argument, incident or phase within autobiography, or profiles within information.

Informed by this new research, let me define "genres" as types of writing produced every day in our culture, types of writing that make possible certain kinds of learning and social interaction. This definition still surprises me. For so long had I thought of genres as convenient categories of literary texts that it has taken me years to internalize a new definition that reveals genres to be essential to thinking, learning, communication, and social cohesion, neither a mere convenience nor, as some English teachers believe, a constraint on writers. This new knowledge has impacted my work as a writing teacher to the same degree that plate tectonics has impacted the work of geologists, or DNA sequencing, the work of biologists.

Recent studies (Bazerman 1988; Ferguson 1994; Coe 1994; Cope and Kalantzis 1993; and Miller 1984) agree about certain basic characteristics of genres. Relying on these studies, we might, for our purposes as writing teachers, consider genres to be social, communal, situational, functional, structured, and stable.

Social. Written genres appear inevitably, predictably, in any literate society or culture. They are not imposed from above by an elite, nor are they the isolated, creative contributions of individuals. Rather, they emerge from social interactions and the need to communicate. Members of a society recognize its genres, benefit from them, and value them. Knowledge of genres is essential to reading and writing, making reading comprehensible and writing possible.

Communal. While genres are broadly social, making possible shared public discourse, they may also be locally or narrowly communal, making possible specialized communication within various communities or groups. English teachers rely on professional journal articles and book reviews, postings to Internet discussion groups made up of other English teachers, well-made assignments, and other genres. Police officers write accident reports and read regulations. Lawyers read legal decisions and write trial briefs and many other kinds of legal documents. Doctors read research reports in medical journals, entries in diagnostic manuals, and explanations of drug benefits and side effects provided by pharmaceutical companies.

Situational. Genres develop in recurring, concrete social situations where people must communicate with one another in writing. These social situations occur in family and community life, school or college, the professions, government, business, leisure, religion, politics—all of the countless occasions for interaction and communication, for conflict and cooperation. Because there are many situations or occasions for writing in any literate society, there are many genres.

Functional. Because genres are situational, they are functional. They serve a particular purpose, filling a recurring social need: stories entertain, revealing other of life's possibilities, and lead to reflection; proposals seek to win support for solutions to problems; explanations make things clear and establish the usefulness of information; reviews evaluate movies or restaurants; thank-you notes express gratitude and show the writer to be a thoughtful person.

Structured. A genre would not be socially useful if it did not have a recognizable structure, realized through a certain set of meaning-making strategies. It makes certain possibilities—and not others—available to writers and imposes certain constraints on them. A genre cannot be reduced to a reproducible formula, yet its main features can be described.

Stable. Genres emerge, merge, evolve, disappear but very slowly, if at all, over many decades or even centuries, even as experimental writers continually push the constraints and boundaries of genres. There are fascinating histories of many genres. Some still-important genres of argument were identified by Aristotle in the fifth century B.C.E. The sonnet appeared in the fourteenth century and is still with us, though now more read than written. The novel in English emerged in the early eighteenth century and, beyond its initial epistolary period, has accommodated itself to many stylistic and thematic variations. The scientific report found its form in the mid-nineteenth century. Movie scripts appeared with the movies after the turn of the twentieth century, newspaper editorials with weekly and daily newspapers toward the end of the eighteenth century.

There is much more to say about genre, but this definition will serve our need for a quick orientation to the significant new knowledge emerging from genre studies. This definition tells us where genres come from, and how they function in (if not create) commercial, religious, civic, political, and professional life. It also establishes that genres are basically social actions and only incidentally textual forms. For English teachers—and indeed for teachers of all subjects—this definition immediately raises a host of urgent questions: How are genres learned? Is this learning explicit or tacit or both? If both, which parts are tacit, requiring merely immersion, and which parts explicit, requiring systematic instruction and conscious learning. Should genres be assigned? If so, might certain genres be more appropriate for particular grade or developmental levels? How might genres be grouped and sequenced to create curricula? Which genres are important to learning an academic discipline and to success at work? How can assignments reflect the fact that genres are purposeful social processes of communication? How can students gain perspective on genres that may seem to them to exclude, constrain, or alienate? I believe these questions deserve the most creative research efforts we can muster.

I have reserved the following three questions as central to my concerns in this chapter: how genre assignments might improve evaluation of writing and extend and enrich what we already know how to do.

- Would genre knowledge enable teachers to give better assignments (or help students think through their own chosen projects) and respond more helpfully to students' drafts and revisions?
- Would genre knowledge enable students to be more thoughtful and critical readers of their own and other students' work?
- Would genre-centered writing instruction complement or contravene expressivist, writing process, or whole language instruction?

Already, in this introduction, I have indicated how I would answer some of these questions, and I will return to them in various contexts throughout the chapter.

Four Genre Examples

Though students' education in our culture's written genres begins and continues at home, in the popular media, and on the streets, schools must broaden and deepen this education, especially if students are to learn to write a wide range of genres that will then be available to them for learning, civic participation, and work. Consequently, it seems obvious to say genres must be assigned and genre knowledge assessed, an assumption of many college writing programs and of California's *English-Language Arts Model Curriculum Standards, 9–12* (1991) and a succession of California statewide assessment programs beginning in the mid-1980s. From one of these assessments, I have chosen essays in four genres familiar to English teachers.

The essays come from a 1990 California Department of Education publication illustrating the range of student performance in eight genres on a statewide writing assessment (*Student Essays Illustrating the CAP Rhetorical Effectiveness Scoring System [Grade 12]* 1990).[1] Reproduced in their original handwriting in the publication, the examples are all first-draft essays written by twelfth-grade students

---

[1]Reprinted, by permission, from *Student Essays Illustrating the CAP Rhetorical Effectiveness Scoring System (California Assessment Program, Grade 12)*, copyright 1990, California Department of Education, P.O. Box 271, Sacramento, CA 95812-0271.

during a fifty-five-minute test period, ensuring at least forty-five minutes of uninterrupted writing time. Students first saw the essay prompt at the beginning of the period. Students wrote independently, without benefit of advice from the teacher or other students, and they were on their own to decide how much time to spend prewriting or planning.

I present the essays here without correcting any spelling and usage errors or editing and clarifying any of the sentences. As you will see, the students, with one exception, made few grammatical errors. Though students were invited to edit and revise by erasing or lining through, their essays show little, if any, evidence of editing or revision. Three of the five essays received a score of 6, placing them in the top 3 percent of essays statewide; one essay received a 5, placing it in the top 18 percent; and one essay, which I have chosen for contrast with a high-scoring essay in only one genre, received a score of 3, placing it in the top 85 percent. Essays were scored by classroom teachers at eight statewide scoring sites, one for each genre assessed. At each site, teachers relied on a scoring guide which focused on the unique rhetorical features of a genre.

The four genres I have chosen to illustrate are recognizably quite different. What I have to say about each genre can be found in numerous sources available to any teacher. I merely want to illustrate genre differences in student writing in order to argue that these differences must be fundamentally important to our work as school or college writing teachers, particularly when we are giving assignments and responding to or evaluating student writing.

Taking a Position on a Controversial Issue

This first essay takes a position on a controversial issue, a familiar genre of argument and a staple of newspaper opinion and editorial pages, magazines of news and opinion, and books on social policy. It may come closest to students' lives as a part of their civic education—learning how to enter the debate authoritatively on some current issue and how to recognize when an important social problem has been addressed thoughtfully or has been oversimplified and distorted for ideological and political reasons.

As you read this essay, notice the confident assertiveness, refutation of some readers' likely objections, and overall plan:

> A vast skeletal dome rises out of the earth. Construction workers, like so many ants, methodically move upon the face of the structure, adding huge slabs of concrete to the partially-completed behemoth. This is the future sight of a nuclear power plant, authorized

by the Nuclear Regulatory Commission. When completed, this plant will replace the outdated natural gas power plants of the area, providing electrical power for thousands. But many are concerned that this nuclear reactor, will put the public and the environment at risk. These concerns, however, are unfounded. As publically held myths, they must be dispelled, so that the true benefits of nuclear power can become a reality for this area.

Many citizens fear that the installation of a nuclear power plant will put not only the environment but the public health and safety in jeapordy. These people feel that the byproducts on nuclear fission will necessitate the creation of toxic waste dumps to contain them. They also think that the presence of a nuclear reactor will kill off the local wildlife. In addition, they worry that radiation from the reactor will put the local inhabitants at risk, especially should a nuclear accident similar to the ones at Chernyobl and Three-Mile Island occur.

These fears are uninformed. The radioactive waste produced by the plant will be very small in volume, and will be easily accomodated by existing safe toxic waste disposal centers. Wildlife will be unaffected by the plant, which will be completely self-contained, and unable to emit harmful harmful waste-heat. The public conception of radiation bursting forth from the plant and harming employees and members of the community is an utter and complete myth. With the tons of shielding surrounding the reactor, far more radiation will be absorbed by employees from the sun than from the fission reaction. Finally, while the above-mentioned nuclear accidents were indeed horrendous, they serve as reminders of the precautions necessary to run a nuclear plant. Thus, safety has in fact <u>improved</u> as a result of these catastrophes, insuring that the odds of such a disaster occuring in this ultra-modern nuclear plant are small indeed. Clearly, these dangers that are seen by opponents of the project are virtually non-existant, and will cease to be a factor once the public is informed.

The benefits of such a plant, on the other hand, are clearly visible to all. A nuclear power plant will be a far more efficient power source that the natural-gas power plants it will replace. Electricity prices will fall and remain constant in the long run, as nuclear power is not vulnerable to the threats of middle-eastern oil lords. In addition, the implementation of such a plant will bolster the local economy by providing hundreds of permanent jobs. The benefits that will be reaped by nuclear power will add immeasurable to the prosperity of the community.

Nuclear power, then, is without a doubt a worthwhile endeavor for this area. The costs of construction of the facility will be repayed many times over by the risk-free benefits afforded by a nuclear power plant. The N. R. C. would clearly be well-advised to proceed at full speed with the development and construction of the power plant.

Stepping into a controversy, the writer immediately identifies the issue and asserts his position. Aware of the sharp division of opinion on nuclear power, he astutely acknowledges opponents' basic reservations—calling them "myths" and "fears"—and attempts to refute them. He is not at all accommodating, conceding nothing at all. He is careful to refute in paragraph 3 each fear he brings up in paragraph 2. Then, he asserts four benefits of nuclear power.

The argument unfolds predictably for American readers who are familiar with this genre. Written like a newspaper editorial on a well-defined local issue already reported on extensively in the editorial writer's newspaper, the argument moves quickly and remains general, asserting specific reasons and refuting objections without concrete and extensive support. Though the argument remains general, it is clear that the writer has more than casual knowledge of the issue. He keeps his focus on trying to convince readers of the plausibility of his position.

Viewing this essay as a first draft and imagining ourselves responding to it in conference or guiding students in responding to it, we can see readily the importance of genre knowledge. What the student has accomplished, and might yet accomplish, can best be talked about in terms largely unique to writing that takes a position: arguing, reasoning, asserting a position, giving reasons, supporting the reasons, anticipating readers' questions and objections, and so on. Only this kind of talk can move the draft forward because so little else needs attention, even if this essay were a revision. The writing exhibits a high degree of syntactic control and fluency; cohesion never breaks down; the hyphen is usually used correctly, an achievement that nearly always comes much later (as it did in my case); and the parallelism in a "not only . . . but also" sentence is managed quite precisely.

With this first essay, I can illustrate the importance of genre knowledge by contrasting two perspectives on evaluating writing, one I'll call "all-purpose," the other "genre-specific." The contrast focuses on a very familiar artifact of writing instruction in all disciplines: the criteria list or scoring rubric. Such criteria serve various purposes: as guides for scoring large-scale assessments of writing achievement, guidelines for the writer at work, guidelines for peer critique, checklists for self-evaluation:

All-Purpose Criteria

Focus and voice established early and maintained throughout;

Organization effective and clearly signaled;

Examples and details relevant to the purpose;

Sentence structure and length varied;

Language and tone appropriate to the purpose and readers;

Conventions observed.

Many school and college writing textbooks and many instructors continue to rely on all-purpose criteria. Because they assume that all writing is the same, they are certainly convenient. They reduce the costs of large-scale assessments. Unfortunately, they are limiting, and even confusing, because they prevent students from learning about the possibilities of specific genres such as taking a position on an issue. I would advocate, instead, genre-specific criteria, which are particularly helpful as guidelines for the writer, for peer critique, and for self-evaluation:

Genre-Specific Criteria: Taking a Position on an Issue

Asserts a clear position on the issue;

Gives specific reasons for holding the position;

Supports each reason with personal experience, examples, statistics, or by quoting authorities;

Provides readers with new, surprising ways to think about the issue;

Shows an understanding of opposing views;

Anticipates readers' objections and questions;

Sequences the argument in a logical step-by-step way.

These criteria focus on what is fundamental to success when a writer takes a position on an issue. They are more meaningful to novice writers because they announce what is to be achieved in clear and useful language. Even experienced instructors find them helpful in focusing their comments when evaluating student work. Instructors can hand genre-specific criteria lists to students, or together they can infer the criteria from close reading of published or high-quality student essays that take a position. Why hide from students what is common knowledge among experienced readers or writers in our culture? Writing that takes a position is realized through unique writers' strategies and text features.

Insisting on the importance of genre knowledge, I do not mean to slight the very great importance of three other kinds of knowledge to a writer taking a position on an issue: the issue itself, its history and the content of the debate; the particular readership for the essay, the readers' knowledge and beliefs; and the status of the issue, its arguability and ripeness for reasoned argument. Nevertheless, genre knowledge remains highly relevant. Like a member of a newspaper editorial board that is seeking to reassert its position on this issue, this writer was asked—or might have chosen on his own in a different situation—to take a position on the debate over building further nuclear power plants. This special writing situation guides how he will select and use knowledge of the debate and of readers in order to achieve his purpose. To succeed, he must rely on his culture's genre for taking positions on issues. To argue that he might instead write a science fiction novel about a golden future with nuclear power does not reduce the importance or usefulness to this writer of the taking-a-position genre. The novel and the argument are simply alternatives. Each genre makes its own special demands on writers—and on readers.

In commenting only on this one example, I do not mean to suggest that there are severe limits or constraints to this genre. In fact, there are a great many options. To give just one example: A writer might take a much more conciliatory approach to opponents by conceding that there is justification for their fear of nuclear power plants. Such a decision would influence noticeably the tone and content and patterning of the essay, but it would still share basic features with this first example.

Let us consider the implications for evaluating a student essay in the same genre that lacks the confidence, authority, and conventional correctness of the first essay. Consider the following essay:

> The American faimly, an apple pie on the sink, boys playing base-ball in the yard, dad taking in a ball game on the couch, and mom baking cookies in the kitchen. These are visions of what might have been.
>
> Yet for millions of wed Americans this dream fails, and a divorce is the answer. A divorce may be extremely dificult for the couple, it is a large part of life gone wrong. Yet as responsible adults, this hurt was brought upon themselves, by themselves. For the children however, this is a enourmous trama that is not deserved. It is the losing of your faimly, thier supposoubly most trusted source.
>
> So when asked whether or not parents should postpone divorce I say a loud and clear yes. It is the parents responsibility to work on thier differences and stick it out until the children finish school. They made a commitment to each other, after all, when they took those marrige vows. And more, by having a child, the parents made an even bigger commitment and must take responsibility for thier actions.
>
> All in all I feel that adults owe it to thier children to provide them with happy, good childhoods. After all, it was thier choice to do all of this, not the child's.

Though the error rate is relatively high, this essay's purpose is quite clear: to convince readers to take seriously the possibility that parents have an obligation to stay together for the sake of their children. The issue remains in focus throughout the essay. There is never any question of where the writer stands on the issue. Because the writer offers reasons for her position and acknowledges that staying together may be difficult for parents, we see clearly the beginnings of a strong argument. Like the first essay, this one is centered squarely in the genre students were asked to write. In both, we have a recognizable issue, a position taken, an argument, and some recognition of readers' predictable objections. Conference or workshop issues should, I believe, be very similar for both essays. Genre knowledge enables us to see the considerable promise of the weaker-appearing of these two essays. Keeping our focus on the possibilities and constraints of the taking-a-position genre, we can feel more cheerful than we otherwise would have about the second essay, and our evaluation of it can lead the writer immediately to substantive revisions.

A teacher who understands the possibilities and pitfalls of taking positions on controversial issues could, in a brief conference, help this writer extend and strengthen the argument. Of course, a strengthened revision is more certain if the student has been reading and discussing essays that take positions and knows the criteria for strong writing in this genre. When the student has revised, and perhaps revised again, she might turn her attention to conventions, with the help of the teacher, other students, and an accessible handbook.

Interpretation of Literature

Several genres play important roles in literary study. Among them are interpretation, evaluation, and the reflective essay. When students write about possible meanings they find in literary works or films, they may rely on the well-established genre of interpretation. If they have been asked to determine the value of a work, or decide whether one work is better than another, or justify their preference for one story in a collection or one film in a film genre or director's *oeuvre*, they lay claim to the evaluation genre. If they have been encouraged to reflect on their response to something in a work, they adopt the reflection genre. Seriously posed, and with high standards of work expected, these are invaluable learning experiences for students in English courses. They are also public genres, written every day by both academic and professional writers, though not always with literary texts as the subject matter.

There is much for students to learn about these writing-about-literature genres. Unfortunately, though we value and assign these and other genres, we rarely arrange for students to read and discuss them as genres before they attempt to write. We immerse them in poetry, drama, and fiction and then expect them to demonstrate their learning by writing in quite different genres.

This first essay about literature offers an interpretation of a poem. The student was asked to assert a meaning or idea she found in the poem and to support that meaning with details from the work. As you read, notice that the student presents a conventional beginning-to-end "reading" of the poem. Notice, also, the inferences the student makes and the way she supports them with details from the poem. Keep in mind that the student had very likely never seen the poem or read anything else by Robert Hayden.

> "Those Winter Sundays" written by Robert Hayden describes the relationship between a father and son, and the lessons learned later in life by the son.
>
> The poem describes an early morning scene, in which a man, who works hard all week long, gets up in the terrible cold to heat the house. It states in the first paragraph, that this deed was done, unselfishly, and was never thanked, or acknowledged by the son.
>
> In the second section, the son reflects on the fear he has of his father and his temper. It is ironic that this young boy would be so fearful of the man who lovingly awoke on a Sunday morning to warm the house for him. The author is making a point to show how easily society takes special tokens for granted.
>
> In the last section of the poem, the young boy, now much older feels the guilt for treating this man so indifferently. The last two lines state, "What did I know of love's austere and lonely offices?" In that, the young boy is saying, "How did I know that these things showed he really loved me"
>
> Hayden is trying to illustrate the infamous lack of communication that occurs between parent and child Here a man who is too proud to hug his son, shows his love by polishing his shoes and building a roaring fire early Sunday morning. Unfortunately, these messages are lost in the fear the boy has of his father. It isnt until later in his life that he can reflect and see the genuine love his father had for him. Now the boys biggest task will be dealing with the guilt of being so bitter and hateful to his father
>
> For centuries relationships such as this have existed, and will continue to do so for years to come, but it is essential that we learn to appreciate one another.

Evaluating this draft, any experienced English teacher will immediately see many opportunities for revision. For example, the student's oversimplification about "lessons learned" in the first paragraph and the generalizations in the final paragraph seem unnecessary. While some teachers might encourage beginning-to-end readings in interpretive essays, others may prefer an analogic approach, with the student arguing to support a series of reasons as to why readers should consider the interpretation plausible. The problem with readings like this one, of course, is that they are often merely summaries and not focused on defending a thesis—an asserted meaning. This essay, I believe, barely manages to avoid summary by naming the lesson learned ("guilt") in paragraphs 4 and 5 and then for the most part keeping the reading focused on this idea. It is not at all a surprising meaning to assert about this poem, but it is truly an inference, though an obvious one. The student names it herself. Hayden does not use the word "guilt."

Like the essay taking a position on nuclear power, this essay is thesis-centered. But notice how different the two theses really are. The taking-a-position thesis arises from a debate over the known physical dangers of a well-understood, concrete (forgive me) phenomenon. In contrast, the interpretive thesis arises from a consideration of possible meanings in ephemeral readings (and rereadings) of a literary text. While both theses acknowledge a material object, the taking-a-position thesis generalizes about many nuclear power plants or a typical plant, but the interpretive thesis points to a particular literary text. Paradoxically, the taking-a-position thesis is more textual because it engages a decades-long debate revealed to a writer in the present, mainly or entirely through countless visual and print texts. While the interpretive thesis represents a much longer, centuries-old tradition of literary interpretation, it very likely arises completely (and, appropriately so, before the college years) in isolation from this tradition and without knowledge of it, particularly without knowledge of even the very few texts concerned with meanings in Hayden's poems.

More generally, the taking-a-position thesis aligns itself in a familiar, public debate, while the interpretive thesis secretes itself within a small, local community of readers—a classroom or a small discussion group or a student-teacher dyad. Rhetorically, the taking-a-position thesis arms itself for a struggle with misinformed, recalcitrant, or fearful readers, while the interpretive thesis offers an idea for sympathetic discussion.

Such abstractions as these are not to be shared with students directly, of course. They are nevertheless fundamental to our work as writing teachers because they enable us to evaluate precisely—and helpfully, because precisely—students' works-in-progress in these two quite different writing situations. Knowing the differences between position and interpretive theses and among other types of argumentative theses is essential if we are to lead our students—especially those with the least experience with written texts—beyond their predictably misdirected, partial, or marginal attempts to write our culture's valued argument genres. These two writing situations—taking a position and interpreting a text—require of students quite different reading, thinking, planning, drafting, and revising strategies. If real learning is to take place, we must offer special resources and guidance in each situation. We need to be prepared to teach not one general writing process but several genre-specific processes. To do so, we need knowledge about genres:

Genre-Specific Criteria: Interpreting a Literary Text

Asserts some meaning the writer finds in the text;

Chooses workable thesis terms and carries them throughout the essay;

Goes beyond mere summary, if organized like a "reading";

Develops logically with one idea leading to the next, if a point-by-point argument;

Makes use of relevant evidence from the text;

Does not ignore or slight contradictory evidence.

Reflection

A second essay based on a literary text illustrates how students can make use of a genre that has been valued in the West since the sixteenth century and the publication of Montaigne's *Essais*. In French, "to essay" means to try out an idea or ideas. Since Montaigne, the reflective or personal essay has enabled writers to explore ideas, usually suggested by specific occasions. The occasion for this student's essay was her reading of a Robert Frost poem, "The Mending Wall." The student was asked to take any idea suggested to her by the poem and to explore its meanings in terms of her personal experience without feeling obliged to reach a conclusion. As you read, notice the continuous grounding in generalized personal experience and in specific personal knowledge.

> I am a paradox when it comes to walls.
> On one hand I say "A room of one's own is best." I might echo Mark Twain's cynical phrase, "Familiarity breeds contempt." There are times when revealing myself to too many people can become exhausting, or just too difficult to maintain. I suppose in these moments—with my cup of tea and book in hand, praying that the phone won't ring—I become more like Frost's primitive "stone savage" than I would like to think. People become not friends, but a hindrance. They bring stories of their anxieties and frustrations, cause complications, or start grating on my nerves. In contrast, a solitary cup of tea with Dickens (who does not grate on my nerves

and even takes the trouble to entertain me) seems comparitively simpler, if lonelier. Good fences may not <u>make</u> good neighbors, but they certainly are a necessary element in maintaining neighbors. There is a certain requisite privace which each person—myself included—*relishes*. There is a fundamental need to seek sustenance from one's solitude, far from the maddening crowd. Thoreau realized that. If not many of us go to his extreme, we at least find walls in subtler forms. . . . In this sense, we all need "a room of one's own." We all need walls.

Yet I switch 180 degrees. I see the viewpoint of Frost's uncomprehending narrator, the man who sees the irrationality in taking walls to an extreme. . . . The harshest walls leave the unpopular child out of the group, challenge the immigrant with "English only" ballots, and ignore the screams of Kitty Genovase [Genovese] in 1962. The horror of building walls is the human appeal for help that they stifle. I think of the Genovase case and wonder how an entire apartment complex could hear and see a girl being attacked without moving a single muscle to help. And the danger of walls is that they are all too easily defended with righteous excuses. "The poor should work themselves." "The foreigner should learn English." Everyone who builds walls should learn a little compassion, I say.

I am a paradox when it comes to walls.

This student not only understands paradox but also manages to quote or refer to Virginia Woolf and Mark Twain. In addition, she knows something about current social issues, allowing herself to make confidently a typical move in the reflective essay from personal experience to social implications. Toward the end of high school, students are ready for the special kind of thinking opened up by the reflective essay. The challenge for students is to learn new strategies for trying out ideas, turning them one way and then the other through contradictions, contrasts, analogies, allusions, and other strategies while maintaining a thematic coherence quite different from the logical, step-by-step coherence of thesis-centered argument. For example, notice how frequently the writer repeats her theme "walls" and how she uses it to frame her essay, in order to maintain coherence.

How can most eleventh and twelfth graders learn to write reflective essays? By acquiring knowledge of the reflective essay's special strategies and features through analyzing and discussing published and student essays, making this knowledge explicit in critera lists, drafting and revising their own essays, and then repeating the cycle again. As with the writing of other genres, there is knowledge for students to acquire. This knowledge does not constrain students because genre knowledge is heuristic. It activates students' creativity, enabling them to make meaning in new ways:

Genre-Specific Criteria: The Reflective Essay

Chooses a subject that will sustain extended reflections;

Presents the occasion(s) for the reflections concretely and interestingly;

States or clearly implies the relevance of the occasion to the reflections;

Develops the reflections through a variety of strategies;

Surprises readers with one or two unexpected insights into the subject;

Moves at least tentatively from personal experience to social implications;

Maintains thematic coherence throughout the essay.

Autobiographical Incident

Contemporary book-length autobiographies unfold through a series of well-focused episodes. One kind of episode is the one-time event or anecdote or incident. Writing an autobiographical incident, the writer seeks to recreate vividly, concretely, and dramatically a brief episode and to understand its significance, which may be either implied or stated directly. Here is an example:

> It was a hot summer day and Chris and I were kicking rocks along the sidewalk. when Chris looked down and noticed a blue-tip match—the kind that could be scraped across any surface producing fire. Of course Chris picked it up being the pyromaniac that he was and handed it to me.
>
> "I dare you to light it," Chris told me.
>
> "No, you light it," I nervously responded.
>
> "What, are you chicken—bock, bock, bock, Chris mocked as he flapped his arms about wildly.
>
> I felt my insides quiver but the smile that came across my face showed old Chris that I wasn't chicken. That was my chance to show Chris how cool I really was—so I thought. I took the match from him and with the thought of it not lighting anyway, struck it across the cold cement. I was startled as a giant flame sparked up on the match and right as that happened, Chris told me to throw it in a bush that was right next to us. Without giving it a second thought I threw the lit match into the bush. Little did I know that bush would start blazing up, causing the whole neighborhood to come running. At that very moment I thought my life was over. Before I could say a word Chris was telling my parents how I found the match and how he supposedly tried to stop me from

lighting the bush. I was so terrified I couldn't even look at my parents but eventually I had to—and boy was that a nightmare.

Keeping in mind that this and the other essays I have chosen were written in forty-five minutes and are little-revised, we can recognize the considerable achievement in this brief essay. It bears the two hallmarks of contemporary autobiography: reconstructed conversation and specific narrative action (people moving and gesturing). Nevertheless, an experienced teacher who also reads contemporary autobiography can readily see issues to take up in a writing conference. For example, the most dramatic moment, the explosive blazing up of the bush, could be detailed; the running neighbors could be shown in action; and the appearance of the parents presents tantalizing possibilities for interpersonal drama. Further, the writer's mentioned embarrassment and terror could be heightened by recalling more specific feelings or by showing those feelings more concretely. All of these possibilities could be either negotiated with the student or simply requested as brief fragmentary experiments to see what might develop. Unlike the reflective essay, which, though it may push off from a personal incident, usually generalizes about experience or refers briefly to a series of related experiences, the autobiographical incident concentrates on realizing the full dramatic possibilities of one brief incident. It is strictly narrative, whereas reflective essays rarely are.

Though middle and high school students have seen and read countless narrative incidents, they nevertheless need supportive, pointed instruction in order to learn how to write them vividly and concretely. Brief, general narratives—even a semester-long journal collection of them—do not allow students to represent their experience in meaningful and deeply satisfying ways. Genre-centered instruction allows them to write the real thing by examining their experience closely through the accessible moves and strategies of contemporary autobiography. These learnable strategies dissipate blandness and reduce predictability. Textual concreteness and vividness enable readers to "see" a persona and to "hear" an autobiographical voice. The writer gains significant personal and genre insights. There is a sense of new learning, of solid achievement. These criteria permit us to guide and describe such achievement:

Genre-Specific Criteria: Autobiographical Incident

Tells an engaging story about a single incident;

Organizes the narrative so that it is easy to follow;

States or clearly implies the significance of the incident;

> Achieves emotional distance from the incident and avoids senti-
> mentality and moralizing;
>
> Presents scene and people concretely and vividly.

If specific genre-focused assignments can enable students to learn
more about written discourse and heighten the usefulness of our
response to their efforts, then we need to ask whether we know how
to classify and describe our culture's valued genres and how genres
might be grouped and sequenced to create curricula.

Classifying and Sequencing Genres

The four genres we examined in the previous section are among many,
many genres that offer the promise of better assignments and evaluation across the school and college years. All of these genres are identified in influential genre classifications. Since these classifications
collect all of writing into a few broad categories, however, they are
quite abstract. After examining two of these briefly, we will look at
much less abstract lists of real-world genres that identify some of the
many actual writing situations in our society. These lists have led
recently to many published assignment sequences for various grade
levels. As we will see, certain genre classifications, while offering lists
of genres that could become assignments, also suggest ways to group
and sequence assignments.

Classifying Genres

Writing teachers have paid some attention to three recent attempts to
classify writing (Kinneavy 1971; Britton et al. 1975; Beale 1987). The most
recent of these, by Walter Beale, proposes the following categories:

> *Deliberative (Rhetorical):* writing that attempts to support opinions
> about issues, policy, or value, for example, taking a position on
> an issue, speculating about the causes of a social crisis, evaluat-
> ing a movie.
>
> *Performative (Instrumental):* writing that delivers public commem-
> orations, celebrations, or declarations for the purpose of reinforc-
> ing the values of a particular community, for example, acceptance
> speeches, obituary notices and essays, political or religious exhor-
> tations to "keep the faith," religious-conversion narratives, the
> Declaration of Independence. (Beale 114–15)

Informative (Scientific): writing that informs and creates interest in its topic, for example, news articles, encyclopedia entries, technical or investigative reports, travelogues, profiles.

Reflective/Exploratory (Poetic): writing that shares, explores, or reflects on human experience, for example, poems, novels, auto-biographies, reflective essays.

Beale's (23–25) ambitious, comprehensive schema focuses on the purposes of writing, its social situatedness and function, its actual human uses. Beale's four encompassing purposes provide a way to categorize all the genres of writing produced every day in our society. Beale calls these everyday genres "de facto genres," the real or actual genres of social life.

Another encompassing schema, that of James Moffett (1992), has for four decades influenced English teachers and curriculum planners. A consummate classifier of de facto genres, Moffett has convincingly demonstrated the importance of genre knowledge in constructing assignments and evaluating student writing (1981). He has also published collections of school and college students' essays categorized by de facto genre (Moffett et al. 1986, 1987a; 1987b; Moffett and Tashlik 1987).

While Beale's schema is based on purpose, Moffett's (1968) is based on the immediacy or remoteness of subject matter and the intimacy or distance between writer and readers. Both Beale's and Moffett's schemas attempt to accommodate all recognized de facto genres in our culture. Even teachers who do not give writing assignments have found Moffett's schema helpful because it enables them to evaluate students' choices and better anticipate problems they may encounter:

Recording (the drama of what is happening), for example, observation, dialogue, monologue, playscript.

Reporting (the narrative of what happened), for example, correspondence, diary, autobiography, prose fiction.

Generalizing (the exposition of what happens), for example, reflective essay, thematic collection of incidents, generalizing about any subject.

Theorizing (the argumentation of what will or may happen), for example, speculation, interpretation, theory.

In a later book, Moffett reclassifies his de facto genres in order to emphasize "how kinds of writing correspond to kinds of thinking" (Moffett, Baker, and Cooper, 1986, ii): *notation* (taking down), *recollection* (looking back), *investigation* (looking into), *imagination* (thinking up), and *cogitation* (thinking over and thinking through).

As writing instructors who must be opportunistic when it comes to theory, we need not be concerned that Beale and Moffett offer quite different discourse theories and classifying schemas. This is actually an advantage because it allows us to choose between theories: one that emphasizes the purposes of writing (Beale) and another, the continua of subject matter and writer–reader relations (Moffett). (A more recent theory classsifies genres as social processes [Callaghan, Knapp, and Noble 1993]).

Grouping and Sequencing Genres

When de facto genres are categorized in some type of classification schema, we may begin to see interesting relations among them. Possible assignment sequences emerge, course plans begin to take shape, and readings begin to suggest themselves. Let me give just two examples, one from Moffett (1992), the other from my work.

Knowing autobiography well as a reader, Moffett recognized that a full-length autobiography collects discrete episodes, loosely assembled narratively or sometimes on the basis of some other principle. (Moffett may also have read Mark Twain on autobiography. Twain pointed out that autobiographers work episodically, beginning with one salient episode and moving on to the next, without any consideration for their chronology. Much later, the autobiographer may or may not arrange the episodes chronologically.) Here is my slightly adapted selection of Moffett's autobiographical genres, taken from the early part of one of his longer sequences:

> *Autobiographical Incident:* a brief incident usually occupying no more than a day, a concise, and vivid narrative.
>
> *Autobiographical Phase:* a period of weeks or months marking a life change or development, a loose narrative of related events.
>
> *Remembered Person:* sketch of a significant person in the writer's life, usually a collection of revealing, brief anecdotes sequenced analogically.
>
> *Remembered Place:* presentation of a significant place in the writer's life, visual details organized either as a tour or from one or two physical points of view.
>
> *Memoir (Human Subject):* presentation of an incident involving other people in which the writer is only an observer, including visual details, a narrative of what happened, and inferences.
>
> *Memoir: (Nature Subject):* presentation of a memorable natural event, restricted in time and relying on visual details and narrative.

Chronicle: presentation of a developing trend or situation in a group (club, team, class, religious organization) important in the writer's life, characterizing different members and narrating revealing events.

Reflective Essay: reflections on the personal and social implications of an idea suggested by a particular occasion that is usually a personal observation or incident. (Moffett 1992, 71–149)

Moffett presents these assignments as a developmental sequence, moving from a smaller to larger scope in time and space. Early assignments develop narrative strategies which fold into later assignments, some of which can be organized analogically. In his rich commentaries, Moffett describes each assignment carefully, situating it in relation to assignments that come before and after. He then lays out workshop issues (his discursive equivalent of my genre-specific criteria in the second section of this chapter). The workshop issues should be central, Moffett believes, to students' and teachers' discussions of essay drafts. The workshop issues following each assignment are a treasure of genre knowledge. They make possible informed evaluation of students' writing. After each assignment, Moffett also discusses possible sources of student reading material in the same genre, thereby encouraging the learning of genres through reading and discussion.

Are Moffett's assignments merely school exercises or de facto genres? They are de facto genres, as Beale defines them, simply because each one of them can be found during the week you are reading this chapter in some newspaper, magazine, journal, or anthology published in the United States. Are they sometimes combined in extended writing? Yes, as I have already pointed out, book-length autobiographies are multigeneric or multiepisodic, necessarily so, because they are conceived and written episodically. That a de facto genre-like incident or place or chronicle of a group may be found collaborating with other genres does not disqualify it as a separate, independent genre that serves its own valued, social purpose. Autobiography, then, is a de facto genre because its book-length manifestations are published every day. Its familiar, predictable episodes, as identified partially by Moffett, are also de facto genres because they, too, are published every day. These episodes should be our focus in giving autobiographical assignments, I believe. How much we as teachers know about these episodes as readers and writers ourselves will determine how successfully we pose assignments, respond to students' works-in-progress, and evaluate students' achievements.

What we know about autobiography applies to argument: There is a book-length de facto genre we have agreed to call "argument" or "persuasion." Most people probably understand this genre to

involve presenting an issue or problem and taking a position on it.
Usually, however, much more is going on: A writer may speculate
about the causes of a social problem, evaluate other peoples' proposed causes, speculate about the consequences of failing to solve the
problem, define and describe a possible solution, outline and narrate
how it might be implemented, and argue for the wisdom of this solution while conceding and refuting likely objections to it. These and
other predictable moves and strategies of argument may also function as de facto genres, fulfilling important social purposes on their
own. For example, a political columnist like George Will or Molly
Ivins, writing over several weeks, might dismiss other people's proposed solutions to problems, take positions on issues, trumpet the
certain causes of social crises, or lament the consequences of legisla-
tion or court decisions. These are some of the de facto genres of
argument, and knowledge of them can lead to effective assignments
and productive evaluations of students' work. Here is an assignment
sequence I have used with both first-year college students and upper-
division writing majors:

> Complaint letter from which you hope to get a response;
>
> Advice letter to someone who will resist the advice;
>
> Solution to a local problem in some group or community you
> belong to;
>
> Speculation about the causes or effects of some phenomenon, event,
> or trend;
>
> Evaluation of some subject, for example, a movie, restaurant, per-
> formance, book, essay, or television series;
>
> Position paper on a local or national issue;
>
> Interpretation of a "text," for example, a story, movie, or statis-
> tical table.

Many middle school and high school teachers in California have
assigned these and Moffett's genres (*Writing Assessment Handbook,
Grade 8* 1990; *Writing Assessment Handbook High School* 1993).

In Chapter 10, Richard Beach classifies high school students'
responses to literature by creating categories of response he calls
"strategies," which, developed and refined by a student writer,
could, I think, be considered some of the de facto genres of our learning community, the discipline we still call "English." These strategies are more than mere exercises or warmups because they fulfill
a personal need and a social function—to express one's response and

share that response in a community of fellow readers—and also because they resemble published responses to the arts. Beach explains how he evaluates students' use of these strategies and describes how students may be encouraged to link response strategies to create extended essays.

A Model for Integrating Evaluation into a Genre Assignment

Since evaluation of writing, as I have defined it, is central to all stages of teaching and learning to write our culture's valued de facto genres, from the beginning of this chapter I have made many comments about teaching and learning. I have, in fact, implied a particular pedagogy, but only in order to illustrate the role of evaluation in a course in which genre assignments are given, a course where students work through a staged writing process and spend a good bit of time at appropriate stages collaborating with other students.

I am aware, of course, that some writing teachers do not give assignments, but allow students to choose and define all of their writing projects; do not make judgments about students' work until the student chooses what to include in a portfolio; show interest only in our discipline's genres of writing about literature; assign little, if any, same-genre reading in relation to writing assignments; eschew reading models; never model writing assignments based on literature; or ignore or slight genre differences in assigning and evaluating student's writing. During my thirty-eight years of teaching writing, I have embraced all of these practices at one time or another, but the romance ended several years ago.

The debate about how to teach writing is heating up, in part, because we have learned so much recently about genres and their role in social life, work and career, and knowledge making and learning in every discipline. We also have a comprehensive, carefully evaluated genre theory of literacy (Cope and Kalantzis 1993). From my perspective, writing teachers who think of themselves as process teachers need not resist a genre-centered pedagogy. My own classroom practice relies on extended, staged activities—from invention through self-evaluation—for every assignment. Teachers who value interaction or collaboration among students will recognize that genre assignments may depend on it. Portfolio advocates will see readily that a portfolio could be an integral part of a genre-centered course in any discipline. "Whole language" enthusiasts need not feel uncomfortable with genre assignments because students read and write only whole, real texts; while students may analyze published texts and their own texts either with genre criteria in mind or in order to discover such criteria, the analysis always occurs within the context of a whole text.

The greatest resistance to the genre theory of literacy comes from expressivist teachers, whose primary goal is to facilitate students' discovery of their voices. They allow students to decide what to write about so that they can feel ownership. They believe that writers must discover unique ways to develop each text. The differences between genre and expressivist approaches run deep because they are based on seemingly antithetical understandings of writing and learning to write. While expressivists believe that learning to write is like learning to talk, genre theorists believe that talk and writing are quite different (as linguists have demonstrated [Chafe 1986]) and that writing must be learned through experience with written texts and guided practice in writing.

Some postmodern language theorists also resist genre classifications and genre assignments by arguing that conventional genres maintain the status quo and protect the privileges and wealth of powerful people. A postmodernist might argue, for example, that the familiar problem-solution genre diverts ambitious policymakers from solvable local problems to more prestigious, but ill-defined and probably unsolvable, national problems, or it leads proposal writers to propose incremental changes rather than radical solutions in order to cater to powerful decision makers who dispense the money to implement solutions. Furthermore, some postmodern theorists argue, the very existence of the genre may lead us mistakenly to assume that any social problem can be solved if we persist in trying out different solutions or even to believe that we have an obligation to solve every problem anyone perceives in the social order.

In all of these ways, the problem-solution genre can be seen to inadvertently undermine its own apparent, social function, and yet few people believe that we can do without a genre that allows us to consider possible solutions to problems small or large, manageable or intractable, technological or social. Even though the problem-solution genre poses dangers and may limit the way we understand problems or think about solutions, it remains essential for social cohesion and political action in a democracy. Social issues like these can and should be raised about every genre we assign. (See the "social dimensions" activity at the end of each assignment chapter in Axelrod and Cooper 1997 for ways to involve high school and college students in considering these questions.)

My own position is that it is time to consolidate what we have learned from expressivism and writing process theory and move on. The new directions will come, I believe, from learning theory and discourse theory, especially genre theory. Our primary subject is written language in all of its amazing diversity. Our curricular and instructional concerns should reflect how students learn about written texts. I believe that there is now reason to argue that we undermine our subject and do students a great disservice to pretend that there is nothing for us to teach about writing. (The October 1993 issue of *Research in the Teaching of English* offers a substantive debate on the teaching and learning of genres [see Freedman, Williams and Colomb; and Fahnestock]).

To consolidate my scattered comments about pedagogy in earlier sections, I want to outline in this section a plan or model for a genre assignment that gives a major evaluation role to students. I have chosen an assignment that asks students to take a position on some local or community issue. (Versions of this plan can be found in the *St. Martin's Guide to Writing* [Axelrod and Cooper 1997] for college students and in California's *Writing Assessment Handbook, Grade 8* [1990] and *Writing Assessment Handbook, High School* [1993]). Classroom research supporting certain stages of this plan has been reviewed by Hillocks (1986). For a recent classroom study of what college students learn from genre models and a bibliography of research on modeling, see Charney and Carlson (1995). See Chapman (1995) for a study of first-grade children learning written genres.

Reading Models

Students begin by discussing brief, accessible published examples of texts that take a position. Three to five carefully chosen examples open up most of the possibilities of the genre. An exemplary student essay or two can be added to the mix. Students can learn about a written genre only if they read it—and reread it and talk about it.

Listing Basic Features

The purpose of reading and talking about models is to begin learning what is possible in a genre and to derive a list of features of that genre. This list can be refined gradually over two or three class meetings focused on models. The teacher may need to classify a scattered list generated from student discussion or to fill in gaps. The final working list need be only descriptive, not evaluative. It should identify the rhetorical and textual characteristics of writing that takes a position: how the text begins and ends, how it is patterned or sequenced, what cues it gives about the sequence, how it shows an awareness of particular readers, what assumptions it makes about readers, what its purpose seems to be what strategies it adopts to achieve its purpose, and so on. The discussion need not be technical, though the teacher can name features and strategies students identify. If the texts are accessible and take up issues students care about, sixth and seventh graders can be very good at this sort of analysis.

The genre knowledge that comes from discussing models establishes goals for learning and leads to criteria for evaluating writing. Most important, it makes invention or prewriting purposeful, and it provides a powerful heuristic for writing, opening up many possibilities for students and leaving countless decisions for them to make as they develop and shape their arguments. Since the genre knowledge is constructed by students and shared among them, evaluation of work-in-progress can be productively collaborative.

Choosing Topics

If students are taking a position for the first time, they will need guidance in choosing topics. With students' help, the teacher lists many possible topics, and asks each student to make a tentative choice. Genre assignments ensure great diversity of topics. If students are choosing their own issues, obviously their topics will differ. If students are writing about the same issue, perhaps with the advantage of shared materials they have explored in discussion, they will be taking different positions, and those students who take the same position on the issue will adopt quite different reasons and support.

Inventing and Researching

The teacher designs a sequence of invention or prewriting activities that engage students in the thinking, problem-solving, and planning required to take a position successfully. Research may or may not be required; it can involve library work or fieldwork (interviews, observations) in order to learn more about the issue. These brief activities are completed in writing so that students accumulate over several days a useful record of ideas and materials on their issues. One activity should allow students to try out their topics and tentative plans on other students.

Two alternatives to guided invention: In one, after some informal thinking and planning, each student writes a "zero draft," a quick, relatively brief draft written in class to see what turns up. In the other, the teacher leads the class in constructing together a draft on a topic no student has chosen. This second activity develops confidence in inexperienced writers, and it can be followed by guided invention on students' own topics.

Planning

Students may work together to plan their essays. By this stage they have developed a considerable amount of material for their arguments, and they know a lot about the genre.

Revising

In pairs or small groups, students read each other's drafts and give advice on revising. Here, a criteria list like those in the second section of this chapter is important. Students can collaborate to develop it from the features list, but whereas the features list is descriptive, the criteria list is qualitative. It identifies what makes a strong argument that takes a position. The criteria list is only the starting point, however. What is needed is some direction, following each criterion, about how to advise the writer on revising, direction the teacher may have to supply at first. For example, for a feature like anticipating readers' objections and questions, students might be encouraged to mark instances of it, advise the writer on how to make each concession or refutation more convincing for the particular readers, and list further likely objections and questions from readers. Such directions provide students with an opportunity to give substantive, genre-specific help toward revising.

Reflecting

Students revise their essays—and may perhaps revise again after another workshop or a conference with the teacher—and then step back to reflect on what they have learned about taking positions on issues. Guidelines are important, I believe, in order to ensure that students think about their writing processes and their achievements in terms of what is special about taking a position. To consolidate what they have learned, they need to use the language of taking a position— issue, position, thesis, argument, reasons, support, readers, conceding, refuting, and so on. They can be asked how they solved certain problems in their drafts, what influence the same-genre readings had on their revisions, what they are most pleased with, what they would continue to work on if they had more time, and so on.

Assembling a Portfolio

At the end of the semester or year, or after a sequence of assignments, students can review their work and make selections in order to present themselves as attractively as possible in a portfolio. Some teachers list what may be included, others provide only general guidelines, while others leave the choices up to students. Most teachers require further revisions on some of the work and a letter or essay presenting the work, justifying choices, and evaluating what has been achieved. Students may help each other with this entire process, and they can be particularly helpful if they have been learning about the same genres together. They understand what is to be achieved in the course, and they have concepts and criteria—substantive rhetorical knowledge—to guide their evaluations of their own and other students' work.

The implications of genre knowledge for writing instruction are certainly not limited to giving assignments in genres like those in the autobiographical and argumentative sequences I have illustrated or to the assignment model I just outlined. I believe genre knowledge is no less important for the teacher and students in situations where students choose to define their own assignments or projects. My own most recent work is with civic literacy assignments, where first-year college students engage in a conversation among themselves based on diverse published materials about a current issue. They record experiences and observations, undertake interviews, and research relevant print and Internet sources. For these projects, we do assign a genre based on our assessment of the status of the issue, so that students' reading and discussion can be purposeful from the beginning. For each issue, however, we offer additional assignments that invite students to try out other genres (Cooper and MacDonald 2000). Similar work (Yagelski 1997) that we admire with high school students allows more than one well-defined, purposeful assignment (i.e., a genre) to emerge during an extended period of exploration, gathering materials, and discussion and planning.

Resources

I have cited several sources, and now I would like to prioritize them for busy teachers who want to know more about genres, assignment sequences, and the new genre theory of literacy. The starting point has to be, I believe, Moffett's *Active Voice: A Writing Program across the Curriculum* (1981). In 148 readable pages it presents more than fifty writing assignments classified into three sequences. Each assignment is carefully posed for students, and then for the teacher Moffett relates each assignment to others in its sequence, discusses workshop issues, and suggests same-genre readings. *Active Voice* also introduces Moffett's fiction writing sequence, which is detailed with readings in *Points of View: An Anthology of Short Stories* (1966). Moffett's assignments slight explanatory, argumentative, and writing-about-literature genres, but those are filled out by Callaghan, Knapp, and Noble (1993), and Axelrod and Cooper (1997).

Moving from assignments toward teaching and evaluation, I recommend the Introduction and Chapters 8 and 9 in *The Powers of Literacy* (Cope and Kalantzis 1993) by an Australian research group. Other chapters present their theory of a genre approach to teaching writing. Another important book combining theory with very general discussions of pedagogy is *Learning and Teaching Genre* (Freedman and Medway 1994). The book's contributors teach writing in Australia, Canada, England, and the United States. For elementary school teachers, I recommend *Exploring How Texts Work* (Derewianka 1990), which is based on the work of classroom teachers whose students were mainly from non-English-speaking backgrounds.

Works Cited

Axelrod, Rise B., and Charles R. Cooper. 1997. *The St. Martin's Guide to Writing.* 5th ed. New York: St Martin's Press.

Bazerman, Charles. 1988. *Shaping Written Knowledge.* Madison: University of Wisconsin Press.

Beale, Walter H. 1987. *A Pragmatic Theory of Rhetoric.* Carbondale: Southern Illinois University Press.

Britton, James N., Tony Burgess, Nancy Martin, Alex McLeod, and Harold Rosen. 1975. *The Development of Writing Abilities (11–18).* London: Macmillan Education.

Callaghan, Mike, Peter Knapp, and Greg Noble. 1993. "Genre in Practice." In *The Powers of Literacy: A Genre Approach to Teaching Writing,* ed. Bill Cope and Mary Kalantzis, 179–202. Pittsburgh: University of Pittsburgh Press.

Chafe, Wallace. 1986. "Writing in the Perspective of Speaking." In *Studying Writing: Linguistic Perspectives,* ed. Charles R. Cooper and Sidney Greenbaum, 12–39. Northridge, CA: Sage.

Chapman, Marilyn L. 1995. "The Sociocognitive Construction of Written Genres in First Grade." *Research in the Teaching of English* 29: 164–92.

Charney, Davida H., and Richard A. Carlson. 1995. "Learning to Write in a Genre: What Student Writers Take from Model Texts." *Research in the Teaching of English* 29: 88–125.

Coe, Richard M. 1994. "Teaching Genre as Process." In *Learning and Teaching Genre,* ed. Aviva Freedman and Peter Medway, 157–69.

Cooper, Charles R., and Susan Peck MacDonald. 2000. *Writing the World.* New York: St. Martin's Press.

Cope, Bill, and Mary Kalantzis, eds. 1993. *The Powers of Literacy: A Genre Approach to Teaching Writing.* Pittsburgh: University of Pittsburgh Press.

Derewianka, Beverly. 1990. *Exploring How Texts Work.* Rozelle, N.S.W.: Primary English Teaching Association.

English Language-Arts Model Curriculum Standards, 9–12. 1991. Sacramento: California Department of Education.

Fahnestock, Jeanne. 1993. "Genre and Rhetorical Craft." *Research in the Teaching of English* 27: 265–71.

Ferguson, Charles A. 1994. "Dialect, Register, and Genre: Working Assumptions about Conventionalization." In *Sociolinguistic Perspectives on Register*, ed. Edward Finegan and Douglas Biber, 15–30. New York: Oxford University Press.

Freedman, Aviva. 1993. "Show and Tell? The Role of Explicit Teaching in the Learning of New Genres." *Research in the Teaching of English* 27: 222–51.

Freedman, Aviva, and Peter Medway, eds. 1994. *Learning and Teaching Genre.* Portsmouth, NH: Boynton/Cook.

Hillocks, George, Jr. 1986. *Research on Written Composition: New Directions for Teaching.* New York: National Conference on Research in English; Urbana, IL: ERIC Clearinghouse in Reading and Communication Skills.

Kinneavy, James L. 1971. *A Theory of Discourse: The Aims of Discourse.* Englewood Cliffs, NJ: Prentice-Hall.

Miller, Carolyn. 1984. "Genre as Social Action." *Quarterly Journal of Speech* 70: 151–67.

Moffett, James. 1968. *Teaching the Universe of Discourse.* Boston: Houghton Mifflin.

———. 1987a. *Active Voices I.* Upper Montclair, NJ: Boynton/Cook.

———. 1987b. *Active Voices III.* Upper Montclair; NJ: Boynton/Cook.

———. 1992. *Active Voice: A Writing Program across the Curriculum.* 2nd ed. Portsmouth, NH: Boynton/Cook.

Moffett, James, Miriam Baker, and Charles R. Cooper. 1986. *Active Voices IV.* Upper Montclair, NJ: Boynton/Cook.

Moffett, James, and Kenneth R. McElhenny. 1966. *Points of View: An Anthology of Short Stories.* New York: New American Library.

Moffett, James, and Phyllis Tashlik. 1987. *Active Voices II.* Upper Montclair, NJ: Boynton/Cook.

Reed, Joseph W. 1989. *American Scenarios: The Uses of Film Genre.* Middletown, CT: Wesleyan University Press.

Rose, Brian G., ed. 1985. *TV Genres: A Handbook and Reference Guide.* Westport, CT: Greenwood Press.

Student Essays Illustrating the CAP [California Assessment Program] Rhetorical Effectiveness Scoring System (Grade 12). 1990. Sacramento: California Department of Education.

Warriner, John E. 1957. *English Grammar and Composition: Complete Course.* New York: Harcourt, Brace & World.

Williams, Joseph M., and Gregory G. Colomb. 1993. "The Case for Explicit Teaching: Why What You Don't Know Won't Help You." *Research in the Teaching of English* 27: 252–64.

Writing Assessment Handbook, Grade 8. 1990. Sacramento: California Department of Education.

Writing Assessment Handbook, Grade 12. 1993. Sacramento: California Department of Education.

Yagelski, Robert P. "Literature and Literacy: Rethinking English as a School Subject." *English Journal* 83: 30–36.

3 Audience Considerations for Evaluating Writing

Phyllis Mentzell Ryder
University of Arizona

Elizabeth Vander Lei
Arizona State University

Duane H. Roen
Arizona State University

Phyllis remembers sitting around a gray seminar table with twelve other graduate students as her professor returned the first essays of the semester. She had written about Emily Dickinson, delving into the poems with a passion that she was certain would be rewarded. When Professor Aiken handed back her essay, Phyllis was startled to see the first comment. Right after Phyllis's opening claim that "In attempting to explore death in Emily Dickinson's poems, we cross into dangerous territory," Professor Aiken had written, "Why should we explore death in E. D.? You need to make the reader care." *Is this blasphemy?* Phyllis wondered to herself. *Isn't this what literature people do—read works and talk about themes? Who would stop to ask "Why?"*

Professor Aiken's question forced Phyllis to see literature professors as a particular kind of audience. When Phyllis tumbled into her office full of questions, Professor Aiken explained that we cannot assume that people will read and analyze literature simply because we think they should. Even among literature folk, debates about which books belong in the canon and which authors should be included in standard curricula have called into question any inherent "literary" value of a text. Literature professors have to justify their choices and persuade readers about the value of texts and the value of analysis.

As a teacher of writing, Phyllis keeps Professor Aiken's advice close at hand. Not only does she tell this story to her students, she also demands that they justify their claims and theses as if they were writing to real readers who need to be convinced about the value of the work. A metaphor comes to mind from Peter Elbow's book *Writing with Power* (1981). Elbow suggests that we picture writers and readers as two people on the same bicycle. As writers, we can steer; but the readers have to pedal. If we don't explain where we are going and why, and if we don't convince them that they should keep pedaling, the bicycle will stop and we'll both tumble off. A text is nothing if readers stop reading.

As writing teachers, we don't often confront our students with this fact. We forget that in the "real world," an essay has to feel significant or readers will toss it aside and turn on the TV. It is easy for us to forget this because when *we* read our students' pieces, we don't have the choice to stop reading: As teachers, we are required to give generous and careful attention to each essay. In fact (as Peter Elbow reminds us), we shelter our students from the brutality of real reader responses, just as Phyllis was sheltered from real literature scholars. Professor Aiken could write, "Why must we read Emily Dickinson?" in the margin, but she still had to read the rest of Phyllis's paper.

As writing teachers, the three of us (Phyllis, Elizabeth, and Duane) have found that recognizing the difference between our responses as teachers and the potential responses of "real" readers is helpful as we evaluate student writing. When we identify the "real" audience of a student essay as someone other than ourselves, we step out of the position of "judge" and into the position of "coach." That is, instead of responding to a text by saying, "This is how it's done; these are the rules," we can say, "Your writing will probably affect your reader in X way," and explain how the author might better reach that audience. We shift out of the role of "antagonist" and into the role of "supporter," a role we like. More important, we believe we are more effective teachers when we can support students' efforts to achieve their purpose for their readers.

We believe that thinking about audience helps students recognize the issues they will have to contend with when they write outside the shelter of our classrooms. In this chapter, we want to invite other writing teachers to pay special attention to the concept of audience as they design assignments and evaluate student work. We will first clarify what we see as the role of readers. Then we will delve into some of the dangers of talking about "audience" as we are most tempted to do—as if all readers are the same. We will then explain the various techniques we have seen both professional and student authors use to accommodate their audiences. Finally, we will show how we use all of this information as we evaluate essays.

The Role of Audience in Writing

One of the fears that writers have when confronted with the concept of audience is that readers will dictate the whole interaction. Phyllis remembers a group of students who rebelled vociferously, saying, "This is me. I am expressing myself through my writing. No reader should be able to tell me how to be myself." While some students refuse to change a word that might compromise their sense of "self-expression," other students want to turn all the decisions over to us. They say, "What kind of writing do you like? Flowery? Candid? Preachy? Timid? Just tell me, and I'll do that." How can we writing teachers respond to these extremes?

One answer is to recognize that there are several kinds of author-audience relationships. The student who writes to express herself might imagine that she is in a *monadic* writing situation. She is both the writer and the audience; no one else need be involved. A second writing/speaking situation is *dyadic*. Such cases, where the writer/speaker is addressing a particular person, are often seen as the most important kinds of persuasion because of the relationship between the author/speaker and reader/listener (Rogers 1961; Teich 1992; Young, Becker, and Pike 1970). Students who ask "What do you want?" might imagine that they are in dyadic situations, assuming that any student's job is to write to the teacher. In their work, they might address us with: "You told me to write an essay about Emily Dickinson."

A third option is a *triadic* situation. Here the author/speaker is one of two opponents before an audience. We see this happen during public debates, when two candidates spar before a crowd. The two are not trying to persuade each other; rather, each is trying to persuade the audience, the third party. To some extent, the audience role in the triadic situation is one that writing teachers find most comfortable. Rather than have students speak to us directly, we prefer that they speak to another audience while we listen in. In this case, students might write, "My English teacher told me to write about Emily Dickinson." More ideally, we are left out of the essay altogether as the student takes on an opponent: "Although some people might not value reading Emily Dickinson, I find that it is important to read her poems because. . . ."

When we pick up stacks of student essays and begin to read, we probably have a sense of which kind of writing situation we expected our students to adopt. In reading journals, we expect monadic situations; it's fine if students talk aloud to themselves. In letters, we expect the dyadic; it's fine if students address us directly. In essays, we expect the triadic. The problems arise when we don't articulate these expectations to our students. If we fail to provide reception-oriented aims for students' writing, we shouldn't fault them if they emphasize the "wrong" qualities of their discourse. For example, the old standby assignment "describe a place that has always been special to you" provokes a private and expression-oriented response. Students might talk about the place as if they were reminding themselves of it, skipping those details that would clarify their experience for another person. Their purpose is to evoke their own emotional response and not anyone else's.

If we want our students to write about this place for readers other than themselves, we need to say so in the assignment: "Think about a place in town that has always been special to you. Imagine that a business is planning to destroy it. In an open letter to the people in town, describe the place in such a way that they will see how important it is and stop the destruction." Here we've given a specific, public purpose to the task. Describing the place to themselves will not be enough: Students have to create emotional responses in the townspeople. Whether we assign the audience or allow our students to choose one, we need to be sure that our students recognize the ways to best address various readers.

Invoking Audience in Writing

One of the difficulties we run into when we broach the idea of a public audience is that it is too easy to imagine a homogeneous group of readers rather than the amorphous, multiple, heterogeneous collection of readers who actually make up "the public." Even when we narrow the field and tell students to write to a very particular person—the author of a story we have read, for example—we must recognize that each person is capable of many different roles (Long 1990). For example, Duane is simultaneously a husband, a father, a writer, a softball player, a Garrison Keillor fan, a professor, a researcher, and a multitude of other things. As a reader, Duane can choose which parts of himself are most appropriate for the text at hand.

While that is true, writers can "invoke" their audience by inserting cues about which role they expect their readers to assume. How exactly does a writer cue a reader, and how can we teachers determine whether or not student writers have done so accurately? First, we have to determine whether the student is writing in a monadic, dyadic, or triadic situation. If the student is writing for himself or herself, we will be given no audience cues. In journal or freewriting, where the student is using the writing to weigh ideas and compare them with personal experiences, the student doesn't need to cue an audience: Writer and reader are one and the same.

Naming Moves

In dyadic or triadic writing, the audience demands are more complex. Students must cue the readers about which stance to take: Are the readers allies? Enemies? Are they indifferent? Writers signal the intended role through "naming moves" which involve particular pronouns, such as you/your or we/our. They also name those groups the readers belong to, using phrases such as "those of us at MADD" or "as administrators of public universities, you . . . " (Hays et al. 1990). In an open letter to the editor, for example, a writer might say, "As women and as Democrats, we cannot allow the Republican-controlled government to take away our right to choose." The audience knows to expect an argument that takes gender and political affiliation into account. In addition, male, Republican, or antichoice readers would recognize that this piece was written to another audience. While they can certainly still read the piece, they do so with an awareness that they are not the primary audience. They use the naming moves to position themselves in relation to the author and intended audience.

Context Moves

A second cueing technique involves background information. These cues arise when the student includes or excludes information on the basis of what the audience already knows. For example, in the assignment to describe a special place for townspeople, the author would have to fully describe the details to ensure that the readers could imagine it. The author would have to linger over those aspects which were most important. But the author would not need to give background or geographical information about where the town itself was located because the audience would know that already.

As teachers, we should recognize that while students can easily incorporate naming and context moves early in an essay, they may have more difficulty considering audience as they move deeper into their argument. This happened, for example, in an essay that Jay wrote. His goal was to convince nongolfers to admire that sport. He invited them into his discussion effectively, taking care to address them respectfully. As he moved deeper into his argument, he tried to consider why people might dislike golf. At this point, however, he seemed to forget whom he was addressing. He dismissed all possible arguments by stating, "Anyone who doesn't like golf is either ignorant or jealous." In the middle of his piece, he insulted the very readers he needed to accommodate. His readers probably stopped "pedaling" and the "essay ride" ended before Jay could steer them where he wanted to go.

Strategy Moves

Clearly, students need to learn techniques for keeping their audience's interest throughout the essay. Professional writers use two other methods—"strategy moves" and "response moves" to do just this. In "strategy moves," writers use tactics which draw on the readers' attributes: Readers are more interested when they believe an argument was compiled for them. In particular, writers appeal to readers' self-interest, state readers' responsibilities, define readers' circumstances, appeal to readers' emotions, suggest readers' choices, praise readers, establish shared features between themselves and the readers, and ask readers to take action (Hays et al. 1990, 254).

Jill Robinson (1994), a first-year composition student, demonstrates some of these moves in her essay on euthanasia. Jill researched this topic to better understand a decision she and her family had made to take her grandfather off life support. She wanted to share how she had arrived at her position, and she felt that the most appropriate audience for her essay was another person who was facing the same decision. Since she didn't know anyone in that situation, she chose to write to an imaginary person, "Mrs. Christiansen." While on the surface this appears to be a dyadic situation, in fact Jill has created a triadic one because Mrs. Christiansen is not a real person: The essay is intended for other readers (in situations similar to Mrs. Christiansen) who read triadically. Jill's strategy is to create an indirect appeal to her real readers—to show she understands without imposing too directly on their lives. In her opening paragraph, Jill uses a number of strategy moves. She establishes her readers' circumstance and appeals to readers' emotions:

> It is with mixed emotions that I am writing you this letter. On the one hand, I feel the deepest sympathy with you in your time of grief over the impending loss of your loved one. It is so difficult to deal with the realization that you are facing the loss of [a] person you have loved so long and hold so dear. You want to do everything in your power to hang on, to not let go of that lifeline holding your loved one to you. But on the other hand, I feel relieved and uplifted

> because I believe I can help you by sharing with you my similar experience and how my family and I made and dealt with the same decision you are facing. (222)

In the next paragraph, Jill tells her own story and establishes shared features with her readers. Throughout the essay, she uses strategy moves to connect with her readers. She also uses "response moves"—that is, she anticipates readers' probable questions or objections.

Response Moves

Response moves can be of several types. In one type, writers simply state the readers' concerns. In another, more complex approach, the writer both states and gives reasons explaining these concerns. Even more sophisticated, the writer might rebut, concede, or accommodate those concerns in the larger argument. Jill sets up her "response moves" in the following paragraphs. Notice how she first explains her readers' concerns and then prepares to respond:

> Your family is now faced with the same difficult decision that my family was faced with. I realize that you do not feel that you, the rest of your family, and the doctors have the power to discontinue treatment because you feel you would be the cause of his death. However, you also admit that you cannot stand to see your husband this way another minute. On the one hand, you don't want to feel guilty for allowing your husband to die, but on the other hand, you don't want to see him in a permanent vegetative state. I believe I can help you to understand why prolonging your husband's life is unnecessary, and why there is no reason to feel guilty when making this decision to stop all treatment.
>   To show you that withdrawing life support from a permanently unconscious person, like your husband, is not considered abandonment or immoral, you must understand the definition of a persistent vegetative state. (224)

Jill continues by providing definitions and reasons that respond to the fears she imagines her readers to have. She designed her essay thoroughly around her reader(s). When students incorporate strategy and response moves, their writing will be more clearly geared to particular readers and, in turn, more persuasive for those readers.

Introducing Questions of Audience

Because writing is an interactive process, an audience has an impact on all parts of a text—the way a topic is developed, the organization, the diction, the tone, and so on. Clearly, then, questions of audience cannot be left to the end of the writing process.

On the other hand, during the first stages of writing, students need to be relatively uncritical as they get words and ideas onto the pages; they need to play with thoughts. Introducing questions of audience too soon may short-circuit this exploration (Elbow 1981; Elbow and Clarke 1987). For example, inexperienced student writers who were asked to consider their readers while drafting produced essays that were judged to be of lesser quality than those written by students who did so while revising (Roen and Willey 1988). The evidence suggests that these students (in this case, first-year college students) need time to generate prose before they package it for others. Once students have identified and perhaps drafted what they want to say, we can ask them how they might need to revise it for readers. As we construct assignments, then, we need to consider how and when to raise questions about audience.

Crafting Writing Assignments

To balance the tensions of writing-for-self vs. writing-for-others, we advocate assignments that prompt students to address the range of audiences along a continuum of private to increasingly more public audiences—that is, audiences who share more or fewer values and experiences with the writer (Moffett 1981). To put it another way, we should develop a range of assignments along a continuum from expression-oriented (monadic) to reception-oriented (dyadic or triadic) writing.

Consider a series of assignments for ninth graders based on Frank Stockton's frequently anthologized story, "The Lady and the Tiger." First, students wrote their initial responses to the story and drew connections to personal experiences or other stories or poems they had read (monadic). Later, they developed their thoughts for an audience slightly removed from themselves, an audience of their classmates. Each student wrote an ending for the story and an argument for why that ending was most appropriate. To help students recognize the ways in which they needed to account for their peers' responses, the teacher had students present their drafts to the class. One student, Gabe, wrote this ending and argument (his response was equally as short as his classmates'):

> **Ending:** The woman walks through the open door. She and the guy get married, have children, and live happily ever after.
>
> **Argument:** This is the ending that the author would have written. I think that the princess loved the man so much that she wouldn't want him eaten by the tiger, which was behind the other door. She will be sad that she can't be married to him, but she will be happy knowing that he is happy.

Gabe's teacher asked six students to read their drafts to the whole class. Three of them had written endings with the woman behind the opened door; the others put the tiger there. The resulting discussion, of course, focused on love, hatred, revenge, happiness, violence, and even literary conventions. In the course of the discussion, Gabe and other students (not only the six who read) recognized that their arguments had relied on assumptions that the whole class did not necessarily accept. In order to revise his essay for this audience, Gabe had to account for these positions and work to convince his peers that his view was right.

In the final assignment in the sequence, students wrote to an audience outside the class. In this case, students wrote to a person who had to make a difficult decision and would use their interpretation of the story to explain how to resolve a moral issue. This time, students needed to articulate the significance of their claims as well as to provide the evidence to support them.

In a sequence of assignments such as this, we can show our students how writing changes depending on the audience. As writing assignments build on each other, students recognize the ways they must adjust their naming, context, strategy, and response moves depending on the intimacy or distance between the authors and their audience.

By now it should be clear that any form of writing can have an argumentative edge. In one sense, every form of writing is working to persuade other people to see the world as the writer does: to see the importance of that special place in town, to understand life and death as the author does, to agree with the author's view of human nature. The more we can help our students to see this aspect of what they write, the more audience will become a factor that shapes their audience.

Whenever possible, though, we need to encourage our students to write explicitly argumentative, persuasive prose because that is the discourse that gets work done in the world. It is the discourse that will serve students throughout their lives—as students, as workers, as citizens—in a democracy. When we fail to assign writing and speaking that persuades, we deprive students of some tools that they need in order to have a full voice in their schools, their jobs, their society. As they write such discourse, students need experiences with a full range of audiences—friendly, general, hostile, multiple, professional—for they will encounter a full range in their lives.

Assigning and Responding to Journals

While we appreciate the ways journals offer students places to explore and write expression-oriented prose, we also advocate journals because they give us opportunities to clarify the multiple levels of our responses to student writing. Through repeated interaction with our comments, students develop a keener sense of us teachers as an audience, and of our ability to shift in and out of invoked audience roles.

Elizabeth required journal writing in her course at Arizona State University. The following extended example demonstrates the ways in which she used the journal to offer varied responses that helped the students consider audience. In the advanced writing class, one student, Leslie Farnsworth, wrote all her course papers on water quality. Her journal entries trace her thinking on the subject. When considering her stance on federal spending on water quality, Leslie recorded the following entry:

> Walt (my husband) asked an interesting question the other night—". . . why would a water quality person want to convince a person of political power to not spend money on water quality???" I explained that this is a paper on comparative risk assessment and that my personal gain really shouldn't be of concern—I also explained that my advisor suggested it and I was desperate to get started, it sounded good, so off I went. But he does have a point. After I finished the rough draft of my definition paper we went to see the IMAX movie <u>Blue Planet</u> and I came away angry as . . . ! Perhaps if our drinking water situation is under control we should consider putting more money into water clean up. It's sickening.

Leslie's struggle—how much should her concerns be central, and how much power should she yield to her potential audience—exemplifies the writer-reader dilemma. If the reader (in this case, the advisor) is given too large of a role, the author's own concerns and questions might become subordinated. In her response, Elizabeth encouraged her to keep her own concerns central in the paper: Elizabeth wrote next to Walt's question: "He's worth keeping around for a while—A really good question!"

As Leslie wrestled with her concerns as a "water quality person" and her stance on continued public funding of water quality improvements, she recognized from Elizabeth's comments that this conflict itself might appeal to her readers. She decided to use the dilemma to establish her persona in her later essay.

At one point in Leslie's journal, Elizabeth directed Leslie to consider her audience more specifically. Leslie's journal entry follows:

> Organization for paper:
>> Brief description of how they are formed
>> Effects of THMs → cancer
>> Show fake #'s to prove how dangerous THM's can be
>> Show real #'s that comply w/current EPA standards
>> Persuasive conclusion

Elizabeth circled the word *cancer* and advised, "Such a strong concept in American thought—it's the dread killer. You need to deal with this fear to get past it and on to your argument of comparative risk." In response to Elizabeth's comment, Leslie added an effective table which illustrated the cancer risk of several actions (the risk from sea-level background radiation was almost one hundred times greater than the risk of THMs in drinking water, for example). Here, Elizabeth was able to intervene during the writing process to suggest that Leslie consider her particular audience.

As she spoke and wrote to Leslie about the project, Elizabeth moved in and out of dyadic and triadic roles: She considered the essay from the role of the invoked reader (Leslie eventually directed her essay to Senator Barbara Boxer) when she suggested that the cancer section might need expansion, and she offered her own response (triadic) during a conference when she spoke of her own concerns as a resident in the Superfund cleanup area. This allowed Leslie to separate the two and understand how Elizabeth was adjusting her role to fit Leslie's audience.

Co-authoring

Another pedagogical tool which gives students experience with both dyadic and triadic rhetorical situations is co-authored writing projects. As co-authors, students negotiate the purpose of their writing and the means by which they will achieve that purpose. This dyadic relationship is especially effective because the collaborating authors have a vested interest in the success of the writing and interact with each other early and throughout the composing process. A co-authored writing project also creates a triadic rhetorical situation that includes the co-authors and the reader of the text. In the same way that Elizabeth and Leslie managed the carcinogenic effects of THMs, co-authors can provide valuable input regarding audience reactions and shared experiences between author and audience that will aid both collaborators when they must write alone.

So that we can assess students' attention to audience, co-authored assignments should contain the following stipulations. First, requiring the co-authors to write a confidential assessment of the collaborative experience helps us instructors determine the success of the dyadic relationship. In such assessments, students should describe the stages at which collaboration was most and least helpful, their evaluation of their co-author's commitment to the project, and what they learned about themselves as writers as a result of this experience. Second, requiring students to keep a collaborative journal provides a window into the co-authors' developing sense of the audience of the writing assignment. We can guide the students' entries by assigning tasks such as comparing audience profiles that the co-authors created individually. The differences between the students' audience profiles can begin a conversation about authorial assumptions regarding audience and initiate the triadic relationship between the co-authors and the reader of the text.

Students as Audiences in the Writing Class

Student writers need to have direct experiences with *audiences*, not just *an* audience. A method for accomplishing this is to have classmates be audiences. The goal is to let students experience a wide range of responses so that they will move beyond their own idiosyncratic thinking (Brown, Mittan, and Roen 1990; Diogenes, Roen, and Moneyhun 1986; Elbow 1973, 1981; Flower 1979).

Peer Feedback

We suggested the benefits of using peer feedback when we discussed Gabe's essay earlier. His peers' responses helped him recognize that his assumptions needed to be further developed in order to persuade his classmates. When classmates offer real feedback, students see the possibilities embedded in their own writing. Here is another example. Abby, a seventh grader, drafted this descriptive paragraph about her hometown, Minneapolis:

> I like Minneapolis a lot. There are many things to do here. My family goes to watch the Timberwolves, the Twins, and the Vikings whenever we can. We try to go to a new ethnic restaurant every week. We see almost all the plays at the Guthrie Theatre. Some Saturday evenings we drive to St. Paul to see Garrison Keillor's show.

When Abby reads her paragraph, her peers' questions suggest that they haven't had the same experiences that she has:

> "How often do you go to the Timberwolves, Twins, and Vikings?"
>
> "Do you also go to college and high school games?"
>
> "What kinds of restaurants are there here besides McDonald's and Burger King?"
>
> "What's an ethnic restaurant?"
>
> "What's the Guthrie Theatre?"
>
> "Who's Garrison Keillor?"

"Are these the things that make you like Minneapolis so much?"

"If you didn't have money to do all these things, would you still like Minneapolis?"

"Do you like the weather here? I hate it."

"Do you like the people here?"

"What don't you like about Minneapolis?"

As Abby listens to these questions, she realizes that she has plenty of decisions to make as she revises the paragraph. Does she want to aim for the least knowledgeable audience, which means that she'll need to add many details? If so, does she want to focus her paper more on Keillor's nationally broadcast radio show, *Prairie Home Companion*, or does she want to keep all of the topics and develop a paragraph for each? Does she want to give a more balanced view of Minneapolis, one that includes what she dislikes about the city? Her classmates' comments have reminded Abby (just as his peers reminded Gabe) of the many decisions to make as she revises her writing for them. In fact, she will first have to decide whom in the class she most wants to address.

To help structure peer-response activities, we recommend the following activity, which was originally proposed by Elbow (1973) and modified by others (Koch 1982; Lyons 1978; Brown, Mittan, and Roen; 1990; Roen 1989). After a writer has read his or her paper, the peers respond in the following way:

1. "I identify with _____ in your writing."

2. "I like _____ in your writing."

3. "I have these questions about what you have written. . . ."

4. "I have these suggestions. . . ."

The first response is a relatively nonthreatening way for peer readers to let the writer know that they have had a common experience—a point at which to begin the conversation. The second response, a positive comment, may be a little threatening for some students, especially adolescents, but the preceding statement of identification paves the way for it. This second response gives the writer an emotional pat on the back before getting down to the hard work required to answer the questions that readers are about to pose. Third, the questions, which need to be genuine requests for information, constitute the heart of the activity. As the writer hears the questions, she or he comes to understand what readers need or want to know. At this point, the writer should answer readers orally and briefly jot down those answers, for they often comprise the bulk of the revisions that follow. The questions serve to notify the writer that at least these readers need more detail in order to understand what the writer wants them to understand. For example, Hanna has drafted a descriptive piece about a visit to her older cousin's farm. In one sentence of one paragraph, she mentions that "The most fun I had on the farm was watching my cousin teach a day-old calf to drink." That single sentence evoked several questions from peers:

> "Don't calves know how to drink when they're born?"
> "How do you teach a calf to drink?"

Hanna's responses to these two questions alone resulted in another lengthy paragraph in which she explained that calves are born with the instinct to suckle, not drink. She further described how the instinct to suckle helps teach a calf to drink:

> Facing the same direction as the calf, stand with the calf's neck between your legs—to keep the critter from wandering away. Then hold a pail of milk in one hand while you let the calf suckle on the three middle fingers of your other hand. Gently lower your fingers into the milk so that the calf ingests mild as it's suckling your fingers. Then slowly remove your fingers from the calf's mouth. Viola. It has learned to drink from a pail.

Finally, the suggestions are optional; they are usually unnecessary if readers have asked enough thoughtful questions.

Teachers' Responses

Clearly, student writers should recognize that the role of audience is integral throughout the writing process. Therefore, when we write our final comments, the question of audience should play a central role as well.

Commenting about Standard Usage

First, consider how an audience-oriented approach determines how we comment on spelling, punctuation, sentence structure, grammar, and other elements commonly found in writing handbooks. If marking these features is our only form of feedback, students may assume incorrectly that content is less important than correctness. When we talk about writing in terms of audience, however, we can discuss the necessity of standard usage on the basis of rhetorical situations.

In monadic situations, "proper" usage is not a concern: The students know what they mean; they are not trying to reach a wider audience. Therefore, we should not address these issues on journals or freewriting. In dyadic or triadic situations, the necessity of following handbook rules depends on how the chosen audience will interpret variations from standard form. Because many readers assume (wrongly, we think) that writers who have poor grammatical and mechanical skills are sloppy thinkers, we need to clarify that proper format, usage, and so on all build up an author's credibility in the eyes of the readers. When we talk about the effect of non-Standard English on various audiences, we emphasize the ethos-building function of Standard English and circumvent the dangerous assumptions that certain forms of speech are *inherently* better than others. In addition, this focus helps us resist the temptation to comment about Standard English on all drafts: We only need address it when students are writing to people who care about proper English.

Commenting on Final Drafts

By the time students are ready to hand in final drafts, they should have a clear sense of whom they are writing for. On a cover sheet, students should explain whom their paper targets and which qualities of their readers they hope to invoke. As the term progresses, they can also indicate which naming, strategy, and response moves they have used to appeal to that audience. As evaluative readers, we should use this knowledge to slip in and out of the role of the invoked/addressed audience and coach our students toward stronger dyadic interactions. Consider, for example, these comments that Phyllis wrote to Anwar, whose essay argued for a code of ethics in business, and whose cover sheet indicated that his audience was "people in management":

> Dear Anwar,
>   As I read your paper [as] if I were in management, I found myself most compelled by those paragraphs in which you addressed "my" position—the discussion of your business (where you and "I" had common awareness of what it means to run a business) and the paragraph where you discussed the possible reasons management might give in to immoral actions.
>   As management, though, I was frustrated by the vagueness of your definitions of "morality" and "ethics." In the first section I felt I was being reprimanded for not being moral, but couldn't get a handle on your definition of "moral." As a result, I resisted your argument.

By stressing that she was playing the role of the intended reader, Phyllis urged Anwar to resee his paper. Furthermore, because she was clear that she was playing the dyadic role in this part of her response, she could shift out of it later in the following response:

> Anwar, I (as me, again, not as management) see that you are dealing with a complex question here. The key to writing persuasively about such touchy topics is to keep your reader in mind. Address the questions your readers will raise; identify with and clarify their points so they feel you have thoroughly considered their position.

Here, in the triadic rhetorical situation, Phyllis can explain to Anwar how she (as the third party) is judging the "conversation" he has initiated with business management. Her emphasis that writing must account for the rhetorical situation, and must use appropriate strategy and response moves, is made explicit when she models the dyadic role and comments from the triadic one.

Making Appropriate Audience Choices for Academic Writing

As students invoke audiences, we must make them aware that not all teachers will be willing to take on all the roles invoked for them. Consider, for example, a case in which a student in an upper-division history course takes a creative approach in a paper which has

> "essentially the tone of a television travelogue commentary" . . . which thus asks the reader, a history professor, to assume the role of the viewer of such a show. The result is as might be expected: "Although the content of the paper does not seem significantly more abysmal than other papers in the same set, this one was awarded a disproportionately low grade." (Pringle and Freedman, qtd. in Ede and Lunsford 1984)

In this case, the writer may have accurately invoked the viewer role, and the argument might have considered the viewer's position, but the projected role was somehow inappropriate for the triadic situation of the classroom assignment. If an assignment fails in this way, we need to clearly indicate whether the invoked role was inaccurately conveyed or whether we, as teachers, are unwilling to take on that role. In addition, we need to indicate to students when they cue invoking roles that other academicians may not be willing to play.

While most composition instructors who make audience a central part of their course may not balk at the invoked role of a television viewer, there are other situations where we might feel uncomfortable.

We might read essays directed to white supremacists who argue that people of other races are inferior. Or consider other scenarios: heterosexual male students writing about their sexual conquests, or "white male students writ[ing] fictional narratives in which a white male antagonist commits violence against a female teacher" (Jarratt 1991, 106). Presumably, the audience for these pieces is composed of other Anglos or other men, but as teachers we have to wonder if it is enough to simply evaluate the writing according to how well it reaches that particular audience.

The triadic role here suggests a way to discuss students' ethical responsibilities as writers. If we receive such essays, we can choose to read them as the intended audience, grade accordingly, and then use the triadic situation to comment on how we, as the third party, reacted. If we are unwilling to adopt the invoked audience role, we can meet with the student to explain clearly why. The student can then redo the essay, this time being aware of the constraints imposed by the triadic nature of academic writing. This triadic situation, which is inevitable in most formal essay writing, gives us a way to discuss writing without having to agree with it.

Conclusion

Perhaps the best reason of all for teaching audience is that students already come to class with many of these skills. As they move up through the grades, as they come into contact with a wider variety of teachers, they learn that *teachers* are particular kinds of readers. They start to play the "figure out what the teacher wants" game. If we acknowledge this and guide students to apply their "detective" skills for a broader range of readers, they will leave our classes learning how to write for more people than just us teachers. At the same time, we can tell them explicitly what teachers want and why: The guessing games are no longer covert but become part of the content of the class.

If we make audience needs and expectations central to our discussions of all writing, students will learn to wrestle with audience negotiations in our classes, and they will therefore be better prepared to analyze the discourse demands they will face once they move on. They won't be surprised if their new readers respond differently than we did. Rather, they will expect it and will be able to draw on analytical skills to determine how to best address each new rhetorical situation. And this is what teaching writing is all about.

Further Reading on Audience

If you are interested in further reading on audience, we recommend the following books: Peter Elbow's *Writing with Power* (1981) is highly accessible. In particular, the "Catalogue of Reader-Based Questions" offers an extensive list of questions that direct students to identify author-reader relationships. James Moffett's *Teaching the Universe of Discourse* (1983) provides cogent arguments for moving students along different continua of distance from audiences. Moffett's companion volume, *Active Voice* (1981), gives detailed, practical descriptions of assignments, following the suggestions of his first book—with special attention paid to audience. Nicholas Karolide's collection, *Reader Response in the Classroom* (1992), offers an accessible explanation of Louise Rosenblatt's theories for responding to texts, as well as a plethora of practical applications of the theory. Meredith Sue Willis's *Deep Revision* (1993) details almost two hundred specific revision exercises emphasizing how students can use responses from audiences to revise effectively. Karen Spear's collection, *Peer Response Groups in Action* (1993), offers ways to encourage students to serve as audiences for one another to generate and effectively revise their work. Gesa Kirsch and Duane H. Roen's *A Sense of Audience in Written Communication* (1990) collects sixteen essays that offer theoretical, historical, empirical, and practical perspectives on audience. And finally, James Porter's *Audience and Rhetoric* (1992) offers theoretical arguments for a community view of audience, with practical suggestions for classroom activities.

Works Cited

Brown, Stuart C., Robert K. Mittan, and Duane H. Roen. 1990. *Becoming Expert: Writing and Learning in the Disciplines.* Dubuque, IA: Kendall/Hunt.

Diogenes, Marvin, Duane H. Roen, and Clyde Moneyhun. 1986. "Transactional Evaluation: The Right Question at the Right Time." *Journal of Teaching Writing* 5: 59–70.

Ede, Lisa, and Andrea Lunsford. 1984. "Audience Addressed/Audience Invoked: The Role of Audience in Composition Theory and Pedagogy." *College Composition and Communication* 35: 155–71.

Elbow, Peter, 1973. *Writing without Teachers.* New York: Oxford University Press.

———. 1981. *Writing with Power.* New York: Oxford University Press.

Elbow, Peter, and Jennifer Clarke. 1987. "Desert Island Discourse: The Benefits of Ignoring Audience." In *The Journal Book,* ed. Toby Fulwiler, 19–32. Upper Montclair, NJ: Boynton/Cook.

Flower, Linda. 1979. "Writer-Based Prose: A Cognitive Basis for Problems in Writing." *College English* 41: 19–37.

Hays, Janice N., Robert L. Durham, Kathleen S. Brandt, and Allan E. Raitz. 1990. "Argumentative Writing of Students: Adult Socio-Cognitive Development." In *A Sense of Audience in Written Communication,* ed. Gesa Kirsch and Duane H. Roen, 248–66. Newbury Park, CA: Sage.

Jarratt, Susan. 1991. "Feminism and Composition: The Case for Conflict." In *Contending with Words: Composition and Rhetoric in a Postmodern Age,* ed. Patricia Harkin and John Schilb, 106–23. New York: Modern Language Association of America.

Karolides, Nicholas J., ed. 1992. *Reader Response in the Classroom: Evoking and Interpreting Meaning in Literature.* New York: Longman.

Kirsch, Gesa, and Duane H. Roen, eds. 1990. *A Sense of Audience in Written Communication.* Newbury Park, CA: Sage.

Koch, Richard. 1982. "Syllogisms and Superstitions: The Current State of Responding to Writing." *Language Arts* 59: 464–71.

Long, Russell. 1990. "The Writer's Audience: Fact or Fiction?" In *A Sense of Audience in Written Communication,* ed. Gesa Kirsch and Duane H. Roen, 73–84. Newbury Park, CA: Sage.

Lyons, Bill. 1978, "Well What Do You Like about My Paper?" *Iowa English Newsletter* (Sep.): 4–5.

Moffett, James. [1968] 1983. *Teaching the Universe of Discourse.* Boston: Houghton Mifflin.

———. 1981. *Active Voice: A Writing Program across the Curriculum.* Upper Montclair, NJ: Boynton/Cook.

Porter, James E. 1992. *Audience and Rhetoric: An Archaeological Composition of the Discourse Community.* Englewood Cliffs, NJ: Prentice-Hall.

Robinson, Jill. 1994. "A Message of Mercy." In *A Student's Guide to First-Year Composition.* 15th ed., ed. Nancy Buffington, D. R. Ransdell, and Phyllis Mentzell Ryder, 222–28. Edina, MN: Burgess.

Roen, Duane H. 1989. "Developing Effective Assignments for Second Language Writers." In *Richness in Writing: Empowering ESL Students,* ed. Donna M. Johnson and Duane H. Roen, 193–206. New York: Longman.

Roen, Duane H., and R. J. Willey. 1988. "The Effects of Audience Awareness on Drafting and Revising." *Research in the Teaching of English* 22: 75–88.

Rogers, Carl R. 1961. *On Becoming a Person.* Boston: Houghton Mifflin.

Spear, Karen, ed. 1993. *Peer Response Groups in Action: Writing Together in Secondary Schools.* Portsmouth, NH: Boynton/Cook.

Teich, Nathaniel, ed. 1992. *Rogerian Perspectives: Collaborative Rhetoric for Oral and Written Communication.* Norwood, NJ: Ablex.

Willis, Meredith Sue. 1993. *Deep Revision: A Guide for Teachers, Students, and Other Writers.* Urbana, IL: National Council of Teachers of English.

Young, Richard E., Alton L. Becker, and Kenneth L. Pike. 1970. *Rhetoric: Discovery and Change.* New York: Harcourt, Brace & World.

4 Coaching Writing Development: Syntax Revisited, Options Explored

William Strong
Utah State University

Because texts are composed of sentences, the teaching (and evaluation) of writing once focused on *syntax*—the rules governing sentences—to the virtual exclusion of other topics. Conventional wisdom called for weeks of grammar exercises, which teachers later "reinforced" with cryptic notations and editorial comments. Of course, the bankruptcy of such an approach became the stuff of legend, an easy target for ridicule. In writing workshops, some of us rolled our eyes when moss-backed traditionalists or uninformed innocents wondered aloud about the role of syntax in instruction and evaluation.

Times have changed. Now, the mantra of the new orthodoxy requires that we work first on fluency and only later on issues of form and correctness; we invoke this formula relentlessly in our professional conversations. But in today's environment—charged by the debate over national standards and multiculturalism—developmental questions about syntax and style seem surprisingly urgent. Only lately, for example, have we begun to ask how we might describe the bewildering array of language in portfolios. And only lately, with increased concern for nonnative and bilingual speakers of English, have we begun to think seriously about how diverse language needs might be addressed.

In addition, the writing process movement has itself matured. Having accepted the utility of prewriting strategies, many of us spend increased time on revision, particularly in workshop-style models of instruction. Now, as we confer with students about drafts-in-progress, focus on texts in computer labs, or work at overhead projectors to demonstrate revising moves, we find ourselves beginning to ask "traditional" questions once again—how we might coach students in matters of style and thereby inform their choice of sentence options.

My aim in this chapter is to consider syntax as a vital dimension of writing development. In doing so, I draw upon "growth sequences" for syntax articulated by James Moffett in *Detecting Growth in Language* (1992). With Moffett's formulations as background, I then identify specific features of syntax that can be viewed developmentally, either when evaluating writing or when coaching students to expand their repertoires of sentence-level moves. Among other things, a developmental view can help us see errors as evidence of syntactic risktaking.

Examples of ethnically diverse writing come from sixth-grade and eleventh-grade classrooms in Honolulu—one taught by Karin Larson, the other by Mary Kay Masters; examples of twelfth-grade writing come from an advanced placement class taught by Patricia Stoddart in Logan, Utah. Toward the end of this chapter, I review certain in-class activities that may prove useful when addressing syntax issues in workshops.

The Facts of Syntax

Few of us doubt that a rich vocabulary, grounded in meaningful experience, enables us both to comprehend meanings and to express them. However, we may be less certain about the case for syntax. To what extent does skill in handling sentences correlate with speech and writing power?

The developmental facts of syntax, based on the research of Hunt (1965, 1977) and O'Donnell, Griffin, and Norris (1967), suggest that written language becomes more structurally complex as children grow older. Moreover, the average length of communication units in writing lags slightly behind those in speech up through middle school or junior high; however, in grades 10 through 12, the reverse trend occurs, with writing showing more elaboration than speech (Loban 1976, 34–35). Finally, features such as increased clause length, depth of modification, and nominalization seem to characterize developing maturity in syntax. Drawing upon Hunt's research, Moffett (1992, 50) summed up key features of sentence growth in this way:

> (1) increasing modification of nouns by large clusters of adjectives, relative clauses, and reduced relative clauses; (2) increasing use of nominalization other than nouns and pronouns for subjects and objects (clauses, infinitival and gerundive constructions); and (3) embedding of sentences to an increasing depth (entailed by 1 and 2).

From the facts of language development, it is possible to make the case that less-successful writers are constrained not so much by deficits of vocabulary or intelligence as by syntactic shackles, a lack of phrase-manipulating skill that makes them understandably reluctant to rework their texts. Successful writers, by contrast, become increasingly adept at manipulating sentence parts to achieve their rhetorical aims; in Loban's words, "They are capable of both simplicity and impressive elaboration" (1976, 72).

For Moffett, syntax assessment must always be situated in meaningful contexts so that judgments about language growth are tied to judgments about appropriateness. He also contends that, when done appropriately, "to be *able* to reduce clauses and embed them in each other . . . indicates fairly advanced growth" (1992, 48; italics in original). Moffett quickly adds, however, that "complexity for its own sake is no mark of maturity" (1992, 49). His position—a cornerstone for what follows—is that "complexity [in syntax] is necessary but not sufficient for fullest growth [of the writer]" (1992, 49).

To assist teachers, Moffett articulates "growth sequences"— standards that define what to look for when evaluating syntactic features or suggesting revisions. One standard deals generally with basic transformations, the other with the broad outlines of an early-to-late developmental sequence (Moffett 1992, 49–50):

Basic transformations:

Toward increasing versatility in constructing sentences, exploiting more nearly the total resources inherent in *modifying, conjoining, reducing,* and *embedding* clauses; and toward increasing comprehension of sentences of such range.

A four-level developmental sequence:

Expanding the repertory of clause-connecting options as follows:

1. String of separate independent clauses, each a sentence
2. Clauses conjoined by coordinating conjunctions (*and, but, or*) and time-space conjunctions
3. Clauses conjoined by logical subordinating conjunctions and fused by relative pronouns
4. Clauses reduced and embedded in each other

These developmental statements focus on what students can *do* with syntax, not on what they can *name*. While Moffett's standards seem to assume a fair level of linguistic savvy on the part of teachers, applying them mainly requires an interest in helping students develop a rich repertoire of sentence strategies and options. Time spent with colleagues in discussing basic principles of style will probably prove more useful than an inservice grammar course. On the other hand—and as Martha Kolln nicely demonstrates in her chapter on cohesion and coherence (Chapter 5, this volume)—adult-level reading focused on syntax and style may lead to unexpected insights, ones that inform day-to-day teaching in powerful ways.

Syntax in the Middle School

Descriptive writing is frequently assigned in middle school classrooms to help children refine their powers of observation. Sixth-grade teacher Karin Larson provided her students with photographs and encouraged them to write as fully as possible about what they noticed. Because many children enjoyed this activity, they chose to put their drafts in writing folders. Here are two samples of children's work that show differing levels of syntactic skill:

Text 1

This is a picture of a village and of a port. In this picture there are sail boats in the port. There is also many buildings. There is a larger boat. Also there are trees, and telephone poles. There are people on sailboats with life vests on. There are also streets that look like tall walls. The buildings have many windows. The buildings are made of brick and cement. The roofs are mostly at a slight angle or flat. There are row boats anchored at the port.

Text 2

This picture is of two stallions. They look like they are playing. The stallion on the left is a light tan color. Its mane is golden and so is its tail. Its front feet are off of the grassy field and its head is cocked up. The legs of the stallion are light brown because of the hair, and its hooves are very dirty. The stallion has kind of small, ovalish ears and its eyes are small. You can see an indentation by its cheek, and its nose is big and black. The tan stallion's mouth is grayish and as it goes down, there are two humps. First by its chin and then by its throat. The stallion seems very smooth. [*A second paragraph goes on to describe the other stallion.*]

Syntactically, the first text appears to be at the first level of Moffett's growth sequence—mainly a "string of independent clauses, each a sentence." There are only four instances of coordination and two instances of relative clauses ("that look like tall walls"; "[that are] anchored at the port"). Of particular importance is the student's reliance on a repeated sentence pattern, almost without variation. This young writer takes few chances with syntax, perhaps fearing usage errors or punctuation mistakes.

The second text uses coordination as a principal strategy (level two in Moffett's growth sequence). Of special syntactic interest is the student's move to embed and conjoin adjective modifiers ("small, ovalish ears"; "big and black [nose]"), thus expanding noun phrases. This writer is not afraid to invert sentences ("and so is its tail") or to use subordinating conjunctions ("because of the hair"; "and as it goes down"). We see clear evidence of syntactic maturity in the fragment sentence ("First by its chin and then by its throat"), which serves to expand a noun phrase ("two humps"). Here is the student's sentence with conventional punctuation:

> The tan stallion's mouth is grayish, and as it goes down, there are
> two humps, first by its chin and then by its throat.

One additional aspect of each text deserves comment—namely, diction. The first text is notable for its factual listing of nouns, with virtually no specification of particulars. In a writing conference, this student could be encouraged first to notice more details and then to embed them into existing sentences; a second step, depending on the response, would be to invite coordination of clauses and experimentation with other sentence patterns. The second text is notable for its series of general-to-specific "snapshots." The general-to-specific movement is a rhetorical strategy, of course, but it is realized through syntax (as in the "tan stallion" sentence above).

With Moffett's growth sequences as background—and the context provided by Text 1 and Text 2—let's now examine a third text, asking ourselves about its development. Where would this text fall along an emerging continuum of syntax in the middle grades?

Text 3

> My picture is in black and white. It has people in it. In front of this
> house is a big bell. This bell has a cross on the top of it. Next to the
> bell is a person on a wagon. The wagon is being pulled by one
> white horse. This wagon has two big wheels and two small wheels.
> The house by the big bell has 16 windows. This home has some-
> one on its steps. It is very big. Next to this house is two other
> homes. One is white and one is black. The white one has ten win-
> dows. It has four people walking by. It has a flag on its roof. The
> black house has eight windows. It has tower like things on its roof.
> On the tower like thing there is a cross. Its windows look like the
> houses we draw.

A case can be made that Text 3 falls *between* Text 1 and Text 2. Why? Because Text 3, like Text 1, relies on a string of independent clauses for its development. On the other hand—and on the positive side, developmentally speaking—Text 3 uses the strategy of inversion ("In front of this house"; "Next to the bell"; "On the tower") to vary sentence beginnings and to create cohesion between adjoining statements. What Text 3 lacks is the use of coordination and the embedding of adjective modifiers. Assuming revision and follow-up, such moves can be encouraged in a workshop-style conference or in marginal comments.

Each of the texts we have discussed offers a specific context for nudging growth in language. Of course, if we invite risktaking and then *penalize* students for making mistakes, we undermine our teaching and thwart long-term growth in syntax.

Syntax in the High School

Understanding the psychological importance of story, many teachers encourage students to write personal narratives, either as stand-alone assignments or as bridges to exposition or persuasion. In the next set of sample texts, from an eleventh-grade classroom, we see students of diverse syntactic ability who are writing to communicate their experience. The first sample comes from a narrative about scuba diving:

Text 4

In the van we talked about how nervous we were. I was worried that I would forget to breathe. Finally we reached Sharks Cove. We unloaded our gear and organized ourselves to make sure that we didn't forget anything. We picked diving buddies and helped each other put on our gear. We all walked down to the beach and sat in the water. We put on our fins and began the long swim out to thirty five feet of water. We lined up in the water and slowly made our descent.

While this text is clear, it depends excessively on coordination, much like the middle school examples. Each instance of coordination occurs in the predicate ("unloaded our gear and organized ourselves"), where it is most easily managed. It is possible, of course, that this writer has used staccato syntax to suggest the tension of the dive. Still, a one-minute writing conference might raise questions about the repetition of *we*, with little variation. On the positive side, from the standpoint of syntax development, there are two noun clauses ("that I would forget to breathe"; "that we didn't forget anything"); once again, these occur in the predicate, not in the more difficult subject position.

Here is another small chunk of narrative, this written deliberately in the third-person, although based on a real-life event:

Text 5

When they entered her brother's room, D. quietly shuddered behind her mother's back. She hadn't been prepared for the sight that she encountered in the ICU room. There on the bed lay K., deathly pale. His jaw jutted out toward the right side, and his face was swollen to twice its normal size. Crusted up on his jaw and mouth was old dried blood. K. lay flat on the bed, but the nurse had raised the head area up so that he could see. Because of his broken jaw, he couldn't greet them. Instead, his exhausted eyes followed them as they walked toward him.

This brief text shows syntactic sophistication. We see a variety of patterns, including a cumulative sentence ("There on the bed") and an inverted sentence ("Crusted up on his jaw"). There are two instances of introductory adverbial clauses, with the second ("Because of his broken jaw") being a reduced clause (level four in Moffett's growth sequence). This student seems quite skilled at framing the scene syntactically and filling in details with nicely chosen adjectives or adverbs ("quietly shuddered"; "deathly pale"). Finally, the control of cohesion between and among sentences is very strong; the transition *instead* actually functions as a reduced clause in context.

With a continuum for eleventh-grade writing emerging, let's consider a third sample. How does this text compare with the other two syntactically?

Text 6

My dad helped me put the engine together, making sure everything was torqued to proper specifications to ensure maximum performance and we got ready to put it in. We found the engine mounts to fit the engine in my car and the 355 easily took the place of the V-6. I spent about two weeks finishing the engine, bolting on the heads, manifold, carburetor, headers, accessories and ignition. I couldn't wait to start it up and drive it around, but we still had to set the timing, adjust the valves and set up an exhaust system. It didn't take long for this and the day came to drive it for the first time. With half an exhaust system, I pulled out of my driveway and stepped on the gas. I couldn't hear a thing because the exhaust sounded like a race car and when I looked in the rearview mirror my whole neighborhood was engulfed in smoke. I had smoked the tires for over thirty yards without even knowing it and I can still see the tracks it left on the road that day.

Punctuation details aside, this text uses a repeated pattern to advance the narrative. Of the eight sentences in the paragraph, six are compound structures. However, this pattern serves as scaffolding for more complex transformations such as participle phrases ("making sure everything was torqued"; "bolting on the heads"), reduced clauses ("With half an exhaust system"), and adverbial clauses ("because the exhaust"; "when I looked"). In addition, the student manages items in a series, both as noun and verb phrases.

Syntactically, this student appears to exercise a greater range of options than the writer of Text 4. On the other hand, this student's facility may not yet match the sophistication evidenced by the writer of Text 5. We would need additional sentences to say for sure. The point of such text-to-text comparisons, of course, is to provide direction for our comments and our coaching with individual students.

Students on Syntactic Thresholds

As noted earlier, researchers have described maturity of syntax in terms of processes (such as embedding, subordination, and nominalization) and products (such as participle phrases, appositives, and absolutes). Their essential point is not merely that clauses grow longer, though this is indeed true; the point instead is that increased fluency and maturity may enable a writer to *say more* in fewer words.

For writing teachers, a developmental view of syntax requires a kind of "double vision." As we focus on what students *do* with texts, we must also note what they *attempt* to accomplish syntactically or rhetorically. Such a view, when taken seriously, radically alters our perception of errors in student work. While some errors result from ignorance of conventions or from simple carelessness, others may result from efforts to cross syntactic thresholds.

Consider the following example of such a threshold, this from an eleventh-grade text in which several coordinate sentences advance the narrative straightforwardly. The student has focused on her dance class and, more specifically, on a dance teacher:

Text 7

> I can go over the motions perfectly in my head, but as soon as I get on the dance floor I flub up and end up making a fool of myself. Then once again she'll demonstrate the combination for us because we can't get it down.
> I watch her with awe, gliding across the floor dressed in her dance clothes which conform to her lean body wishing I could dance as she does. Every motion done with such concise precision and energy, her toes pointed every time they are lifted off the floor, she finishes the combination with such ease.

The two sentences that conclude Text 7 are by no means perfectly crafted; on the other hand, they reveal a student attempting new syntactic moves, perhaps like those just encountered in a novel or a contemporary essay. Her efforts at phrasing ("concise precision and energy") and at depicting physical movement ("her toes pointed") suggest that she is testing a threshold.

This student has a sense of the cumulative sentence. All she needs is coaching and encouragement. In a brief conference, we might praise the two sentences and ask the student to read them aloud. Then, focusing on the first sentence ("I watch her with awe"), we might ask, "Who is *gliding* and *wishing?*" The student could be helped to see that because *gliding* refers to the teacher and *wishing* refers to the speaker, confusion may result. Seeing this problem, the student would probably try different revisions, one of which appears below:

> Wishing I could dance as she does, I watch her gliding across the floor, dressed in dance clothes which conform to her lean body.

The concluding sentence in Text 7 demonstrates a very advanced construction (level four in Moffett's growth sequence). Notice that the main clause ("she finishes the combination with such ease") is preceded by parallel absolutes ("Every motion done . . . with energy"/"her toes pointed"). Structurally, this sentence has essential features of the modern cumulative sentence. While further shaping of the sentence might be desirable, this occasion might also be one when we resist the temptation to teach. Moffett's (1983, 172) observation remains valid—that "children's sentences must grow rank before they can be trimmed."

The writing tasks that students undertake may either invite or suppress certain structures. In Text 7, for example, the participle phrase ("wishing I could dance as she does") emerges naturally as the student works on *narrative*. As the student shifts to *description*, two absolutes emerge. Later in the essay, when the student again attempts description, the absolute ("eyes wide open") reappears—this time more problematically:

Text 8

> Her lips are pursed together, eyes wide open staring intensely at herself in the mirror which she has chosen as a focus, she completes a flawless turn.

Here, problems of punctuation are linked to syntax. However, there is much to praise as this sentence is read aloud, and we help the writer refine what she has written. First, we might ask whether the absolute is related to the "lips" clause or to the main "she" clause. After discussing punctuation briefly, we might also ask whether the relative clause ("which she has chosen as a focus") is really essential. The student's revised (and tightened) multilevel sentence might look something like this:

> Her lips are pursed together. With eyes wide open, staring intensely at herself in the mirror, she completes a flawless turn.

Or perhaps she might create two parallel absolutes ("her lips pursed together and her eyes wide open"), a syntactic *tour de force* to mirror her teacher's pirouette:

> With her lips pursed together and her eyes wide open, staring intensely at herself in the mirror, she completes a flawless turn.

And what about the safe, error-free writing we considered in Text 1 and Text 4 above? Such texts remind us that many students are deeply reluctant to exercise stylistic options. We should especially encourage these writers to combine sentences, add details, and take syntactic risks. Whatever errors these students make should be welcomed as evidence of their efforts to *develop* their writing skills rather than play it safe.

Syntax in Service of Rhetoric

In addition to permitting the "showing detail" we associate with narrative, facility with syntax seems to move students toward certain habits of mind, ones we associate with explanation and argument. Just as jokes require punch lines, narratives often demand a "point" or follow-up comment. Of course, in commenting *about* narrative events—whether in our own lives, the lives of others, or in literature—we necessarily assume a detached role, one of informed observer or spectator.

Let's now consider high school writing in which *description* and *narrative* serve broader discourse aims. In the example shown below, an eleventh-grade student has taken on reportage—first, observing and interviewing a person of interest, and then weaving field notes into an informative essay. The subject of the piece is a highly skilled bike rider, one with "sweat droplets lining the top of his wide forehead" and "dark wet circles under the armpits of a yellow and black shirt" as he does his stunts:

Text 9

> To begin, M. stands relaxed and comfortable atop one side of the U-shaped ramp. He seems to be pondering his next move and appears to be completely oblivious to what is going on around him. The descent begins. He rolls over the side of the ramp and then

pedals through the middle. He does this several times, back and forth to gain speed. Then suddenly, he will start lifting his bike away from the ramp and be at a standstill about four feet above the ramp. Down he goes again to repeat the prior events until he falls off or "bails his bike."

Here, syntax mirrors reality. Opening with an infinitive phrase ("To begin"), the student sets the scene. Then language drops away abruptly ("The descent begins"). Rhythmically, the next two sentences echo the rider's movement, with a free modifier ("back and forth to gain speed") used to good advantage. The penultimate sentence, like the biker "at a standstill . . . above the ramp," seems to hover. Then, the writer takes us *down*, literally, with the inverted syntax of the final sentence.

Rhetorically, description and narration can set up judgments and commentary. Notice the detached stance that the writer of Text 9 assumes in the following paragraph, one that provides an interpretation of the subject:

Text 10

When M. makes his way along the road to Kailua, he is definitely the pride of the pack. The most daring and often the most reckless, he furiously pedals to reach a good speed before soaring into the air with a simple tug at the handlebars. The wheels go round and round over bumps, holes, and up the curbs. The average man or woman would think that the curb would be an obstacle to the average biker, but M. isn't the average biker. He craves the tiny ditches and cement curbs of the main roads. They symbolize a way to show his talent and superiority over the other riders.

The syntactic interest lies in the student's use of subordination ("When M. makes his way"), the appositive used as a sentence opener ("The most daring and often the most reckless"), and the use of nominalization ("that the curb would be an obstacle"). Notice also, however, how the writer uses a negative ("but M. isn't the average biker") to create intersentence cohesion. Phrases such as "pride of the pack" and "symbolize a way" reinforce the image of a writer in syntactic control, reflecting on the *meaning* of specific observations.

Of course, in writing tasks that call explicitly for explanation or argument, we would expect to see *fewer* participles or absolutes, even from syntactically able writers. The demands and constraints of such tasks—an essay like this one, for example—lead almost inevitably to an increased frequency of adjective and adverb clauses. As students develop syntactically, we can expect increased nominalization, first in the predicate and later in the subject slot. Developmentally speaking, reduced clause structures (such as the appositive) will *follow* nouns before they precede them. Here are four examples of such syntactic moves from the preceding sentences in this paragraph:

Adverb Clause	*as students develop syntactically*
Nominalization	*The demands and constraints of such tasks*
Appositive	*an essay like this one, for example*
Reduced Clause	*first in the predicate and later in the subject slot*

The implications should be clear: If the nature of the task invites certain syntactic moves and constrains others, we have strong support for encouraging *all* types of writing, not just autobiography or reportage on the one hand, or literary analysis and research reports on the other. Simply put, encouraging a wide range of modes and genres will help students explore their syntactic resources; conversely, in-class practice with a range of sentence options will facilitate writing in multiple genres.

The Syntax of Argument and Interpretation

As noted above, when we ask students to explain or argue in writing, we are implicitly asking for certain kinds of sentences—ones that students may not have fully internalized, particularly if their reading background in nonfiction is weak. Ironically, too, most imaginative literature does not model the sentence patterns or registers of language that students are expected to use in essays *about* literature.

Let's first examine syntax in which certain flaws reveal opportunities for instruction. In Text 11, the student argues that mountain bikes should be allowed into wilderness areas, where horses are currently permitted. Part of the argument is that horses are more destructive than bicycles:

Text 11

When out on the trails horses are a great danger. Not only to the rider but to all those around. A horse has a mind of it's own. It could be spooked by nearly anything. If a horse decides to take off on a mad rampage and trample all of our lovely wilderness, who's going to stop it?

On the positive side, developmentally speaking, is the student's use of subordination ("When out on the trails"; "If a horse decides"). However, this student's writing will be improved by revisiting the connection between syntax and punctuation. The writer needs to hear problems of missing punctuation in the first sentence as well as the problem of a detached free modifier ("Not only") punctuated as a sentence. Paying close attention to verb tense (substituting "can" for "could") might be another recommendation in a syntax-focused writing conference.

Consider now a second example of argumentative writing, this from a student who demonstrates considerable prowess in crafting sentences. Perhaps with tongue in cheek, the writer contends that "a well-regulated gambling establishment would greatly enhance our city's reputation and overall atmosphere":

Text 12

> To fully understand the actual effects of betting upon society, a distinction between the reasons for gambling must be made. People gamble for two reasons: to have fun and to make money. Those who bet as a pastime and social activity are usually just out to enjoy themselves. They are not the ones that end up making trouble and breaking laws. Problems arise from those who are out to get rich and often wager their whole pocketbooks in an obsession for money.

Not only is Text 12 technically flawless, but it also reveals a very high level of syntactic sophistication. In the first sentence, for example, note the introductory infinitive phrase ("To fully understand") as well as the complex noun phrase ("a distinction between the reasons for gambling") in the subject position. In the second sentence, consider how the writer rivets the reader's attention, using both a colon and parallel infinitive phrases ("to have fun and to make money"). Finally, study how restrictive relative clauses ("those who"; "ones that") provide additional evidence of writing skill.

Let's now move to a different genre—that of the "critical essay," with literature serving as the subject. Typically, students are expected to make sense of their responses as readers and to explain certain text features such as character or theme. For better or for worse, such assignments are part of the culture of English/language arts classrooms, although many students remain uncertain about how to handle the syntactic or rhetorical demands of these tasks. Obviously, if students cannot manage the conventions of paraphrase, direct quotation, or allusion to other works, they are likely to have difficulty demonstrating their ability to interpret.

Retelling the narrative is one strategy frequently used by students who are syntactically unsure of themselves. Because narrative patterns are rhetorically familiar and safe, students often fall back on retelling unless encouraged to use their powers of analysis and interpretation. For example, in a paper that otherwise uses retelling as virtually the exclusive strategy for dealing with Robert Penn Warren's *All the King's*

Men, one student finally tries something new, an interpretive risk. Notice how flawed syntax in Text 13 signals the student's effort to make sense of Willie Stark.

Text 13

Stark was a hick. Not only a hick, but a hick with morals who appealed to the country folk. If Stark ran, he would split the hick vote and Harrison would win the election.

Here, a decision is called for: We can mark *fragment* in the margin, or we can regard the appositive noun phrase ("not only a hick, but a hick with morals") as an effort toward elaboration—an interpretive act. The choice, in other words, is to penalize the student as she moves to interpret text or to celebrate her effort to make an appositive with specific, encouraging feedback. One approach will exacerbate her strategy of narrative retelling and "playing it safe"; the other will encourage further risks, both in interpretation and syntax.

For purposes of contrast, let's consider a second example of interpretive text, this composed by a student whose language is mature and richly developed. The following two sentences open an essay of remarkable clarity and power:

Text 14

The belief that everything one does affects someone else's life is the most important lesson Jack Burden learns in Robert Penn Warren's book, *All the King's Men.* With the help of Cass Mastern, and through the belief and disbelief of the spider web theory, Jack concludes that the theory is true.

Nominalization, reduced relative clause, appositive, introductory prepositional phrase, parallel structure—this is language at the upper reaches of the syntactic ladder described by Loban (1976) and Moffett (1992). Equally important, facility with syntax has literally *enabled* this young writer to engage in full interpretive reading, not just in textual retelling. We owe her teachers thanks for a job well done.

Syntax-in-Action Workshops

Writing conferences encourage syntactic facility, but workshops can also prove useful, especially when done as mini-lessons. So how do we encourage risktaking—an exploration of sentence options—without a return to the grammar exercises of yesteryear? After all, according to the research, there is no reason to think that grammar study will facilitate growth along the lines studied by Loban (Hillocks 1986, 133–41).

Various forms of sentence-combining (SC) activities provide a useful (and motivating) alternative to grammar study. These materials may be derived from student papers, in-class reading, or textbook sources. They may be presented in either "open" or "cued" formats for large-group, small-group, or individual practice. All such activities invite "hands-on" syntax manipulation, which many students seem to learn from and enjoy. Happily, too, many research studies suggest that SC not only promotes sentence fluency and maturity, but also can lead to significant gains in writing quality (see Hillocks [1986, 141–51] for a summary of relevant research).

One SC approach is to use sentences like the one in Text 8 in workshops. Clearly, such workshops will require an atmosphere where we have communicated, by word and deed, that mistakes are opportunities for learning, not occasions for public humiliation. When students are applauded for putting problem sentences before their response groups—as well as on transparencies or the chalkboard—skills cannot help but improve over time.

Shown below is a student-centered exercise based on the underlying propositions in Text 8. To construct such an "open" exercise, one simply analyzes a sentence into its constituent kernel (or near-kernel) sentences and lists them:

1. Her lips are pursed together.
2. Her eyes are wide open.
3. Her eyes stare intensely at herself.
4. She stares in the mirror.
5. She completes a turn.
6. The turn is flawless.

Working in pairs or small groups, students might tackle this exercise orally to combine its sentences; subsequently, the class would write out their "best sentences" individually. As a final step, volunteers could share their options, using the chalkboard, acetate transparencies, or networked computer screens.

Such an activity draws upon—and extends—a group's collective knowledge of syntax. After exploring "basic" approaches to combining, students will invariably attempt more complex transformations. Of course, the goal of combining is to produce *good* sentences, not merely long, cumbersome ones. When students question whether the SC cluster contains *too much* information for one sentence, encourage them to make two sentences. Also, try sharing the larger paragraph context so that students see and hear the "fit" of sentences they combine. In general, whole-discourse exercises—those which situate combining in a paragraph context—help to keep the focus on the *appropriateness* of various options. Teachers who use "kid watching" to set goals will be fascinated by the syntactic struggles (and triumphs) of a typical workshop group.

A more directive "cued" approach for the preceding SC exercise might center on the cumulative sentence, a structure found at level four of Moffett's growth sequence. In *Crafting Cumulative Sentences* (Strong 1984a), such activities provide students with models for imitation, closure clues for practice, and open exercises to consolidate understanding. Using this approach, students learn how to use participle phrases, appositives, adjective clusters, and absolutes as free modifiers. Shown below is a closure clue "scaffold" for the earlier SC exercise, with phrases and clauses set off in "levels" as recommended by Christensen (1967). Basically, the scaffold shows the architecture of a target sentence, with the main clause set off at level one and subordinate elements set off in relation to that level:

> 2   With _____,
>
> 2   her _____,
>
> 3   staring _____,
>
> 1   she _____.

With just a little coaching, many high school students will figure out how to delete the "be" verbs in the first two sentences of the SC cluster, thus shaping a pair of absolutes; their next task, embedding a third-level modifier, results in a participle phrase:

> 2   With her lips pursed together,
>
> 2   her eyes wide open,
>
> 3   staring intensely at herself in the mirror,
>
> 1   she completes a flawless turn.

Such scaffolding becomes unnecessary, of course, as students develop increased proficiency with syntax and confidence in their technical skills.

Although used here to illustrate a cumulative sentence, closure clue prompts can be adapted to SC exercises at *any* level, including syntax appropriate for ESL and bilingual learners. For example, as part of a unit on "Everyday Heroes," a middle school ESL teacher might present learners with a pair of kernel sentences whose logic demands a *contrast* relationship; the following three prompts—each increasingly difficult—could be put on an acetate transparency to help students understand their syntactic options:

1. Some heroes make headlines for their deeds.

2. Many others do not achieve public recognition.

    A. Some _____ ,

        but _____ .

    B. Although _____ ,

        _____ .

    C. _____ ;

        however, _____ .

It is important for students using this approach to write out *complete* sentences, with correct punctuation, and not merely fill in the blanks on a worksheet. The sentence chosen by each student serves as an opener for follow-up writing on "Everyday Heroes."

To further assist young writers with this task, a teacher might have learners specify information for the following sentences, which would then be combined. (The second sentence calls for a relationship—for example, "my mother," "a friend of our family," or similar identifying phrase.)

3. One example of an unsung hero is _____ .

                                       [Person's name]

4. This person is _____ .

                         [Relationship]

After combining this cluster of sentences, students would be encouraged to identify heroic qualities of the individual they have chosen and to develop their writing as fully as possible.

Of course, grammatical terminology is optional as students work collaboratively to solve syntax problems. See, for example, *Practicing Sentence Options* (Strong 1984b), *Creative Approaches to Sentence Combining* (Strong 1986), or *Writer's Toolbox* (Strong 1996). The latter textbook uses SC exercises to illustrate basic and advanced grammar concepts as well as usage and punctuation principles (twenty-six mini-lessons in all).

The oral and collaborative aspects of such language-learning activities deserve emphasis, especially with students whose skills are underdeveloped. Oral language provides a way for students to try out sentence options with writing partners. One especially powerful activity for teaching stylistic decision making begins by dividing a whole-discourse exercise into separate clusters, each of which becomes the "property" of a student team. Each team's task is to construct at least three "quality options" for their cluster, writing these sentences on an acetate transparency. As the teams take turns presenting their options to the class, the stylistic issues of rhythm, sentence variety and length, emphasis, and cohesion are suddenly made concrete. Using context as their guide, the class votes on "best sentences."

While SC exercises are no panacea for instruction, they do provide instructional focus as well as an opportunity for students to refine their syntax skills. Marion Crowhurst (1983, 70) stresses the importance of maintaining "realistic expectations" for activities like sentence combining: "Quality improvements are most likely to result if substantial time is spent on open, rather than cued, exercises, on whole-discourse problems, and on discussing the rhetorical effects of the various versions produced." The aim of such work is for students to flex new linguistic muscles and to make informed judgments about style.

As we noted above, grammar study alone simply cannot produce the gains in fluency, maturity, and elaboration that seem to be associated with increased language power. Various exercises in given language, on the other hand, may help some students gain access to an inner repertoire of sentence options, even as they discover syntax to be mastered later (Strong 1983). Of course, such activities should never serve as a busywork curriculum.

Syntax in Perspective

Coaches of tennis, skiing, and many other sports know that learners must develop a "feel" for target behaviors. They therefore use visual imagery and modeling to help their students understand the moves that lead to a desired performance. When done successfully, the teaching is in context and tied to what Vygotsky (1978) referred to as the learner's "zone of proximal development." Coaching assumes that whatever learners can do with the help of others, they will eventually be able to do on their own.

The teaching of writing can be viewed analogously. When we look carefully at syntax—and encourage our classes to do the same—we are developing images of the "shape" and "feel" of different moves at the sentence level. With such instruction, we focus not so much on the overall writing process as on specific phrase-to-phrase options that result in rhetorical effects. Put another way, our goal is to help learners develop an "ear" for options within their developmental range. Workshops and writing conferences provide ideal contexts for practice because of their ethos of collaboration, rehearsal, and risktaking.

Some teachers may regard attention to syntax as a kind of arcane diversion or frill—not really essential to the development of authentic voice or to features of text such as logic, coherence, and organization. Yet all these elements of composition are realized *through* syntax (Strong 1985). For teachers to dismiss issues of syntax as "mere technique" is to shortchange students in profound ways. In fact, writing instruction will always remain basically incomplete if not grounded, to some extent, in syntactic options. Perhaps this is why Donald Murray (1995, xiv) defines writing as rewriting and goes on to make the following point:

> Writing is a decision-making process. As we revise, considering each word, each piece of punctuation, each phrase, sentence, paragraph, page, we make decisions that lead to other decisions. We don't work by intuition but by craft.

Murray's emphasis on *craft* as a basis for decision making serves to remind us that syntactic knowledge—a sense of options—is absolutely basic to growth in written language.

And where can we turn for help? For further reading on syntax, style, and sentence combining, the following resources may be of special interest. All provide elaboration for the pedagogical and linguistic matters discussed in this chapter:

> Christensen, Francis. 1967. "A Generative Rhetoric of the Sentence." In *Notes Toward a New Rhetoric: Six Essays for Teachers,* 1–22. New York: Harper & Row. As readable now as it was thirty years ago, this essay explores the cumulative sentence, a main clause with one or more free modifiers.
>
> Daiker, Donald A., Andrew Kerek, and Max Morenberg, eds. 1993. *The Writer's Options: Combining to Composing.* 5th ed. New York: HarperCollins. This useful text offers an array of whole-discourse SC exercises, all designed to help students internalize grammatical and stylistic principles.
>
> Lanham, Richard. 1991. *Revising Prose.* 3rd ed. New York: Macmillan. In a wry, anti-academic style, Lanham shows how his "Paramedic Method"—a way of analyzing syntax—can help make the world safe from "prose sludge."
>
> Miles, Robert, Marc Bertonasco, and William Karns. 1991. *Prose Style: A Contemporary Guide.* 2nd ed. Englewood Cliffs, NJ: Prentice-Hall. This well-written book not only covers all major topics of

syntax and style, but also provides many useful classroom examples and exercises.

Quirk, Randolph, Sidney Greenbaum, G. Leech, and J. Svartvik. 1985. *A Comprehensive Grammar of the English Language.* New York: Longman. A grammar for grownups, this volume provides an in-depth analysis of English syntax and explores many topics related to prose style.

Strong, William. 1996. *Writer's Toolbox: A Sentence-Combining Workshop.* New York: McGraw-Hill. Utilizing a writing process and portfolio framework, this textbook offers whole-discourse exercises and twenty-six mini-lessons in basic and advanced grammar, usage, and punctuation.

Weaver, Constance. 1979. *Grammar for Teachers: Perspective and Definitions.* Urbana, IL: National Council of Teachers of English. This teacher-friendly resource provides a point of departure for those needing a foothold on the slippery slope of syntax.

William, Joseph M. 1994. *Style: Ten Lessons in Clarity and Grace.* 4th ed. New York: HarperCollins. Humane and intelligent, this book is a classic in the field; see Chapters 8–10, in particular, for insights about syntax.

Above all, of course, attention to syntax should be viewed as a means to an end, not an end in itself. By developing the language competence of students, we strengthen their confidence to initiate and sustain a range of writing tasks, in school and beyond. The bottom line of this chapter is that syntax practice can help young writers develop what Sondra Perl (1983) has called a "felt sense" of composing—a sense that enables them to pause without panic, listening to an inner voice, and to reread their own texts with interest, looking for ways to extend and clarify their own thinking.

Works Cited

Christensen, Francis. 1967. *Notes toward a New Rhetoric: Six Essays for Teachers.* New York: Harper & Row.

Crowhurst, Marion. 1983. "Sentence Combining: Maintaining Realistic Expectations." *College Composition and Communication* 33: 65–72.

Hillocks, George, Jr. 1986. *Research on Written Composition: New Directions in Teaching.* New York: National Conference on Research in English; Urbana, IL: ERIC Clearinghouse on Reading and Communication Skills.

Hunt, Kellogg W. 1965. *Grammatical Structures Written at Three Grade Levels.* Urbana, IL: National Council of Teachers of English.

———. 1976. *Language Development: Kindergarten through Grade 12.* Urbana, IL: National Council of Teachers of English.

———. 1977. "Early Blooming and Late-Blooming Syntactic Structures." In *Evaluating Writing: Describing, Measuring, Judging,* ed. Charles R. Cooper and Lee Odell, 91–106. Urbana, IL: National Council of Teachers of English.

Loban, Walter. 1976. *Language Development: Kindergarden through Grade Twelve.* Urbana IL: National Council of Teachers of English.

Moffett, James. [1968] 1983. *Teaching the Universe of Discourse.* Boston: Houghton Mifflin.

———. 1992. *Detecting Growth in Language.* Portsmouth, NH: Boynton/Cook-Heinemann.

Murray, Donald M. 1995. *The Craft of Revision.* 2nd ed. Ft. Worth: Harcourt Brace.

O'Donnell, Roy C., William J. Griffin, and Raymond C. Norris. 1967. *Syntax of Kindergarten and Elementary School Children—A Transformational Analysis.* Urbana, IL: National Council of Teachers of English.

Perl, Sondra. 1983. "Understanding Composing." In *The Writer's Mind: Writing as a Mode of Thinking,* ed. Janice N. Hayes, 43–51. Urbana, IL: National Council of Teachers of English.

Strong, William. 1983. "How Sentence Combining Works." In *Sentence Combining: A Rhetorical Perspective,* ed. Donald A. Daiker, Andrew Kerek, and Max Morenberg, 334–50. Carbondale: Southern Illinois University Press.

———. 1984a. *Crafting Cumulative Sentences.* New York: McGraw-Hill.

———. 1984b. *Practicing Sentence Options.* New York: McGraw-Hill.

———. 1985. "Linguistics and Writing." In *Perspectives on Research and Scholarship in Composition,* ed. Ben W. McClelland and Timothy R. Donovan, 68–86. New York: Modern Language Association of America.

———. 1986. *Creative Approaches to Sentence Combining.* Urbana, IL: National Council of Teachers of English and ERIC Clearinghouse on Reading and Communication Skills.

———. 1994. *Sentence Combining: A Composing Book.* 3rd ed. New York: McGraw-Hill.

———. 1996. *Writer's Toolbox: A Sentence-Combining Workshop.* New York: McGraw-Hill.

Vygotsky, L. S. 1978. *Mind in Society: The Development of Higher Psychological Processes,* ed. Michael Cole, Vera John-Steiner, Sylvia Scribner, and Ellen Souberman. Cambridge, MA: Harvard University Press.

5 Cohesion and Coherence

Martha Kolln
Pennsylvania State University

If Miss Jane Marple—or, more likely, Ms. Jessica Fletcher, the ex-English teacher turned sleuth—were investigating the topics of cohesion and coherence, she might be tempted to call the caper "the case of the missing concepts"—especially if she conducted her search in current composition textbooks. Oh, she'd probably find an index entry for "coherence," which would lead her to a description of paragraph patterns. And she'd spot a few key points, sometimes discussed in connection with coherence, sometimes not: a list of transition words, warnings to avoid pronoun-antecedent problems, the pitfalls of parallel structure, commentary on the use of synonyms and repetition. But despite twenty years of research and publication on cohesion and coherence by linguists and composition specialists, the handbooks and rhetorics for both secondary- and college-level composition classes continue to overlook some of the most valuable lessons that the research has to offer.

Distinguishing Cohesion and Coherence

Obviously cognates, from the Latin *cohaerere*, "to stick," the two words *cohesion* and *coherence* are not always clearly distinguished in the literature. In some early writings especially, the two seem not to be differentiated at all, with coherence generally used to cover both the broad rhetorical aspects of a text as well as the cohesive ties between sentences. The accepted distinction in current work can be summed up by a heading that appears in *Style: Ten Lessons in Clarity and Grace*, by Joseph M. Williams (1994): "Local Cohesion and Global Coherence."

The word *cohesion* refers to the categories of ties that connect sentences as described by M. A. K. Halliday and Ruqaiya Hasan in *Cohesion in English*, published in 1976.[1] Their categories of cohesive ties include not only the familiar handbook lists of transition words, but also personal and demonstrative pronouns, comparative signals, repetition, collocation (words that generally co-occur), and ellipses. (These ties are discussed more fully under "Research on Cohesion" later in this chapter.)

In contrast, then, we can define *coherence* as "cohesion on a global scale," taking into account those features other than sentence-level ties that work together to produce a unified text. Such features include not only the development and arrangement of sentences into paragraphs, but extratextual rhetorical considerations as well. The reader brings expectations and knowledge to the writing situation, both of which play a part in the judgment of whether a text is coherent or incoherent. A coherent text also includes the conventions of a particular writing genre: The funding proposal, for example, includes a budget; a dissertation includes a review of the literature; a position paper considers the arguments of the opposition.

Composition Textbooks: Lagging Behind the Research

No matter what we call the features of prose that provide the sticking power and the flow (two seemingly incongruous metaphors that describe cohesion and coherence), textbook authors have been especially slow to incorporate research findings on these concepts in a positive and organized way. Of the fifteen books I examined—five of which were for high school juniors and seniors, ten for college freshmen—three, all college texts, had no index entry for *coherence;* and only one, also a college text, included the word *cohesion* as an entry.

None of the texts that do discuss coherence have gone very far beyond the description found in Warriner's *English Grammar and Composition* (1982), that middle and secondary school stalwart, first published in 1951:

> A paragraph is coherent when its sentences are logically and clearly related to one another and their total effect is the clear development of the paragraph topic. One way of achieving coherence is by arranging the details in a paragraph in a clear and logical order. . . . Four plans, or orders, for the arrangement of the details in a paragraph are chronological order, spatial order, the order of importance, and the order required to bring out a comparison or contrast. (331)

This description of coherence is clearly the standard. In several of the books, this paragraph is reproduced almost verbatim.

Although my survey was by no means exhaustive of the genre, it did include the leading books in the field, written by well known authors.[2] All fifteen discuss transition devices; some bring up the positive features of parallelism and repetition, while others discuss only the pitfalls of these strategies. And one of the rhetorics—but only one—includes the cohesive categories as described by Halliday and Hasan. What the textbooks for our courses ought to do is to combine those parts under one umbrella and, what is more important, to bring into the discussion the cohesive features of language that linguistics has illuminated for us, features now essentially ignored that can make the concepts of cohesion and coherence the useful tools for writers that they ought to be.

It is also time for textbooks to delete from their pages some of our profession's cherished myths. Two of the most commonly repeated myths actually undermine the concept of cohesion: the directive to avoid the passive voice and the blanket warnings to avoid wordiness.

Halliday and Hasan's *Cohesion in English* (1976) has provided researchers with a functional tool for measuring cohesion. And many researchers have made use of it in their attempts to identify those features of prose that lead to judgments of writing effectiveness. One conclusion we can draw from their findings is that ours is a highly cohesive language.

Halliday and Hasan classify cohesive ties into five major categories, along with a number of subcategories; they also label the ties according to the distance between them, as immediate or remote. Following is a brief description of the five categories. Although most are familiar, there may be some you hadn't thought about before in connection with cohesion.

1. **Reference:** (A) PERSONAL PRONOUNS (*I, me,* etc.); (B) DEMONSTRATIVES (*this, that, these, those*); (C) COMPARATIVE SIGNALS (*same, different, other, better, more, less,* etc.).

2. **Conjunction:** (A) ADDITIVE (*and, or, besides, by contrast, furthermore, likewise, on the other hand,* etc.); (B) ADVERSATIVE (*yet, but, though, however, instead,* etc.); (C) CAUSAL (*so, then, for, because, to this end,* etc.); (D) TEMPORAL (*then, next, first, later, finally,* etc.).

3. **Lexical cohesion:** (A) REITERATION (repetition of the same word; synonyms and near-synonyms; superordinate words [more general class: *suit/clothes,* etc.]; general words [*people, child, thing, stuff, objects,* etc.]); (B) COLLOCATION (words that generally co-occur: *climb/ascent; boy/girl; stand up/sit down; order/obey; king/crown,* etc.).

4. **Ellipses:** parts of the sentence that are left out, or "understood" (*Tim ate two pancakes, and Shelley [ate] four; I am older than you [are old]; He asked me to go with him but I didn't [go with him]*).

5. **Substitution:** words that are substituted for other structures *(Tim served pancakes, but I didn't want* any; *Pat thinks our test will be easy, but I don't think* so [or, *I think* not]).

Clearly, these categories go beyond the words and phrases that we see listed as "transition devices"; such lists are generally limited to the conjunction category. When we consider all of these lexical ties, it is not surprising to discover that most texts, in terms of numbers at least, are highly cohesive.

Research on Cohesion

When Stephen P. Witte and Lester Faigley (1981) examined the cohesion of low- and high-rated essays, they reported a significant difference in the frequency of ties, but even in the low group they found a cohesive tie every 4.9 words: 20.4 percent of the words contributing to cohesion. They found an astonishing 31 percent in the high-rated essays. Marion Crowhurst (1987), in examining grade levels (6, 10, and 12) and modes (argument and narration), confirmed these high numbers of total ties with frequencies between 20 and 25 percent at all levels. Interestingly, the mode made more difference than the grade level, with the highest number, 25.54 percent, in the narratives of sixth graders.

Numbers, of course, don't give the whole picture: Quantity is not necessarily quality. For example, as you might expect, a high percentage of the ties that Crowhurst found in narratives signaled time, especially in the writing of sixth graders. The number of these temporal conjunctions decreased from grade 6 to 10 to 12, but that decrease was due largely to the decreasing frequency of the word *then*. That one word accounted for 61 percent of the temporal conjunctions for sixth graders. And in examining the temporal conjunctions used in argument, Crowhurst reports that even though total numbers showed no significant difference between grades 6 and 12, word choice was decidedly different. The sixth graders used only two temporal conjunctions: *then* and *soon*. Twelfth graders developed their arguments with *first of all, next, for one thing, meanwhile, all in all,* and *finally.* Crowhurst reports similar differences in the use of adversative conjunctions, with the sixth graders relying mainly on *but,* and the twelfth graders using a much wider range.

It's obvious that not all cohesive ties are created equal. Crowhurst reports that Halliday and Hasan's categories of repetition, synonyms, and collocation also showed significant differences for grade level, with synonyms and collocation increasing with age: "Greater use of these two kinds of lexical cohesion by the two upper grades seems to reflect the ability to use diverse vocabulary" (1976, 192). George A. McCulley (1985), in an investigation of the relationships among features of cohesion and primary-trait assessments of writing quality, also reports that the vocabulary measures—synonyms, hyponyms [*chair:furniture; dog: animal*] and collocations—"contribute most to judgments of writing quality and coherence" (278). Witte and Faigley report that high-rated essays had significantly more collocation than did the low-rated essays.

These findings come as no surprise. Vocabulary develops with age, and certainly the students with the widest-ranging vocabularies are the best writers in our classes—and they're the more experienced readers as well. These findings, of course, also suggest that we have work to do in helping students explore their vocabularies: Sixth graders certainly have more than those two temporal adverbs, *then* and *soon,* in their lexicons.

Witte and Faigley cite the following paragraph to demonstrate the collocation exhibited in a high-rated essay, which, they point out, is rarely found in the low-rated papers. The assigned topic had to do with changes in behavior, why people act differently in different situations:

> It is a job that really changes our behavior. Among other changes, we change the way we dress. In many jobs college graduates want to look responsible and mature, projecting an image of competence. The college student who wore faded blue jeans is now in three-piece suits. He feels the need to be approved of and accepted by his boss and associates. While he talked of socialism in college, he now reaps the profits of capitalism. While in college he demanded honesty in the words and actions of others, on the job he is willing to "kiss ass" to make friends or get a promotion. Indeed, working can change behavior (1981, 198).

Witte and Faigley point out how the writer "extends the semantic domain of the concept *behavior*" by supplying "examples of types of behavior, which are linked to the topic by a series of lexical collocations (e.g., *behavior, dress, look responsible, blue jeans, three-piece suits*)."

Interestingly, the better writers also use more repetition, a finding that at first might seem incongruous, given that it's the less-experienced writers who find our "rep" notations in the margins. However, as Crowhurst points out, the better writers elaborate more; they stick longer to a particular paragraph theme, so they're bound to repeat certain words.

I would suggest, too, that better writers recognize how repetition enhances the text. They understand the difference between repetition as redundancy and repetition as a cohesive device. Good repetition also goes along with another important cohesive device: parallelism. In the previous example, the writer has elaborated with some nice parallel touches, in the contrasting ideas of then and now. The two *while* clauses are especially effective, illustrating the past and present in parallel form.

Both of these contributors to cohesion—repetition and parallelism— are features of good prose that we can and should take time to teach. Perhaps the exceptional writers and prolific readers in our classes will use them without our help; but most of our students will not—not unless we identify them as tools and give students instruction and practice in using them. Happily, these tools are fairly easy to teach.

In evaluating our students' writing, we can point out possible candidates for good repetition in sentences that include compound structures. In other words, an *and* signals a possible candidate, because within the sentence a compound structure nearly always includes deletions. Here is a sentence from the "behavior" paragraph, a sentence with two *and*s:

> He feels the need to be approved of and accepted by his boss and associates.

With the simple addition of another "to be" and another "by his," the sentence will send a "Listen to me!" message:

> He feels the need to be approved of and to be accepted by his boss and by his associates.

This revision gives a deliberative tone to the sentence, fitting in with the two *while* sentences that follow.

Sometimes a more effective connection is the correlative pair of conjunctions: *both-and; either-or; neither-nor;* and *not only-but also* (or *as well*). These two-part conjunctions can connect all compounds, both complete sentences and structures within the sentence. An alternative to the revision we just considered might be a correlative in the second compound: "by *both* his boss *and* his associates" or "*not only* by his boss *but also* by his associates." Obviously, that kind of emphasis will not always be appropriate (and the latter suggestion probably is not).

There are, of course, other places for expanding ideas with parallelism and repetition besides compound structures—especially when sentences call for further details. However, this simple technique for examining compounds is easy to teach and to learn; it can be a successful revision exercise in a workshop class with peer groups. When students are evaluating one another's papers, they can be instructed to look for compounds, which they can then consider revising with correlatives or other expansions.

Two caveats go along with the use of correlatives: (1) The correlatives change the rhythm of the sentence, calling attention to the structures they connect, especially the second of the pair, so they can't be used just anywhere; they should be reserved for those ideas that need such attention. (2) The correlatives are easy prey for unparallel constructions: Students must be taught that the two parts of the conjunction introduce identical forms:

> Parallel: by *both* his boss *and* his associates
> (two noun phrases)

> Unparallel: both by his boss and his associates
> (prepositional phrase and noun phrase)

Because error correction and error avoidance constitute the traditional focus of the grammar lessons in textbooks, this second caveat is the only message in most of those I examined. Only three of the fifteen devote space to the positive values of parallel structures.

The Known-New Contract

Of all the concepts that have emerged from the scientific study of language, the most neglected by handbook and textbook writers—and certainly among the most useful for both evaluating prose and revising it—is the known-new contract. This method of analyzing sentences and paragraphs considers not only structural features such as subjects and predicates, but also the kind of information that those structures contribute—the roles they play.

In a coherent paragraph, every sentence after the opening one will generally include known information. In most cases, that information will fill the subject slot; the new information—the real purpose of the sentence—generally comes in the predicate. Linguists have found this known-new sequence to be so pervasive a feature of prose that it has come to be called a contract. The writer has an obligation, a contract of sorts, to fulfill expectations in the reader and keep the reader on familiar ground by connecting each sentence in some way to what has gone before. Consider how often the subject slot is filled by a pronoun; that pronoun, of course, stands for an antecedent known to the reader, a previously mentioned noun, noun phrase, or other nominal structure. The vague use of pronouns, especially *this* and *that* and *it*, which we sometimes find in students' papers, is actually an example of breaking the contract. In the following passage, for example, the second sentence has two pronouns, neither of which has a specific noun phrase or nominal as its antecedent:

> Yesterday, without warning, my roommate announced she was
> dropping out of school and hitchhiking to Colorado. *That* really sur-
> prised me, and I know *it* will shock her parents.

There's no problem of communication, of course. The reader understands that the pronoun refers to the whole idea of the preceding sentence. But the writer has put the problem of connection in the reader's
hands. An easy solution is to turn the demonstrative into a determiner
and to supply a noun headword:

> *That decision* (or *Her announcement*) really suprised me.

With that change, the pronoun *it* has also acquired an antecedent.

Readers expect pronouns to be known information: When they see a
personal or demonstrative or relative pronoun, they have a right to
assume an antecedent. We have traditionally described this problem as
a "pronoun-antecedent agreement" problem; it might be more useful to
think of it in terms of the reader, as a problem of missing information.

The Role of the Passive Voice

Now consider what happens when the known element in the sentence
is not the active subject—when it is not the agent, the actor, but rather,
the object. In such a situation, the passive voice may get put into play.
The passive transformation enables the writer to "front" that object—
that is, to put it in subject position, the position of known information.
Note the passive structure in the second sentence of the following passage from an article in *Time*:

> If Americans are truly interested in saving the rain forests, they
> should move beyond rhetoric and suggest policies that are
> practical—and acceptable to the understandably wary Brazilians.
> Such policies cannot be presented as take-them-or-leave-them
> propositions. If the U. S. expects better performance from Brazil,
> Brazil has a right to make demands in return. (emphasis added)
> (Lemonick 1989, 85)

In the first sentence, *policies*, in direct object position, is the new information; in the second, where it has become the known information, it
has been fronted, shifted to subject position. This change in sentence
function is, in fact, a common reason for choosing the passive voice.
Yet this purpose is ignored in our textbooks. Instead, such passives are
dismissed as weak and/or wordy.

This condemnation of the passive is not only misinformed; it is hyp-
ocritical. The textbook authors themselves use the passive extensively—
as they should—and elaborate as needed, disregarding their own advice
about the weakness and wordiness of the passive. As experienced writers

and experienced readers, they write cohesive prose, complying with the known-new contract intuitively. But their students, the readers of these texts, are not experienced writers—and most are not experienced readers either. They haven't developed an intuitive "feel" for language. They need good advice. Yet not a single one of the fifteen texts I examined discusses the contribution to cohesion that the passive voice makes, its role in the known-new contract.

Applying the Known-New Contract

In my composition classes, advice about the known-new contract has been especially useful for helping the good writers become even better. Although I always felt blessed whenever I discovered really good writers in my classes, I sometimes worried that I had nothing to teach them. Of course, every first draft can be improved, but it's not always easy to put your finger on the weak spots. However, after I introduced the known-new contract into my teaching, and combined it with the concept of sentence rhythm (another concept from linguistics that is ignored in our texts), I was able to identify problems that had escaped me and to suggest improvements. Often, those improvements are subtle, but they are meaningful. Many of my good writers have asked, "Why wasn't I ever told about this before?"

Here, for example, is a well-organized opening paragraph from one of those good writers. (I have numbered the sentences for convenience.)

> (1) Created by Congress in 1980, the 17.9 million acre Arctic National Wildlife Refuge (ANWR) lies in the northeast corner of Alaska, bordered by Canada's Yukon Territory and the Arctic Ocean. (2) The refuge was founded about ten years after the massive oil find at Prudhoe Bay, west of the refuge. (3) Geologists suspected there was oil on the Coastal Plain of the ANWR as well. (4) Quickly an environmental conflict was born. (5) Pro-development forces, noting that the country had just gone through tripled gas prices, argued the country needed the deposits to reduce dependence on foreign imports. (6) Conservationists countered that the wildlife and habitat of the Arctic represented a resource just as precious as petroleum.

The writer has made good use of subordination; he also uses strong verbs. But—But what? There's nothing particularly awkward here—not exactly—but the paragraph could be smoother, whatever that means. And saying that to the writer would certainly not help him—not if that was all I could say.

When I analyzed the sentences in terms of the known-new contract, I discovered a problem in sentence 3, where the subject slot contains new information, and the main stress is on known information. We know, of course, that when oil is found geologists are involved, so in that sense the information is understood. However, *geologists* is still a different subject, so it's the place to start thinking about revision. I was also bothered a bit by the modifier at the end of the second sentence. At first reading—momentarily, at least—I thought it was adverbial, modifying *founded*. Just to avoid that possible problem, I suggested turning it into a relative clause, so that it would clearly modify *Prudhoe Bay*. And the repeated *refuge* could easily be cut:

> The refuge was founded about ten years after the massive oil find at Prudhoe Bay, which lies to the west.

Maybe that third sentence just needs transition; a time phrase would help, with *geologists* kept as the subject. The new information, the purpose of the sentence, is the oil in the ANWR, so it would help to get *oil* at the end:

> At the time, geologists suspected that the Coastal Plain of the ANWR would also prove to be rich in oil.

With these suggestions, along with his awareness of the known-new contract and sentence rhythm, the student was able to accomplish the changes himself.

Sentence Rhythm and End Focus

The known-new pattern is clearly related to sentence rhythm, the valleys and peaks of stress in our language that make up its intonation contour—a feature of English that native speakers rarely think about. As speakers we manipulate the peaks and valleys to coincide with the message, reserving the loudest stress, the highest peak, for the new information, our main point of focus. And the peaks are what we as listeners pay attention to, knowing that those are the places where we will hear the important—the new—information. We want our readers to do the same, to read our prose with their peaks of stress in the right places.

Because the subject of the sentence is generally old information, it is likely to be a valley in the rhythm pattern; the main stress, the new information, will be a peak near the end of the sentence, often the last or next to the last structural unit.

Here is a simple example to illustrate this concept of end focus and reader expectation. When you read a sentence like this one, without a context,

> Barbara wrecked her motorcycle yesterday.

you probably give the main stress to *motor*:

> Barbara wrecked her MOTORcycle yesterday.

And in the following context, that reading would be the natural one:

> Did you hear what happened? Barbara wrecked her motorcycle yesterday. She was on her way to work when the car in front of her stopped suddenly—and she didn't.

Here, the sentence about Barbara is new information, both subject and predicate. But listen to the intonation of that sentence in a different context, when the known information has changed:

> Pete told me that Barbara had an accident this morning on her way to work. But I think he got his facts wrong. She wrecked her motorcycle yesterday.

The principle of end focus is still operating, but in reading this version, you probably delayed the main stress until *yesterday*; in this new context it would make no sense to stress *motorcycle*. Try reading the passage that way, either silently or aloud, and you will easily recognize the problem: The information in the last sentence up to the word *yesterday* is already known. "She wrecked her motorcycle" repeats the idea, albeit more specifically, of "Barbara had an accident." As a reader, you know intuitively that it's not time to apply stress until you get beyond that old information, until you get to *yesterday*, the new focus.

Now consider the awkwardness that would result if we shifted *yesterday* to the beginning of the sentence:

> Pete told me that Barbara had an accident this morning on her way to work. But I think he got his facts wrong. Yesterday she wrecked her motorcycle.

Although the reader might recognize the opening adverb as the new information and give it the main stress it deserves, the passage will have lost its natural rhythm. In fact, that placement for *yesterday* is typical of the unnatural rhythm that is likely to prompt that unhelpful "awk" in the margin. And, unfortunately, sometimes as teachers we may unwittingly encourage that awkwardness by suggesting that our students begin their sentences with something other than the subject—just for the sake of variety. But if what gets shifted to the opening position is the new information, it's in the wrong place.

It's not unusual for adverbial information, such as *yesterday*, to be the new information, the purpose of the sentence; when that's the case, its natural place is at the end, in the position of end focus. If that information is already known, however, it may very well belong in the opening slot as a cohesive link. We added such a link in the ANWR paragraph: "At that time" connected to the previous time phrase, "about ten years after the massive oil find." Notice what else the added prepositional phrase does. It provides an unstressed valley at the opening of the sentence, so that the subject will be in line for a slight peak of stress; the highest peak, however, still occupies end-focus position. This feature of adverbials, their movability, makes them highly versatile tools by enabling the writer to change the rhythm pattern. It makes them important contributions to cohesion.

Controlling Rhythm and Focus

The known-new contract calls for new information to come at the end of the sentence, in the position of main stress. But, of course, not all sentences are alike; not every sentence has end focus. In speech, especially, the focus is often shifted elsewhere. A speaker can easily stress the new information, no matter where in the sentence it appears. Consider, for example, these alternative ways of saying the motorcycle sentence, the variety of messages that are possible:

> BARBARA wrecked her motorcycle yesterday. [Not someone else.]
>
> Barbara wrecked HER motorcycle yesterday. [Her own; not someone else's.]

And we can add extra stress to *motorcycle:*

> Barbara wrecked her MOTORCYCLE yesterday. [Not her car.]

Or we can give the whole sentence added emphasis:

> Barbara DID wreck her motorcycle yesterday. [Believe me; I'm not making this up.]

Clearly, the spoken language is powerful, and the speaker is in control of the message.

But the writer is certainly not powerless—far from it. Writers don't use capital letters for emphasis, but there are other handy tools for making sure the reader understands the message. As mentioned earlier, the careful writer can take control simply by understanding the reader's expectations about the sentence and by making sure that the new information coincides with the prominent stress. You'll recall the version of the motorcycle passage in which the sensitive reader would almost certainly delay the stress until the new information *yesterday*. But in the following revision, the writer has left nothing to chance:

> Pete told me that Barbara had an accident on the way to work this morning. But I think he got his facts wrong. *It was yesterday that she wrecked her motorcycle.*

In this version, it is impossible for the reader to avoid putting the stress on *yesterday* with that *it* construction, known as a cleft sentence. The *it* cleft enables the writer to shift the emphasis to any slot in the sentence, forcing the reader to focus on the structure following *it was* (or *is, has been,* etc.):

> It was Barbara who wrecked her motorcycle.

> It was her own motorcycle that Barbara wrecked.

Another kind of cleft sentence uses a *what* clause in subject position:

> What Barbara wrecked was her motorcycle.

And another common transformation for changing sentence stress—probably our most common—is the *there* transformation:

> There was an accident at this intersection yesterday.

Remember that the normal subject position, the opening slot, is usually an unstressed valley in the intonation pattern. The addition of the expletive *there*, called the "existential *there*," delays the subject, putting it in line for a peak of stress. The expletive *there* actually has many uses in English, one of which is to enable the speaker or writer to introduce a new topic in a sentence that may not include known information.

Unfortunately, the uses of cleft and *there* sentences are rarely taught. In fact, the opposite is true: They are more likely to be *un*taught, to be discouraged, condemned as empty phrases or excessive words. In several of the texts I examined, the *it* and *there* sentences were labeled "wordy" or "fat" (as opposed to "concise" and "lean"). And examples are always presented with no context—as if context made no difference. One text claimed that

> It is entirely possible that the lake is frozen.

> [and]

> The lake may be frozen.

are synonymous, so the one with fewer words and a simpler construction is the better choice. But clearly these two sentences would occur in different contexts.

Of course, it's easy for inexperienced writers to overuse there and it constructions, just as it's easy to find unnecessary passives—even in our own writing. But this is true of every structure: They can all be overused. And, of course, we should pay attention to that overuse and help our students recognize it. But when the *there* and *it* transformations are well used, they provide efficient—and almost foolproof—ways for the writer to direct the reader's focus.

Evaluating for Information, Rhythm, and Focus

The following excerpt is part of an essay on the special excitement and competition and entertainment value of the major league baseball playoffs. Written by a college freshman in a first-semester composition course, it is probably typical of the writing of many high school students as well. As you read and evaluate the passage—the third and fourth paragraphs of a three-page essay—consider the cohesive ties and the known-new pattern of information. (I have added the sentence numbers.)

> (1) Another major reason people flock to playoffs is that they know how high a level of competition will be involved. (2) They know that these are the four best teams in all of Major League baseball, and that they are competing for the highest honor in baseball—the World Series. (3) This best of seven game series is so brutal because of the players' competitive drive to be the best. (4) In America, this kind of intense competition is something that is taught when we are young. (5) Success at what we do is possibly the most important goal of our society. (6) In every aspect of life we are expected to be competitive, even fighting our own death. (7) The competitiveness of the teams in the playoffs is at a level that most Americans can identify with; therefore, many people turn more attention to playoffs than the rest of the season. (8) But the playoffs offer entertainment too.
>
> (1) Baseball, America's national pastime, was originally intended to provide entertainment. (2) In this nation, where entertainment is such an important matter, baseball is just such a source. (3) More than any other part of the season, the playoffs supply a great deal of entertainment, drawing the fans from everywhere. (4) The players are paid outrageous sums of money to provide this entertainment, so the fans expect a lot from them—especially during the playoffs. (5) The playoffs always provide just the entertainment that people expect, and sometimes more.

Clearly, there's no lack of cohesive ties here; the number probably comes close to those of the high-rated essays in the research discussed earlier. The very first word, *another*, connects the paragraph to the previous text. The subject pronoun of the second sentence obviously refers to *people* in sentence 1. In reading sentence 2, I was struck by the rhythm pattern of strong stress falling on *four best teams* with a series of three fairly equal beats—an unusual stress pattern for a three-syllable phrase. In the same sentence there's another stressed phrase: *highest honor.* These two phrases supporting the paragraph's theme, "high level of competition," simply cannot be read without main stress. An important part of what makes this a well-written sentence is that the writer is in charge of the way the reader reads it. I would like to believe that the author heard its rhythm pattern in his head—and liked the sound of it. Because I teach my students to listen for stress and focus, I would use a passage like this one for a class discussion.

Now look at the cohesive ties in sentence 3. It's loaded: *best of seven game series, players' competitive drive, best.* In fact, just about the only word not connected to prior text is *brutal,* yet it is probably the one the writer intended to stress. But notice where it is—buried in the middle of the sentence. And what occupies the position of end focus? The old information in that *because* clause. The writer has used a forceful, even arguable, description for baseball—*brutal,* a word more often associated with football or hockey. But placed as it is there in the middle of the sentence, the word simply gets lost. It has another problem too—the qualifier *so,* which leads us to believe that we've heard about brutality before, when, in fact, we have not. The writer has not crafted the sentence with either the message or the reader in mind.

In our comments to the writer, we can suggest, then, that *brutal* be given end focus. If he agrees, what are the possibilities he might come up with?

> Because of the players' competitive drive to be the best, the best of seven series is brutal.

The main stress now falls where we want it, on *brutal,* but we've introduced a different problem with that side-by-side repetition of *the best.* But that one is easy to fix: The writer can either end the *because* clause after *drive* or simply say *the series*—although "best of seven" does serve to emphasize the pressure. The first choice is probably the better one:

> Because of the players' competitive drive, the best of seven series is brutal.

Notice, too, that in this revision the word *drive,* now followed by a comma, is in line for strong stress. (We could also suggest an *always* to add emphasis and give the reader more time on *brutal.*)

There are other possibilities as well: How about making *competitive drive* the subject?

> The players' competitive drive makes the best of seven series brutal.

In both of these rewrites, the reader is forced to put the main stress where it belongs—on *brutal*. And by cutting down sentence length, we have given *brutal* even more emphasis. (And, yes, *best-of-seven* should be hyphenated.)

The next two sentences conform to the known-new contract, living up to the reader's expectation, with the known information in the subject slots and the new information—"taught when we are young" and "important goal of our society"—in the predicates. Now look at sentence 6. I call that a problem sentence. Although the main clause says nothing new, there is new information in the participial phrase—the idea about fighting death; and it's in the right position for new information, at the end. But is that information appropriate? Is it really an example of competition? In our marginal comment, we might raise that question—with the hope, perhaps, that the author will decide to delete it. The paragraph can end with sentence 7, a summary statement. Sentence 8 is a typical ending sentence for inexperienced writers—foretelling what's coming in the next paragraph. But it's unnecessary here; it really belongs with the next paragraph.

Obviously, there are other changes the writer could make to improve this paragraph. The ones suggested here are the kinds of cohesive concepts that can be taught—and can be applied in the workshop or peer-review session. A peer reviewer—or the writer himself—looking for examples of the known-new contract would probably have spotted the problem with sentence 3.

The weakness in the second paragraph of the passage is easy to see—or hear: five instances of the word *entertainment* within five sentences (six, if we add the last sentence of the previous paragraph to this one.) In your evaluation, you might be tempted to write the marginal comment "Work on repetition"—and that is precisely what the instructor, a colleague of mine, actually wrote. But does "repetition" really pinpoint the problem?

Let's examine the sentence with the known-new contract in mind. Look at the information supplied in sentence 2: The only thing resembling new information is the *where* clause—and it has been placed in the middle of the sentence. In end-focus position we find the main clause, which is a clear repetition of the first sentence: known information. Is there anything new in sentence 3? The idea of fans is not only known to the reader, it is implied by *entertainment*; the sentence does nothing to further the topic of entertainment. Sentence 4 introduces the subject of money, but again the point of the sentence is lost as the reader comes to a second clause filled with known information.

"Repetition" in the margin simply doesn't help this writer revise the paragraph. In fact, the message is likely to be misinterpreted: It could mean "Don't use the word so often; find another." Our students, after all, have a handy helper when they're confronted with "rep" messages: the thesaurus. They can find lots of synonyms for *entertainment*. Even a message such as "Use specific details" may not help this student recognize that the problem lies in the known-new contract. Here he has broken it by leaving out the new information.

This paragraph is loaded—overloaded, as it turns out—with cohesive ties. And, clearly, the repetition of *entertainment* is only a symptom of the problem. The real problem is the dearth of ideas, of new information. The only new idea, the one about money, comes in sentence 4— and it's simply left hanging. You might have noticed that the word *originally*, in the first sentence, is also left hanging; it sets up an expectation in the reader that simply doesn't get fulfilled. The writer may have intended to pursue the subject of today's high salaries, the idea that money has changed baseball's purpose or fans' expectations: a then-now contrast. In evaluating this paragraph, the instructor can make good use of the known-new contract and the reader's expectations.

Understanding Cohesive Ties and Commas

We generally equate the comma in writing with the pause in speech— although of course not every pause calls for a comma. But clearly many of our students' punctuation errors can be attributed to that misunderstanding. A more useful observation, and one that can help writers in using some of the cohesive ties to better advantage, is the relationship between commas and peaks of stress. To make sure that a reader will put strong stress on a word, the writer can look for a way to follow that word with a comma.

This advice, of course, doesn't mean that we simply toss in commas. But many of the cohesive devices in Halladay and Hasan's conjunction category are movable, and most can be set off by commas. Look at the "of course" in the first sentence of this paragraph (and compare it with the same phrase in the first sentence of the previous paragraph—the "of course" without commas). Listen especially for the effect the comma has on your reading of the word *advice*: It is louder and longer because of that insertion. Compare your reading to this one:

> This advice doesn't mean that we simply toss in commas, of course.

In this version it's the word *commas* that gets the attention—not *advice*.

There are many such movables in that list of cohesive ties. Much of the power of conjunctive adverbs like *however* and *moreover* and such cohesive phrases as *for example, on the other hand,* and *in any case* derives from their ability to shift the stress.

When we teach students about the cohesive power of sentence rhythm, we are teaching them to listen to their language. Most of us encourage our student writers to read their papers aloud; these lessons tell them why to listen and what to listen for.

Reader Expectation

In an article entitled "An Appetite for Coherence: Arousing and Fulfilling Desires," Kristie S. Fleckenstein (1992) discusses the connection between writer and reader:

> Helping students create coherent texts is one of the most difficult jobs that composition teachers have. Part of that difficulty lies in the fact that coherence is as much a reader-based phenomenon as it is a writer-based creation. (81)

She emphasizes the importance, and the difficulty, for a student

> to step out of his or her shoes as a writer and examine the passage as a reader. Writers need to perceive the desires or expectations their texts arouse in their projected readers and then check to see if those desires are satisfied. (82)

Reader expectation can be turned into a practical editing tool by means of a classroom exercise. Ask a student to read the opening sentence of a paragraph; then ask the class to predict what comes next, what the subject of the second sentence will be. (This can also turn into a lesson on pronouns—as well as a follow-up lesson on known and new information.)

Fleckenstein describes a more elaborate version of this reader-based exercise in which the students respond to an opening sentence by explaining "(a) what they think the idea of the sentence is, (b) what they think will come next, and (c) what they think the entire essay will concern" (83). In working with peers the students are also instructed to "stretch out" a paragraph or two when they write their essays—that is, leave space after each sentence for the peer-partner's response.

Considering what the reader expects to come next can be especially helpful when evaluating those texts in which the known-new contract doesn't seem to apply. And it's certainly true that it doesn't apply in every case. In a narrative, for example, or in the description of a process, where the movement is chronological, temporal ties (*first, second, then, next, finally, eventually, at last*) generally connect the ideas.

Reader expectation and rhythm—two basic R's—are cohesive factors in every text. As teachers, we can enhance the evaluation skills we bring to our students' papers by recognizing their importance. They work hand in hand with cohesive ties and the known-new contract.

Raising Cohesion Consciousness

For the most part, students who can speak English sentences can write them by the time they reach the upper grades of elementary school. And for the most part, these writers—given a topic and a purpose and an audience—will demonstrate cohesion in their prose. So a great deal of what we teach them can be classified as revision. And revision is a matter of consciousness raising. Our job as writing teachers, then, should be to raise our students' consciousness, to teach them to recognize the strengths of their prose and to strengthen the weaknesses, to help them understand the tools of the writer's craft.

We can enhance our own evaluation and revision skills—and our teaching skills as well—by understanding and applying the many facets of cohesion outlined in this chapter: the lexical and grammatical ties, the known-new contract, reader expectation, and sentence rhythm. And when publishers ask our opinions of their textbooks, perhaps we should clue them in about those missing concepts.

Meanwhile, you can read more about cohesion and coherence and their classroom applications in the following books and articles:

Brostoff, Anita. 1981. "Coherence: 'Next to' Is Not 'Connected to.'" *College Composition and Communication* 32 (1981): 278–94.

Christensen, Francis. 1967. "A Generative Rhetoric of the Paragraph." In *Notes Toward a New Rhetoric: Six Essays for Teachers,* 52–81. New York: Harper & Row.

Donnelley, Colleen. 1994. *Linguistics for Writers.* Albany: State University of New York Press.

Fahnestock, Jeanne. 1983. "Semantic and Lexical Coherence." *College Composition and Communication* 34: 400–16.

Fleckenstein, Kristie S. (See Works Cited.)

Holloway, Dale. 1981. "Semantic Grammars: How They Can Help Us Teach Writing." *College Composition and Communication* 32: 205–18.

Kolln, Martha. 1996. *Rhetorical Grammar: Grammatical Choices, Rhetorical Effects*. 2nd ed. Needham Heights, MA: Allyn & Bacon.

Noguchi, Rei R. 1991. *Grammar and the Teaching of Writing: Limits and Possibilities*. Urbana, IL: National Council of Teachers of English, 1991.

Vande Kopple, William J. 1982. "Functional Sentence Perspective, Composition, and Reading." *College Composition and Communication* 33 (1982): 50–63.

Williams, Joseph M. (See Works Cited.)

Notes

1. Some researchers maintain that any list of sentences connected by cohesive ties constitutes a cohesive text. Here is a simple example:

> My computer is on my desk.
> My desk is made of oak.
> Tall oaks from little acorns grow.

This kind of passage is sometimes used to distinguish the two concepts, cohesion and coherence. In other words, the passage is considered cohesive because each sentence is tied to the previous one by a lexical tie. It is not coherent, however, because there is no situation for such a text; it has no unity, no meaning. For me, the problem with calling the passage a cohesive text lies in the assumption that such a passage should be called a text at all. I suspect it might be a problem for Halliday and Hasan as well. They define *cohesion* and *text* in a somewhat circular manner: Cohesion is that which produces a text; a text is any sequence of sentences that demonstrates cohesion, that forms "a unified whole"—a "unit of language in use" (1976, 1). It is a stretch, indeed, to label that chain of unrelated ideas a unified whole.

2. I have not included the titles and authors of the books I surveyed, except for the one by Warriner. My purpose in this chapter is not to critique individual textbooks; it is, rather, to emphasize how much more there is to know about cohesion and coherence than the textbooks of our profession tell us, with the hope that future editions will reflect that knowledge.

Works Cited

Crowhurst, Marion. 1987. "Cohesion in Argument and Narration at Three Grade Levels." *Research in the Teaching of English* 21: 185–201.

Fleckenstein, Kristie S. 1992. "An Appetite for Coherence: Arousing and Fulfilling Desires." *College Composition and Communication* 43: 81–87.

Halliday, M. A. K., and Ruqaiya K. Hasan. 1976. *Cohesion in English.* London: Longman.

Lemonick, Michael D. 1989 (Sept. 18) "What Can Americans Do?" *Time,* 134 (12): 85.

McCulley, George A. 1985. "Writing Quality, Coherence, and Cohesion." *Research in the Teaching of English* 19: 269–82.

Warriner, John E. 1982. *English Grammar and Composition.* Franklin Edition. New York: Harcourt Brace Jovanovich.

Williams, Joseph M. 1994. *Style: Ten Lessons in Clarity and Grace.* 4th ed. New York: HarperCollins.

Witte, Stephen P., and Lester Faigley. 1981. "Coherence, Cohesion, and Writing Quality." *College Composition and Communication* 32: 189–204.

6 Assessing Portfolios

Sandra Murphy
University of California–Davis

As a teacher, I have long since learned to be suspicious of any attempt to judge student writers on the basis of a single piece of writing collected on a single occasion. Experience has taught me, and research has confirmed, that it may not be possible to take a student's performance on a single occasion and use it to predict what will happen on others, in other contexts, in other genres. Interest, prior knowledge about the subject, engagement in the task, time and support for writing, familiarity with different kinds of text structures—these are only a few of the things that contribute to changes in the way a student performs from one occasion to the next. When I taught high school English and, later, when I taught composition at our local community college, I could assess an individual piece of writing in relation to a particular assignment and compare it with papers written by other students, but it was more difficult for me to see whether my students were improving over time, how they fared in one domain of writing compared with another, and how their writing and their writing processes varied from assignment to assignment. Missing in the stack of papers I carried home each night, all written by different students to the same assignment, was evidence of the breadth of my students' capabilities across different domains. Nor did the stack of papers tell me what my students thought about the processes they were using, or the progress they were making, or their lack of it.

Portfolios, because they are *collections* of student work, have given us a new way to look at student writing and an opportunity to gather new information about our students. In addition to analyzing papers written by different students to the same assignment, we can now look at several papers written by the same student, collected over time and in a variety of situations. Portfolios can help us see how a student performs in different circumstances and in response to different tasks, revealing in the process the highs and lows of the student's performances, shedding light on the scope of the student's work, and making known what the student sees and values in her writing. For

114

teaching, this kind of information is useful, because it helps us know how to guide students to the next steps in their growth as writers. We can learn, for example, which writing strategies or genres a student has under control, and which call for more work and more instructional support. We can learn what our students think about their writing and how they see themselves as writers.

Depending upon its purpose of the portfolio, and the specifics of its design, a portfolio of student work can also show us many things. If we ask students to collect writing over time, we can watch how they are developing as writers. If we ask them to include evidence that they have accomplished challenging and complex tasks, we can examine in-depth learning. Because the portfolio is a collection, we can ask students to show us that they can write for different audiences, both public and private, and for varied purposes. We can also ask students to include information about the processes and strategies they use, and from this evidence, we can learn about our students' awareness of those processes and strategies (Camp 1990, 1992; Paulson, Paulson, and Meyer 1991; Wolf 1989). Equally important, we can use portfolios to engage students in reflection, making assessment a learning experience. When we give students opportunities to reflect on their own work and writing processes, they learn to exercise judgment about their own work, monitor their own processes and progress, set goals for themselves, and present themselves and their work to others (see Camp 1992; Murphy and Smith 1991; Rief 1990; Wolf 1989; Yancey 1992).

In sum, then, portfolios offer definite assets. They can help us gather information that has been relatively unavailable in other approaches to evaluating writing, in particular, information about the processes students use, about what they think and value, and about their accomplishments across a range of different writing experiences. We can also use portfolios to encourage students to reflect on their work, engage in self-assessment, and learn how to exercise judgment and responsibility. When it comes time to assess portfolios, however, the assets they provide pose serious challenges:

- How do we evaluate a portfolio containing diverse kinds of writing composed under diverse conditions?
- How do we assess the unique kinds of information about processes and self-assessment that portfolios can provide?
- What kinds of assessments encourage students to exercise judgment about their own work?

One approach to evaluating portfolios is to use what we already know about assessing writing. Various approaches—holistic, primary trait, analytic scale, etc.—are described in the literature on writing assessment (see, for example, Diederich 1974; Cooper and Odell 1977; Faigley et al. 1985; Lloyd-Jones 1977). My purpose is not to describe these various methods. However, I will begin by discussing two of the scoring methods originally developed for use with individual pieces of writing, holistic, single-score assessment and genre-specific assessment, which have been adapted for use with portfolios. As useful as these two approaches are for assessing individual pieces of writing, when it comes to assessing portfolios, I think they have limitations. Rather than adopting methods designed for use with individual pieces of writing, I think we should be using and developing methods that tap the rich and unique kinds of information that portfolios offer about writing performance. Later in this chapter, I will make suggestions about promising approaches.

Holistic, Single-Score Assessment

Early efforts to assess portfolios have somewhat naturally relied on well known methods for assessing writing. In some portfolio projects, for example, teachers have turned to sets of criteria that emphasize generalized features and mechanics (Gearhart and Wolf 1994). Similar sets of criteria have appeared in dozens of district- and state-level writing assessments in the past—criteria which address generic features of writing such as organization, idea development, usage, mechanics, sentence variety, etc. As one example of a holistic, single-score rubric, consider the following description for the next to highest level of performance on a four-point scale. (The rubric from which this example was drawn was used in review training for scoring single samples of writing in the explanatory domain in a statewide writing test.)

> SCORE POINT 3 = These responses are well developed and have enough information to complete the writing task. The information is presented clearly, and irrelevant information does not interfere with details.
>
> • These responses contain some specific details that more than adequately explain the topic, although some details may not contribute to the development of the explanation.
>
> • The organizational plan is established and generally maintained.
>
> • The writer addresses the intended audience [specified in the prompt for writing].
>
> • Errors in sentence formation, if present, do not interfere with meaning.

- Errors in spelling, usage, punctuation, and capitalization, if present, do not interfere with meaning.

Although this particular rubric was created for the scoring of single samples, it is not difficult for one to imagine how a focus on generic characteristics of writing might be adapted for portfolios. Following typical holistic scoring procedures, for example, we might rate the portfolio as a whole.

Essentially, this is the approach adopted at Miami University in Oxford, Ohio, where portfolios are read holistically and given a single comprehensive score on a six-point scale (6 = high, 1 = low). For example, the *Miami University Portfolio Assessment Program 1992 Scoring Guide* describes a midrange portfolio (score point 3) as:

> A portfolio that is *fair* in overall quality. It suggests the competence that a "4" portfolio demonstrates. Strengths and weaknesses tend to be evenly balanced—either within or among the four pieces. One or more of the pieces may be too brief or underdeveloped. There is some evidence of the writer's ability to handle varied prose tasks sucessfully and to use language effectively, but it is offset by recurring problems in either or both content and style. A "3" portfolio often lacks both a clear sense of audience and a distinctive voice. (*Miami University* 1992)

Faculty at Miami University have found this scoring approach useful in their voluntary program for awarding advanced placement and credit. However, holistic, single-score rubrics are not very useful for guiding the growth of young writers or for helping teachers diagnose students' instructional needs. Because a holistic rubric relies on a single, comprehensive score and employs generic descriptors, it obscures distinctions among strategies appropriate for different genres, audiences, and purposes for writing which might be highlighted for young writers. For example, it does not help student writers understand how texts take different forms with variations in social purpose or how register and the need for background information might vary when different audiences are addressed. For teachers, then, this kind of rubric makes it difficult to diagnose a student's strengths and weaknesses. A student writer might be adept at organizing but troubled by errors in sentence formation, and while a student may be accomplished at developing narrative, he or she may be less adept at developing other kinds of writing.

More to the point for a discussion of portfolios, this kind of rubric reflects a very limited view of what the field now sees to be involved in writing. Holistic, single-score methods for assessing writing address only a small portion of the skills and strategies represented in emerging theoretical constructs of writing. New views of writing move beyond a focus on the formal characteristics of texts to include attention to the processes students are using to create them. As Grant Wiggins explains, assessments which support learning "educate teachers and students alike as to the qualities sought in finished products and the processes deemed likely to yield exemplary products" (1994, 130). New views of writing also acknowledge that different modes and purposes for writing draw on different knowledge, skills, and strategies and conceive of writing not as an isolated activity performed by an individual, but one embedded in social and communicative contexts (Camp 1993a; Witte and Flach 1994). Portfolios can provide us with information about the processes student writers use in composing, their versatility, their ability to engage in self-assessment, and their ability to exercise judgment and responsibility, but holistic, single-score rubrics do not address that information.

Genre-Specific Assessment

Holistic, single-score methods fall at one end of the continuum of methods designed for evaluating individual pieces of writing. At the opposite end are genre-specific assessment rubrics which focus on the characteristic features of particular genres or domains of writing. To chart development in writing, some portfolio researchers and teachers have turned to this kind of rubric. For example, the "Writing What You Read" narrative rubric employed in studies conducted by Maryl Gearhart and Shelby Wolf (1994) focuses on particular components of narrative and the ways developing writers orchestrate those components. In the rubric for narrative, the components are "theme," "character," "setting," "plot," and "communication," a category dealing with the author's audience awareness and crafting of style and tone. Descriptions of different levels of performance emphasize the interaction among components. As one example, the highest level of the "setting" category describes ways students at this level integrate setting with other components:

- Setting fully integrated with the characters, action, and theme of the story; role of setting is multifunctional—setting mood, revealing character and conflict, serving as metaphor. (75)

In comparison, less successful narratives at the second level reveal less sophisticated uses of setting:

- Skeletal indication of time and place often held in past time ("once there was . . ."); little relationship to other narrative elements. (74)

Criteria such as these, which focus on important rhetorical features of a particular genre, and which articulate the orchestration of those features, can provide a powerful tool for examining the development of competence over time, since the levels describe characteristic stages of development in that particular genre. Such rubrics also give us opportunities to effectively integrate assessment with instruction because they explicitly describe features of texts which are designed to accomplish particular social purposes. Students need to learn that "how a text works is a function of what it is for" (Cope and Kalantzis 1993, 7). We can use rubrics which explicitly describe *how texts work* to help students learn how to achieve the purposes they intend.

Genre-specific rubrics have also been used to assess individual pieces of work in portfolios. For instance, as part of an effort to devise new ways of assessing the verbal skills of third-year undergraduates, researchers at the University of Wisconsin–Madison used Applebee's (1981) system for classifying informational uses of school writing to categorize pieces of writing in the students' portfolios (Nystrand, Cohen, and Dowling 1993). Individual pieces of writing in each portfolio were categorized by genre as report, summary, analysis, theory, or persuasion and then scored with two modified scales drawn from the work of Britton et al. (1975) and the National Assessment of Educational Progress (Applebee, Langer, and Mullis 1990).

In some cases, genre-specific rubrics have also been used to guide students in the process of portfolio construction. This approach was employed by the New Standards Project, a partnership of states and school districts involved in the development of a large-scale portfolio assessment system. During the 1995–96 field-trial year of the project, students were asked to choose four entries for the writing exhibit in their portfolios from a list of six possibilities. Students could include a piece that "responds to literature," a piece that "demonstrates proficiency in a literary genre" (e.g., a play, a poem, etc.), a "narrative account," a "report," a "narrative procedure," and/or a "persuasive essay." Descriptions of requirements for specific pieces, called "entry slips," provided information about how each piece would be evaluated. For example, students were advised that their persuasive essays would be assessed according to how well they could

- engage the reader by establishing a context, creating a persona, and otherwise developing reader interest;
- develop a controlling idea that makes a clear and knowledgeable judgment;

- create and organize a structure appropriate in terms of the needs, values, and interests of a specified audience, arranging details, reasons, examples, and/or anecdotes effectively and persuasively;
- include appropriate information and arguments and exclude information and arguments that are irrelevant;
- anticipate and address reader concerns and counterarguments;
- support arguments with detailed evidence, citing sources of information as appropriate;
- use a range of strategies to elaborate and persuade, such as the following: definitions, descriptions, illustrations, examples from evidence, and anecdotes. (*New Standards Portfolio Field Trial* 1995)

When students constructed their NSP portfolios, they looked for pieces of writing that met the criteria.

On the whole, genre-specific rubrics seem more useful in instruction than holistic, single-score rubrics because they can be used to offer explicit guidance to students about rhetorical features of their writing (see the "Further Reading" section for other examples). They are consistent with theories that describe writing as a meaning-making activity that requires the coordination of diverse skills and stategies which vary with audience and purpose (Langer and Applebee 1987; Odell 1981; Camp 1993a, 1993b). They are supported by research which indicates that different genres or purposes for writing draw on different linguistic abilities, cognitive operations, and different skills and strategies (Durst 1987; Langer and Applebee 1987; Pringle and Freedman 1985; Witte and Cherry 1994). When they are accompanied by exemplars, genre-specific rubrics can become points of departure for discussions about what texts are for and about ways the structure of a text can support its purpose. With care that instruction does not become simply a formulaic exercise to transmit the "correct" way to write a particular genre, they can be a powerful tool for helping students learn how the features of texts can be used to accomplish social purposes.

However, because each genre-specific rubric focuses on the characteristics of a single kind of writing, by themselves these rubrics do not tap the unique information available in a collection of student work. They are not very useful evaluating the student's use of processes and resources for writing, for assessing the student's ability to evaluate his or her own writing, or for capturing information about the breadth of a student's abilities. These three components of performance are now seen as essential to the development of writing ability (Camp 1993). But they are not tapped by traditional methods for assessing individual pieces of student writing. In order to gather information relevant to this broader concept of assessment and what should be assessed, approaches which can be used with collections of writing have potential. One of these approaches is dimensional scoring.

Dimensional Scoring

Assessments based on dimensions of performance or learning derived from curriculum standards provide an open-ended alternative to prescriptive menus of portfolio contents, that is, a certain number of specified kinds of pieces such as letters, poems, or essays. In contrast, guidelines for putting together a portfolio based on dimensions of learning ask students to submit evidence of the knowledge, abilities, or habits of mind that are encompassed by the identified dimensions. Not to be confused with batteries of skills, dimensions are broad in scope and few in number. They describe selected, but essential elements of the execution of a particular kind of work, action, or deed, much like length, width, and thickness describe essential elements of space.

In some large-scale assessment efforts, dimensions of learning and performance have been used to guide students in the construction of their portfolios. For example, this approach was employed by the New Standards Project during the 1994–95 field trial. In a yearlong process prior to the field trial, teachers, researchers and language arts specialists from the participating states, working with staff from the Project, had generated statements about expectations for performance, and for portfolios, expressed as "standards" ("New Standards Project Takes a Close Look" 1993). Students who met the standards for writing were expected (1) to "communicate clearly, effectively and without errors"; (2) to "write for different kinds of readers using different writing styles"; and (3) to evaluate [their] own work (New Standards Project 1994a). When students constructed their portfolios, they put together sets of evidence to demonstrate their accomplishment in dimensions of performance for writing, reading, speaking, and listening.

Using a similar approach to the one employed by the New Standards Project during the 1993–94 field-trial year, teachers, administrators, and other educators in California, working with members of the Portfolio Task Force of the California Learning Assessment System (CLAS), generated dimensions of learning and performance in reading and writing. The guidelines asked students to demonstrate their ability to "construct meaning"—that is, to "respond to, interpret, analyze, and make connections within and among works of literature and other texts, oral communication, and personal experiences"—and to "compose and express ideas"—that is, to "communicate for a variety of purposes, with a variety of audiences, and in a variety of forms" (California Learning Assessment System 1994, 1).

The Pacesetter English Program, an advanced-placement program for English language arts sponsored by the College Entrance Examination Board and the Educational Testing Service, also uses a dimensional approach for scoring student portfolios. In the area of writing, assessors look for evidence in portfolios that students "use their own voices," "develop and present texts," "demonstrate technical command," and "reflect on and evaluate" how their "own texts are created and presented" (Sheingold et al. 1998, A1–A4). Each dimension is scored on a five-point scale as beginning, developing, promising, accomplished, or exemplary.

In addition to these large-scale assessment efforts, several schoolwide programs have adopted a dimensional approach for assessing portfolios. A well-known example is the portfolio program at Central Park East Secondary School (CPESS), where dimensions of learning and performance, called "habits of mind," have been incorporated into a rubric for scoring portfolios that students construct to meet graduation requirements. "Habits of mind" include dimensions such as the student's ability to take a position and show "in-depth understanding," to organize texts so that "all parts support the whole," to provide "credible" and "convincing" evidence, to create engaging texts that show "lively use of language" and an awareness of the reader, and to present texts that are "legible and intelligible" (Darling-Hammond, Ancess, and Falk 1995, 38–39).

The approaches taken in these projects have been attempts to gather information about important dimensions of learning and performance which have not been tapped by methods for assessing individual pieces of writing.

Assessing Breadth and Versatility

Information about the scope of a student's expertise has not been available in traditional, single-sample approaches to assessing writing. However, when portfolios "contain multiple samples representing a variety of performances and addressing different audiences and purposes" (Camp 1993b), they invite students (and evaluators) to observe how performance varies from occasion to occasion, how particular strategies and techniques can be adapted for different writing situations, and how writing varies across genre, audience, and purpose (Murphy and Smith 1992). Because they encourage us to examine the ways in which writing varies across situations, portfolios can help to bring our assessment practices more in line with current theories of writing.

Our experience as teachers, combined with research on writing, has led us to think of writing as a complex, multifaceted activity which varies according to the genre, the audience (from private to public), the purpose of the writing, the knowledge of the writer about the subject, and the writer's interest in it (Camp 1993a; Dyson 1989, 1993; Nystrand 1989; Witte 1992; Witte and Flach 1994). We have learned that writing is not just a matter of grammar and mechanics and that it is important for student writers to learn how to adjust their writing for different audiences and purposes. Dimensional scoring offers us one way to address these complexities.

The New Standards Project explored ways to assess breadth and versatility, in particular, students' ability to write for different kinds of readers using different writing styles. For example, an early draft of the high school version of the rubric for collections of writing included the following description of a level-four performance on a 1 to 4 scale:

- Provides evidence of an awareness of diverse audiences; the writer's attention to public and private audiences matches his/her varied purposes for writing.

- Demonstrates the ability to communicate for a variety of purposes; there is ample evidence of the ability to use a variety of genres, forms, and topics in written communication.

- Provides substantial evidence that the student's skillful control of a variety of distinctive voices makes the portfolio richer, more interesting, and more focused.

- Provides substantial evidence that the student has attempted to create a portrait of himself/herself as a learner by experimenting, attempting imaginative or unusual pieces, or approaching a topic or text in an innovative way. (New Standards Project 1994a)

While other rubrics focus attention on individual pieces of writing within portfolios, this one asks the evaluator (and the student) to look at the collection as a whole and at the student's accomplishments across a variety of different writing situations. When we assess this dimension, we ask questions such as: Can the student communicate effectively for a variety of purposes and audiences and in different genres? Can she write poetry as well as prose, stories as well as essays, letters as well as reports? Can she write for a distant audience as well as she writes for herself? The student's accomplishments cannot be determined by examining any single piece of writing within the portfolio. Rather, we must look at several pieces and assess the student's versatility. Putting a premium on versatility as a dimension of performance encourages us to provide students with rich and diverse writing experiences.

Another important feature of the dimensional approach to assessing portfolios is that the evaluation criteria can guide students in assembling their portfolios. Instead of requiring students to submit particular types of writing, or a certain number of specified pieces (for example, a narrative, a letter to a friend, a business letter), when we use a dimensional approach we challenge students to decide, with the guidance of their teachers, how to demonstrate the dimensions of performance on which they are to be evaluated. Many different kinds of evidence might be offered, then, as long as the particular dimensions are demonstrated. The 1994 NSP student handbook (New Standards Project 1994c), for example, provided explicit criteria to guide students in assembling their portfolios, which, in turn, were keyed to the dimensions assessed by evaluators. With respect to breadth, students were asked to show that they could

- Write for a variety of purposes.
- Write for a range of audiences.
- Write in a range of styles and formats. (New Standards Project 1994a, 14)

Students responding to these guidelines could approach the task in different ways. One student, for example, put the following pieces in her portfolio:

- an essay in response to Macbeth
- a personal narrative about Christmas
- a satire modeled on "A Modest Proposal"
- a character analysis written in a timed test in response to a specific prompt
- a letter to President Truman about the atomic bomb

This student demonstrated a clear understanding of what it means to write for different audiences. The narrative about Christmas had a personal voice. The recollection seemed written solely for the writer, and the reader of the piece seemed secondary. The audience for the timed prompt and the Macbeth essay, on the other hand, addressed a limited audience—the teacher and the assessor—while the letter to President Truman revealed a public voice. Another student, in contrast, chose the following:

- a narrative written in emulation of Edgar Allan Poe
- a poem with biblical allusions
- dialectical journals (notes and reflections on assigned readings)

- a reading log (a list of books and pages read)
- a reflective essay about the death of the father of a friend

While the selections were very different from those of the first student, this student also demonstrated breadth.

Assessing Metacognition

Portfolio assessment, as F. Leon Paulson and Pearl Paulson say, is neither instruction nor assessment. Rather, it is both instruction and assessment, and it occurs at the intersection of the two (1990, 1). It has the potential to be a powerful force in student learning because it fosters self-assessment, a dimension of learning that is at the heart of learning to write. Key elements of learning to write are learning to exercise judgment, to apply standards to a performance, to choose effective strategies for accomplishing one's intentions, and to make decisions about appropriate revisions. Research has demonstrated the importance of students' own awareness in monitoring their processes and strategies for writing (Bereiter and Scardamalia, 1987). In addition, reflecting, or looking back, on the experience of writing a piece is, according to Roberta Camp (1992), an integral part of becoming a more accomplished writer. When students are asked to reflect on their work, they have opportunities to make learning conscious, and teachers have opportunities to learn about what their students see and value in their writing (Camp 1992; Howard 1990, 1993; Johnston 1983; Reif 1990).

Students can be asked to provide information about their own assessment of their work and their agendas as writers. As one example, in the New Standards Project *Student Portfolio Handbook: Middle School English Language Arts,* students were told that they needed to "learn how to judge your own performance in order to set goals and improve" and were asked to "show us you can"

- recognize the strengths and weaknesses of your own writing . . .
- review your progress and set goals for improvement . . .
- explain the strategies you have used to make your writing better. (New Standards Project 1994c, 15)

Like the NSP guidelines described above, guidelines for assembling portfolios in many other projects emphasize reflection and self-assessment to encourage students to assume control of their own development as writers. Donald Daiker and his colleagues at Miami University in Oxford, Ohio, for example, suggest that teachers working with portfolios should "ask students for their *reflections*—on their portfolio, on their writing process or history, or on themselves as writers" and "offer important *choices* to the writer" (Daiker et al. 1996, 257). Similarly, guidelines for portfolios proposed by F. Leon Paulson and his colleagues indicate that "portfolios should provide opportunities for students to engage in self-reflection" (Paulson, Paulson, and Meyer 1991, 60).

Some rubrics for scoring students' portfolios focus on the students' ability to assess their work and to make effective choices for their portfolios. For example, a draft version of the NSP High School English Language Arts rubric for writing that was developed during the 1994 pilot year includes the category "reflective analysis." Portfolios at level four of a 1 to 4 scale on this dimension are described as follows:

- Provides substantial evidence of the ability to assess the strengths and weaknesses of [the student's] own work, processes used, and progress; overall, these self-assessments are both accurate and insightful.

- Provides clear, thoughtful, thorough explanations of decisions about the reasons for including particular portfolio selections; these explanations reflect an understanding of the portfolio's purpose.

- Provides substantial evidence that the student makes connections in order to reflect on ideas and to analyze and interpret across texts, disciplines, and genres, among language processes, and between experiences in and out of school. (New Standards Project 1994a, 1)

When this dimension is assessed, evaluators look for clarity and detail in the students analyses of their work and of their reasons for selecting pieces for their portfolios. For example, in a letter of introduction, the student who wrote the Macbeth essay clearly stated her goals for writing: "[The 'Macbeth' essay] is an example of what I can do when I work at editing and restructuring until I get a combination that is pleasing to the ear as well as the mind." In contrast, other students may not go beyond "I put this in because I liked it," when explaining their reasons for selecting a piece for their portfolio.

Portfolios in the Pacesetter English Program (1995, 1) have been scored on a similar dimension. Assessors make judgments about how well students "reflect on and evaluate how [their] own texts are created and presented." Rubrics which attend to this dimension of performance give teachers information about how well students are learning to judge their writing, to evaluate the processes they use, and to assess the progress they are making. Combined with guidelines for assembling portfolios which ask students to provide the evidence, they promote an important goal in instruction: helping student writers assume more responsibility for learning.

Assessing Technical Competence

In emerging alternative assessment models, even the familiar kinds of evidence about "formal" aspects of competence are defined in subtly new ways. Indeed, many of the chapters in the present volume provide insightful ways to describe aspects of technical competence such as control of syntax, awareness of audience, or students' understanding of a particular genre. In a dimensional approach to scoring, evaluators look for these kinds of evidence of technical competence throughout the collection. For example, in the New Standards field-trial approach to assessing writing, meeting the standard for "technical competence and effectiveness" meant more than mastery of correct spelling, mechanics, grammar, usage, paragraph structure, and punctuation. Although mastery of these skills was necessary, it was not sufficient for an exemplary rating. Students also had to show that they knew how to organize different kinds of writing coherently. Writers who met the standard for this dimension were also expected to demonstrate that, like professional writers, they could use a variety of writing strategies—appropriate for audience and purpose—to accomplish their intentions. For instance, in the New Standards Project's draft rubric, portfolios at level four of a 1 to 4 scale on this dimension were described as follows:

- Provides substantial evidence that the student can effectively organize ideas and *use a range of organizational strategies appropriate to audience and purpose* in order to create unified texts.
- Demonstrates clear command of various types of sentence structures.
- Demonstrates clear command of conventions and mechanics.
- Provides clear evidence that the student's word choice and use of language *is appropriate to audience and purpose,* and enhances the overall effectiveness of the portfolio. (1994c, 1; italics added)

The language of the rubric acknowledged that word choice is dependent upon audience and purpose and that different strategies might be employed in different genres, such as foreshadowing to build suspense in stories, or effective examples to persuade. Evaluators were to look for "a range of organizational stategies appropriate to audience and purpose." Thus, the draft rubric for this dimension of performance made it clear that evaluators were examining a *collection* of pieces, not making inferences on the basis of a single sample. Technical competence, then, was defined in terms of a body of work.

Assessing Processes Used in Creating Text

In the new, alternative models for assessment, students perform complex and meaningful tasks that are themselves valuable for learning (Camp 1993a; Mitchell 1992; Wiggins 1989). The papers that result are not, as Roberta Camp points out, "the exclusive focus for evaluation" (1993a, 67). Rather, the evaluation includes observations of the "essentials of performance, including the strategies and processes used to bring it about" (67). In many portfolio projects, teachers assess processes as well as products. Information about students' writing processes and strategies can be useful to instruction because it helps teachers and student writers alike to know about the ways that a writer's processes and strategies contribute, or fail to contribute, to successful writing.

In the New Standard Project's 1993–94 field-trial guidelines for assembling portfolios, high school students were advised that in order to meet the standard for technical competence, that is, to "communicate clearly, effectively, and without errors," they would have "to plan . . . draft, revise and polish . . . , and finally edit and proofread to eliminate errors" (1994c, 20). Suggested evidence for meeting the standard for "technical competence and effectiveness" was "one essay with multiple drafts in which you demonstrate that you have revised to improve clarity and effectiveness, as well as edited and proofread to correct errors" (22). Thus, students were expected not only to produce effective writing, but to demonstrate that they knew how to execute the processes that can bring it about. Assessments such as this encourage students to reflect on the processes and strategies they use and to gauge the effectiveness of those processes.

Some rubrics for scoring focus the attention of evaluators and students alike not only on the processes students use, but on the resources they draw from during those processes. In the Arts PROPEL Project in Pittsburgh, for example, scorers evaluate students' "use of processes and resources for writing" on a 1 to 4 scale ranging from "inadequate" to "outstanding." Students are expected to demonstrate

- awareness of strategies and processes for writing
- use of processes: prewriting, drafting, revision
- awareness of features important to writing
- ability to see strengths and opportunities in [their] own writing
- ability to describe what one sees and knows about writing

- use of the classroom social context for writing
- use of available experience and resources (one's own, the school's, the community's). (Educational Testing Service and Fellows of Harvard College 1993, 5)

To assess this dimension of performance, evaluators look for notes, outlines, or semantic maps as evidence of planning. They compare early drafts with later ones to see whether revision, as the students understand it, means restructuring or simply recopying. They look for evidence that the students have responded to feedback from the teacher or from peers about ways to improve their writing—for changes the students may have made in response to comments. In the students' reflective letters, evaluators look for evidence that the students are aware of the processes that work well for them, as well as the practices that impede their progress. In the students' chronicles of the processes through which the individual pieces were created, evaluators look for documentation that the students have made connections with other resources—the library, books, interactions with teachers and students—in developing their material for writing. Evidence about processes is, like other dimensions of performance, threaded throughout the portfolios. It is found in the comments of students about their work, in the bits and pieces of notes leading to drafts, and in the changes they make or don't make *between* initial drafts and revisions. It is evidence of an important component of writing performance.

Conclusion

One clear advantage to the dimensional approach is that it gives us a way to examine the unique kinds of evidence that portfolios can provide. These unique kinds of evidence include

- multiple samples representing a variety of performances and addressing different audiences and purposes;
- evidence of the processes, including interactions with others, used in creating text;
- evidence of students' awareness of the processes and strategies they have used and indications of what they value in the writing. (Camp 1993b, 191)

Other approaches to assessing writing, including holistic, single-score and genre-specific rubrics, are not designed to assess these kinds of evidence.

Another advantage of the dimensional approach is that it highlights and explicitly communicates key aspects of performance that are considered important for students by educators and the community at large. In this respect, the dimensional approach differs in an important way from other approaches to writing assessment, in which a topic for writing is *expected* to elicit a particular kind of writing or evidence of a particular aspect of performance—even though the expectation may never be made explicit to the students who are taking the test. Students creating portfolios for dimensional scoring are given explicit instructions about the dimensions of performance they are expected to demonstrate. This explicit connection between the criteria and the guidelines for assembling the portfolios enhances the instructional potential of the portfolio; it invites the student to self-assess in relation to the relevant dimensions of performance, and it invites teachers to teach the dimensions to the students. When teachers make the dimensions clear to students at the outset, the dimensions can be used for formative, as well as summative, evaluation.

Teaching to dimensions, however, is not the same thing as teaching to a test. Typically, a test is not flexible. Students must write to the prompt they are given or search for right answers. In contrast, the dimensional approach to assembling and scoring portfolios gives students and teachers both the responsibility and the authority to make choices about how to best demonstrate the dimensions of performance. That is, students are not required to complete identical tasks. Instead, students can take a variety of approaches to demonstrate accomplishment in a particular dimension. When students have some latitude in making decisions about the conditions for writing and about selecting the contents for the portfolio, they can be encouraged to assume some responsibility in the assessment process. Exercising control and responsibility encourages the personal development of students. For this reason, many portfolio practitioners highlight the importance of the students' role in generating the contents of the portfolio and in deciding how their work will be represented to external audiences.

The flexibility of this approach fills an important need in curricular reform (Murphy 1994). For decades, formal assessment has relied on assumptions that require uniform methods of test administration and a uniform set of test items (Eisner 1985). In turn, preoccupation with control and measurement has encouraged assembly line instruction. Under the press of standardization, there is little incentive for teachers to adopt individualized forms of teaching or to allow students to explore their own topics for writing. Rather, teachers experience pressure to pay particular attention to the content of the test and to the form of the test question—multiple-choice, short-answer, essay—and they adapt their instruction accordingly (Corbett and Wilson 1991; Loofbourrow 1994). Tests call for a particular content to be covered, and dictate when it should be taught (before the test administration). In tests, only certain responses are acceptable. As a result, tests impart a sameness to the educational enterprise, a sameness which runs counter to individualism and the development of personal initiative.

Portfolios, in contrast, can be generative. If they are not defined by rigid menus which dictate particular assignments, portfolios leave room for creativity and for students to play some role in the planning of their educational program. They help us see students as individuals who have important things to say, things that are of interest to them. They provide a useful complement to other assessment techniques available to the classroom teacher and a powerful alternative to "prepackaged," bureaucratic kinds of large-scale assessment that have the potential to dictate the curriculum and disempower both teachers and students (Darling-Hammond 1989). In sum, the flexibility that these approaches provide may be one of their most attractive assets. Similar—and rigorous—challenges can be presented to all students, but accomplishment can be demonstrated in multiple ways.

Further Reading

I think that readers will find *The Powers of Literacy: A Genre Approach to Teaching Writing,* edited by by Bill Cope and Mary Kalantzis (1993), to be an insightful exploration of the theory and practice of teaching via genres. For additional examples of rubrics focusing on specific types of writing, I recommend *The Writing Report Card, 1984–1988,* by Arthur Applebee, Judith Langer, and Ina Mullis (1990), and *A Measure of Success: From Assignment to Assessment in English Language Arts,* by Fran Claggett (1996). For general information about teaching and assessing with portfolios, I recommend *Portfolios: Process and Product,* edited by Pat Belanoff and Marcia Dickson (1991), and *Writing Portfolios in the Classroom: Policy and Practice, Promise and Peril,* edited by Robert Calfee and Pam Perfumo (1996). Secondary teachers of writing who want a general introduction to portfolio practice may find *Writing Portfolios: A*

Bridge from Teaching to Assessment, by Sandra Murphy and Mary Ann Smith (1991), to be a useful resource.

Works Cited

Applebee, Arthur. 1981. *Writing in the Secondary School: English and the Content Areas.* Urbana, IL: National Council of Teachers of English.

Applebee, Arthur N., Judith A. Langer, and Ina V. S. Mullis. 1990. *The Writing Report Card, 1984–1988: Findings from the Nation's Report Card.* Princeton, NJ: National Assessment of Educational Progress.

Belanoff, Pat, and Marcia Dickson, eds. 1991. *Portfolios: Process and Product.* Porstmouth, NH: Boynton/Cook.

Bereiter, Carl, and Marlene Scardamalia. 1987. *The Psychology of Written Composition.* Hillsdale, NJ: Lawrence Erlbaum.

Britton, James N., Tony Burgess, Nancy Martin, Alex McLeod, and Harold Rosen. 1975. *The Development of Writing Abilities (11–18).* London: Macmillan Education.

Calfee, Robert, and Pam Perfumo, eds. 1966. *Writing Portfolios in the Classroom: Policy and Practice, Promise and Peril.* Hillsdale, NJ: Lawrence Erlbaum.

California Learning Assessment System. 1994. *Dimensions of Learning in Language Arts.* Emeryville, CA: Educational Testing Service and Center for Performance Assessment.

Camp, Roberta. 1990. "Thinking Together about Portfolios." *Quarterly of the National Writing Project and the Center for the Study of Writing* 12: 8–14.

———. 1992. "Portfolio Reflections in Middle and Secondary School Classrooms." In *Portfolios in the Writing Classroom: An Introduction,* ed. Kathleen Blake Yancey, 61–79. Urbana, IL: National Council of Teachers of English.

———. 1993a. "Changing the Model for the Direct Assessment of Writing." In *Validating Holistic Scoring for Writing Assessment: Theoretical and Empirical Foundations,* ed. Michael Williamson and Brian Huot, 45–79. Cresskill, NJ: Hampton Press.

———. 1993b. "The Place of Portfolios in Our Changing Views of Writing Assessment." In *Construction versus Choice in Cognitive Measurement: Issues in Constructed Response, Performance Testing, and Portfolio Assessment,* ed. R. E. Bennet and W. C. Ward, 183–212. Hillsdale, NJ: Lawrence Erlbaum.

Clagett, Fran. 1996. *A Measure of Success: From Assignment to Assessment in English Language Arts.* Portsmouth, NH: Boynton/Cook.

Cooper, Charles R., and Lee Odell, eds. 1977. *Evaluating Writing: Describing, Measuring, Judging.* Urbana, IL: National Council of Teachers of English.

Cope, Bill, and Mary Kalantzis, eds. 1993. *The Powers of Literacy: A Genre Approach to Teaching Writing.* Pittsburgh, PA: University of Pittsburgh Press.

Corbett, H. Dickson, and Bruce L. Wilson. 1991. *Testing, Reform, and Rebellion,* Norwood, NJ: Ablex.

Daiker, Donald, Jeffrey Sommers, and Gail Stygall. 1996. "The Pedagogical Implications of a College Writing Portfolio." In *Assessment of Writing: Politics, Policies, Practices,* ed. Ed White, William Lutz, and Sandra Kamusikiri, 257–70. New York: Modern Language Association of America.

Darling-Hammond, Linda. 1989. "Accountability for Professional Practice." *Teachers College Record* 91.1: 59–80.

Darling-Hammond, Linda, Jacqueline Ancess, and Beverly Falk. 1995. *Authentic Assessment in Action: Studies of Schools and Students at Work.* New York: Teachers College Press.

Diederich, Paul. 1974. *Measuring Growth in English.* Urbana, IL: National Council of Teachers of English.

Durst, Russell K. 1987. "Cognitive and Linguistic Demands of Analytic Writing." *Research in the Teaching of English* 21: 347–76.

Dyson, Anne Haas. 1989. *Multiple Worlds of Child Writers: Friends Learning to Write.* New York: Teachers College Press.

———. 1993. *Social Worlds of Children Learning to Write.* New York: Teachers College Press.

Educational Testing Service and Fellows of Harvard College. 1993. *Arts PROPEL: A Handbook for Imaginative Writing.* Boston: Educational Testing Service and Fellows of Harvard College.

Eisner, Elliot W. 1985. *The Educational Imagination: On the Design and Evaluation of School Programs.* 2nd ed. New York: Macmillan.

Faigley, Lester, Roger Cherry, David Jolliffe, and Anna Skinner. *Assessing Writers' Knowledge and Processes of Composing.* Norwood, NJ: Ablex.

Gearhart, Maryl, and Shelby Wolf. 1994. "Engaging Teachers in Assessment of Their Students' Narrative Writing: The Role of Subject-Matter Knowledge." *Assessing Writing* 1: 67–90.

Howard, Kathryn. 1990. "Making the Writing Portfolio Real." *Quarterly of the National Writing Project and the Center for the Study of Writing* 12: 4–7, 27.

———. 1993. "Portfolio Culture in Pittsburg." In *Fire in the Eyes of Youth*, ed. Randolph Jennings, 89–94. St. Paul: Occasional Press.

Johnston, Brian. 1983. *Assessing English: Helping Students to Reflect on Their Work.* Sydney: St. Clair Press.

Koretz, Dan, B. Stecher, and E. Deibert. 1993. *The Reliability of Scores from the 1992 Vermont Portfolio Assessment Program.* Tech. Rep. no. 355. Los Angeles: University of California, the Center for Research on Evaluation, Standards, and Student Testing and the Center for the Study of Evaluation.

Langer, Judith A., and Arthur N. Applebee, eds. 1987. *How Writing Shapes Thinking: A Study of Teaching and Learning.* Urbana, IL: National Council of Teachers of English.

Lloyd-Jones, Richard. 1977. "Primary-Trait Scoring." In *Evaluating Writing: Describing, Measuring, Judging,* ed. Charles R. Cooper and Lee Odell, 33–90. Urbana, IL: National Council of Teachers of English.

Loofbourrow, Peggy Trump. 1994. "Composition in the Context of the CAP: A Case Study of the Interplay between Composition Assessment and Classrooms." *Educational Assessment* 2: 7–49.

Miami University Portfolio Assessment Program 1992 Scoring Guide. 1992. Oxford, OH: Miami University.

Mitchell, Ruth. 1992. *Testing for Learning.* New York: Free Press.

Murphy, Sandra. 1994. "Portfolios and Curriculum Reform: Patterns in Practice." *Assessing Writing* 1: 175–206.

Murphy, Sandra, and Mary Ann Smith. 1990. "Talking about Portfolios." *Quarterly of the National Writing Project and the Center for the Study of Writing* 12: 1–3, 24–27.

———. 1991. *Writing Portfolios: A Bridge from Teaching to Assessment.* Markham, Ontario: Pippin.

———. 1992. "Looking into Portfolios." In *Portfolios in the Writing Classroom: An Introduction,* ed. Kathleen Blake Yancey, 49–61. Urbana, IL: National Council of Teachers of English.

New Standards Portfolio Field Trial 1995–96 Workshop Edition: High School English Language Arts. 1995. Washington, DC: National Center on Education and the Economy; Pittsburgh: University of Pittsburgh, Learning Research and Development Center.

New Standards Portfolio Scoring Profile, English Language Arts, High School. 1996. Washington, DC: National Center on Education and the Economy; Pittsburg: University of Pittsburg, Learning Research and Development Center.

New Standards Project. 1994a. *Draft Rubric for High School English Language Arts.* Washington, DC: National Center on Education and the Economy; Pittsburgh: University of Pittsburgh, Learning Research and Development Center.

———. 1994c. *Student Portfolio Handbook: High School English Language Arts Field Trial Version.* Washington, DC: National Center on Education and the Economy; Pittsburgh: University of Pittsburgh, Learning Research and Development Center.

———. 1994c. *Student Portfolio Handbook: Middle School English Language Arts Field Trial Version.* Washington, DC: National Center on Education and the Economy; Pittsburgh: University of Pittsburgh, Learning Research and Development Center.

"New Standards Takes a Close Look at Portfolios." 1993. *Council Chronicle* 3: 1, 2

Nystrand, Martin. 1989. "A Social-interactive Model of Writing." *Written Communication* 6: 66–85.

Nystrand, Martin, Allan Cohen, and Norca Dowling. 1993. "Addressing Reliability Problems in the Portfolio Assessment of College Writing." *Educational Assessment* 1.1: 53–70.

Odell, Lee. 1981. "Defining and Assessing Competence in Writing." In *The Nature and Measurement of Competency in English,* ed. Charles Cooper. 95–138. Urbana, IL: National Council of Teachers of English.

Pacesetter English Program. 1995. "Aspects of Performance Assessed in Portfolios." Pittsburgh: College Entrance Examination Board and Educational Testing Service.

Paulson, F. Leon, and Pearl R. Paulson. 1990. "How Do Portfolios Measure Up?" Paper presented at the Aggregating Portfolio Data Conference. Union, WA: Northwest Evaluation Association.

Paulson, F. Leon, Pearl R. Paulson, and Carol Meyer. 1991. "What Makes a Portfolio a Portfolio?" *Educational Leadership* 48: 60–63.

Pringle, Ian, and Aviva Freedman. 1985. *A Comparative Study of Writing Abilities in Two Modes at the Grade 5, 8, and 12 Levels.* Toronto, Ontario: Ministry of Education.

Rief, Linda. 1990. "Finding the Value in Evaluation: Self-assessment in a Middle School Classroom." *Educational Leadership* 47: 24–29.

Sheingold, Karen, Joan Heller, Barbara Storms, and Athena Nunez. 1998. "Pacesetter English Portfolio Assessment: Final Report." Princeton, NJ: The College Board and Educational Testing Service.

Wiggins, Grant. 1989. "A True Test: Toward More Authentic and Equitable Assessment." *Phi Delta Kappan* 70: 703–13.

———. 1994. "The Constant Danger of Sacrificing Validity to Reliability: Making Writing Assessment Serve Writers." *Assessing Writing* 1: 129–39.

Witte, Stephen. 1992. "Context, Text, Intertext: Toward a Constructivist Semiotics of Writing." *Written Communication* 9: 237–308.

Witte, Stephen, and Roger Cherry. 1994. "Think-Aloud Protocols, Protocol Analysis, and Research Design: An Exploration of the Influence of Writing Tasks on Writing Processes." In *Speaking about Writing: Reflections on Research Methodologies,* ed. Peter Smagorinsky, 20–54. Sage.

Witte, Stephen, and Jennifer Flach. 1994. "Notes Toward an Assessment of Advanced Ability to Communicate." *Assessing Writing* 1: 207–46.

Wolf, Dennie Palmer. 1989. "Portfolio Assessment: Sampling Student Work." *Educational Leadership* 46: 35–39.

Yancey, Kathleen Blake, ed. 1992. *Portfolios in the Writing Classroom: An Introduction.* Urbana, IL: National Council of Teachers of English.

II Assessing Writing-to-Learn in Four Disciplines

The chapters in Part II focus on the ways writing might be assigned and evaluated to enhance students' learning in four centrally important academic disciplines: science, math, history, and literature. The Part II authors know that writing both reveals what students learn and enables that learning to occur. While the authors implicitly accept a constructivist theory of learning, their proposals for assigning and evaluating writing are based on a profound understanding of their own disciplines. They have specific ideas not just about what they want students to learn, but also about how well they want them to learn it. They are interested in standards of achievement and in criteria for evaluating writing against those standards.

The Part II authors are necessarily concerned with assignment making because, as they argue, evaluation can be most helpful if assignments are made and sequenced with particular kinds of learning in mind.

The authors believe that writing-to-learn must steadily engage students' personal experience and knowledge—an essential element of "constructing" new knowledge—but through carefully scaffolded activities and assignments. No matter how informal the writing, it must serve the purpose of learning about a discipline by bridging from the student's experience to the discipline's concepts and principles. Evaluation of informal writing must sustain a dialogue, these authors agree, but a special kind of dialogue, a conversation between a novice and an expert in which the expert guides the novice toward a specific kind of learning and achievement. Writing enables, sustains, and reveals that learning.

Denise Levine, in Chapter 7, focuses on the importance of writing in learning science. She argues that students learn science concepts best when textbook explanations are brought together with hands-on class-room experiments and that writing provides irreplaceable impetus for this learning as well as evidence of it. Levine advances this claim and supports it in an interesting way—by telling the story of her own education about the role of language in learning. She illustrates her story copiously with the writing of both elementary and secondary school students. Discovering that she "could assess students' understanding of scientific concepts by their use of generalizations, specific examples, and the connections they made to personal experience and prior knowledge," she set out to help them develop language to consolidate their learning and express their achievements. She offered sentence starters—what she calls "word strings"—to support all of her students in learning a "pattern of language behavior" that would enable them to engage science more fully and to provide evidence of their science learning. As a science teacher, Levine's concern is not so much with language in general as with a certain kind of language that helps her students learn science. She came to rely on the science portfolio as a way for students to demonstrate their learning and to reflect on it. Levine tells not just an inspiring story but one supported by current language theory.

Levine's chapter and the next one, by math educator Richard S. Millman, should dissolve any remaining skepticism that writing has a major role to play in students' learning of science and math. Both chapters make clear that there is already a substantial literature on assigning and evaluating writing in these disciplines. Equally important, there is solid theory (or "philosophy," to use Millman's term) and careful classroom research supporting such practices.

Adopting a topical instead of a narrative strategy, Richard S. Millman, in Chapter 8, emphasizes two benefits of writing for students studying mathematics: writing provides their teachers with irreplaceable knowledge about what students are learning and how they are learning it, and writing enables teachers to readjust the focus and pace of instruction. From his perspective, evaluating writing benefits the teacher as much as the student. Addressing English teachers directly, he advises us on how we might help our colleagues in mathematics to consider using writing in their classes. Millman relies on research in his own college math classes and his collaborative research in school classrooms to offer many concrete examples of writing in the service of learning math. Like Levine, Millman notes the importance placed on writing in his discipline's Goals 2000 national standards.

Kathy Medina, in Chapter 9, focuses on her own high school history classes to provide a rich, comprehensive review of many possible uses for writing in history. Through specific writing assignments and a full sampling of her students' writing, she demonstrates how she evaluates students' journal writing, in-class essay exams, and "formal history papers." Medina takes us on a complete tour of the ways in which she helps her students "reason historically" through carefully formulated assignments and searching but engaging responses to their work. She demonstrates convincingly how she involves students in evaluating their own and other students' writing. English teachers will be impressed with the way Medina makes use of pedagogies and evaluation strategies developed by colleagues in our own discipline. She sets a high standard for us in evaluating students' writing in ways that increase students' engagement with course materials and concepts and enhance their learning.

Richard Beach, in Chapter 10, relies on several decades of productive research on students' responses to literature in order to propose ways to evaluate writing about literature. He offers a comprehensive scheme of student "response strategies"—ranging from retelling to interpreting—with criteria for evaluating each strategy. Relying on student writing from Grades 9, 11, and 12 about diverse literary selections, Beach demonstrates possible teacher responses designed to sustain students' engagement with literature, elaborate their responses further, broaden their range of responses, and connect various response strategies in extended writing. The student responses come from brief and extended journal entries and from essays. Beach advocates giving writing assignments with specific criteria for students' achievement in mind. In the last part of his chapter, he turns to the possibilities of portfolios for assessing students' growth in using response strategies— growth in the use, range, linking, and elaboration of strategies. This approach makes possible an evaluation not only of participation in classroom activities or dimensions of performance, but also of achievement in writing about literature. Beach stresses the importance of involving students in evaluation by asking them to write reflections on their responses. There are, of course, other ways of conceptualizing literary study and achievement in literature than reader response, but Beach has carefully followed out its implications for evaluating students' achievement through their writing.

7 How to Read a Science Portfolio

Denise Stavis Levine
University of Pittsburgh Institute for Learning

I was always interested in science, although not the kind we did in elementary school, which—when we studied it at all—only involved reading a book and answering questions at the end of a chapter. Nor am I thinking of the high school physics class in which science was reduced to memorizing formulas for the mechanical advantage of a pulley system or an inclined plane. What I am referring to is what I heard young children call "the project thing"—the get-your-hands-dirty investigative science that helped me win first prize in the elementary school science fair for the model of a rocket control panel that I researched and created *at home*; and the project in junior high school, which allowed me to uncover concepts about molecular structure by growing crystals *at home*; and the experiments that made Mendel's law come alive for me when I mated guppies *at home*. I'm thinking about the hands-on, trial and error, continual experimentation of *doing* science. For me, the doing happened *at home*.

When I became a teacher, I realized that little had changed since I was in school. Even now, some twenty-five years later, this continues to be the case. In many classrooms, science is still teacher directed and dominated, outdated textbooks drive the curriculum, laboratory supplies needed for the doing of science are nonexistent, and students have few opportunities to pursue their own questions about scientific phenomena. In an address delivered at the University of New Mexico, Vice President Gore (1992) likewise observed, "We give outdated books to children sitting in quiet rows, rather than allowing them to plunge their hands into the mysteries of growing plants or crystals. And then, as our students become more sophisticated in their abilities, we increasingly divorce 'science' from real life and experience, and from the other disciplines they are studying."

The author gratefully acknowledges Marguerite Straus, principal of PS 1, Pamela Chin and Alice Young, bilingual teachers par excellence, and the students of PS 1, for allowing her to visit and work in their classrooms.

Early Inquiry

It was while I was teaching middle school science, and studying for my doctorate in language and learning, that I began to consider the role language plays in understanding the concepts of science and, more broadly, in learning itself. Since beginning that metacognitive journey, I have focused on the question of what learning looks like, and language's role in the process. Early on, with only a tentative understanding of the works of Britton (1970) and Vygotsky (1962), I postulated that if I pretaught the technical vocabulary of science, my students would own the concepts as well. What I discovered was that my students learned the language of science not by my preteaching technical vocabulary in isolation, but through the hands-on experiences in which we engaged (Levine 1982). It was interesting to see my first notions about the doing of science borne out in actual classroom-based research. However, in retrospect, what is more interesting is that the more I learned about thinking and learning, the more my ideas evolved as to what constituted solid evidence of learning.

After reading an article about concept development by Ehrenberg (1981), I began to look for evidence of students' ability to make generalizations about what they were learning, and their ability to provide specific examples of scientific understandings in their writing. I reasoned that if they provided generalizations and examples, they must have ownership of the concepts. This excerpt from Andi's seventh-grade science journal was written after a hands-on laboratory class focusing on the properties of metals:

> The way you might be able to tell if an element is metallic, you might use a dry cell to see if the object conducts electricity . . . Most metals are malleable . . . Also, some are ductile which means they can be drawn out into thin wire. Copper is a good example of ductile wire . . . electrical wires are made from copper therefore it is a good conductor of electricity too.

Andi's use of the word "most" indicated a generalization about the properties of metals, and her example of copper as a ductile metal used for electrical wires demonstrated her grasp of the concepts involved in this lab.

My students' writings also made it possible for me to detect when they did not understand something or were struggling to make sense of the concepts embedded in a lab. Laurel, also a seventh grader, was grappling with the notion of elements as the "building blocks of matter" and with the difference between elements and compounds. Her text-based homework assignment was meant to extend the understandings developed in the hands-on lab and to set the stage for the next day's work. In this case, however, it had clearly caused her confusion:

> I don't understand what they mean by compounds have different properties than elements. If oxygen and hydrogen are both gases then how can they form a liquid? How do oxygen, hydrogen and other elements differ?

Laurel was in touch with her own confusion. She provided an inside view of her learning as she continued writing her way toward understanding during the next week. After watching a demonstration of the electrolysis of water, and conducting her own tests for the presence of hydrogen and oxygen, she wrote:

> What I learned is how to tell the difference between hydrogen and oxygen. If the test tube filled with gas makes a popping sound when a burning stick is put into it, then it's hydrogen. If it becomes a flame when a glowing stick is put into it, then it's O.

She also returned to her original journal entry on the building blocks of matter, adding (in a different color ink) that

> The answer to the question about how hydrogen and oxygen form water/since they're both gases is that the elements can be different forms.

While it was clear that Laurel had come to understand that elements can be identified by their different states and properties, she still had not demonstrated an understanding of the difference between an element and a compound, and she missed the idea that when elements combine chemically to form a compound, the elements lose their original properties.

About a week later, she begins to makes sense of previously tangled ideas in this double-entry journal:

Reactions, Ideas, Ques.	Summary
What about water?	Of all the elements only 2 are
It's a compound!	liquids at room temperature,
	mercury & bromine.

With her answer to her own question about water ("It's a compound!"), she was reminded of her earlier questions. At this point, she pulled together what she had seen and done in the lab with what she had read in her text. She returned to her journal entry from the preceding week, chastised herself, and wrote "WRONG!" alongside her earlier note about elements coming in "different forms." Instead she declared that

> Water is a compound. Compounds gain all new properties. Their
> old elements lose their properties.

And that is precisely how two gases can alter their state when chemically combined! At last, Laurel demonstrated an understanding of what
a compound is and "what they mean by compounds have different
properties than elements."

Making Connections

Not too long after reading Ehrenberg, I came across Mayher, Lester, and
Pradl's (1984) work and was convinced that learning could be defined
as the connections we make, whether between the new and the known,
to personal experience. When I examined the journal writings of
Lucinda, a ninth grader studying acceleration in her physical science
class, I knew from her connection to a personal experience that she
understood the concepts involved. She wrote that

> This whole study reminds me of what happened last week. I knew
> I was in trouble when my elevator began to decelerate and it should
> have been accelerating, I thought. Then, we stopped . . . BETWEEN
> FLOORS. I was stuck!

This is authentic learning at work. Lucinda's understanding goes
beyond memorizing a formula for acceleration ($a = v/t$), which would
tell us nothing about the meaning she is making. Instead, she provides
a window on her thinking by making a connection between what happened when the elevator began to slow down ("decelerate"), or lose
velocity (v), during the time (t) when it should have been picking up
speed. In applying the concept to a real experience in her life, she made
sense of it and understood it, whether or not she had memorized the
shorthand formula.

In fact, Lucinda's method of coming to understand concepts embedded in a formula is not unlike the way in which scientists actually
derive formulas in the first place, and it is not unlike the way in which
young children, who are natural scientists, discover things about their
world. Vice President Gore (1992) explained it this way: "The kinds of
inquiries that have intrigued scientists throughout history are the daily
thoughts of childhood. 'How many stars are there?' 'How does that
seed make a flower?'" Grumbacher (1987), a physics education
resource specialist for the American Association of Physics Teachers,
concurs: "Physics begins to make sense for students as they connect
physics concepts with experiences from their lives: walking backwards

on a boat, watching a golf ball, recognizing the Aristotelian nature of a childhood belief" (327).

I was fleshing out my theories of teaching science as well as my framework for what constituted learning. Now, I could assess students' understanding of scientific concepts from their use of generalizations, specific examples, and the connections they made to personal experience or prior knowledge.

Building a Theory

When I was working in elementary schools to test out my understanding of whole language philosophy and emergent literacy theory, I found that the science writings of the schoolchildren contained much of the same evidence of learning that was found in the writing of the middle and high school students. Here is a journal entry from Carl, an inner-city fourth grader who had just returned from a four-day field trip to Connecticut:

> I remember tracking with Rick. It was fun. We learned that there are many ways to track deer. For example, deer [hoof] prints, bark eaten off trees, bushes sagging . . .

Like the middle and high school students, Carl demonstrated what he had learned by providing specific examples that helped to illustrate his understanding.

I began to make some connections of my own. My learning about language and cognition, my teaching, and my own methods of assessing students' learning came together when I realized that certain phrases kept appearing in students' journals. I speculated that perhaps these phrases might be evidence of specific kinds of learning or thinking. Because it was clear to me that no standardized test was able to measure this, and because my assessment had to keep pace with changes in my teaching and learning, I turned to portfolios.

Negotiating Portfolios

What I needed was an assessment that could be adapted to a curriculum comprised of authentic tasks negotiated between students and teachers. I wanted to look at my students' critical thinking—the speculation, analysis, synthesis, and evaluation that my students, from elementary to graduate school, kept telling me was at the heart of what it means to learn. So, each semester, as a matter of routine, I began the portfolio process in my classroom by asking students to "reflect on what we value in this class." Whether I presented that task to third graders, middle or high school science students, or inservice teachers, the response always came back as "thinking and learning."

The next step was to move students toward developing standards for evaluating evidence of thinking and learning. They needed to articulate what learning and critical thinking might look like in their portfolios. On the basis of their responses, we negotiated the criteria for evaluating the portfolios. After several trial semesters, the criteria for evaluation usually boiled down to some version of the following list:

- evidence of making connections between texts, to previous knowledge, or to personal experience;
- evidence of observing and raising questions, wondering or speculating;
- evidence of analysis or explanations of how and why;
- evidence of synthesis or pulling it all together—usually in the cover letter to the portfolio.

It soon became apparent that I was learning even more from my students than they were learning from me.

Reading Portfolios

As I read students' portfolios each term, I was repeatedly struck by the notion that certain oft-repeated words or phrases did, in fact, signal specific evidence of students making connections, observing and speculating, analyzing, synthesizing, and evaluating information, theories, and concepts. The more I read their work, and the more I spoke with students, the longer my list of phrases or "word strings," as I thought of them now, grew. Finally, I had a working document (see Figure 1).

Outcomes or Habits of Mind

I began mining the portfolios for data with which to test my theory about word strings as indicators of various kinds of learning and thinking, but I soon came to realize that I was working with descriptors rather than categories. Often, there was overlap, especially in analysis and synthesis; frequently, the metaphors used by students were more indicative of their analysis than of their having made a connection. Since the groups of word strings were not always discrete, I came to

Word Strings Demonstrating Thinking and Learning

1. Making Connections

"This reminds me of . . ."
"I remember . . ."
"This is like . . ."
Analogies, metaphors, and similes

2. Observing and Speculating (Raising Questions)

"I noticed . . ."
"I wonder . . ."
"What if . . ."
"If I were . . ."
"Why do/does . . ."
"How do/does . . ."

3. Analyzing (Explaining, Making Comparisons)

"This means that . . ."
"This is/happens because . . ."
"I think that . . ."
"The reason . . ."
"It works by . . ."
"It happens because . . ."
"Compared with . . ." "In comparing/comparison with . . ."

4. Synthesizing (Pulling It All Together)

"All in all . . ."
"As a result/consequence . . ."
"Thus . . ."
"Therefore . . ."

Figure 1. Word strings demonstrating higher-level thinking and learning strategies.

think of them as being descriptive of the ways in which students were thinking and learning, rather than representing hard and fast categories. Yet, I was also struck by the fact that sometimes these word strings indicated a much deeper analysis and synthesis than at other times. There seemed to be more to it than merely categorizing learning. What was I missing?

At about this point in my research, I came across an article on language outcomes by Roseanne DeFabio (1992), of New York State's Department of Education. The word "outcomes" was being used by the state education folks to describe language usage that becomes habit, those instances in which evidence of a definite *pattern of language behavior* exists. Once again, what I was learning about language education fit my notions about writing, learning, and assessment in science. And, once again, I found evidence for this thinking about habits of mind in classroom-based research, only this time, the classroom belonged to a colleague and friend.

Writing to Learn Science in Chinatown

I had been working with teachers at PS 1 in Chinatown (in New York City's Community School District Two) ever since I had had the good fortune to teach there beginning in 1990. The teachers and I were specifically interested in how we could document our bilingual students' many language competencies, instead of succumbing to the depressing picture of deficits and inadequacies painted by the standardized test already in use. For three years, two of the bilingual teachers, the principal—who strongly believed that theory-driven language and learning strategies work equally well with native and nonnative speakers of English—and I brainstormed ways to link assessment and instruction, as well as alternative ways to report progress to parents. The outcomes of this collaboration, which continued after I moved on to direct my own school, can be seen in the story of Annie.

Annie was a student in Pam Chin's bilingual fourth-grade class when I came to visit early in the fall term. I didn't notice her right away. What I did notice was that Pam had taken a series of starters for literary responses and displayed them on a large piece of oaktag, which was hanging from a clothesline that ran from one end of her classroom to the other. This was meant to help her students, for whom English was a new language, to get started writing after they had done some independent reading. The chart was a means of scaffolding their learning and thinking in English. Figure 2 shows what was on the chart.

What I loved about the chart was that the prompts seemed to provide for responses to nonfiction as well as they did for fiction. I was eager to show Pam my work on word strings (descriptors which might indicate evidence of thinking and learning) because it seemed to dovetail well with what she was already doing and might provide a natural link between her instruction and assessment.

I'd like to know . . .

This story reminded me of . . .

I felt . . .

I think . . .

I didn't understand . . .

I was surprised by . . .

I was confused by . . .

I learned that . . .

It would help me if . . .

I realized that . . .

If I were . . . I would . . .

Figure 2. Literary response starters in Pam Chin's bilingual classroom.

While I was trying to explain all of this to Pam, she was busily call-ing Annie over with her science journal to show me her writing. "You won't believe what this girl can do. I'm so proud of her!" she exclaimed. What she showed me was very interesting in light of my reading and thinking about outcomes. Annie had definitely internal-ized Pam's chart of reading-response starters, and she was using them each time she wrote in her reading-response log. She was also mak-ing astute personal connections with what she was reading, as in the following excerpt, which she wrote after reading a book whose theme was broken promises:

> It reminded me of my brother promise to go with me to my grand-mother's house and tomorrow when I ask him to go to my grandmother's house and he say no . . .

Clearly, this demonstrated that Annie understood what she had read. However, the best evidence for her speculative thinking becoming an outcome, or habit of mind, was found in her science journal.

Like many good teachers, before starting on a new project or topic in science, Pam invited her students to write about what they already knew. On October 1, Annie wrote in her science journal, beginning with a reading-response starter:

> It reminded me of my mother bought a plant. I think plants need sunshine. . . .

It appears that remembering her mother's plant purchase enabled her to recall what it was they had to provide for the plant. Two weeks later, she made further connections to previous experiences:

> Today I learn many kinds of seeds. . . . It reminded me of China I plant flowers and vegetables. I think planting is fun because you can get the vegetables to eat. I learn that the world has different kinds of seeds and when the seeds grow you have different kinds of vegetables.

Annie came to understand the notion of different seeds growing into different vegetables by connecting her previous experiences with growing and eating vegetables and what she was currently learning about seeds. As she continued to make detailed observations of her plants, she was full of wonder and began generating lots of terrific questions, evidence of real speculative thinking at work. Again, she used a reading-response starter to begin:

> I wonder why the small seeds grow faster that the big ones. I see that the vegetables are coming out from the seeds. . . . I wonder why so many roots are in one seed. . . . I wonder why some seeds doesn't grow.

This process of observing, speculating, reflecting, making connections to prior experience, synthesizing it all in order to construct new understandings, and finally coming up with new questions and wonderings is now a habit or outcome for Annie, the direct result of the rich language-learning and teaching strategies employed by her teacher.

Pam is not alone in applying rich language-learning strategies to science education. In *Science Workshop*, Saul (1993, 2) and her colleagues raised the issue of what might happen if they brought "some of the wisdom of the whole language workshop to bear on science instruction." They understood that "science is a way of thinking, a way of viewing the world, an approach to problem solving." They found "much of what they have come to understand about working with children . . . serve[s] them well as they go about teaching science" (2).

What Really Counts

After we had pored over Annie's writing together, Pam asked me to point out exactly where and how the evidence of learning was manifested in her work. It was so clear to me that I was surprised by her question. "The research indicates that Annie's use of those word strings to make personal connections, to connect the known and the new, and to construct her own meaning, not only at your suggestion in reading, but on her own in science, too, is hard data, proof she's learned a strategy *and* the content matter." Pam's reply is still fixed in my mind: "But that can't count; I taught her that!"

Way back at the beginning of this story, when I was a middle school teacher, I taught my students to keep double-entry journals to respond to the science readings assigned for homework. After they had been using the notebooks for a while, I asked them if they might consider using double-entry journals to respond to literature. They couldn't see what sense that made. So I explained that the idea for the double-entry journal had originally come from an English professor, which was why I had asked the question. One seventh grader took offense. He declared, "That's not fair. You're our science teacher, and you showed it to us for [making sense of] our *science* textbooks. Now, if our English teacher had shown it to us, we probably wouldn't see the value for science!"

I tell this anecdote to make a point about Annie and about Pam's statement. What really counts is not a score on this year's language-assessment battery, but the integration of instruction and assessment in Pam's classroom. It is the climate she creates for learning, one in which Annie has become smart about transferring a strategy that works in one subject area to another. And it is the writing Annie does in her science journal, which proves beyond a doubt that certain ways of thinking about, thinking through, connecting, and coming to know have become habits of mind for her in literature, in science, and in life.

It is precisely this kind of thinking that the recent push for high standards and more rigorous curricula in the sciences is trying to foster. The National Committee on Science Education Standards and Assessment (National Academy of Sciences 1996) has developed standards for science education in grades K–12, which are based on six general principles. These include the following:

1. All students have the opportunity to study and learn science.

2. All students can learn science with the appropriate opportunity.

3. Students should use modes of inquiry similar to those of scientists in order to understand the natural world.

4. Learning is an active process that best occurs when learners work together as a community.

5. We need to reduce the factual science knowledge that all students are expected to learn in favor of developing greater depth of understanding of scientific concepts and processes.

6. Science content, teaching, and assessment need to be considered within the context of and relationship to one another. (19–21)

I think they've really hit the nail on the head in terms of what really counts for science students of all ages.

Others who are beginning to focus on what really counts in science teaching, learning, and assessment include the American Association for the Advancement of Science. The Association's publication *Benchmarks for Scientific Literacy*, which grew out of Project 2061, addresses the issue of what students should know in terms of science content and what they should be able to do as far as carrying out investigations and scientific processes at each grade level. New Standards Performance Standards (National Center on Education and the Economy 1997, 80–105) in science have been internationally benchmarked and address the question of how well students should be performing in science—that is, "How good is good enough?"

In closing, I want to recommend two more resources for those who are interested in the points raised here. The first is Zemelman, Daniels, and Hyde's (1993) *Best Practice: New Standards for Teaching and Learning in America's Schools*. The section on science (91–107) is especially helpful. The second is Hein's (1991; Hein and Price 1994) work on "active assessment for active science," which will provide much in the way of food for thought, and isn't that what this is all about?

Works Cited

American Association for the Advancement of Science. 1993. *Benchmarks for Scientific Literacy.* New York: Oxford University Press.

Britton, James N. 1970. *Language and Learning.* New York: Penguin.

DeFabio, Roseanne Y. 1992. "An Attempt to Define Language Outcomes." *English Education* 24 (3): 168–87.

Ehrenberg, S. 1981. "Concept learning: How to make it happen in the Classroom." *Educational Leadership* 39: 36–43.

Gore, Albert. 1992. "Science Education for All." Address given at the University of New Mexico, Albuquerque, NM.

Grumbacher, J. 1987. "How Writing Helps Physics Students Become Better Problem Solvers." In *The Journal Book*, ed. Toby Fulwiler, 323–29. Upper Montclair, NJ: Boynton/Cook.

Hein, George E. 1991. "Active assessment for active science." In *Expanding Student Assessment*, ed. V. Perrone. Alexandria, VA: Association for Supervision and Curriculum Development.

Hein, George E., and Sabra Price. 1994. *Active Assessment for Active Science: A Guide for Elementary School Teachers.* Portsmouth, NH: Heinemann.

Levine, Denise Stavis. 1982. "Subject Specific Vocabulary in School." Unpubl. Paper. Bronx, NY: Fordham University.

Mayher, John, Nancy Lester, and Gordon M. Pradl. 1984. *Learning to Write/Writing to Learn*. Upper Montclair, NJ: Boynton/Cook.

National Academy of Sciences. 1996. "National Science Education Standards." Washington, DC: National Academy Press.

National Center on Education and the Economy. 1997. "New Standards Performance Standards." Washington, DC: 80–105.

Saul, Wendy, et al. 1993. *Science Workshop: A Whole Language Approach.*

Vygotsky, L. S. 1962. *Thought and Language*. Cambridge, MA: MIT Press.

Zemelman, Steven, Harvey Daniels, and Arthur A. Hyde. 1993. *Best Practice: New Standards for Teaching and Learning in America's Schools*. Portsmouth, NH: Heinemann.

8 Using Writing to Assess Mathematics Pedagogy and Students' Understanding

Richard S. Millman
Whittier College

The purpose of this paper is to give both a philosophical basis for the use of writing in mathematics and specific suggestions for the inclusion of writing assignments in mathematics courses. I will place special emphasis on the use of writing as a tool to evaluate the learning of mathematics. I am not, however, trying to persuade you, an audience of people who teach English, of the virtue of this approach. Rather, I will present discussion points to use in your efforts to persuade math teachers to use writing in their courses. The most succinct summary of my thesis is to let mathematics itself and mathematicians themselves persuade your colleagues!

The two overriding themes of this discussion are that (1) the reason to do writing in mathematics courses is to use writing as a diagnostic or evaluative tool *about the mathematical knowledge of the students,* not just about their "English," and that (2) such assignments allow math teachers to see how to change the way in which they teach so that their students may learn better.

After making philosophical points in favor of using writing to teach mathematics, I will offer some practical suggestions to help mathematicians assess students' writing. It is really the lack of practical suggestions that is a major stumbling block for mathematicians who are willing to try writing in their classrooms. The six main points of this discussion are that

1. Writing provides an assessment of what an individual student understands.

This paper was presented at the NCTE Annual Convention in Louisville, Kentucky, in November 1992.

2.   Writing can increase both the personal and the mathematical self-esteem of students (and lessen math anxiety).

3.   Writing can shed light on cultural aspects of learning mathematics.

4.   Writing can effect changes in pedagogy.

5.   Mathematics education known as "the Standards" of the National Council of Teachers of Mathematics (NCTM).

6.   There is a significant literature on the subject of writing as a tool for learning and assessing mathematics.

Writing Provides an Assessment of What an Individual Student Understands

Writing affects student learning and adds to the teacher's assessment of class understanding. For example, writing allows for diagnosis of a student's misconceptions. What is a writing exercise that could show how well a student can solve a linear equation? Let's ask a student to find x in the equation $3x + 7 = 22$. The student may solve it correctly in the following manner:

$3x + 7 = 22$

$3x = 15$

$x = 5$

Of course, the student will get full credit for the problem. On the other hand, another student who is asked to respond in writing to that question, may present something like:

> I subtract 7 from both sides to get $3x = 15$, and then I divide by 3 because the teacher always divides by whatever is in front of the x.

The second half of the sentence makes a math teacher wonder whether the student has understood the material. Suppose that the student had ended up with $(x + 1) = 15$—would that student have divided by $x + 1$? Does the student realize that "whatever is in front of the x" has to be a number ("the coefficient"), and not a variable?

Although both students got the correct numerical answer, there is certainly a difference between the two students' understanding of the solution—one which is only uncovered through use of writing. The teacher can do some real diagnosis and reinforce what the second student is doing well, while also working to correct misconceptions. The instructor can now teach the second student a lot about the process of solving equations. Asking the student to write ("even though this is a math class") clearly gives the teacher an alternative diagnostic tool.

A second example of how writing can be used to identify student misconceptions comes from factoring, a concept which is studied at the middle school or early high school level. Students usually do not have a lot of trouble with multiplying two polynomials together. A typical question, for example, is to ask for the product of

$$(x + 1)(2x - 3) = ?$$

Students should "multiply out the terms" and obtain

$$(x + 1)(2x - 3) = 2x^2 - 3x + 2x - 3 = 2x^2 - x - 3.$$

On the other hand, when we teach factoring, we start with a polynomial like

$$P = 2x^2 - x - 3$$

and ask, what two polynomials multiply together to get P? The answer in this case is clear if we look at the last displayed equation, because it shows that $P = (x + 1)(2x - 3)$. Really, if you multiply two polynomials to get an answer, then factoring could be thought of as starting with the answer and asking what the original question was. The question and answer dichotomy can be phrased more formally by saying that the two processes, factoring and finding a product, are the reverse of each other.

Cynthia Nahrgang and Bruce Peterson (1986) asked their students to discuss the following statement: "Factoring and finding a product are reverse processes." We hope to see in student responses that they are comfortable mechanically with both factoring and multiplying (as shown through an example) and that they realize that to do one process is to undo the other. The responses of three students follow.

Student C

Factoring and finding a product are reverse processes. They result as reverse processes, but the way you go about it isn't reverse because the opposite of multiplication is division. The equations are interchangeable though and can be called . . .

Student D

I believe that factoring and finding a product are reverse procedures. When you find a product of two binomials, that is to multiply:

$$(x + 2)(2x - 1) = 2x^2 + 3x - 2$$

When you factor a trinomial you end up with two binomials:

$2x^2 + 3x - 2 = (x + 2)(x - 1)$

Student E

Combining factors to find a product is an application of algebra that allows factors to be combined into either monomials, polynomials, or trinomials, or whatever. Factoring is the process of taking monomials, polynomials, binomials, trinomials, or whatever and reducing them to the terms that multiply together to form them. Thus, factoring is taking polynomials apart, while finding the product is putting them together. Actually, the two are very similar in the process used. One used primarily, multiplication, the other division.

It is very instructive and a good introduction to the use of writing in mathematics to ask math teachers from grade 8 and above to discuss what they feel Students C, D, and E understand. Most math teachers would evaluate the work of the three students by saying that Student C is quite confused. C has mistaken undoing a process ("the opposite of") with the simpler idea of inverting ("division"). I would ask C what the word "interchangeable" means and use that discussion to segue to the different ideas represented by two equations being the same and two equations having the same solutions. (An example: $2x = 2$ and $2 = 2x$ are the same equation, whereas $2x = 2$ and $3x = 3$ are different equations. They all have exactly the same solutions, $x = 1$.)

Student D has gotten the example right, but there is no prose to show that D understands the connection between factoring and multiplication. D should be asked for more explanation. Student E has a firm understanding of the relationship between the concepts. Note that E talks about division (as C did), but only in an essentially parenthetical way.

A third and final example of how writing can be used to assess mathematical learning concerns the definition of a *limit*. "Limit" is a concept taught in the first calculus course and not generally understood until after the last one. The formal mathematical definition of limit is extremely difficult. In most calculus courses, an informal approach is taken that I will now explain. Suppose that y is a function of the variable x, so that $y = f(x)$. This means that for each value of x there is a corresponding value of y, for example $y = x^2 + 1$. Note that when x gets closer and closer to zero, then the first term (the x^2) gets closer to zero (or "approaches zero"). Thus y approaches $0 + 1 = 1$. We would say that the limit of $x^2 + 1$ (or of $f(x)$) is 1.

For another example, as x approaches 1, the value of $f(x) = 1 - 1/x$ gets closer to 0. Thus, the limit of that function is 0 as x approaches 1. A third example begins with you at a distance of one yard from the wall.

Every minute, you go exactly one-half of the distance to the wall. You never get to the wall, but you come (as time goes on) as close to the wall as possible. The wall then becomes the limit of the function as time becomes very large.

A reasonable working definition of the term *limit* is

> As x approaches a, the *limit* of a function f(x) is L means that as x gets closer to a, then the value of f(x) gets closer to L.

In a first-semester calculus class, I asked the students to help me grade a problem from another section. The formal instruction was "What do you, as a calculus student, think of the definition of limit that Student A made? Does he understand the concept?"

Student A

> Quantities, as also ratios of quantities, which constantly tend toward equality in any finite time, and before the end of that time, approach each other more nearly than with any given difference whatever, become ultimately equal.

My student responses were really interesting. They ranged from a detailed attempt to understand Student A's definition to a comment that I was paid to grade papers, so the students should not have to. Reading the papers gave excellent insight into a student's understanding of limit! Returning the papers gave a wonderful opportunity to discuss what a limit is and what the misconceptions of the class were. For example, the students were tremendously confused about the difference between the value of the function at its limit point—a [in mathematical notation, f(a)]—and the limit of the function as x approaches a.

The punch line of the exercise is that the identity of Student A is that giant figure of mathematics and physics, Sir Isaac Newton (1642–1727)! The invention of calculus is an exciting subject in its own right. Newton, along with the philosopher and mathematician Gottfried Wilhelm von Leibniz (1646–1716), are certainly the two major figures in the history of calculus. Thus, not only can be make the point to our mathematical colleagues that they can assess their students' understanding of the term "limit," but they can also teach a little bit of history.

Writing Can Increase Both the Personal and Mathematical Self-esteem of the Student

The preceding limit example can also be used to increase students' self-esteem. If a superb mathematical scientist like Sir Isaac Newton had trouble with the concept of limit, then, certainly, the concept must be difficult for mere mortals. The limit assignment is one of my favorite types of writing. It interweaves the history, the content, and the "effect" of mathematics into one exercise. Note how different this homework is from that which asks students just to write a biography of a mathematician. If you suggest to your colleague a simple biography as a meaningful exercise, you will most assuredly receive the valid response "that's history or English."

A significant exercise is created when history, biography, and the mathematical content mix together. Personally, my students find some lives quite fascinating—people such as Evariste Galois (1811–32), about whom the myth is that he died in a duel over a prostitute, and Emmy Noether (1882–1935), who was denied her proper place in the university because she was a woman. (The Galois story—romantic or foolhardy though it may be—is probably fiction. See Rothman [1982].) The point here is to give substantive assignments—ones that demonstrate the mathematics being studied in the course and bring the historical and social issues of the day into the discussion. You can then assess the student's understanding of math and also discuss "social issues" surrounding math. It may also be that the social relevance places the mathematics within the student's immediate world.

A writing assignment that has substantive content is one that mathematicians will like. Carolyn Mahoney, professor of mathematics at California State University–San Marcos, designed and implemented a course called "Women and Mathematics." It has a significant number of exercises that commingle mathematics and social issues. Some other sources for original historical material with significant mathematical content are Grattan-Guinness (1970)—which is at the level of mathematical analysis—and original source material such as that found in Smith (1959) or Struik (1986).

Another way in which writing can increase the self-esteem of both the student and the teacher is collaborative writing whose final product is a journal article. In an advanced undergraduate geometry course, I had the experience of assigning a paper that ultimately became a published article (written jointly with a student, Ramona Speranza) in "Mathematics Teacher." Ms. Speranza was quite interested in art and wanted to teach both art and mathematics in the middle school. We worked up a presentation concerning elementary geometry for students whose visual ability was very good, but whose mathematical ability was not. The amount of enjoyment and self-esteem that my student colleague derived by having a journal article published was enormous. (For description of the original writing assignment, see Millman [1990]; for the published paper itself, see Millman and Speranza [1991].)

Writing Can Shed Light on the Cultural Aspects of Learning Mathematics

It is only recently that we mathematicians have realized that different cultural groups learn mathematics in different ways. Philip Uri Treisman's (1992) work (for which he was named to the MacArthur Fellows program) is an example. Treisman's work demonstrates the complexity of assessing the learning of mathematics. The same argument can be made for any subject.

While teaching calculus at the University of California–Berkeley, Treisman noticed the poor grades of African American students, especially when compared with Asian Americans. He then did a careful study that included his getting involved in the lives of his students outside of the classroom (Treisman 1992). He found, among other things, extraordinary cultural differences that affected how the students performed on their homework. After working individually, the Asian American students would work together in study groups, whereas the African Americans would not. In fact, when he talked with the latter group, he found that they did not think it "acceptable" to work together. This notion of nonacceptability came, not from the university standards, but from the students' own cultural background. From this insight, Treisman designed a learning strategy that proved very effective. He initiated a calculus course that required students to put in fifteen hours a week working either in the classroom or in small groups. By making collaboration a part of the course, he was able to effect an enormous improvement in the performance of all the students.

Writing can be used to understand the cultural issues that are present in a mathematics classroom. Because of some comments that I had heard teachers make about the mathematical level of the Latino American students in their middle school and high school classes, I decided to use writing to assess the level of these students. For this project, I worked with Bernardo Estrada, a California State University–San Marcos student, and Yolonda Mendoza, a high school teacher and director of the Newcomers program at Vista High School, in Vista California. Together we designed an in-class experiment to see how well the students were doing in both mechanical skills and "word problems," by asking them to write in both English and Spanish.

Most of the students who participated in this math project were from Mexico and had been in the United Sates for less than a year. Their mathematical skills varied greatly. Some of them only knew basic math, which consisted of how to add, subtract, multiply, and divide. Other students had taken the "Math "A" course, which, in California, covers much of the same material as does basic algebra but introduces concepts through practical problems. In this course, students, besides learning the mechanics of basic math, learned math through applications and by writing. Other students had taken basic algebra. In that class, the students learned the concepts of rational and irrational numbers, the real-line number, exponents, etc.

We designed two exercises for these students. The exercises were written by a California State University student whose first language was Spanish. The first consisted of a mechanical problem and a word problem. For this test, the students were divided into three groups. One group was given written questions in English, and asked to answer the questions in English. The second group was asked the first question in English and the second question in Spanish. The third group was asked to answer both questions in Spanish.

The second test consisted of two word problems, both given in Spanish. For this test, the students were also divided into groups, but this time one group had to answer the first question in English and the second in Spanish. The other group was asked to answer the first question in Spanish and the second in English.

What we found wasn't surprising. If you read the English version of the students' answers, you would conclude that they couldn't do mathematics. However, the Spanish version showed whether or not they could really do the material. We certainly hope that those who determine which "track" students belong in look not just at the mathematical manipulations, but also at the mathematics expressed in the student's native language. One surprising revelation: Our students had more trouble with the mechanical "multiply the fraction" problem than they did with the word problem!

Following are two examples from the Vista High School class exercise. They represent typical responses from students who knew what they were doing, but who still exhibited some misunderstanding:

Exercise 1

Question:

1. Escribé una explicacíon en palabras de como evaluar

    2 2/3 × 9/10

Student's Response:

To value this problem you have to know the basic mathematics. To resolve this problem first, put the fractions in decimal order. Then multiply.

Question:

> 2. Cada carro puedo tomar 5 personas al juego de football. ¿Si hay 23 personas en mi casa, cuantos carros necesitare para llevar a cada uno al juego? Explica en palabras que hicistes para obtener esta repuesta.

Student's Response:

Se necesitan 5. Divide las 23 personas entre los 5 carros y el resultado dan 4 carros pero te quedan 3 mas, entonces tíenes que tomar otro carro.

It surprised me that nearly all of the students realized that there had to be five cars, rather than the "arithmetic" answer of 4.6. It would have been interesting to have assigned the problem without asking for the response as a written paragraph. How many of the students would have responded 4.6 without writing being required?

Exercise 2

Question:

> 1. Tu compras un pantalon pro $25.00 y una camisa por $30.00. La tienda ofrece el 15% de descuento para los estudiantes. ¿Cuanto es el total que le debes a la tienda? (Explica en palabras como obtubistes la repruesta.)

Student's Response:

Si yo compro una camisa y un pantalon pro $25.00 y por $30.00 el costo total seria $55.00 pero si hay un descuento de 15% entonces el total que debo seria $40.00.

That student is subtracting the discount (after first converting it to dollars) from the total price of an object. He does not understand the whole idea of percentage and needs to work on it from the beginning.

Question:

> 2. ¿Tu compras una Television que cuesta $120.00 y le das al vendedor $200.00. Si el impuesto es 6%, cuanto te regresara? (Explica en palabra como obtubistes la repuesta).

Student's Response:

First I have to add $120.00 plus .6 the result will be $126.00 then I have to add $200.00 then I have to subtract $200 and $126.00 the total of my change will be $24.00.

The last student is very confused about all of the operations involved in the question. In each case, it is clear to the math teacher what misconceptions the students in the preceding examples have. The instructor can now give targeted help to both of the students.

Writing Can Effect Changes in Pedagogy

One of the criticisms of writing a tool for learning mathematics is that the evidence in its favor is merely anecdotal. In fact, much of the Sterrett (1990) volume is concerned with just such evidence. There is also a careful, scholarly study by Diane L. Miller (1992), which appeared recently in the prestigious *Journal for Research in Mathematics Education.* I will now sketch the contents of that article.

Miller considered the question of what effect students' writing has on teachers. For her study, she chose three teachers in Algebra 1 and 2 from a large, racially and socioeconomically mixed high school in a metropolitan area of southern Louisiana. There was a total of 85 students in the classes. The students were of varying mathematical ability. There were also two university professors (one in mathematics eduation and one in writing) involved in the study.

The study team considered the following two principal questions:

a. What can teachers learn about their students' understanding of school mathematics from reading their responses to in-class impromptu writing prompts?

b. Are instructional practices of teachers influenced as a result of reading students' responses to the prompts? (Miller 1992, 330)

The writing technique which she used was that of "writing prompts." A writing prompt consists of giving a phrase, sentence, or equation and asking the students to write for a few minutes about that prompt. A good writing prompt is one that deals with a key concept—a way of reinforcing the material already taught, or the way in which the students are trying to learn the material—or one that asks for explanation of a subtle point. Experienced teachers will easily find excellent prompts once they think in those terms. Examples from Miller's article include the following.

a. Division by zero exercise: Explain the differences or similarities.
$$0/5 \text{ vs. } 5/0 \text{ vs. } 0/0$$

b. Explain the use of the property of zero: Write about how you would evaluate the following:
$$(5 + 7 \times 13 - 6) \times (36 - (3 \times 12))$$

c. Tell everything that you did to prepare for the class/test.

  d.   What are x and y in $4x = 28$ and $4y = 28$? Are they the same? (Miller
       1992, 338)

The last prompt is an example of writing about subtle points. In an
expression like $x^3 + 2x^2 + 1$, there is no value assigned to x—it is a variable. On the other hand, the variable x in the equation $4x = 28$ can take
only one value in order for the equation to be true. This prompt gets
some interesting responses because students usually don't realize the
subtlety of the difference between a *variable* (like x or y) and the *value*
of the variable (the answer is 7, of course, no matter what you call the
variable in the equation).

   The study team's method was to design writing prompts (some of
which are listed above). Five-minute writing assignments from these
prompts were done on four out of five class days. Thus, writing was
an integral part of the course. There was no grading of the writing, nor
were the assignments mandatory.

   What impressed me most was the change in the pedagogy implemented by the teachers because of the study. Those actions included
the following:

  a.   Teaching the same material again, immediately, as indicated by the
       writing assignments.

  b.   Delaying an exam because the responses to the writing prompts
       showed a lack of understanding.

  c.   Designing and adding more reviews.

  d.   Initiating private discussion with individual students.

  e.   Using prompts *during* a lesson, rather than to *start*, to see if the stu-
       dents understood the new concept.

  f.   Teaching study skills (see the fourth item, above). (Miller 1992, 338)

   Below is an example that is quite persuasive because it shows a fault
in the teacher's pedagogy. The difficulty was easy to correct, but would
not have been recognized without the writing exercise:

      Factor: $6b^2 + 7b$ Answer: $(6b + 7)b$

Most students responded that factoring is a "subtractive process." For
example, a student wrote "because $7 + b$ is $7b$ the b [can be] taken
out." Of course, $7 + b$ and $7b$ are not the same (the latter is multiplication of the value of b by the number 7, whereas, the former just adds
7 to the value b). The other difficulty that the student was having is
indicated in the language "taken out." That phrase shows a subtractive process too.

As a result of this exercise, the teacher concluded that she needed to be extremely careful about her choice of words during instruction in factoring. Statements like "when factoring, look for a number or letter that can be taken out of each term" can confuse students because they will equate factoring with subtraction ("taking out"). Actually, the key to factoring is recognizing a common term in each polynomial, and that is the point to emphasize. This teacher learned about teaching and charged her pedagogy as a result of using writing in mathematics.

From the results of the study, Miller concluded the following:

a. Writing and the individualized instruction that accompanies it helped the students to know that someone cared. They also realized that they could ask a question in private, thus making it easier to understand those mathematical concepts that were unclear.

b. Since there was no grammar, etc., involved, it was sometimes difficult to understand what the students meant. Oral comments and individual help were useful. This means that written comments do not always adequately show what the students know.

c. Written comments provided a unique and continuous dialogue for the teachers about the process of teaching and learning—one from which they and the university people learned a great deal.

d. Assessment is difficult with this vehicle because of students' varying writing skills.

e. Teachers are reluctant to share their understanding in writing. We need to work on the NCTM's Standard 2 with teachers.

Another example in which writing in mathematics can give information about curricular reform is provided by Richard Bullock and Richard Millman (1992). More specific than Miller's article, its major thesis is that student writing can be used to assess the quality of a math textbook. An important corollary of that article is that much more care has to be taken in the choice of textbooks. In particular, the intended audience of the book needs to be involved in the process of selection. These articles should be thought of as pointing to the power of writing in curricular change because they indicate the way in which courses should be taught and planned.

Writing Is Included at All Grade Levels in the NCTM Standards

In 1986, the Board of Directors of the National Council of Teachers of Mathematics established the Commission on Standards for School

Mathematics, in an effort to improve the quality of K–12 mathematics instruction. The discussions involved classroom teachers, supervisors, educational researchers, teacher educators, and university professors. The wide range of backgrounds is what led to the extraordinary quality and the universal adoption of the recommendations (called, simply, "the Standards"), which have been endorsed by fifteen major scholarly societies and have also gained support from thirty others. The development of the Standards is often cited as a way to effect systemic change in the teaching of a discipline. When talking to a mathematician about a mathematical issue, to be able to quote from the Standards adds tremendous force to your position.

In the middle school and high school Standards, writing plays an important part. For example, the Standards for grades 5–8 state that

> These more open-ended problems can have several correct answers and can promote opportunities for students to write about their ideas, discuss interpretations, and expand their understandings.
>
> An interchange occurring between common and mathematical language builds on the existing structure and logic of common language, and connects student's experiences and language to the mathematical world. Terms whose meanings change from one language to anther must be addressed straightforwardly. For example, the use of such terms as "improper fractions" and "right angle" as mathematical descriptions can be misleading to students, who relate them to the common meanings of the words "improper" and "right." (Standard 2)

The Standards for grades 9–12 are even more explicit.

> Techniques used to teach writing can be useful in teaching mathematical communication. The view of writing as a process emphasizes brainstorming, clarifying, and revising; this view can readily be applied to solving a mathematical problem. The simple exercise of writing an explanation of how a problem was solved not only helps clarify a student's thinking but also may provide other students fresh insights gained form viewing the problem from a new perspective.
>
> Students should be encouraged to keep journals describing their mathematical experiences, including their reflections on their problem-solving thought processes. Journal writing also can help students clarify feelings about mathematics or about a particular experience or activity in a mathematics classroom. These activities can foster students' positive attitude about mathematics, particularly if the journal entries are accompanied by discussions about any negative feelings and ways to deal with unpleasant experiences. (Standard 2)

There Is Significant Literature on the Subject of Writing as a Tool for Learning and Assessing Mathematics

Nothing is more persuasive to teachers and scholars than the existence of a body of literature. To that end, Appendix A of this paper presents a bibliography, through January 1993, of literature about writing in the mathematics classroom. The first work that should be consulted by your mathematical friends is Sterrett (1990), and the second is Connolly and Vilardi (1989). I have tried to make the bibliography as complete as possible, but, inevitably, there will be articles that I have missed. The accompanying works cited listing also includes mathematical books that have writing exercises in them. One of them is Millman and Parker (1991).

Although it most certainly is not for a mathematical audience, there is one other book that I would like to single out: Randy Moore's *Writing to Learn Biology* (1992). The book is well written and contains many ideas that are transferrable to mathematics or any science.

Suggestions for Convincing Mathematics Faculty to Use Writing in Their Classrooms

Mathematics faculty need to be given examples of what types of writing are used and what specific topics could be given. The most popular types of exercises for mathematics can be found in the literature cited in this paper.

Those who teach English certainly believe that writing is a process. Unfortunately, mathematicians need to be convinced of that approach. Sterrett (1990), however, is especially helpful in this regard. With the help of the references listed in this paper, suggest topics to your colleagues and emphasize that papers are to be done in multiple-draft format. The effect of such assignments can be interesting and unexpected. Urge the mathematicians to consider the changes in the drafts as anecdotal evidence that writing is an integral part of the NCTM Standards. Furthermore, the Standards make specific reference to writing as a process (as quoted earlier). Because mathematicians are unaware that writing figures so prominently in the Standards, giving a precise reference can be very persuasive.

When you suggest historical subjects, give something that is substantive from a mathematical viewpoint or that has interesting social implications.

There are modern mathematical topics about which students can write even if they are not going to be mathematicians. Examples include chaos theory, the geometry of fractals, mathematical anxiety, the role of abstract groups in the "real world" (symmetry), applications of math in the student's favorite discipline, the breaking of secret codes through number theory (cryptology), the use of the computer in proofs, and many more.

One word of caution: There is no question that giving writing exercises increases the time the teacher spends with the class assignments. This work load increase must be acknowledged up-front by faculty and administration. However, the quality of the results obtained makes the time spent well worth it.

Invite a mathematician or scientist who likes to write and who has an established reputation as a scientific scholar to come to your college or school and give two colloquia, one in her discipline and the other in writing. As one of our own is far more persuasive than someone from another camp, this technique works extremely well in changing the attitude of some of the faculty in a mathematics or science department.

Works Cited

Bullock, Richard, and Richard S. Millman. 1992. "Mathematicians' Concept of Audience in Mathematics Textbook Writing." *Primus* 2: 335–47.

Connolly, P., and T. Vilardi. 1989. *Writing to Learn Mathematics and Science*. New York: Teachers College Press.

Grattan-Guinness, Ivor. 1970. *The Development of the Foundations of Mathematical Analysis from Euler to Riemann*. Cambridge, MA: MIT Press.

Miller, Diane L. 1992. "Teacher Benefits from Using Impromptu Writing Prompts in Algebra Classes." *Journal for Research in Mathematics Education* 23: 329–40.

Millman, Richard S. 1990. "Writing in a Non-Euclidean Geometry Course." In *Using Writing to Teach Mathematics*, ed. Andrew Sterrett, 134–37. Washington, DC: Mathematical Association of America.

Millman, Richard S., and George Parker. 1991. *Geometry: A Metric Approach with Models*. 2nd ed. New York: Springer-Verlag.

Millman, Richard S., and Ramona Speranza. 1991. "Artists' View of Points and Lines." *Mathematics Teacher* 84: 133–38.

Moore, Randy. 1992. *Writing to Learn Biology*. Philadelphia: Sanders College.

Nahrgang, Cynthia L., and Bruce T. Petersen. 1986. "Using Writing to Learn Mathematics." *Mathematics Teacher* 79: 461–65.

National Council of Teachers of Mathematics. 1989. *Curriculum and Evaluation Standards of School Mathematics*. Reston, VA: National Council of Teachers of Mathematics.

Rothman, Tony. 1982. "Genius and Biographers: The Fictionalization of Evariste Galois." *American Mathematical Monthly* 89: 84–106.

Smith, David E. 1959. *A Source Book in Mathematics*. New York: Dover.

Sterrett, Andrew E., ed. 1990. *Using Writing to Teach Mathematics*. Washington, DC: Mathematical Association of America.

Struik, Dirk J. 1986. *Source Book in Mathematics*. Princeton, NJ: Princeton University Press.

Treisman, Philip Uri. 1992. "Studying Students Studying Calculus: A Look at the Lives of Minority Mathematics Students in College." College Mathematics Journal 23: 362–72.

Appendix A: Selected References on Writing as a Tool for Learning Mathematics

Books

Connolly, P., and T. Vilardi. 1989. *Writing to Learn Mathematics and Science*. New York: Teachers College Press.

Sterrett, Andrew, ed. 1990. *Using Writing to Teach Mathematics*. Washington, DC: Mathematical Association of America.

Articles

Davidson, David M., and Daniel L. Pearce. 1988. "Using Writing Activities to Reinforce Mathematics Instruction." *Arithmetic Teacher* 35: 42–45.

LeGere, Adele. 1991. "Collaboration and Writing in the Mathematics Classroom." *Mathematics Teacher*. 84: 166–71.

Maurer, Stephen. 1991. "Advice for Undergraduates on Special Aspects of Writing Mathematics." *Primus* 1: 75–86.

Miller, Diane L. 1991. "Writing to Learn Mathematics." *Mathematics Teacher*. 84: 516–21.

Millman, Richard S. 1991. "Writing around Humor as a Tool to Learn Mathematics." *Mathematics in College* (fall/winter): 3–10.

Rishel, Thomas W. 1991. "The Geometric Metaphor: Writing and Mathematics in the Classroom." *Primus* 1: 113–28.

Rose, Barbara. 1989. "Writing and Mathematics: Theory and Practice." In *Writing to Learn Mathematics and Science*, ed. P. Connolly and T. Vilardi, 15–32. New York: Teachers College Press.

Schmidt, Don. 1985. "Writing in Math Class." In *Roots in the Sawdust: Writing to Learn across the Disciplines*, ed. Anne Russles Gere, 104–16. Urbana, IL: National Council of Teachers of English.

9 Evaluating Student Writing about History

Kathleen Medina
University of California–Davis

As a teacher of American and world history at the high school level, I want my students' writing to express their own beliefs and perspectives about historical and social issues, but I work to make those expressions informed, thoughtful, and critical. My teaching program asks students to "reason historically" from various, often conflicting, sources of evidence. The act of weighing evidence, of adopting a critical stance, and of creating a narrative out of bits and pieces of information is best accomplished in writing. So, from the first day of class, I place an emphasis on written expression.

I get students into a writer's mode by asking them to write on a daily basis in response to startling propositions, to "what-ifs," to troubling historical events, or to burning social issues. They gradually make the transition from informal journal-type writing to essay examinations and formal papers. How well they progress as writers is important to me, but how well they develop as historical thinkers is what's most important. As a history teacher, I am willing to struggle along with a developing writer in order to produce a historical reasoner. How I evaluate and support my student's writing will be the focus of this chapter.

Some of my high school history teacher colleagues have said to me, "You teach writing?!" I am afraid they mean it not as a compliment, but as an accusation: I somehow diminish the profession by doing so. Everyone knows it is the English department's job to teach writing. If I needed additional proof, I need only consult with my students. Sophomore boys, new to the regime, inevitably wail, "Mrs. Medina, this isn't an *English* class."

Evaluating writing is always a delicate process: Sometimes the force and momentum of a developing student writer's narrative will cause the writer to sacrifice history for the sake of a good story; sometimes thoughtful historical reasoning will only be suggested by jumbled lines of awkward prose; sometimes the developmental stage of the writer will transform a clear, straightforward communicator into a stilted, verbose one. When students experience "growth spurts" in either vocabulary or conceptual understanding, the awkward stage of transition will be reflected in their writing.

It is usually a surprise (and relief) to students to learn that they may go through typical stages in their development as writers, stages that other students have experienced. To learn how to assist my students in their development, I began by asking, what are the traditional obstacles for students as writers? What are their stages of language development? If they are learning new words or concepts, what kinds of awkwardness might their writing exhibit? What does it look like when a beginning writer experiments to gain greater command of the language? And always, what unique power, grace, or insight does a student exhibit as a writer/historian that I can identify and encourage?

When I comment on a student's work, I do it with a goal of strengthening that student's next effort. With the exception of the revision processes we use for formal papers, I make comments designed to move students forward to the next assignment, rather than stalling and urging them to invest more work in a failed piece. My strategy is to make the student a partner in the critical process. I highlight, photocopy, group together, and read aloud particularly striking examples of strong opening sentences, of conclusions that work, of budding "arguments" or points of view supported by evidence, and examples of sentences that reveal unique insights. I teach students to look for structure, strong statements, clear sentences, and meaty content in their writing about history.

As I share examples of my students' writing in the following pages, I will describe why I use certain strategies, what I look for, and how I advance students as writers and historical thinkers.

Encouraging Informal Writing: The Daily Journal

Like many of you, I begin each class by asking students to write informally. We call such writings "journals," but their variety and nature expands the usual definition of the word. The writing is always directed by me in response to a topic we are studying, a question, or a source. When students enter the classroom, the journal topic is on the board. Journal writing refocuses students on what we are studying, puts them in a more reflective state of mind (after the more engaging stimuli of the passing period), and allows them to write in a fail-safe way. Students who have spent a few minutes in written reflection on a topic will have something thoughtful to contribute to either a small- or whole-group discussion. When the journal topic for the day asks them to critically analyze a primary source (written or visual), they gain guided experience at doing so. Frequent practice will produce astute critical judges of source materials by the year's end.

If I required myself to read and respond to each journal entry by my students—or even most of the entries—I would not be able to have a journal program at all! My goals are to provide a space for thinking and regular practice in writing. When I scan groups of student entries I ask myself,

- Is this a thoughtful, authentic reponse to the question or source?
- Is the student making a connection between his or her own experiences and history?
- Did the class, as a whole, "get it"?

If students repeatedly seem to be "going through the motions" for my benefit, I critically evaluate my own approach, and prod them to share what they really think about the topics. If students need more structure (and some do) I require that they write a certain number of sentences and follow a format until they feel more confident as writers and critical thinkers.

Consider the following examples from beginning journal writers in a regular (heterogeneous) sophomore world history class.[1] During a study of the debate over the structure of government during the French Revolution, I sensed that students were both stumped and bored (the two often accompany one another). In an attempt to salvage the lesson, I grouped students and asked them to choose a governmental model from the following: democratic republic, monarchy, or dictatorship.

At the end of the eighteenth century, the philosophical debate over natural rights and the structure of government was a hot political issue; but today that passion has faded. I hoped that by asking students to choose a government, they would at least have to think deeply enough about it to rationalize their choice. By the end of class, groups had established five fictitious countries: two democratic republics, two dictatorships, and one monarchy. While walking to class the following day, it occurred to me that if we were to consider those countries as existing in a hypothetical world, we could imagine how migration patterns might flow and what the implications would be for a country's policy toward dissent—all issues for the French at that time, as well as for us today. Most high school students have not had the opportunity to make a connection between the job a person holds and that person's political views, between the religion of a family and their country of origin, between dissent and the stability of the government or the role of the military, between all of these and migration patterns. These are the kinds of historical inferences I want students to make.

As you read the following examples of student responses, keep in mind that we are entering protected territory. Journal writing is not intended to be evaluated as writing, any more than one would evaluate a shopping list or the notes we make for ourselves to prepare for discussion. Journals can be highly abbreviated. However, since students use journals to gain writing practice, it is often possible to recognize an analytical or intellectual growth spurt in a young author. Consider the following excerpt from Susan:

> When including the types of governments such as Democratic Republic, Dictatorships and Monarchy, I feel there would be obvious patterns of immigration. I think people would be most likely to move to a country under a Democratic Republic. Next they would immigrate to a country of monarchy. Lastly, and perhaps least appealing to people would be dictatorships. As this form of government leaves the least amount of freedom and power for the body of citizens.

Susan is a thoughtful, wordy fifteen-year-old who is making a transition from writing a simple narrative to more complex forms of analytical writing. This has caused her sentence structure to seem somewhat pretentious for an informal journal. About dissent she added that

> An advantage of tolerating dissent is that it may enlighten new ideas to the government, that are not necessarily bad or wrong but just have never been thought of before. Disadvantage to tolerating dissent are that there would be less order within the country and the government may feel they have less power.

I chose Susan's example because although the ideas expressed may seem straightforward to an adult (teacher), this could be the first time Susan has ever considered the relationship between the form of government and the resultant lifestyle enjoyed by its citizenry. In other words, there is more thinking going on here than meets the literary eye. Susan has also presented, albeit awkwardly, a two-sided view of the effect of dissent on a populace. I have achieved my goal: Susan is prepared to discuss the complexities of dissent. If I were to comment on Susan's writing, it would be to validate her reasoning as important and correct. We could easily identify situations in history in which leaders have weighed these options. In this way, informal writing helps me to build individual and group understanding of the intricacies of history, and presents the opportunity to relate what we have learned from one situation to others in history or to current events.

Another student, Jim, was a member of a group that had chosen to form a dictatorship. In contrast to Susan, Jim is a young man of few words, with a different perspective:

> They will try to go to the dictatorship but will be forced to stay if already there. Allowing protests can get the government into trouble because more and more people will question them.

Jim's writing needs to be unpacked. What he has done is to make notes to himself about main points that he will want to explore in discussion. Often, journals are condensed versions of more lengthy thought processes. Because Jim's group had chosen to establish a dictatorship in their hypothetical country, they were faced with the task of defending their choice to students like Susan. Jim imagined that a powerful and effective dictator would attract loyal followers (a historical inference from readings by Machiavelli, and vague impressions of Napoleon, Mussolini, and Hitler). Written reflection helped Jim prepare for class discussion by allowing him to realize what his own views were. He had views on the power of dictators both to attract and control and the danger of tolerating protest.

A third classmate, Mary, combined notions (post-1944) about Hitler's Germany with her knowledge of present-day immigration issues. She also provides us with an example of sound thinking without clear writing:

> In a dictatorship, (for example Adolph Hitler,) no one would want to immigrate to Germany, but many of those in Germany would want to immigrate to safe countries. In many cases if people from other countries want to immigrate into a different country because of a poor government or being mistreated, then laws are made to keep them out. The people are then forced to come in illegally, but they do it anyway. The country receiving the immigrants often have a hard time tracking them down and costs a lot of money.

I know what Mary wants to say, even though she does not express herself clearly. She draws an inference from a situation like the one she imagines existed in Germany during World War II, to the immigration situation in our country today. With regard to the disadvantages of harboring dissent, Mary properly assessed the role of the military:

> You would need stronger police (military) forces, many people would disagree with each other and the government might lose power.

In the ensuing discussion, Jim was quick to point out to Mary that not all Germans wanted to leave Germany. Mary was able to raise the issue of the role of the military in Germany, and also in France at the time of the French Revolution. From the range of views expressed by

Jim, Susan, Mary, and others, we were able to have a sophisticated discussion that connected specific historical situations to current world conditions after only a few minutes of reflective writing.

At the end of a unit of study, I use journals to find out what students judge that they have learned about a subject. All too often as teachers and students, we leave a subject behind without stopping to identify the big ideas or general impressions we have formed. I always read these because they help me to evaluate my own teaching. Following a review of the age of exploration, Jeremy, a sophomore, wrote the following:

> I also learned why Columbus went west. I did not know why, but I did know that he did. I learned the main reasons for explorations: spices, trade, dyes, religion, and territorial power. I also learned of how the two hemispheres were like two different worlds. Not until the age of exploration did they meet. I learned of the Columbus trade and the importance of it. The main thing I learned was how important this period was to how today's world is now! Also, the controversial discussion of Columbus Day, who discovered American first, why did he get credit, why wasn't this acknowledged back then?

This general impression will remain with Jeremy long after he has forgotten the specifics of the review. I was pleased to find that he recognized the significance of the meeting of the hemispheres, the controversy surrounding the event in history, and made links to today's multicultural debate.

Journal entries can be saved and used by students in many ways: to review and prepare for exams, to recall points of view or arguments for culminating essays or debates, or to include in their portfolios as evidence of growth in writing or thinking.

Writing History on Demand: The In-class Essay Exam

I invest considerable time and effort in developing my students' ability to perform on in-class essay examinations because I know that those who learn to write confidently on demand will have an edge in college and in the job market. College history courses require that students be proficient at writing essay examinations and papers. If I were to let college be the first time my students confronted an essay exam in history, they would be at a distinct disadvantage. But more important, the process required to create a historical narrative out of a variety of source materials, impressions, discussions, and lectures is the process of learning history: It requires students to synthesize the course material into an interpretation of their own. Writing about history makes the process of learning history a conscious one.

Essay exams ask students to distill information we learned from many sources into a coherent narrative. As a class, we prepare to answer broad culminating questions from the first day of each unit. Rather than beginning with the textbook version (where all of the thinking has been conveniently done for us), we instead proceed like historical detectives. Depending on the event or era we are tackling, we might examine primary-source data such as letters, official proclamations, traveler's journals, public or published accounts, demographic statistics, public records (like wills, inventories, census data, voting registers), or cultural evidence like music, art, architecture, households, habits, and belief systems.

On an in-class essay exam, I expect students to present the event or issue in a historical context, to draw inferences, to support their opinions, or to sometimes make a prediction. When I evaluate, I ask myself the following:

- Does the student demonstrate a general historical understanding of the subject in question—can she sort the foreground from the background and the significant from the insignificant?

- Does the student have the ability to analyze the historical age, event, or issue in terms of the perspectives of those involved, and can he relate those perspectives to cultural, social, political, or economic roots?

- Does the student demonstrate an understanding of the incentives and motives of various groups?

- Is the student aware of economic or geographic determinants?

- Can the student judge the situation in terms of who has power or influence and who does not?

- Does the student understand what the function and role of government is for the society?

In the beginning, I try to reduce my students' anxiety about essay examinations by structuring their preparation. Two days before the exam, I model for students how to prepare for the exam by means of a skit I perform with the assistance of a student. In the skit, we speculate about what might be on the exam and create a strategy to prepare for it. This is followed by class time for preparation in groups. On the day before the exam (as a journal topic), I ask students to list sources they will use to review. We combine our responses as a class and discuss the relative merits of the different sources and what they can contribute. We then discuss together what kinds of significant questions I might ask on the exam about the unit we have completed and what the key organizing idea for a response might be.

Because there is always the potential for writer's block on essay exams during the first semester, I allow students to bring with them a list of ten things (a simple list, no more) they may want to include in their essay, to refer to as they write the exam. I also require that they bring one primary source document which they would like to quote in their essay.

The results of essay exams early in the year are usually disappointing. A student will invariably raise a hand to ask, "When are we going to have a real test, Mrs. Medina?" Others will express their amazement (and delight) that I am interested in their own "b.s." interpretation of history. Students who have never spent an entire class period (fifty minutes) thinking and writing will shake cramped hands and throw me pained looks throughout. As a safety net during these early months, I allow students to rewrite failed attempts as a take home essay, for which they can earn a "C." But by Thanksgiving, most students have settled into the routine, and all eventually produce well-developed historical essays in one draft under time pressure.

From the beginning of the year, I follow each exam by reading good opening paragraphs or particularly strong sentences to the class. For example, one student used the strong opening line, "It all began in 1450 when people started thinking about life on earth rather than life after death." I choose examples from a variety of student levels and writing styles with the hope of presenting enough models for everyone (and showcasing the work of writers who need encouragement). I try to photocopy the short excerpts or sentences I share with the class so that they can read them from the page. There is a difference between written and oral language, and I don't like to confuse the two. Portions of papers I read aloud to the class will sound more impressive (and thus less attainable) with the benefit of the auditory cues I can provide. I want them to think, "I can do that," not "How did he write that!?"

Some budding historians are self-conscious about early attempts at writing. For example, consider the following excerpt from a bright fifteen-year-old who thought of himself as an "A" student. Matt had always excelled at quantitative tests and was severely disappointed when he received a B– from me on his first essay exam:

> I'm going to try to do better on this essay than my last one you didn't like. That's a start. I feel this period of time was called the Enlightenment period because people were enlightened. Brilliant, huh? Before this time they all lived with a blanket over their heads, (a figure of speech). They were ruled by the church (we learned about earlier) and only heard about what the church wanted them to know. This is when people really start thinking and discovering.

> The discoveries of Chris Columbus affected these people because
> it showed them they didn't know everything and there are still
> things to be learned. I feel this would be enlightening. Not a bad
> start if I do say so myself.
>   Now let's try brilliant thinkers. My favorite is Jean Jacques
> Rousseau. . . .

I chose this example to encourage you to be tolerant if a student
should begin an exam in this manner. Beginning paragraphs are difficult for everyone, but I am encouraged by this type of response from
my students: Matt is being honest about his feelings and fears of writing. In the margin of Matt's opening paragraph I only commented
about his previous exam: *I liked it.* In the second paragraph, my marginal comments reinforced Matt's review of Rousseau's beliefs, but, in
a conversational response to what he contributed about Rousseau, I
tried to push him beyond merely reporting that these were nice ideas
by explaining that they were dangerous ones at that time. The fervor
inspired by Rousseau and others eventually culminated in a reign of
terror in France. Matt went on to write an adequate four-page essay in
which he reviewed the major players, the political and social history of
the time, and made a prediction about upcoming events in France and
Europe. His grade on this and subsequent essays continually improved
until he reached his goal. When he did, he understood why. Students
like Matt—who have conquered multiple-choice tests (and the routine
motions of school)—need to be reassured that they will conquer essay
exams as well.

During an in-class essay examination it is difficult for students to
monitor the form of their written expression. Historical ideas tend to
flow or not flow, and that must be their first concern. Most students do
not possess the level of reflection or distance required to assess, evaluate, and revise writing in progress. As a result, I don't do line editing
of students' *in-class* writing. I save any critical comments I have for the
end of the paper, with the intention of improving their next effort. On
Matt's paper, I encouraged him to seek a middle ground between a tone
that was too chatty and too formal. Matt's witticisms disappeared from
his essays once he realized that his history was being taken seriously
by his reader.

Students' first attempts at in-class essays exhibit a range of common problems. Another student, Warren, began his essay with a broad
leap which captured the spirit of history as change over time, and I
complimented him:

> When people grow up, they change. That little boy who never said
> anything in class may turn into a TV evangelist. People change. Not
> unlike people, nations and/or countries change too. Europe is, or

was, an excellent example of this. In the years of 1450 to 1650, Europe underwent many changes. Both political and religious. Plus economically and intellectually. The change was split up, basically into two major happenings. First the artistic Renaissance and then the ever-changing time known as the reformation. I will attempt to cover how one led to the other, plus how Europe was changed and who the main players were. Ready to go? Yes!

In marginal comments throughout the rest of Warren's paper, I tried to raise his consciousness about what he did well: "yes, science caused doubt," "nice approach to use," "this is to the point," "good intellectual reasons for change," as well as "good use of quote" when he made effective use of a quote as evidence to support his discussion.

I require the use of quotations in student writing because it allows students to support assertions with evidence (a hallmark of writing history). Here is an example from a student, Wendell, who used a quote so gracefully that I read it to the class:

> Unhappy with the way the church was taking money from its parishioners in the form of indulgences, Martin Luther drew up a document denouncing indulgences and many of the church's other policies and nailed it to the church door. One of the things Martin Luther said was, "The Pope can remove only those penalties which he himself imposed on earth. . . ." He believed the Pope had no power to free souls from purgatory.

If the beginning is difficult for students, so is the ending. Fifteen-year-old (and older) students have internalized the story format so powerfully that it is difficult for them to make the switch to expository writing. Add to that the fact that American students unconsciously believe that history equals progress. In other words, we are all smarter or better off at the end of the story than we were at the beginning. The next student's work illustrates what I call "the happy ending" syndrome. Sandy presented an excellent review of the causes, issues, and events in the French Revolution on an in-class exam, but she could not resist tying up loose ends in her concluding paragraph.

> These major events changed France forever by ending years of hard times and struggles, high taxes, non-equality and the right to be yourself. France was now a land of people who for once in their lives could walk streets freely. Pay equal taxes, make as much money as they wanted and own their own land. The French society was now living the way that many only dreamed of. And they are still living freely and equally today.

On some level, Sandy knows she is making exaggerated and overly general statements, but she is riding a galloping rhetorical horse. It is absolutely okay to challenge and correct her history in such a way that acknowledges your recognition of the problem: She wants to sum things up for all time! That isn't necessary, but it isn't fatal, either. I want to encourage students to retain the style and appeal of the narrative, without letting their rhetoric run away with their reasoning.

Some fifteen-year-old students are just not ready to abandon the narrative style, but instead relate to history most effectively as a dramatic story. This can be done well. The following creative offering is from a bright sophomore, Amy:

All For Gold

> The noise was amazing. Shouts, screams, the buzzing made by thousands of people talking at once, animals making all manner of sounds, it was a terrific din. It was normal for this time of day, and I had heard the same things many thousands of times. Everything had been this way for as long as we could remember, and we had no reason to think that it would ever be different. We were the Aztecs, the greatest. We would soon learn that there were others even more ethnocentric than we.
> The Spaniards came to shore at dawn. . . .

Amy's first few lines carried this priceless sidebar: "P.S. I wrote with my left hand here to make all the rest seem very neat." She wanted the visual presentation of her paper to somehow represent the tremendous impact of the Spanish arrival on the chronicler—a change she envisioned as moving from variety toward order. I understood this and told her so. I had few suggestions to make to Amy because I thought her combination of creative writing and historical narrative was effective.

Often, a student's (or anyone's) first reaction to a historical situation is an emotional one. My goal is to help the learner get beyond the initial gut reaction, to examine the forces and causes acting upon the various players. Even when historical positions or actions seem morally repugnant to students, I want them to understand how the historical actors characterized or rationalized their positions, how they represented their views to others, and what world view, goals, or capabilities led them to hold that perspective.

The opening paragraph from Jennifer's essay exam on the French Revolution combines an emotional analysis with some new vocabulary:

> The French Revolution, in my opinion was due to selfishness, some maybe needs but mostly selfishness. Mostly the first and second estates are what I'm getting at. All of them had their wants and needs, but what you get and what you want may not fall so closely together.

Jennifer's emotional analysis (selfishness) handicaps her from pursuing a fuller understanding. The danger of this kind of judgment is that it can allow her to dismiss the entire event on moral grounds. I suspect that what is really behind her confusion is failure to understand a connection I made between rising social expectations, an economic downturn, and revolution. I asked the class to considered (as a journal topic) a graph of the "J-Curve Hypothesis." Developed by James C. Davies, the hypothesis predicts that revolutions are more likely to happen after a period of fairly steep social and economic growth, followed by a sharp downturn. This situation creates an intolerable gap between public expectations and what the political and economic conditions provide. The internal sense Jennifer made of the J-curve came out sounding more like Mick Jagger's famous line, "You can't always get what you want." Jennifer recognized that there was something significant about a link between rising expectations and revolutions, but she was not able to make sense out of it.

Later on in her essay, however, Jennifer did produce a savvy historical statement (below) that I seized upon and encouraged. Students who bring an emotional perspective to history tend to be drawn to situations in which historical actors form sympathetic alliances across social or class lines:

> The lower first estate felt sincerity for the third estate and helped them get more votes and helped their people.

Jennifer has hit the nail on the head. Poorer members of the clergy did abandon the ranks of the first estate to support the cause of the peasantry. Alliances across estates which reorganized society and defined new social classes are a significant development. Jennifer, bless her heart, concluded her essay with the following, touching statement:

> From then on French society changed forever. The laws eventually got fairer and the tax systems did too. *This is my favorite history event because it illustrates how you can always achieve what you want if you feel that strongly about it, as the third estate did.* They complained, rebelled, protested, did whatever they could to be equal. Unfortunately violence was involved but that got them mostly no where, only ambition and courage led them to their desired goal.

Don't assume that the J-curve hypothesis was simply too difficult a concept for a student like Jennifer. A classmate of Jennifer's with similar ability, Debbie, grasped the concept behind the J-curve hypothesis and expressed it more clearly. Following is a portion of her opening paragraph:

> The third estate, which accounted for about ninety-seven percent of France's total population, wanted the same rights as the higher estates. They wanted their votes, thoughts, and opinions to count

with the King. *In time, the gap between what the people wanted and what they got was so intolerable that everyone's blood boiled.*

These two young ladies have demonstrated why I tread cautiously when responding to writing: Heaven forbid that I should discourage imagery like "everyone's blood boiled," or unwittingly discourage Jennifer's enthusiasum for her favorite event in history.

While on the one hand I urge students to use historical and analytical terminology, on the other hand I fear they will do so only to please me, without having internalized the implications of the terms or their helpfulness as organizational tools. If I find the words *social, intellectual,* and *economic* in a student's paper (or *politically* and *religiously,* as we saw in an earlier sample), you can bet that I worked with the class to organize our thinking about a subject in those terms. As students learn a new conceptual language, they will apply labels without understanding them.

For example, in studies of war, many history teachers distinguish between "fundamental" or underlying causes for war and "immediate" incidents which spark an outbreak of war. Distinctions like this work best when they enable students to generalize about many wars. Such teaching tools backfire when they trap students in a "nonthinking" mode, by doing all of the analysis for them. I found that I had overemphasized this way of looking at the French Revolution in one class, when I received at least a dozen papers which began much like the following:

> In this essay I will discuss the fundamental and immediate causes of the French Revolution and how the society was changed.
> Fundamental causes were many. First, the peasants . . .

Using this distinction, Aaron was able to categorize the causes of the French Revolution without struggling with the confusion of issues and forces which prompted this great event—without doing any real thinking. And because I had defined the task and taught him to do this, I was left with the uncomfortable duty of granting him an "A" for a technically correct endeavor.

Although responses such as Aaron's make me sigh, I know such students will be on familiar ground the next time a discussion of the fundamental causes of war arises. It may take time before they are able to judge the usefulness of our trite ways of organizing history.

Although in-class essay exams might appear to be rather limited in terms of design possibilities, they actually present the same creative possibilities that journals do, with the added bonus that, during a test, students are heavily invested in the task before them. In one interesting experiment (with experienced essay writers), I asked students to trade test papers with a partner after writing on a question for about twenty-five minutes. They were then asked to respond to the answer/argument presented by the first writer. Did they agree? What would they add? This idea came to me as a way to help students focus upon the perspective of another writer and on the idea that historical interpretation is, in an important sense, argument/conjecture. We differ greatly on how we view the past. But more important, the past avails us of many interpretations. This process had the added bonus of exposing students to each other's knowledge during the most teachable moment of all: the testing situation.

Assessment of such an assignment can be made more interesting by including the students. When students read each other's answers and comment on them, they are applying a kind of mental rubric. When we talked about creating a rubric for this type of exam, my students were interested in the amount and veracity of historical information provided by the initial writer—they have learned *that* is history. They also could see how a coherent essay focused around a key idea, and supported by historical evidence, was better than one that was rambling or awkwardly written. Since they had all just finished writing about the question, they all had something in mind to measure against what their partner had written. And if they had found themselves short of time on the first go-round, they were often in a position to add more information to their partner's version. Because the time spent reading and critically evaluating what the first writer had written was as important as the time spent writing a response, the actual written responses by students were fairly short and were graded leniently. Did they enlarge upon or successfully contest the first writer on one or more points? Did they agree and provide an example or explanation to illustrate agreement?

Every class of mine has had a few students who are challenged as writers for reasons other than beginner's status. It is entirely possible for students who are considered "learning disabled" to progress through school without ever being asked to write. If given the opportunity, however, they can and will learn to write a coherent in-class examination, and their accomplishment becomes even more important when we consider what is at stake for them: a high school diploma, future employment, the ability to represent their views in an effective letter, and so forth. These students need much more support and encouragement than others (and possibly open-ended time) because they know very well what a painful process writing is for them and have learned to avoid it like the plague. If any students are seeing a resource teacher, I arrange for them to have extra time to complete their essays.

I have found that the historical information such students include is generally correct and sometimes sophisticated, but they have trouble expressing themselves coherently in writing given the time pressure. My students respond well to comments designed to illuminate and expose the structure of their writing (where they return to a theme that helps focus their essay) and comments that encourage them to add examples, quotes, or more explanation in the appropriate places. I try to make my feedback general and valuable enough to apply to any writing situation the students encounter—so that they are learning about writing an essay as we go along. Students need to feel that they are making progress, that their writing contains promising elements. The following excerpt from Dave, a resource student, illustrates how an awkwardly written piece can nevertheless contain valuable and insightful information:

> But before this the black plague, famine, and other things took many lives. Because before there was to many people and to little food. Nobles were born into the noble family and the poor was exploited. During the Reformation the church was attacked openly. It was very corrupt. Greed was a very prominent figure in the church. Indulgences were being sold to pay for the basilica of St. Peter. Martin Luther said, "Indulgences are positively harmful to the recipient because they impede salvation by diverting charity and inducing a false sense of security." Martin Luther then went and create another branch of faith.
>
> I believe that a lot of good came out of the Reformation. Just think about great minds like Gallieo and such. Artists like Leonard de Vinci. Also, Individualism popped up out of the dark. . . .

You can see Dave's natural sense of imagery all through this excerpt: "Greed was a very prominent figure"; Individualism popped out of the darkness." He uses his quote very effectively. It would be tragic not to encourage such a student to write. In Dave's case, his fears about writing (and my emphasis upon it) were making him give up on the class—he hadn't bothered to prepare for the exam. I was encouraged by the fact that, although he did very little written work either in class or at home, he had still managed to pick up historical information from participating in class. I tried to reassure him by noting sentences that I thought were lyrical and by urging him to bolster his writing with more concrete historical information. Dave did not receive a good grade for this attempt, but I wanted him to understand that it was not because of his writing, but because his historical content was too general, not specific or explicit.

The Formal History Paper

When I evaluate formal papers, I use criteria similar to those I use for in-class essay examinations, but with the addition of high expectations for the style and mechanics of the finished piece. I inform students that I want to receive a paper that exhibits the following:

- The paper begins with an interesting title and opening paragraph that forecasts the discussion.
- Issues and events are placed in time and set in a historical context.
- Historical evidence or quotes support claims made by the author.
- The writer's interpretation includes/explains/accounts for competing historical perspectives. (This is the most difficult for students and requires guidance, support, and examples.)
- The paper's structure is coherent and focused, with a summary in the concluding paragraph.
- Presentation, style, and mechanics enhance, rather than detract from, the paper.

This is the time to pull out all the stops, to have high expectations for student writers, and to insist that your expectations be met. I spend a considerable amount of time going over the rubric with my students and sharing examples of how their finished product should look. I have found that rubrics or grading guides work most effectively when they are *specific* to the assignment in question and understood thoroughly by students.

By the time I receive a formal paper to read, it has usually undergone several readings and revisions on the basis of responses from one or two classmates, or from a parent and usually from an outside (lay) reader. A lay reader can be a hired reader or a teaching colleague who has agreed to exchange student papers with you for the purpose of providing feedback on a draft. If we use a lay reader, students can experience a trial run with the scoring rubric because the reader will use it to approximate their grade based on their unrevised draft.

High school students are very good at playing the game of school, and included in the rules is the aphorism that term papers are to be hammered out the night before they are due. There are good reasons for this rule. Why prolong such an agonizing process? The night before the paper is due adrenaline flows; classmates commiserate; short-term memory cells are available to organize and dump out information without disturbing more personally relevant, long-term data banks. There is no incentive for a student to prolong a task which is, after all, the concern of an external agent.

Of course, my goals and expectations come up hard against such natural tendencies toward efficiency, but I try to work with, rather than against, the tide. My students still write the night before, but what they are writing is their first draft. A student without one writes while others begin the response process.

The assignments I give for papers delineate what students must include and also give them a few choices for constructing the paper. For example, when we had completed a unit of study on American Indians and their ultimately devastating encounters with settlers in the nineteenth century, high school juniors were required to respond to three broad questions and were allowed to choose a focus for their papers from four others. It was at that point that we also became familiar with the scoring guide (rubric) for the essay.

Once we have a rough draft in hand, the real work begins. I tell my students, you don't have to be a great writer; you just have to be a great rewriter. The transformation of writing from being writer-based (decipherable by the author) to being reader-based (understandable to an audience) involves a major leap in perspective for a student writer.

When students arrive in class with their rough drafts, I provide them with an explanation of what it means to change their drafts from being writer-based to reader-based. I ask them to read through their own rough drafts and begin to think globally about the written construction and historical goals of their work. Students then follow a series of steps with their work: They sum up the main theme of their essays in three or four sentences, and they make a list of the concerns and questions they have about their rough drafts. Student (author) questions can be as vague as the following: Is my paper too short? Does my overall plan make sense? Do I support big statements with details, examples, quotes? And so on. Before they give their papers to a peer reader, I have them underline all of the words they know are misspelled. That way the reader does not have to worry about calling attention to details that the writer can correct herself.

Once the students all understand the response process from the perspective of a writer (i.e., what they each want to know from a reader about their paper), they are ready to receive their instructions as readers responding to another student's paper. Reader response works because each student plays both roles. Readers are instructed to read the author's statements and questions about the draft before they read it and then to read through the piece, underlining words which are misspelled, misused or unclear, and placing question marks wherever they fail to get the writer's drift. They then respond to the writer, both orally and in writing, in terms of the following: measuring the paper in terms of the assignment; identifying strengths; noting problem areas and omissions of information and providing suggestions for revision.

It is important to give students permission to be critical of each other's work. I tell the class that we will begin from the position that every paper has merit and while it is helpful to point out specific strengths, in the draft stage it is *most* helpful to point out where you don't understand what the writer is getting at. It is also valuable to the author to learn what information he or she may have left out that is crucial to an understanding of the situation, argument, or issue being presented. In the case we will consider, I had specifically required that each student provide information about the philosophical, cultural, and occupational conflicts that occurred between the white settlers and the Indians. If they did not present a clear analysis of both positions, a reader should point out the deficit.

Although the process seems on the surface to be writer-centered, actually the student learns more as a reader than as a writer. In the draft stage, many writers are aware of the major weaknesses of their work. They can benefit from having their use of indefinite pronouns pointed out to them, or from getting feedback about the structure of the paper, but so much depends upon the skill of their evaluator. It is as a reader that the scales begin to fall from their eyes to reveal what constitutes effective essay writing. Readers automatically react by mentally judging their own effort in relation to other papers. They learn firsthand about the possibilities for variation in structure, in use of information, in point of view, and about how a writer can confuse the reader by failing to communicate an idea clearly. Readers gain experience in looking for strength and weaknesses in positions, and they learn to recognize effective reasoning. They also learn how deadly dull writing can be when a writer just goes through the motions, or how a reader's mind will automatically turn off if it cannot understand the meaning.

Following are a few examples of student work at each stage of this process. This was the class's first use of reader response. The first set of examples consists of authors' summaries of the main idea of their papers. The intent of asking the writer to do this is to help him or her focus a wandering paper:

Writer #1

The Indians were harassed by the White settlers because they possessed land that the settlers wanted. This resulted in violence and resentment among the two forces. Finally the whites overcame the native resistance and moved them onto reservations to keep them out of the way.

Writer #2

My essay is about the end of the Indian Era. It tells about how and why the Indians were eliminated in America. I try to show, prove and do that the Indians didn't have much of a chance against the US government and white settlers.

Writer #3

Indians were treated badly, partly because they were different.

These students are at different stages of development in thinking about their papers. Although they won't say so, their papers probably meant little to them—except that they were burdensome writing assignments for a history class—until they were asked to characterize their work. Student responders are encouraged to help the writer clarify and strengthen the focus of the work by voicing their own confusion/impatience/lack of interest in what the writer really means as it is currently expressed.

The following comments are representative of the kind of self-criticisms (really pleas for help) expressed by my student writers:

It's too short, nothing about Manifest Destiny or the Dawes Commission.

It doesn't go in sequence.

I need to write a conclusion.

[Even] "Needs to be less boring and make more sense."

Students were not very good at asking specific questions of readers about their own work at this stage. One wrote: "Spelling? Organized? Clear? Run-ons?"

In response to these pleas for help, the student readers responded to writers with constructive comments like:

Need to work on some of the awkward places I marked—make it more clear.

Should have more on the motives for Manifest Destiny.

Settler's opinion of Indians kind of weak. Opinionated when talking about white's treatment of the Indians.

Re-arrange introduction. Split essay into paragraphs. Support statements with more detailed facts.

A sample of sentences students marked or underlined as not understandable included the following:

> Which hardly happened.
>
> They came and killed them for purposes they didn't need.
>
> The government, however, still owned this land and were soon forced to sign off 80% of their land and go and live on over populated reservations.
>
> The white men differed philosophically, culturally, and occupationally to the Indians which also brought about the attitudes which were developed.

This process saves me from encountering such sentences in final drafts.

I can't emphasize enough how everyone is learning to play a new role in this initial situation. Students are learning how to think critically about their own work—actually to take ownership of it. Readers are learning about what they should look for and what kinds of comments they can make that will be most helpful to the author. The critical comments students make on papers are modeled after the comments teachers have been making on their papers for years—even though students may never have understood what those comments really meant. As I passed one of the response group, I had to smile when I overheard one student remark to another, "I'm not sure why, but I think that you have committed a major faux pas."

Final papers are due about one week after a response session. In this case, on the day that students showed up with their final papers, I asked for a show of hands of those who had read through the final product. Only about three or four students (from a class of thirty-three) raised their hands! Needless to say, I had them spend the first few minutes of class reading through their final drafts. No sooner had they begun than a few bottles of White-Out® surfaced and were circulated feverishly around the room.

The following excerpts from final products illustrate the level of thoughtfulness and investment of those who have undergone the response process, but they continue to illustrate the difficulties that are endemic to developing writers.

The first writer, Erika, chose to focus on the work of Angie Debo, a writer and historian who detailed the processes whereby Plains Indians were systematically defrauded of land in Oklahoma following the discovery of oil. Her opening paragraph leads smoothly and skillfully into a focus on Debo's work.

> The tragedy of the American Indians began in 1863 with Carson forcing the Navajos on the "Long Walk". It ended a mere twenty-seven years later in the almost complete destruction of the culture of the American Indian. Most of the damage was done in the name

of destiny, or by defrauding the Indians and covering it up. Many government officials were involved or informed of this terrible tragedy and yet did not see the long range consequences or dismissed the Indians and their vastly different civilizations as unworthy of preservation. This form of corruption was especially widespread in Oklahoma, where even the Governor was involved in defrauding the Indians. Ironically, the person who uncovered this scandal and dared to write about it is one of the leading citizens of Oklahoma, Angie Debo. . . .

Erika is introducing a position she has taken on a twenty-seven-year period of history that she has studied. She is equipped to be challenged by classmates who studied another period or group in-depth. Throughout Erika's paper, I reinforced the things she had done well: I appreciated her recognition of the ecological disaster that the slaughter of the Buffalo represented for the Plains Indians and her blunt conclusion that "both the Buffalo and the Indian were considered disposable by the white settlers." Erika internalized the nature of my assignment rather than plod (like some others did) from one of the guiding questions to the next—this is worth noting. At the end of her paper, I told her how much I appreciated

> the way in which your ideas flow logically, one from the other. In the end you have said all that needed to be said, but as a reader I was not conscious of an awkward framework or the forced inclusion of some historical fact.

Contrast Erika's smooth introduction with an opening paragraph by Amanda, another good student who is undergoing an analytical "growth spurt." Her desire to include the right terminology alongside a review of the main points in her paper made her beginning a grab bag of disjointed sentences:

> It all started when Columbus first stepped on American soil and spied the first Indian. The philosophical, cultural and occupational differences which led to the destruction of Indians were all justified by the white man's idea of "manifest destiny". There are many false reports in sources in which the Indians are portrayed. Only a few unique historians told the actual truth about the Indians and their ways. Angie Debo was among those historians. She included all of the political dirty dealings besides the Indian lifestyle in her books. Like the Blacks, the Indians were treated with no understanding or respect and were taken advantage of just because of their ethnic differences.

I commented that "Your first sentence is direct and clear but your first paragraph is a bit choppy. You do sum up your main premise, however." Amanda went on to relax and write a very fine paper, which included the following strong, direct statements: "The only occupation that Indians had was survival," and "The Government needed an

excuse to break the treaty with the Indians that said that land was rightfully theirs. *That excuse was called, 'Manifest Destiny.'"*

Another intelligent student, Jan, was experiencing a similar growth
spurt in terms of associative thinking. As students become more experienced at both writing and historical thinking, they will be tempted to
make playful associations and apply sophisticated-sounding terminology they have heard used elsewhere to the situation at hand. Such
anachronistic applications usually make for bad history. It is a bit tricky
to encourage the development of associative thinking while discour-
aging the misapplication of unique ideas. We find an illustration of this
in the beginning of Jan's paper:

> The Indians marked the beginning and the end of an era for the
> United States of America. However, the United States wasn't so
> united, but divided between two cultures. These two *"separate but
> equal"* denominations of people were the American Indian and
> other white settlers of the United States.

I responded by writing "Interesting comparison with another situation involving discrimination but best not to do this. You may distract
or confuse the reader." It is important and valuable for students to make
associations from one historical situation to another, but I wanted Jan
to think about how she applied language.

Another student, Mabel, a Chinese national, could speak English
quite well, but made the kinds of structural writing errors that are the
hallmark of the English-language learner:

> They could not hold on to their land because whites produced
> documents that prevented them to live in certain areas. White set-
> tlers did not care about the Indians. They went on invading Indian
> lands, many treaties were broken. The whites abide to US laws
> while Indians were bounded by traditional authority.

Because Mabel had received both student and lay-reader feedback,
I was actually relieved to see that she was clearly responsible for writing the final essay. In this case student readers were too lenient by not
letting Mabel know where they failed to understand her point. I did
not want Mabel's student friends to write for her, but I did want them
to let her know when she was not communicating with them. "I'm not
sure what this means—I'm intrigued" was my comment alongside a
sentence that stated, "It is a misconception that whites were considered
the dominant race among others."

The subject of race and the exertion of white power in the name of
manifest destiny was an emotionally charged one for Mabel, but in her
concluding paragraph, she made a statement which seemed to argue
against her position:

> The Indians did not complain for the treatment they received. Instead they tried to talk with reason in a peaceful manner; but failed. The whites should be more aware of the racial issues that had caused pain to everyone. *They have to accept the fact that this is the land of melting pots.*

Who does she mean by "they"? Since I was fairly sure by the way she had presented her case that Mabel did not mean to say that the Indians should have been willing to give up their indigenous identity and adopt American customs, I both wrote and talked with Mabel about what the term "melting pot" suggested. As with my other students, I grade students like Mable primarily on the basis of their historical understanding, not their language (or writing) fluency.

Writing a history paper is hard work, but it can be immensely satisfying if student authors are encouraged to make a personal investment in their subject, if they have the opportunity to share their new knowledge with others in discussions or read-arounds, and when they can take evident pride in their accomplishments.

I hope that this discussion of some of the ways in which I have used writing to facilitate an understanding of history will serve as a point of departure for more experimentation and dialogue about the intriguing work we do as teachers. Children are born to learn. If we can somehow convince them that school is as appropriate a place to do that as anywhere else, and that the topics we study can have meaning and relevance for their lives, then we will have made a start toward renewing the nature of school. If I had to sum up what I try to do in one sentence, I would say that I look for literary and historical merit in student writing (however nascent), and I go from there.

Further Reading

For short readings about assessing writing in social studies, I recommend three articles from the periodical *The Social Studies* (which can be accessed through a university library). "Social Studies Research Papers: A Writing Process Approach" (November/December 1987: 264), by Robert Gilstrap, uses student examples to illustrate the four stages of a writing process used effectively in a fourth- and fifth-grade social studies classroom. "Using Informal Writing in Large History Classes," by Henry Steffens (May/June 1991: 107), describes Steffens's strategies for personalizing a large history class by infusing writing and discussion on traditional lecture situations. Another article by the same author, "Discovering the Historian's Voice: Interesting Students in Historical Subjectivity" (July/August 1991: 148), describes Steffens's process for enabling students to recognize a historian's (and their own) "voice" when writing about history. Steffens tackles the thorny question of objectivity and subjectivity in student (and historians') writing that are at the heart of the historian's craft, but are all too often skirted in high school history courses.

For book-length forays into the subject of writing and history, I recommend Henry J. Steffens and Mary Jane Dickerson's *Writer's Guide: History* (1987). The book includes a chapter by Toby Fulwiler and was written for an audience of students and teachers. Steffens teaches at the college level, but I found his insight, suggestions, and resources to be equally applicable to teaching from middle to high school, and to be easily adaptable to the elementary grades. Two books that I found practical and insightful are *Connecting with the Past: History Workshop in Middle and High Schools* (1994), by Cynthia Stokes Brown, and *History Workshop: Reconstructing the Past with Elementary Students* (1993), by Karen L. Jorgenson. These books were written about experiences in elementary and high school classrooms where the authors initiated a "workshop" or inquiry method for teaching history through writing. Both include examples of student writing accompanied by the teacher's analysis and reflection.

Recently, a number of scholars in education have become interested in the different ways in which history is viewed, understood, and practiced by students, teachers, and historians. Charles A. Perfetti et al.'s *Text-Based Learning and Reasoning: Studies in History* (1995) presents the results of a study of how students reasoned and wrote about history on the basis of their study of documents surrounding the U.S. acquisition of the Panama Canal Zone. Perfetti's work makes a substantial contribution to research done by Sam Wineberg at the University of Washington. Wineberg examined students' and historians' differing perceptions about the usefulness and reliability of various kinds of historical sources. Another, even more interesting collection of writings about this subject is *Cognitive and Instructional Processes in History and the Social Sciences* (1994), edited by Mario Carretero and James F. Voss. Don't be discouraged by the awful title. The book is an engrossing account of the views students from elementary school to college have about history, as evidenced, in part, by their writing. I particularly recommend the chapters by Bill McDiarmid, Charles Perfetti (who summarizes the Panama study), and Sam Wineburg. And finally, to achieve a philosophical perspective on the nature and goals of student assessment, I recommend Grant P. Wiggins's *Assessing Student Performance: Exploring the Purpose and Limits of Testing* (1993). Chapters six and seven are particularly useful because they describe how to give effective feedback to students about their writing, and how to design scoring guides that are authentic and valid measures of student understanding.

Note

Samples of student writing have not been altered in any way, with the exception of nonsubstantive corrections in spelling. Pseudonyms have been assigned to student work irrespective of gender. Emphasis, if present, has been added. Students samples are typical, not remarkable.

10 Evaluating Students' Response Strategies in Writing about Literature

Richard W. Beach
University of Minnesota

In this chapter, I will discuss techniques for evaluating students' writing about literature, writing that includes both informal journal writing and formal essay writing. In evaluating students' writing about literature, teachers are assessing what their students are learning from practicing new ways of responding to literature, for example, applying psychological or sociological concepts to analysis of texts; relating their own autobiographical experiences to texts; or describing the cultural norms operating in texts.

I will also discuss ways of defining criteria for evaluating students' use of various response strategies and then suggest ways to assess changes in students' use of strategies over time. I also stress the need to understand why students are responding in particular ways—to recognize that the quality of students' responses depends on the quality of the assignments and social context in which the students are responding. Understanding this context requires ongoing inquiry about students' knowledge of literature, attitude, ability, interest in the text, understanding of the assignment, or sense of purpose and audience in shaping their responses. For example, my own University teacher-preparation students, fresh from reading Rosenblatt ([1938] 1983), are most willing to express their engagement or aesthetic responses. However, they often describe their engagement in general, even clichéd, terms such as "I was really caught up in the story." They seem reluctant to explore publicly the complexities of their particular emotional experience, perhaps because they do not trust the validity of their own particular experience as uniquely different or divergent from others. Fearing some raised eyebrows from peers who may judge expression of unusual engagement experiences as self-indulging, they opt for more truncated, familiar descriptions of their engagement. I therefore try to create a safe environment for expression of engagement responses.

And, in reacting to their responses, I react with my own "reader-based" descriptions of their responses (Elbow 1981; Johnston 1992), describing how their engagements evoked my own engagement responses. I am therefore modeling the very response processes I want my students to employ. I am communicating *what* I value in their responses through *how* I respond to them.

In addition to my reactions, I provide students with activities and assignments based on heuristics or systematic ways of thinking about their responses to texts. These heuristics are built on the following response strategies (Beach 1993; Beach and Marshall 1991):

> *Engaging.* Entering into and reflecting on one's experience with the text, focusing on *how* one is experiencing a text.
>
> *Recalling/Recounting.* Describing, recalling, or recounting the events or characters.
>
> *Inferring/Explaining.* Inferring characters' traits, beliefs, knowledge, plans, and goals or aspects of setting in order to explain characters' or speakers' actions.
>
> *Understanding the Text as a Cultural World.* Constructing the social and cultural contexts of texts by determining conventions constituting appropriate behavior in a particular text world.
>
> *Connecting.* Connecting and contrasting one's experience of a text with related autobiographical experiences or other texts.
>
> *Interpreting/Judging.* Inferring larger thematic meanings; judging characters' actions or the quality of a text.

These strategies are derived from numerous research studies on response to literature designed to identify different types of responses (Purves and Beach 1973, 15–20; Beach and Hynds 1991, 453–91). None of these strategies is necessarily more desirable than any other strategy. They serve as a framework or taxonomy for organizing instruction and evaluation designed to encourage students to go beyond simply retelling and interpreting texts to entertain engagement with texts, connections with autobiographical and intertextual experiences, interpretations of the social and cultural forces constituting their responses, and judgments of characters' actions and authors' literary quality.

In addition to acquiring the use of a range of different strategies, students also need to learn how to link these strategies effectively. For example, recalling may be linked to connecting, which is linked to explaining and interpreting. An assignment may begin with students' describing characters' experiences, followed by drawing connections to their own experiences. Students then infer beliefs about the similarities between their own experiences and events in the text, and then use those beliefs to interpret the text. In addition to reacting to students' use of individual strategies, teachers also need to react to students' ability to link these strategies. For example, to link explanations of characters' actions with interpretations of those actions, students need to be able to develop reasons for characters' actions that then provide valid interpretations for them.

Responding to Students' Use of Strategies

To illustrate how I would respond to students' use of response strategies, let me cite some responses of secondary students who were members of an elective literature course for ninth to twelfth graders at South High School in Minneapolis, Minnesota. In that course, the teacher, Emily Lilja, taught the novel *A Yellow Raft in Blue Water,* by Michael Dorris (1988), a Native American writer. The novel depicts the conflicts between three generations of Native American women: Rayona, a fifteen-year-old; Christine, her mother; and Ida, Christine's mother. Each of these characters tells her life story in a separate section of the novel. In her section, Rayona describes her alienation from her mother and her childhood living with estranged parents. She then leaves home to work in a state park, where she is sexually abused by a Catholic priest. In her section, Christine describes her own version of conflicts with Rayona; her husband, Elgin; and her presumed mother, Ida. She could never understand why Ida was reluctant to love her. Christine and her brother, Dayton, develop a close relationship, but then he is killed in the Vietnam War. Later, when Christine's marriage to Elgin falls apart, she is left to fend for herself in raising Rayona. In the final section of the novel narrated by Ida, Ida reveals that she is not Christine's real mother; rather, she is the daughter of Ida's father and a woman who came to live with the family. To avoid embarrassment to the family, Ida then raised her, along with her actual son, Dayton. At the end of the novel, Ida describes her partial reconciliation with Christine.

In teaching the novel, Ms. Lilja provided instruction in the use of various strategies by modeling her own strategies for responding to the novel. She also devised discussion questions based on the use of different strategies so that students were using these strategies in their discussions. And, over the period of two weeks, she assigned a series of journal entries based on these strategies. Students described their engagement with one of the characters; created their own version of events in the novel as told through the eyes of a character; explained one of the character's actions in terms of reasons for those actions; compared a character's experience with conflict with their own experience with conflict; described the cultural norms operating in the novel; and analyzed a conflict in the novel in terms of differences in cultural norms. Ms. Lilja responded to these entries in a conversational mode, posing questions and giving her own reactions in an attempt to provoke further thinking about the responses to the novel. These journal entries serve as guided preparation leading up to a final essay assignment on the conflicts between the characters as related to differences in family, gender, or culture.

In the following section, I give some examples of how I, had I been their teacher, would have evaluated students' responses by describing students' use of strategies using reader-based" reactions (Elbow 1981; Johnston 1992) such as "I liked the fact that you are [name a strategy]." These reactions are designed to praise the student's use of a strategy, to bolster students' confidence in the validity of their own responses, and to model a vocabulary for them to use in reflecting metacognitively on what they are doing when they respond.

I also invite students to entertain some further, potential development of their responses. As Peter Elbow notes, "I increase the chances of my liking their writing when I get better at finding what is good— or *potentially* good—and learn to praise it" (1993, 202). I show students how to develop their responses by sharing my own responses and describing how I extend them. For example, Lorna describes her engagement thus: "One thing I really like about this book is that its not predictable." I react by stating, "I had the same experience of constantly being surprised by unexpected events." I then model how I extend my response by citing reasons for my engagement: "I think that one reason I was surprised was that I kept hoping that relationships would improve, but they usually did not."

My dialogic reactions also serve to model ways of carrying on peer-written conversation about a text in dialogue-journal or e-mail exchanges, written conversation that is a central part of my class (Anson and Beach 1995). The quality of these written conversations often depends on students' ability to provide thoughtful, descriptive, dialogic reactions, something that many students need to be shown how to do. Given the amount of time involved in providing reader-based feedback, and given the need to model dialogic reactions, I record my reactions on a cassette tape, which generally takes less time than writing comments. I ask students to submit a tape with their journal or essay and to number the lines of their writing in the margins. I dictate my reactions, referring to specific numbered lines and starting and stopping the tape using an on-off microphone. I have found that using the tape encourages me to adopt a more dialogic, conversational style than when I write comments, so that, in some cases, I share my own responses to a text. Again, *how* I respond—with dialogic, divergent reactions—serves to convey *what* I value in their responses.

I also judge students' effectiveness in using a strategy and in linking strategies, according to explicit criteria that constitute the value of using certain strategies. For example, in responding to a student's comparison of her own mother and the mother/daughter conflicts in the novel, I explain why I liked the fact that she elaborated on the similarity to her own relationship: that her elaboration about her relationship with her mother helped her to define her own love/hate attitude toward her mother, which then helped her to interpret the love/hate relationship in the novel. This conveys to her the fact that had she not elaborated on these similarities, she would not have formulated as rich an interpretation as she did. These reasons also imply those criteria or ground rules for what constitutes successful use of strategies. As illustrated in Figure 1, each strategy can be evaluated according to different criteria, criteria having to do with the specificity, elaboration, relevancy, verification, or validity of their responses. While this figure should not imply a hierarchy in the use of these strategies, they do, however interact with each other, suggesting the need to formulate further criteria regarding students' ability to link them. These criteria could be simplified or elaborated upon, depending on students' level of sophistication. And, in assigning essays, it is helpful to openly discuss and negotiate these criteria with students so that they understand how they apply to their writing in a particular assignment.

Making explicit these criteria or ground rules (Sheeran and Barnes 1993) also conveys to students that I am evaluating their writing according to some shared criteria, or what is known as criterion-based evaluation. Many students assume that they are being evaluated according to their performance relative to a group norm, or norm-based evaluation. In a criterion-based approach, I am encouraging all students, regardless of their ability levels, to demonstrate change relative to their initial starting point. I am therefore evaluating students against themselves, rather than against some group norm. All of this serves to reduce students' fear of failure derived from labels such as "below average" or "low ability." When asked by students if their work was not "good enough," the poet and teacher William Stafford replied, "That will be impossible: in this class, by definition, what you can do is all right. Here, you start where you are and go somewhere" (McCarthy 1993, 18a).

Strategy	Criteria
engaging: identifying, empathizing with or defining attitudes toward a text	specifies one's description of an experience with a text; degree of awareness of stance and attitudes shaping one's experience
retelling/recounting story events or plot development	describes story events or plot development in detail in order to make inferences, define relationship of events to other strategies, or interpret meaning of events
inferring/explaining characters	infers a range of optional factors: beliefs, knowledge, goals, context; generates valid explanations based on these inferences and awareness of text-world conventions
understanding the text as a cultural construction	defines perceived patterns of behavior to infer cultural norms; explores alternative cultural perspectives without imposing one's own cultural perspective
connecting texts with autobiographical experiences or other texts	infers relevant connections; elaborates on connection to define beliefs and attitudes; uses the perceived connections to interpret the original text
interpreting text meaning	formulates original, valid interpretations; cites supporting evidence from the text and related connections
judging characters' actions or text quality	states a clear judgment; cites supporting evidence based on awareness of relevant criteria

Figure 1. Criteria for Evaluating Response Strategies.

Evaluating Students' Use of Response Strategies

Let me illustrate ways of responding to students' use of response strategies by describing how I would react to Ms. Lilja's students' journal and essay responses.

Engaging

Ms. Lilja's students wrote about their experience of liking, disliking, being enthralled or moved by, annoyed with, or overwhelmed by a text as part of an *aesthetic* experience (Rosenblatt [1938] 1983) with the novel. In my reactions, I would focus on students' ability to describe their emotional or aesthetic experience in some detail, evoking the criteria of specificity. Lorna describes her experience of reading the opening section of the novel:

> One thing I really like about this book is that its not predictable. Besides that one episode with Father Tom, I have pretty much been surprised at what happens. For instance, being liked by Evelyn and getting a job, but most of all, when she rides Babe! I never would have guessed that. It makes it fun to read, and I'm anxious to find out what Christine has to say.

I would tell Lorna that I like the way she describes specific feelings about how the novel sets up and plays with her expectations, expectations that may or may not be fulfilled. I would also convey the value of describing her engagement with the novel as a potential link to judging the quality of the novel's story development.

Students may also describe their experience of empathizing or identifying with a character. In response to the journal assignment in which students adopt a character's perspective and retell parts of the novel through the eyes of that character, Maria adopts Christine's perspective and describes Christine's recollection of her relationship with her own brother Lee:

> I remember back when Lee and I were younger about high school years and we'd get into some trouble. You must know one thing to understand, Lee and I, we were the best of friends. It was like that our whole life. Wherever he went I'd go. Lee was the one and only stable thing I knew I would depend on in my life. We did all of the rebellious stuff parents don't like.

I would react to Maria's entry by noting the she effectively adopts Christine's perspective as an adolescent girl who loves her brother, a love that she never finds in her relationships with other characters. I am therefore noting how Maria links her engaging strategy—adopting

Christine's perspective with her explaining strategy—giving reasons for Christine's actions.

Retelling/Recounting

Students may also recount or retell what happened in the text, recounting or retelling that triggers other response strategies. I evaluate recounting/retelling on the basis of the degree of elaboration of events, noting that I want to know more about what happened in the event. As in any effective storytelling, in recounting and elaborating events, students begin to explore their beliefs or attitudes about those events, and this serves to link those events to use of other strategies: connecting events to their own experiences, explaining characters' actions, or interpreting/judging the event. For example, Chris recounts Christine's departure from the reservation:

> Christine ultimately left the reservation for a job in Seattle, although many events had been building up to her departure— her feelings of neglect from Aunt Ida, her friendship with Lee becoming rocky, Dayton taking Lee away from her, etc. She met Elgin in Seattle, by accident actually. Christine is always running from her past. Didn't she say that she threw away the old Christine when she met Elgin?

In reacting to Chris's recounting of Christine's actions, I note that describing specific actions leads him to infer a pattern in her behavior—the fact that she is "always running from her past," which helps him explain her behavior. I am therefore praising him for his specificity and for his ability to link his recounting to his explaining of characters' actions.

Inferring/Explaining

In inferring/explaining, students use characters' actions to infer characters' traits, knowledge, beliefs, plans, and goals. They then use those inferences to explain a character's actions, inferring that, for example, Christine hates Ida because she believes that Ida never loved her as a child.

The quality or validity of students' explanations often depends on their ability to consider a range of different characteristics. Students who base their explanation on only one minor characteristic may not develop as valid an explanation as a student who cites a range of different, prominent characteristics. In the following response, Roman uses his inferences about Rayona's traits and needs to explain her difficulty in communicating her feelings to others:

> Rayona was always getting "dumped around" by Christine. She was the kind of girl who accepted the things that were said to her. She kept them inside of her and didn't have anything to say back. She didn't have any close friends in Seattle. She kept to herself all of the time. She also did not have a father to go to. She was in need to a father to be with because Ida always had a sister and other family members living with her. Ida had someone to communicate with everyday. Christine had Lee, Dayton, and some of her own friends. Rayona only had Christine to talk with.

I would react to Roman's explanation of Rayona's behavior by noting that he cites a number of different characteristics to explain Rayona's insularity—her treatment by Christine and her lack of either friends or a father, and that he bolsters his explanation by contrasting Rayona's loneliness with Ida's and Christine's connections with others.

In some cases, students may explain a character's actions by imposing their own real-world assumptions onto texts, failing to recognize the assumptions operating within the world of the text. For example, in his journal, Roman criticized Rayona for quitting her job at the state park: "I don't see what Rayona quit the job at the state park. I think she should've stayed a little while longer working because she was getting a lot of money. The way Rayona was saving money she could've bought a new house." I would tell Roman that he needs to consider whether his real-world assumption that Rayona wants to buy a house is consistent with her desire to quit her job—that forces operating in the real world may not necessarily be operating in the same manner in the text world of the novel. At the same time, Roman also provides an alternative explanation, that "she left because she missed her mother and she needed her back," an explanation more consistent with text-world assumptions. I would also cite my criterion—that explanations need to take into account the conditions or conventions constituting the text world.

Understanding the Text as a Cultural World

As they enter into the world of the text, students need to be able to construct that world as a culture constituted by certain norms and conventions. Understanding, for example, the early-nineteenth-century world of *Pride and Prejudice* requires some understanding of how social behaviors were perceived as appropriate for certain social classes—the aristocracy, the landed gentry, the mercantile middle class, the military, and the working class.

Students contextualize texts as cultural worlds by drawing on their everyday experience of having to size up and define the norms and conventions operating in peer-group encounters, classrooms, organizations, workplaces, and ceremonies. For each of these, which they detect differences in the social genres and discourses that constitute the meaning of events in these contexts. For example, during the school day, as they move from class to class, they experience different microcultures operating according to different norms and conventions. They learn to interpret events in each class according to these norms and conventions. A student challenging a teacher may be interpreted as totally unacceptable in one class but a normal, routine event in another class.

Similarly, students learn to contextualize the different social and cultural contexts operating within a text world. In responding to *Yellow Raft*, students defined differences between the Native American, Caucasian, and Catholic cultural worlds. They contrasted the Native American, Caucasian, and Catholic beliefs about the same events in the novel. In his essay, Chris wrote about the conflict between Father Hurlburt's Catholic world and Ida's Native American world. He focused his analysis on Ida's braiding her hair as a metaphor for differences in cultural understanding:

> At the very end of the book, Father Hurlburt and Ida are sitting on the roof of Ida's house. Ida lifted her hands and started to braid her hair. This action of braiding was foreign to him and he had to ask what Ida was doing. The book says that Father Hurlburt had short hair and so he could not identify with Ida's actions. Because it was foreign to his culture, Father Hurlburt did not recognize the action of braiding nor could he have comprehended the rich heritage and tradition behind the braid.

Later in his essay, Chris discusses the conflict between attitudes associated with displays of American patriotism and the attitudes of Native Americans on the reservation:

> Many of the people on the reservation felt that the American patriotism was an intrusion on their privacy and more importantly, their culture. This, unfortunately, has been an all-too-common theme in American history. An example of this tension between cultures is seen when Christine describes the flag-bearing Color Guard parading through the reservation gym before every social event: "It isn't till they leave, out of the light or the room or the gym, that you hear a kind of sigh pass through the crowd" (p. 142).

In this response, Chris contextualizes Ida's braiding or the Color Guard's parading within the competing Native American and Caucasian cultures. He describes these images as two distinct cultural codes—braiding as weaving together different aspects of life and the Color Guard as celebrating military might and control.

I evaluate students' construction of cultural worlds according their ability to detect signs of honesty and deception within a context (Witte and Flach 1994); define relevancy and significance within a context; discern appropriate behavior within that context; note how characters include and exclude other characters according to positions of authority or status; and determine characters' beliefs and values. Part of constructing cultural worlds entails the ability to perceive patterns in characters' behaviors that suggest that certain cultural conventions are operative. In reacting to Chris's response, I would note that he effectively detects a pattern of racist behavior in the white people, a pattern he uses to explain Christine's resistance to that culture.

I also evaluate students' ability to recognize how their own cultural beliefs and attitudes are shaping their construction of these worlds. Students who can discern their own bias may be more open to accepting different or alternative cultural perspectives portrayed in a text.

Connecting

Students also connect their responses to related autobiographical experiences or other texts. However, they may simply note that a text reminds them of a related experience or another text without developing or elaborating upon this. By elaborating on the meanings of connections with related experiences and texts, students are then able to apply the meanings back to understanding the current text. For example, Gayle responds to the fact that Christine expresses love for Rayona, love she never received from her own mother, Ida. In describing this mother/daughter relationship, Gayle is reminded of an episode in her own life:

> When she [Christine] said that she never wanted her [Rayona] to be anybody but who she was I can recall a time when I was in grade school. My best friend's name was Annie. She was smart, sweet, good at everything she did. Well one day in the car my mom kept talking about how great Annie was and I said something like what do you wish Annie was, your daughter. She turned and looked at me and said, honestly, sometimes I've wished you were Annie or just like her. That really hurt. To think that your own mother would say a thing like that. I got over it and forgave her but it still lingers in the back of my mind. So the relationship that Ida and Christine had reflects on Rayona and Christine's life.

I would react to Gayle's connecting response by noting that she employed a series of steps: She empathized with Rayona's feelings about her mother; she elaborated on her own similar experience with her mother; and she used the similarity between her own and Rayona's experience to explain Ida's failure to express her love to Christine, modeling the different steps involved in the connecting process.

Similarly, a twelfth grade student, Wendy compared her family experiences with that of Rayona's relationship with Christine:

> I think I have a personal connection with Rayona. Her dad left her and all she had was a few memories and a bunch of broken promises.
>
> My dad left me for another woman and that's what it sounds like Elgin did. I didn't see my dad for almost two years after he left the first time. He called and wrote and even sent postcards saying things would work out and he'd come see me soon. Well that was a joke. Christine made it worse than it was and that's exactly what my mom did and still does. Sometimes my mom will look at me and start yelling about my dad. I went through mood swings and attitude changes and I grew further away from my mom. I think Rayona went through the same thing. Even though my mom stayed and my dad left, I thought it was my mom's fault deep down.

In this entry, Wendy compares Rayona's strained relationship with her parents with her relationship to her own parents. She then used this comparison to explain Rayona's sense of alienation as stemming from her parents' marital conflicts. In reacting to her response, I would note that by elaborating on her conflict with her mother, she clarified her own ambiguous attitude toward her, which enhanced her understanding of Christine's and Rayona's attitudes toward their own mothers. For both Gayle and Wendy, I am emphasizing the criterion of elaborating on connecting experiences as enhancing their understanding of the mother/daughter relationships in the novel.

Interpreting

In interpreting a text, students are inferring the larger symbolic or thematic meanings of events or characters' actions. In some cases, this involves relating the text to larger issues or themes associated with the need for power, freedom, identity, love, etc. For example, Evan interprets Rayona's actions as representing an internal conflict between freedom and responsibility:

> I know many kids who would use the kind of freedom Rayona had to get away with doing all kinds of things. They would take advantage of all that freedom. Rayona didn't take advantage of her freedom. She accepted the responsibility that comes with freedom. I think Rayona is disappointed at the amount of responsibility that her mother places on her shoulders, especially at her young age. Rayona feels that it is unfair treatment but she doesn't fight her mother about it. She sees herself as the person who must take care of her mother, so she is careful not to cause problems for her.

In his interpretation, Evan perceives Rayona as caught between the need for freedom versus responsibility to her mother. A central criteria in evaluating interpretation is the degree of supporting evidence from the text. I would note that Evan draws on Rayona's actions as well as his own experiences with his peers to analyze Rayona's willingness to assume responsibility, which, for Evan, contributes to her maturity.

Students also need to be able to interpret differences in characters' own interpretations of text-world events. Characters' interpretations serve as "metamessages" that shape their social definitions of events and their actions in those events. These "metamessages" frame events that define the type of activity involved, definitions of the situation that serve to guide behavior in those situations (Tannen 1993). One character perceives a conversation as a "friendly chat," while another character perceives the same conversation as a "sharp disagreement." A student must then determine which character's interpretation or frame is the most valid relative to the text world as constructed by other characters. Evan is able to interpret Rayona's perspective because he has some sense of her relative perspective on the text world as defined by not only Rayona, but also Christine, Ida, and the other characters. This requires students to determine a character's ability to interpret or misinterpret what may be "really" happening in the text world and the reasons for that character's ability or inability to make valid interpretations. As the text unfolds, students therefore need to be open to entertaining new, alternative versions of text-world "reality." Rather than prematurely latching onto one version, they need to synthesize and assess the relative validity of multiple, competing versions of text-world "reality." In comparing college freshmen's and graduate students' writing about literature, Elise Earthman (1992) found that the freshmen "made up their minds very quickly [as to] what a story or poem was 'about,' and then stuck to it even when the text invited them to revise their understanding" (379). In contrast, the graduate students were more likely to continually reexamine their initial interpretations by entertaining alternative perspectives.

To evaluate students' interpretations of character's interpretations, I therefore consider their ability to weigh the multiple, competing perspectives constituting the text world relative to a character's own perspective.

Judging

Related to interpretation of characters' actions or interpretations is students' ability to judge characters' actions or talk as appropriate, insightful, sincere, truthful, sufficient, ethical, or moral. Judging characters' actions requires some reasons based on consistent patterns of characters' actions or talk. A judgment based on multiple instances is generally more valid than one based on a single instance. I therefore evaluate students' judgments of characters' actions according to their ability to defend those judgments with valid reasons derived from analysis of consistent patterns in characters' actions or talk.

Students also judge the quality of writing related to a text's coherence, development, literary merit, or writing style. As in judging characters' actions, students need to be able to cite reasons for judging writing quality, reasons not only having to do with criteria based on literary form, but also the ways in which the use of form or technique serves to enhance their experience with the text. In this manner, judging is linked to engaging. In her journal response, Hadley judges the quality of the novel's plot:

> I feel that this plot is very well thought out and set up nicely. The only thing is when the story repeats itself in a few places. In a way, it a waste of time to read the same thing over again. But it is also through a different point of view, because we're dealing with another character's thoughts and feelings at that exact moment of the situation. For example, when Christine and Rayona are in the car headed back for Montana and the car breaks down. In each story, both are thinking of each other even though they really don't say it, show it, or express it.

I would react to Hadley's judgment by noting that she relates her judgment of Dorris's use of multiple retellings of the same events to her own engagement with Christine and Rayona's perspectives—the fact that the retellings encouraged her to empathize with Christine and Rayona's unspoken feelings about each other.

In responding to judgments, I may also impute assumptions implied by the cited reasons. For example, in response to "this poem fails because there are no symbols," I would impute the implied assumption—that "successful poems contain symbols"—and then ask the student to explore that assumption. Imputing assumptions serves to challenge students to examine their own questionable or dubious reasoning.

Evaluating Strategies in Extended Journal Entries and Essays

In writing extended journal entries or essays, students are learning to link these various strategies together in a systematic, sustained manner. Teachers may then evaluate students' ability to link together multiple strategies, for example, to use their recounting of events to generate an explanation of a character's actions. Students then evaluate whether they have effectively developed one strategy in order to link that strategy to another, whether, for example, they have done enough relevant recounting to make a valid explanation. For students to anticipate potential uses of strategies requires their ability to perceive some purpose in why they are using certain strategies. Students may be able to recount events, but if they perceive little purpose in the recounting, they may then perceive it as a meaningless exercise. For example, Sarah devoted a lot of her initial freewriting and journal writing to retelling of events in the novel, but with little reflection about the meaning of those events. She was adopting what Hunt and Vipond (1992) define as a "story-driven" stance. She is so engrossed in the story world, in the experience of "what happens next," that she has difficulty stepping outside that world to adopt a "point-driven stance"— inferring larger meanings of a text as opposed to a "story-driven" stance in which students simply describe their experience with a text. Hunt and Vipond argue that inferring the "point," as in the "point" of a conversation, is mutually constructed through social interaction with others—unless participants in a conversation stick to the "point," their contributions are deemed as "pointless." Defining the "point" therefore involves more than simply inferring the theme or gist of the text itself. It's meaning is constituted within the social context of writing for a teacher or peer, who may recognize that a strategy in not "pointless," that it has some purpose.

Teachers' evaluations play an important role in helping students perceive some purpose for using strategies to link with other strategies. To help Sarah further explore her journal recounting, Ms. Lilja posed a series of questions designed to encourage her to adopt a "point-driven" stance, questions such as "What is Dorris saying through all of this family conflict?" or "What is Christine's point of view on the possibility of resolution?" Then, as Sarah was writing her rough draft, Ms. Lilja encouraged her to formulate her thesis and use that thesis to reflect on her retelling. By her final draft, Sarah organized her retelling around underlying patterns in the story, representing a shift from a "story-driven" to a "point-driven" stance. In her concluding paragraph, she describes this pattern: "that all three women made a wrong turn somewhere and tried their hardest to overcome that mistake and followed through to make that mistake worthwhile or change completely." In her writing, Sarah is linking together strategies according to Ms. Lilja's explicit criteria for defining a conflict and providing supporting evidence.

Let me illustrate how I evaluate students' uses of multiple strategies by discussing my reactions to an essay written by Dawn, an eleventh-grade student. In her essay, Dawn argues that "the root family conflict is dependent upon the personalities of the characters involved. The beginnings of family conflict can be traced back to Ida's younger days, when she naively took on a huge, lifelong burden." In the first section of the paper, she discusses the conflict between Christine and Ida. She argues that because Christine was not Ida's daughter, Christine was not only resentful of her, but she also had difficulty communicating with her given their differences in personality. In evaluating this essay, I describe my perceptions (in italics) of Dawn's use of specific response strategies. Then, at the end of the essay, I comment on the audiotape about the ways in which she was able to combine her use of different strategies.

> As Christine grows up a conflict develops between Christine and Ida. This conflict is a result of similarities in their personalities. Ida and Christine are both very closed to the people around them. They have a difficult time expressing positive feelings to the ones they love. When Christine returns to the reservation for the first time after Lee's death, this characteristic of their personalities is illustrated in their first interaction with each other. When they meet, Ida says to Christine, "Give me three good reasons why I should be happy to see you" (page 30). Christine responds "One, Mother, I'm your daughter, your only living child. . . . Two, I need someplace to stay. . . . Three, go fuck yourself anyway" (page 31). This conversation had the potential to turn out much better, if either of them could have let go of their old habits and told the other one what they really felt, love.
>
> Through time, and in certain circumstances, we see the beginning of resolution. When Ida visits Christine at Dayton's house to tell her that Rayona has run away, she says, "You call for me. . . if you want to" (page 275). This is not an all out gesture of consideration or love, but it can be looked at as an indicator that the two characters may drop their defenses. It is Ida's way of saying that she will be there for Christine.

> *Dawn, I like the way you use your recounting of Ida's visit to explain her flexibility and interpret a shift in Ida's attitude toward Christine.*

> Christine expresses a change in this aspect of her personality later on in the book when she invites Ida over to Dayton's for dinner. During the first part of the book Christine tells Rayona how lucky she is ". . . since her mother drives her crazy" (page 14). During the dinner situation, Christine and Ida get along very well. Christine does not say anything negative about Aunt Ida during this time. This indicates that Christine is finally able to show Ida that she does care.

> *Here you explain the conflict between Christine and Ida as due to their shared personality traits—that both had difficulty expressing their feelings. By recounting shifts in Christine's attitude towards Ida, you are developing information that supports your larger thesis that conflict*

derives from personality traits. I do wonder if Christine's difficulty in expressing her feelings derived from being raised by Ida or from other factors outside her home life.

While the conflict between Ida and Christine seems to be rooted in similar personality traits, the conflict between Christine and Rayona seems to be rooted in bad communication, differences, and misconceptions. Rayona and Christine do not effectively communicate their thoughts to one another. This is expressed with the hospital scene. When Rayona describes the situation she says "I want to leave but mom would hit the ceiling and tell me I'm not polite" (page 3). This is how Rayona sees her mom (Christine) thinking about the situation, while actually Christine is thinking that she wants Rayona to leave. Her thoughts were ". . . Rayona would arrive on the button and stay the whole time. More than anything I wanted to be alone to think things over . . ." (page 236). Christine also states that "Rayona would wonder if I sent her home early" (page 238). This is a classic example that they do not communicate well.

The differences in personality traits between Rayona and Christine are a constant source of conflict between them. As a result of these differences, they misunderstand the other's actions. Christine is very wild and does not really need to feel that she has roots, or a permanent place or support. To Rayona, family is important and although she accepts change, she does not necessarily want that in her life.

You explain the breakdown in Rayona's relationship with Christine as due to their personality differences, more evidence to support your larger thesis that conflict derives from personality traits.

Christine's feelings about change are expressed when she describes her first months in Washington. She says "For months I bounced around western Washington from Everett to Olympia. . . . I came to think of myself as the song 'Tumbling Tumbleweed.' One of these days I was going to blow against something good and hang on, and there was no rushing it" (page 173). When Christine describes this, she does not give the impression that this was a negative time in her life, but rather something that she enjoyed.

Rayona's resistance to change is expressed when she says "The last thing I need is to leave Seattle and be stuck on some reservation with people I don't know" (page 14). This attitude is considerably different from the one that Christine has about change, and because they don't try to understand each other, there is a resulting conflict.

Rayona's need for family becomes evident in her actions involving the letter from Ellen's parents to Ellen that she found in the park. After finding the letter, Rayona says "This scrap of paper in my hand makes me feel poor in a way like I just heard of rich. Jealous" (page 81). Christine does not see that family is important to Rayona. She does not understand that Rayona wants a true family, instead of just biological parents.

You effectively contrast Christine's and Rayona's beliefs about change and family, recounting events to illustrate the differences in their beliefs.

As with most novels, everything turns out pretty well in the end. Conflict resolution is not achieved by discussing problems or going to therapy. Instead, each of the three characters learns to accept and love the other ones, regardless of their differences, on a common ground. They learned, essentially, that their lives represented three parts of one whole. Ida states it best, ". . . the whispers of coming and going, of twisting and tying and blending, of catching and letting go, of braiding" (page 372).

As a reader, I wanted some more evidence that Christine and Rayona actually learned to accept each other; here you provide evidence that Ida and Christine reach some conciliation.

Overall, I liked the way you compared the two relationships themselves; that allows you to argue that the conflicts between these characters were rooted in basic personality differences that shape their relationships. With the exception of the Christine/Rayona reconciliation at the end, you also documented your explanations of conflict with illustrative examples from the novel. Based on your ability to link your specific recollections of events with thoughtful explanations to interpret reasons for the conflicts, you therefore earned an "exceptional" evaluation.

Note that during the essay, I focus on describing what I perceived to be this student's effective use of response strategies—recounting, explaining, and interpreting personality conflicts. Then, at the end of the essay, I evaluate how effectively she was able to combine her use of these particular strategies.

Formulating Criteria for Use of Strategies

When faced with an assignment such as "Analyze the main character's development in a novel we read in this course. 500 words," many students have no sense of what specific strategies to employ or what constitutes a successful essay response. An alternative, guided version (Axelrod and Cooper 1997; Beach and Marshall 1991) of this assignment specifies a series of activities (listing, freewriting, mapping, etc.) and strategies involved in analyzing character development. Each activity prepares students for subsequent activities. For each activity, the assignment also states the purpose for using that strategy along with criteria for assessing its successful use. By explicating these criteria, as did Ms. Lilja, students then have an understanding of the expectations or ground rules for effective use of strategies (Sheeran and Barnes 1993; Witte and Flach 1994). These assignments therefore model ways of assessing purposeful uses of strategies, as illustrated in the following, guided version of a character analysis assignment:

- Describe the main character's actions in the beginning, middle, and end of the novel. Develop your description in enough detail so that you can make inferences about the character's traits, beliefs, or goals.

- Define a pattern in the character's actions for each of the three sections on the basis of perceived traits, beliefs, or goals. From this pattern, infer some consistent traits, beliefs, or goals. For example, in the beginning of the novel, the character is consistently avoiding other characters, implying his difficulty in communicating with others.

- Compare and contrast these traits, beliefs, or goals from the beginning versus the end of the novel.

- Explain reasons for these changes in terms of the influences of other characters, events, or social contexts within the novel. Describe these influences in enough detail so that they serve to adequately explain the changes.

Using Feature Analysis to Evaluate Overall Entries or Drafts

In addition to evaluating links between strategies as they develop their responses, students also need help in evaluating their overall entry or essay draft. I provide them with a list of features that constitute effective use of multiple strategies relevant for a particular type of analysis. I first consider the various strategies involved with that type of analysis. Take, for example, an assignment involving retelling a story's events through the eyes of a character other than the main character or narrator. To complete this assignment, students need to be able to empathize with this other character in order to understand that character's point or view or beliefs—engaging, explaining, and interpreting strategies. They also need to be able to discern the difference between this other character's perspectives and that of the main character or narrator—contrasting and judging strategies. And they need to translate their understanding of the other character's beliefs and perspective into their own fictional version, creating a different language that captures the character's perspective—interpreting and connecting strategies.

I then generate a list of features that constitutes effective use of these strategies, for assessing the student's reconstruction of the character's version of events, a retelling that:

- reflects an understanding of the other character's beliefs and point of view;
- uses language and descriptions that capture the other character's beliefs and point of view;
- differs from the main character's or narrator's perspective.

On the basis of these criteria, students then assess the extent to which their entry or draft achieves these features. Both the student and I may then evaluate each feature as "excellent," "completed," or "needs work." The mismatches in evaluations may then stimulate students to consider further revisions. If a "needs work" is noted, then both the student and I suggest revisions or additions that would serve to fulfill the criteria. In suggesting revisions or additions, I can model ways of extending or linking strategies.

Self-reflection on Beliefs, Attitudes, and Stances

In addition to reflecting on ways of extending or revising responses, students also need to stand back and reflect on their responses in terms of their own beliefs, attitudes, or ideological stances. Such reflection helps students recognize that their responses are shaped not only by their own beliefs and attitudes, but also by the beliefs and attitudes of their peers, classroom, family, or community. For example, in a study of the responses of high school students from three different schools to multicultural literature (Beach 1996), I found that many students adopted stances of resistance to reading and responding to such texts. They were resentful of implied challenges to their sense of white privilege; they were reluctant to adopt alternative cultural perspectives; and they assumed that racial differences can be bridged simply by changing how people perceive or feel about each other as opposed to perceiving differences as defined by institutional forces. In reflecting on these stances of resistance, students recognized how their own school culture, particularly the culture of the largely white suburban schools, shaped their attitudes toward multicultural literature. The suburban students noted that they were uneasy about discussing issues of diversity because there was little diversity in their schools and suburban communities. Through such reflection on their stances, these students recognized that their responses were influenced by their school's and community's attitudes and assumptions about what constitutes appropriate responses.

To encourage this self-reflection on factors influencing their response, I ask students to draw circle maps representing different groups or institutions in their lives. Within each group or institution, students then list a few norms or conventions that define appropriate behavior or attitudes for that particular group or institution. As is the case with a "you are here" map in a store or building, students then put a star for the place(s) in the circles they *most* prefer to be versus a square where they *least* prefer to be. They then discuss with peers how they learned the norms or conventions constituting a group or institution and the actions or behaviors that marked them as a bona fide member within that context. Finally, they reflect on their own or others' written or oral responses, to answer the question "Who is speaking here?" In answering that question, students are determining what Bakhtin (1981) describes as the different "voices" representing the language or perspectives of their teachers, authors, characters, peers, critics, parents, or textbook (Recchio 1991). In some cases, students adopt the formal, authoritative voice of a literary critic or a "teacher talk" discourse that reflects "the voice of the teacher's manual" or "the voice of the curriculum" (Wertsch 1991, 144).

I also ask students to identify instances of different, competing voices within the same journal entry or essay, voices reflecting ideological tensions in their own lives. They then link these different voices to the different groups or institutions on their maps. For example, in reflecting on his responses to *Yellow Raft*, John drew a map of the groups in the novel that included "Native Americans," "Catholics," and "Whites." Then, in his own real-world map, which included his school, home, church ("Protestant"), as well as groups—"White/male" and various persons in his life—he placed his "here I am" designator in the "White/male/Protestant" circles. In reflecting on his map, he discovered conflicting allegiances to different aspects of these competing worlds. His allegiance to a "Protestant" world led him to sympathize with Rayona because of her mistreatment by the Catholic priests, priests he perceived to be "outsiders." At the same time, his allegiance to a "White/male" world led him to reflect on one Catholic priest's sense of male dominance that led him to take advantage of Rayona. Through reflecting on each character's own "voice" or stance, John recognized tensions among his own voices that reflect the tensions between the characters in the novel.

In addition to having students reflect on responses in individual pieces of writing, it is also important to have them reflect on consistent patterns of thinking in their responses across different pieces of writing. They may discover that they are consistently grappling with particular issues or topics or are adopting certain consistent stances. For example, throughout Ms. Lilja's course, Donna was concerned with her gender stance. In some cases, she had adopted a traditional male stance that was invited by much of what she was reading, while in other cases, she had adopted a feminist stance. By reviewing all of her writing in the course, she recognized the tensions between these different stances as representative of different aspects of her own self. As James Zebroski (1994) argues that "Instead of a singular writer producing plural texts, why can't we think of a plural writer producing a singular text" (54). Across their different writings, students are producing what Zebroski describes as "life-text" (54) themes that reflect the tensions of their "plural" selves.

Consistent with the idea of portfolio self-evaluation, students may also reflect on change and growth in their use of response strategies from the beginning to the end of a course. By comparing their written responses in their journal entries or essays at both the beginning and end of a course, students begin to appreciate the fact that they have actually changed in their use of response strategies. For example, in the beginning of a course, a student might note that her responses consisted simply of retelling the story. By the end of the course, the student might recognize that she went beyond retelling the story to explain, interpret, and connect story events.

In asking students to examine changes in their response, I caution them not to necessarily expect dramatic, marked changes within a relatively short period of time, for example, in writing two or three papers. In his discussion of portfolios, Jeffrey Sommers (1991) notes that teachers hold to a "myth of improvement," assuming that, given their instructional efforts, their students must be improving. Rather than change their responses, it may simply be the case that students are establishing a habit of responding in a certain, consistent manner.

Assessing Growth in Response Strategies

To help students reflect on change or growth in their response strategies, I provide them with some criteria and directions for organizing their review. For their final paper in a course, students write a letter to me in which they describe changes in their responses, with documented evidence taken from their writing throughout the course.

Amount. Students may change simply in the amount of response— from a few lines at the beginning of a class to a more extended text by the end. By counting the number of lines of response from beginning, middle, and end, students simply record the changes in amount. While change in the amount of response may not necessarily represent a change in the quality, the very fact that students are writing more may mean that they are more likely to explore different aspects of their responses.

Use of specific response strategies. Students may change in their ability to employ specific response strategies. For example, at the beginning of a course, a student's explanations for characters' actions may rely solely on traits—for example, that a character did something because she was lazy, lonely, angry, naive, etc. By the end of the course, that student's explanations may now include characters' beliefs and knowledge about other characters, as well as consideration of the social context. To chart changes in the use of strategies, students label their use in the margins by means of a coding system, i.e., "e" for engaging, "r" for recounting, and so on. They then select the same strategies from the beginning and end of the course and compare their use.

Range of response strategies. Students may also employ a wider range of different response strategies than they did at the beginning of a course. At the beginning of a class, they may be only recounting/retelling, while, by the end, they are adding more engaging, connecting, and interpreting strategies. Using the labeling system noted above, students create a chart that allows them to compare the types of strategies employed at the beginning and the end of a course.

Linking of strategies. Students may not only employ a wider range of strategies, but they may also change in their ability to link their use of different strategies. At the beginning of a course, students may recount story events without connecting that recounting to explaining, constructing cultural worlds, connecting, interpreting, or judging texts. By the end of a course, students may link their recounting of story events to these other strategies. Having used a coding system to label their use of strategies in an initial and later piece of writing, students draw lines between codes that represent links between strategies. They may then find that, in an initial entry, the strategies are generally unrelated—a string of random, unconnected thoughts. In contrast, in a later entry, the strategies are more directly related together.

Elaboration/extension of response. Related to the amount of response is the extent to which students change in their elaboration or extension of their responses. In their initial entries, they may respond with only vague, superficial responses: "I really liked this story"; "This was a dumb poem"; "The main character was a real loser"; and so forth, without elaborating on or extending those responses. In their later entries, they may be more likely to elaborate on these responses, citing reasons for their engagement responses or inferences. Or, they may move beyond vague, global descriptions of responses to specify the particulars of their experience with a text. Rather than respond with "I just didn't understand this story," they describe their experiences in some detail: "I was confused about what happened in the end"; "I didn't like the way she described the crowd"; or "I didn't understand what the title had to do with the poem." In comparing the degree of elaboration or extension of their responses, students circle responses they perceive to be vague or superficial and put boxes around responses they perceive to be more elaborated or extended, recording the extent to which they changed from circled to boxed responses.

Adapting responses to different contexts. As they reflect on changes in their responses—rather than compare their responses across time to what may be quite different assignments—students may compare their ability to adapt or vary their responses according to the demands of different contexts or assignments. Writing about their engagement with a short poem may be a totally different task from writing an extensive critique of a long novel. In comparing their responses, they may sense that they adopt different "voices" or stances, shifting from the voice of a detached "critic" to one of an engaged "reader." One "voice" is not necessarily better or more authentic than another. These variations simply represent different ways of adapting their responses to different contexts. This presupposes that writing quality has much to do with writers' ability to reflect on learning new genres or on ways of knowing required to meet the demands of new or different rhetorical contexts (Witte and Flach 1994). For example, in his eighteenth-century literature course, Russell Hunt (1994) asked students to share their responses with each other on a computer network. As the students became more accustomed to exchanging their responses in what was often a conversational, informal mode, they recognized that they were responding in a different voice or discourse. One student, Barb, began the course by writing in a formal mode—for example, "Ultimately, the relationship between comedy and its audience cannot be measured because society is not homogenous in nature . . ."(254). Toward the end of the course, after much experience with computer exchanges, she wrote, "From what I've read about the often diseased food at the time, I don't think I would have wanted to have eaten back then" (254). In reflecting on the differences between her more formal and her informal responses, Barb noted that

> I found my initial report to be more formal. I think we were trying to impress you, the professor, rather than our classmates because that is what we are used to doing . . . we try to sound as academic as possible. When we write for the benefit of our classmates, we know that they are at the same academic level, so we

> don't have to sound so professional. The writing in class is more
> friendly; more personal and less formal. (254)

Barb relates the differences between her formal essay writing and her more informal computer-exchange writing to differences in purpose and audience—impressing the professor versus sharing responses to inform her classmates. She is learning that the very fact that she recognizes the differences in these contexts is itself an important aspect of learning literature.

Summary

In summary, responding to students' writing about literature is a complex, dialogic process. From a transactional perspective, the meaning of this feedback is constituted by a transaction between myself, students, and their texts, within a social context constituted by a set of ground rules. I therefore provide "reader-based" descriptions of their responses, highlighting what I like about their response. I also anticipate potential directions for further development of their responses. And I ask students to reflect on their own stances as readers. In addition to reacting to specific writing, I also react to change and growth in their responses. And using portfolio evaluation, I encourage them to evaluate their own change and growth in the amount, elaboration, or use of response strategies; the range and linking of strategies; and their self-reflection on their beliefs, attitudes, interest in texts, contexts, and voice. In all of this, my evaluation hopefully serves to foster development in the quality of their responses.

Recommended Further Reading

For reading on literary-response theory applied to teaching literature, I recommend my own two books, *A Teacher's Introduction to Reader Response Theories* and *Teaching Literature in the Secondary School* (with James Marshall); Kathleen McCormick's *The Culture of Reading and the Teaching of Literature;* and Teresa Rogers and Anna Soter's collection, *Reading across Cultures: Teaching Literature in a Diverse Society.* For more specific discussions of evaluating writing about literature, I recommend *Exploring Texts: The Role of Discussion and Writing in the Teaching and Learning of Literature,* edited by George Newell and Russel Durst; and Yanini Sheeran and Douglas Barnes's, *School Writing.*

Works Cited

Alexrod, Rise B., and Charles R. Cooper. 1997. *The St. Martin's Guide to Writing.* 5th ed. New York: St. Martin's Press.

Anson, Chris, and Richard Beach. 1995. *Journals in the Classroom: Writing to Learn.* Norwood, MA: Christopher-Gordon.

Bakhtin, M. M. 1981. *The Dialogic Imagination: Four Essays,* ed. Michael Holquist. Trans. Caryl Emerson. Austin: University of Texas Press.

Beach, Richard W. 1993. *A Teacher's Introduction to Reader-Response Theories.* Urbana, IL: National Council of Teachers of English.

———. 1997. "Students' Resistance to Engagement in Responding to Multicultural Literature." In *Reading Across Cultures: Teaching Literature in a Diverse Society,* ed. Teresa Rogers and Anna O. Soter, 69–94. New York: Teachers College Press.

Beach, Richard W., and James Marshall. 1991. *Teaching Literature in the Secondary School.* Orlando: Harcourt Brace Jovanovich.

Beach, Richard W., and Susan Hynds. 1991. *The Handbook of Reading Research, Vol. 2,* ed. Rebecca Barr, Michael Kamil, Peter Mosenthal, and P. David Pearson. New York: Longman.

Dorris, Michael. 1988. *A Yellow Raft in Blue Water.* New York: Warner.

Earthman, Elise Ann. 1992. "Creating the Virtual Work: Readers' Processes in Understanding Literary Texts." *Research in the Teaching of English* 26: 351–84.

Elbow, Peter. 1981. *Writing with Power.* New York: Oxford University Press.

———. 1993. "Ranking, Evaluating, and Liking: Sorting Out Three Forms of Judgment." *College English* 55: 187–206.

Hunt, Russell. 1994. "Speech Genres, Writing Genres, School Genres, and Computer Games." In *Learning and Teaching Genre,* ed. Aviva Freedman and Peter Medway, 243–62. Portsmouth, NH: Boynton/Cook.

Hunt, Russell, and Douglas Vipond. 1992. "First, Catch the Rabbit: Methodological Imperative and the Dramatization of Dialogic Reading." In *Multidisciplinary Perspectives of Literacy Research,* ed. Richard Beach, Judith Green, Michael Kamil, and Timothy Shanahan, 69–90. Urbana, IL: National Council of Teachers of English.

Johnston, Brian. 1992. *Assessing English.* Milton Keynes, England: Open University Press.

Many, Joyce, and Carole Cox, eds. 1992. *Reader Stance and Literary Understanding: Exploring the Theories, Research, and Practice.* Norwood, NJ: Ablex.

McCarthy, Colman. 1993. "Poet Helped Many Find Their Way." *Minneapolis Star and Tribune.* Metro Edition. Sept. 11, 1993, 21: 18a

McCormick, Kathleen. 1994. *The Culture of Reading and the Teaching of English.* New York: St. Martin's Press.

Newell, George, and Russel Durst. *Exploring Texts: the Role of Discussion and Writing in the Teaching and Learning of Literature.* Christopher-Gordon Publishers.

Purves, Alan, and Richard Beach. 1973. *Literature and the Reader: Research on Response to Literature, Reading Interests, and Teaching of Literature.* Urbana, IL: National Council of Teachers of English.

Recchio, Thomas. 1991. "A Bakhtinian Reading of Student Writing." *College Composition and Communication* 42: 446–54.

Rogers, Teresa, and Anna O. Soter, eds., 64–94. *Reading across Cultures: Teaching Literature in a Diverse Society.* New York: Teachers College Press.

Rosenblatt, Louise. [1938] 1983. *Literature as Exploration.* 4th ed. New York: Modern Language Association of America.

Sheeran, Yanina, and Douglas Barnes. 1993. *School Writing.* Philadelphia: Open University Press.

Sommers, Jeffrey. 1991. "Bringing Practice in Line with Theory: Using Portfolio Grading in the Composition Classroom." In *Portfolios: Process and Product,* ed. Pat Belanoff and Marica Dickson, 153–64. Portsmouth, NH: Boynton/Cook.

Tannen, Deborah. 1993. "What's in a Frame: Surface Evidence of Underlying Expectations." In *Framing in Discourse,* ed. Deborah Tannen, 14–52. New York: Oxford University Press.

Wertsch, James. 1991. *Voices of the Mind: A Sociocultural Approach to Mediated Actions.* Cambridge: Harvard University Press.

Witte, Stephen, and Jennifer Flach. 1994. "Notes toward the Assessments of Advanced Ability to Communicate." *Assessing Writing* 1: 207–46.

Zebroski, James Thomas. 1994. *Thinking through Theory: Vygotskian Perspectives on the Teaching of Writing.* Portsmouth, NH: Boynton/Cook.

III Supporting the Writing of Dual-Language Students

Our classrooms are increasingly multicultural in two ways: Students born in the United States come from many different cultural or ethnic groups, some of them speaking home and neighborhood languages or dialects that are different from mainstream English; and students who have immigrated from many different countries bringing their own languages as well as diverse cultural and social practices and political ideologies. The authors in Part III seek to increase our understanding and respect for these dialects, languages, and cultures. They offer advice on how we might help these students move from the language and discourse they bring to the classroom toward mainstream conventions, genres, and rhetorical stances. The authors focus not so much on error or control of the conventions of Standard Edited English as on cultural understandings, gains in oral language, and learning about diverse writing situations or genres. They recognize that speakers of nonstandard dialects and of other languages must struggle for years to master the conventions of English, but they insist that this struggle must go on simultaneously with broad cultural and composing instruction.

Arnetha Ball, in Chapter 11, is concerned with helping all English teachers better understand the language of their African American students who speak African American Vernacular English (AAVE), a dialect of global English spoken by "many—though by no means all—lower- and working-class African American youth throughout the United States and . . . by many African American adults . . . [among] family and close friends." Early in her chapter she offers a richly detailed linguistic description of an essay by an AAVE-speaking high school student. From this description comes a table that teachers will almost certainly find helpful when evaluating writing influenced by AAVE. This table explains the AAVE features of nineteen different expressions in the student essay, a partial but nevertheless very useful introduction to the linguistic features of AAVE. Asking the question about what teachers can do to broaden this student's control of written registers and genres, Ball offers a "reconceptualization" of the writing conference and outlines several principles that might guide our evaluations of AAVE-speaking students' writing. She urges teachers to take the time to study what linguists have discovered about the home dialects spoken by students.

Guadalupe Valdés and Patricia Sanders, in Chapter 12, aim to help non-ESL teachers understand the writing difficulties faced by recent Latino immigrants and to improve mainstream course support for these students' writing development. Valdés and Sanders report results from an impressive two-year study of two middle school students who arrived in the United States with "zero" English. They describe in detail the instruction these students received and their development as writers during the two-year period. (The larger study included eight students.) Relying on sixteen separate writing samples, Valdés and Sanders document how one student made little progress as a writer while the other made impressive progress. These two stories are extremely revealing about the chances for literacy development of immigrant students who must start out in ESL classes. From the study came a seven-level description of stages in the writing development of students learning English that all writing teachers will find interesting and useful. At the conclusion of their chapter, the authors provide guidelines for evaluating the writing of students like those in the study.

Guanjun Cai, in Chapter 13, demonstrates how the writing in English of students from other cultures can be influenced by the social, political, and ideological perspectives that make up a world view. Relying on the college coursework of a Chinese student in the United States, Cai demonstrates how, even after she achieves fluency and correctness in written English, her writing continues to reflect fundamental aspects of the Chinese culture of her formative years in the 1970s and 1980s. Cai's impressive command of Chinese cultural history, particularly the history of writing, enables him to contrast clearly the social and political perspectives in one of the student's essays with the expectations of her American instructor. Cai argues that teachers need to acknowledge and respect immigrants' cultural and rhetorical traditions—a particular challenge when the traditions are non-Western—and to help them learn more about American culture and American readers' expectations.

11 Evaluating the Writing of Culturally and Linguistically Diverse Students: The Case of the African American Vernacular English Speaker

Arnetha F. Ball
University of Michigan

> Our secret language extended our understanding . . . and gave us the freedom to speak to our brothers . . . ; we polished our new words, caressed them, gave them new shape and color, a new order and tempo, until, though they were the words of the Lords of the Land, they became *our* words, *our* language.
>
> —Richard Wright (1941, 40)

In 1979 a federal court judge in Detroit ruled that to meet federal guidelines for nondiscrimination, a school must consider the language of a student's home culture, even when that language varies from the linguistic system used by most middle-class Americans. The challenge for teachers then and now has been to find ways to support the learning of all students in a culturally and linguistically diverse society. Teachers' long-standing concern has been to develop evaluation practices that promote equity in opportunity and accessibility to learning for individuals across the social boundaries of class and ethnicity. Acting upon this concern can be difficult, however, for many teachers feel overwhelmed when faced with the task of evaluating the writing of students who speak African American Vernacular English (AAVE), a linguistic system used by more than twenty million African Americans in the United States. Sociolinguists use the term AAVE to refer to the highly consistent grammar, pronunciation, and lexicon that is the first dialect learned by many—although by no means all—lower- and working-class African American youth throughout the United States, and is used in much the same way by many African American adults in their most intimate settings with family and friends (Labov 1969).

AAVE is a linguistic system that many teachers may not fully understand. Often, teachers encounter what Richard Wright refers to as a "secret language"—one that, although similar to academic English in many ways, is extended to include new words, new shapes, colors, order, and tempo. Wright expounds on his notion of a "secret language" by explaining that many lower- and working-class African Americans have developed a language that, among other things, "assigns to common, simple words new meanings"—meanings that enable AAVE speakers to communicate in the presence of non-AAVE speakers without those other speakers being aware of subtle meanings (1941, 40). Most teachers, including many African American teachers, are unaware of the subtle features that characterize AAVE as a distinct linguistic system.

Generally, those who have not been socialized with AAVE styles of rhetoric, traditions of linguistic creativity, uses of African and English words and grammatical constructions in intimate communications, or traditions of African American preaching fail to fully understand that these experiences influence the linguistic practices of AAVE-speaking students. Sarah Michaels (1987) refers to some of these practices when describing some of the oral strategies African Americans use, including implicit linking of topics in the discourse, shifts in focus, and topic relationships which must be inferred by the message receiver. Teachers encounter these linguistic practices every day when they serve students who are native speakers of AAVE, and many wonder how they can best evaluate or respond to these students' written texts. Although linguists and anthropologists have assured teachers that AAVE is a logical language with systematic patterns of expressions, many educators have trouble seeing and appreciating these patterns. Instead of patterns, they see only "mistakes"; instead of "efficacies"—powerful resources that are part of an oral tradition that students can use to produce an effect—they see only "errors." This is sometimes understandable since the writing of AAVE speakers, like the writing of any group of students, may indeed contain errors—features of language or organization that are, from any perspective, mistakes that need to be corrected. But sometimes what seems like a simple error may be more than that. It may be part of a linguistic code that has considerable social or cultural value.

This leaves teachers and evaluators with two questions: How can they distinguish between random instances of inept writing and valid, predictable, and systematic patterns that are a part of students' cultural and linguistic background? And how can they best work with students whose writing displays these patterns? We can all agree that our ultimate goal is to enable all students to express their ideas in a wide range of registers and discourse styles. But the question remains, how to accomplish this goal without causing some students to feel negative about the linguistic resources they bring from home. In an effort to begin answering these questions, this chapter brings together longstanding research on the oral and written linguistic behaviors of urban AAVE-speaking youth and recent research on their language use in classroom and nonclassroom settings.[1] It is divided into three parts. Part one provides a sample case study, focusing on a text written by an AAVE-speaking student. It also provides a brief historical review of how this student's text may have been evaluated in past decades, as well as current perspectives to guide an evaluation of the text today. Part two describes how the student's oral language features are reflected in the written text. Part three discusses key principles that underlie the successful work of several classroom and nonclassroom instructors as they provide students with opportunities to develop discourse behaviors that are appropriate in a variety of contexts—behaviors that empower students as they attempt to cross borders between familiar and unfamiliar discourses.

My interest in the evaluation of the writing of culturally and linguistically diverse students stems from my experience as a classroom teacher, bidialectal African American, and university researcher. Before becoming a university professor, I taught preschool, elementary, secondary, and postsecondary students for more than fifteen years. Those experiences, in conjunction with my recent collaborations with secondary classroom teachers and community-based organization leaders, provide me with countless examples of the linguistic properties of today's AAVE speakers that writing instructors seek to understand. They also provide numerous examples of students and teachers who are frustrated by the history of failure and miscommunication that marks the writing experiences of AAVE speakers. Fortunately, the writing profession is undergoing a period of change and reformation. This chapter provides some useful principles for addressing changes that can help writing instructors who seek to support students in their writing.

A Sample Case Study: Historical and Present-day Perspectives for Looking at Students' Texts

In order to provide a brief review of how a student's text may have been evaluated from a range of historic and present-day perspectives, I asked a dear friend and writing teacher with whom I have been collaborating for more than a year to give me a student's paper that she found to be particularly challenging. I wanted a text that this exceptional, European American teacher found interesting—one that she was drawn to—yet one that she found difficult to understand. Following is the paper that my friend shared with me. This paper, written for a creative writing class portfolio by an AAVE-speaking high school sophomore, proved to be particularly suitable for my purposes because it revealed an unusually wide range of features commonly found in AAVE oral language:

"On The Corner"

(1) Down on the corner at the store on Holister sometimes the
(2) Arabs call this man says things that shouldn't be said like
(3) "Nigger." The man is tall with a little fuzz on his chin. Bugs
(4) say things like "Go get a job Nigger." Everything he says
(5) and has "Nigger" at the end of it. Doug be trying to tell and
(6) make him do something and dogging Doug out but then
(7) sometimes they do him with respect but I say to Bugs
(8) sometimes "Don't say that." I'll say "don't say that because
(9) that ain't cool." The Arabs keep saying that and I'll get mad
(10) and madder because the Black man don't do or say nothing
(11) but "thats all right." He will say some jokes and smile about
(12) it. He willn't call me a nigga. I'll whip his "ass" because I
(13) don't say anything for him to say that nigga or other things
(14) bout me. Back to the Black man he don't say anything for
(15) him to call him a nigger either. Well the Arab look kinda big
(16) with a lot of fuzz and fat. Bugs wear his gear everyday. He
(17) will look and look like you will still. Then bout 11:00 pm
(18) then everyone will go home from chilling on the corner and
(19) talk to your homies.

The paper, "On The Corner," was the final draft of a short story written by Jelani, an African American male who attended high school in a West Coast metropolitan area. The public high school that he attended served approximately 2,500 students from primarily lower- and working-class communities. The school's student body was approximately 35 percent African American, 30 percent Latino, 30 percent Asian American, and 5 percent European American and other. Approximately 20 percent of the teachers at the school were persons of color.

The teacher assigned the writing of a short story retelling an incident, in one or two pages, about a time when the students experienced prejudice. In writing their fictional account of the incident, the students were free to skip long introductions, far-reaching conclusions, and almost all plot advancement. Instead, they were to focus on the heart of the story, vividly describing exactly what happened by appealing to the five senses, using nouns and verbs, and dialogue to show the reader what was on the author's mind. This version of the story followed the teacher's written notations on multiple drafts, three writing conferences with the teacher, and workshop sessions with his peers, study hall supervisors, and computer lab paraprofessionals. Even with evidence of support from concerned adults and peers, Jelani's text poses a number of challenges to the reader. Some of those challenges emanate from the fact that Jelani uses African American Vernacular English (AAVE).

Historically, researchers and educators have viewed AAVE primarily from four perspectives: those of language deficit, language difference, language proficiency, and language resource. During the 1950s, the text would most likely have been viewed from a *cultural-deficit* or *deprivation-perspective*. From this perspective, "On The Corner" would be considered written by a speaker with a culture that was dissonant with and generally inferior to the culture of mainstream society, and the writer might be referred to a speech/language pathologist to have his language "fixed" or at least improved. This perspective implicitly denied the legitimacy of AAVE and attempted to eradicate it.

During the late 1960s, "On The Corner" might have been viewed from a *language-difference perspective*. From this perspective, the text would be considered written by a speaker with a language system that was not deficient but, rather, different from other varieties of American English. This perspective concluded that AAVE was indeed systematic, structured, and rule governed. However, because it was assumed that contrasts between AAVE and global (mainstream, academic, middle-class) English caused AAVE-speaking students to produce large numbers of unacceptable sentences in oral language and written compositions, "On The Corner" would most likely have been viewed as reflecting a dialect interference. Since proponents of this perspective failed to offer teachers practical strategies for evaluating AAVE speakers' writing, most teachers' behavior remained unchanged. In fact, the tendency to focus on AAVE as interfering with other varieties of English demonstrated the continued view of AAVE as a negative influence.

During the 1970s, "On The Corner" might have been viewed from a *dialect-proficiency perspective*. This perspective went beyond the general goal of arguing for the adequacy of the AAVE speaker's linguistic system, and illustrated that African American students possessed a sophisticated knowledge of the grammatical, phonological, and speech-community norms of both AAVE and global English. Many educators and scholars referred to this ability to communicate in two varieties as "bidialectalism." As a result, many educators may have used second-language methodology as a model for instructing students to write "On

The Corner" in academic English as a second dialect for AAVE speakers. The proponents of this perspective advocated bidialectalism as an educational goal for African American students.

Since the 1980s, "On The Corner" might be viewed from a *language-resource perspective*. This perspective builds on sociocognitive and sociocultural views of writing evaluation and pedagogy, and recognizes that students bring language resources to the classroom in the form of different patterns of discourse from which everyone can learn. Attempts to develop formal and academic language skills from the discourse patterns students bring to the classroom, while maintaining the student's culturally influenced language skills, have become more common as educators design systematic approaches to written composition that serve to broaden the range of acceptable writing patterns. Proponents of sociocognitive and sociocultural perspectives advocate the building of bridges, rather than barriers, between the language resources students bring to the classroom and the skills teachers want students to learn. They encourage instructors to note characteristic patterns in spoken AAVE and to use them as scaffolding devices to improve students' writing (Applebee and Langer 1983). Suggestions about how this scaffolding might be constructed are discussed in the later sections of this chapter.

Guided by these sociocognitive and sociocultural perspectives, today's writing instructors are beginning to recognize the accomplishments in texts written by AAVE speakers. For example, teachers might recognize that the author of "On The Corner" demonstrated mastery of the academic rules of punctuation and capitalization and that he completed the assignment and turned it in. They might also recognize that this student has remained somewhat focused on his topic, expressed an account of a series of complex social activities, and successfully captured a variety of personal reactions to the episode being discussed. Guided by these perspectives, today's writing instructors can view the skills that students bring to the classroom as language resources rather than deficits.

Description of Oral Language Patterns in "On The Corner"

According to Georgia García and David Pearson, one of the keys to meeting the assessment needs of a diverse student population is a "dramatically improved teacher knowledge base" (1991, 254). In order to become knowledgeable, teachers need an understanding of what is already known about the characteristic patterns in the spoken linguistic systems of their students. This step is crucially important for improving evaluation and the instructional process. A close examination of the written text by this AAVE speaker reveals four oral language influences: (1) syntactic patterns (the student's grammatical choices); (2) semantic patterns (the student's vocabulary or word choices); (3) phonological patterns (spelling variations); and (4) stylistic patterns (the student's discourse styles and expressions).

Syntactic Patterns

Some speakers of AAVE do not use the third-person singular, present-tense inflection. In lines 4, 15, and 16 of "On The Corner," Jelani uses forms of third-person singular that are characteristic of the AAVE syntactic linguistic system, e.g., "Bugs say__," "the Arab look__"; and "Bugs wear__his gear." Since AAVE does not require the use of the -*s* present-tense marking following a third-person singular, Jelani does not use one in these instances. Although final [s] and [z] both function as noun plural, noun possessive, or third-person singular, present-tense markers in global English and in AAVE, the likelihood of their being present in the surface structure of an AAVE speaker depends on their function. While most AAVE speakers seem to use -*s* to indicate the noun possessive, plural, and present tense (e.g., the dog's food; four cats; cuts), many do not use the third-person singular form (e.g., he say__). Since [s] is used only for the third-person singular present (she walks, but I, you, we, they walk), the verb inflection -*s* really does not indicate tense so much as the "number" in global English. But even here it is redundant. The fact that we are talking about more than one thing is usually indicated by a noun, not by the verb, to communicate effectively. Some speakers of AAVE, therefore, do not use the third-person singular, present-tense inflection at all. Others use a verb inflection that on first sight seems to correspond to the global English one, but it is used with all persons (e.g., "I walks" and "they walks") and in fact functions as a present-tense marker, not as an indicator of whether the noun is singular or plural. For AAVE speakers who use the -*s* as a present-tense marker, the verb inflection may or may not be present. In helping students acquire global English, teachers must be aware that AAVE speakers have to learn not only to use the form more frequently, but also to assign a different function to the inflection. Elsewhere I have discussed how explicit instruction that clearly pointed out the form and function of the verb singular -*s* morpheme effectively enhanced students' use of this morpheme (Ball 1995b). This research also confirms that, when teaching other -*s* morphemes to AAVE speakers, more interactive techniques like a literature-based approach to instruction may be more effective than using techniques that draw heavily on worksheets and explicit instructional models.

In line 5 of "On The Corner," Jelani uses what is referred to as the "habitual *be*" in AAVE when he writes "Doug *be* trying to tell." In the global English variety, only adverbs are used to distinguish something that happens on an ongoing basis from something that does not. In AAVE, however, the distinction can be made by using the "habitual *be*" Thus, an AAVE speaker might say, "Doug be trying to tell . . .", while a global English speaker might say, "Doug is often trying to tell. . . ." The habitual *be* is most often used where a speaker of global English might use adverbs like *sometimes, often, always,* and *whenever.*

There is another "invariant *be*" with quite a different function—that of expressing intention in AAVE. Jelani's *be* in the phrase "Doug be trying to tell . . ." could also be interpreted as meaning that "Doug is intent on trying to tell . . ." or that "Doug has the intention of trying to tell. . . ." Many European American speakers do not understand this *be* unless they know AAVE well. This form of *be* usage originated in the pidgin and Creole languages spoken by African American slaves in the seventeenth and eighteenth centuries.

Another characteristic of AAVE is the inflected *be*-verb, frequently called a "copula." The copula is not often present in the surface structure of AAVE if it signals present tense. Consequently, the form "The man is tall" seems somewhat formal in line 3 of Jelani's text. Although the word "is" is most common in AAVE following a full noun phrase like "the man," the form used more often in casual AAVE speech is "He tall." When I inquired about the formal nature of this line, Jelani's teacher told me that he added this sentence to his text after her repeated requests for more vivid descriptions that showed the reader what was on his mind.

Line 10 of "On The Corner" contains an example of the AAVE system of using multiple negation, particularly common in AAVE. In other English varieties, multiple negation is largely used for emphasis, as in "Nobody doesn't like Sara Lee." For such speakers the multiple negation is optional. However, for some speakers of AAVE, it is nonemphatic and required, which seems to be the case for Jelani when he uses the phrase "the Black man don't do or say nothing. . . ." Those who proscribe multiple negation on the grounds that two negatives make an affirmative (just as two minuses make a plus in mathematics) are confusing surface structure with underlying function.

Line 11 of "On The Corner" contains another feature of AAVE syntax: where AAVE uses "There's . . . , It's . . . , or That's . . . " as a device for making an indefinite noun phrase the theme in certain sentences. In the sentence "Thats all right," *that's* is usually pronounced [das] (with "long s"). This form appears not to be understood as "that" plus contracted "is," but rather as a unit word, "das," that functions as an indefinite subject of the sentence.

Semantic Patterns

Much broader and more in-depth than an ethnic slang, the AAVE semantic system represents African Americans' longstanding historical tendency to appropriate English for themselves and their purposes. AAVE semantics is broadly conceived to encompass the totality of idioms, terms, and expressions that are commonly used by African Americans. Geneva Smitherman (1977, 35–72) notes that there are over-arching principles that describe the general characteristics of contem-porary African American semantics. African Americans' semantic patterns have traditionally crossed generational and class lines, and are grounded in the common linguistic and cultural history of their West African language background and experiences of oppression, music, and the traditional black church.

Lines 6, 12, 16, 18, and 19 of "On The Corner" display varying exam-ples of the AAVE semantic system. When a global English word like "dog" is used in an African American semantic pattern, the word is given an African American interpretation, and the range of interpreta-tions for this word increases. In line 6 of "On The Corner," the word *dog* could mean "to degenerate morally or physically" or "to have an unhappy or harassed existence." The use of the words *chilling* in line 18, meaning to relax, and *gear* in line 16 are similar cases of AAVE speakers' tendencies to give broadened interpretive meanings to words. Judging from the word's context, Jelani's use of *gear* could have several possible meanings. It could refer to a name brand of shoe wear, the tra-ditional dress or clothing of the Arab, or, more likely, a gun or other type of weapon.

The AAVE practice of transforming words to have multiple levels of meaning holds true for the use of curse words and the word *nigger*. In African American semantics, curse words take on multiple meanings and purposes and are often used as either a complimentary term, an obscenity, a term denoting negative personal characteristics, or an empty word or filler in a communication. In African American semantics, the word *nigger* holds negative connotations when used by European Amer-icans, as in lines 3, 4, 5, 12, 13, and 15 in "On The Corner." But when used by an African American, it can be regarded as either a term of endearment or solidarity, an expression of disapproval of one's actions, or a neutral reference to all persons of African American descent.

Many African American semantic terms are used as in-group terms that are appropriately used by African Americans to refer to other African Americans, e.g., *homies* in line 19 of Jelani's text. Use of such terms by most European Americans would be inappropriate and considered an act of overfamiliarity. Generally speaking, when African American semantic terms are adopted into the American mainstream of vocabulary, they serve to enrich the general language of all Americans. Words like *dig* (to understand or appreciate), *mean* (a positive reference to an extraordinary person or event), and *fat mouth* (to talk too much) have come into global English from AAVE. When this adoption takes place, however, the words usually lose their linguistic value in the African American community and are replaced by other words. For example, when middle-class Americans began using the term *cool* on a regular basis, AAVE speakers sharply decreased their use of the term. Not long thereafter, African American youth began to use the term *fresh* or *fonkie fresh*, which had a similar meaning to the term used earlier, *cool*. Thus, new terms are constantly being coined and African American semantics are in a constant, dynamic state of change.

Phonological Patterns

AAVE has been recognized as a linguistic system with phonological features that distinguish it from global English. Research indicates characteristic features that tend to be found more consistently and more frequently in AAVE than in global English. For example, AAVE speakers tend to systematically pronounce the /th/ sounds differently from global English speakers. Lines 14, 15, and 17 of "On The Corner" contain instances where characteristic phonological patterns of AAVE exemplify themselves as spelling variations, e.g., *bout* for *about, kinda* for *kind of,* and *still* for *steal* in Jelani's written text. AAVE speakers generally have patterns of usage that differ from global English speakers for the following sounds: *r*'s that follow vowels (e.g., *po'* rather than *poor*); use of *-in* rather than *ing* for the present participle (e.g., *runnin'* rather than *running*); voiced and voiceless *th* sounds in the word-initial and word-final position (e.g., *dem* or *mouf* rather than *them* or *mouth*); word-final *l* (e.g., *ol'* rather than *old*); and word-final consonant clusters like *st* (e.g., *tes* rather than *test*). As Bruce Cronnell (1973) demonstrates, these phonological patterns are especially likely to appear in the writing of very young children, accounting for 61 percent of the spelling variations in the work of AAVE second graders. Patrick Groff (1979), however, found that by the middle grades, few features of AAVE continued to have a significant effect on AAVE-speaking students' spelling patterns. Those AAVE-related spelling patterns that do persist into the middle grades include words that rhyme with *spill*, words that have the suffix *ed*, and words that end in *s* (64–75). Consistent with this finding, Jelani spells the word *steal* as *still* in line 17 of his text. Lines 14, 15, 17 of "On The Corner" exemplify instances of what might be a universal phenomenon of rapid speech, when unstressed vowel sounds are not attended to in the spelling of words, e.g., *bout* for *about* and *kinda* for *kind of.*

In line 12 of "On The Corner," Jelani uses the sentence, "He willn't call me a nigga." This author's use of *willn't* may be an example of what Walt Wolfram and Marcia Whiteman (1971) refer to as the phenomenon called "hypercorrection." Hypercorrection results from the writer's attempt to produce academic patterns with which he or she is not completely familiar. Because of this unfamiliarity, the writer incorporates items not only where they are appropriate, but in inappropriate places as well. This phenomenon appears in spelling, vocabulary choices, and syntactic structures, and is not exclusive to AAVE speakers.

Stylistic Patterns

Research confirms that systematic differences in language and discourse styles are evidenced in African American populations as a result of cultural experiences. Variations in style include the AAVE speakers' use of ritualized ways of expressing their ideas. Line 12 of "On The Corner" contains an example of the AAVE stylistic forms called "boasting" and "bragging." These terms refer to vocal self-praise or claims to superiority over others. African American boasting is a source of humor, not intended to be taken seriously. In AAVE these exaggerated claims of self-praise or superiority need not correspond with reality, and there is no obligation that their truth be proved. For example, "I'm so fast, I can hit you before God gets the news" is a phrase made famous by the former heavyweight boxing champion of the world, Muhammad Ali (see Smitherman 1977). Unlike boasting, African American bragging is a serious form of self-aggrandizement that has an element of accountability present. African Americans view bragging about one's abilities somewhat negatively unless the bragger is capable of demonstrating the claims. Under those circumstances, the bragger is viewed with admiration, e.g., "No brag, just fact." Bragging about one's possessions, social achievement, or children, on the other hand, is viewed negatively even though the claim may be true (Kochman 1981, 61–73). Jelani's use of the phrases "He willn't call me a nigga. I'll whip his 'ass'" in line 12 could fall into either of these categories, depending on the seriousness of the writer.

Table 1 summarizes how a wide range of oral language features of AAVE are reflected in "On The Corner." Organizing the information

from "On The Corner" in such a grid can assist teachers during the evaluation process to make clear distinctions between random errors in the
student's written texts and patterns of expression that are a reflection
of the student's culturally influenced oral-language patterns. Using
such a rubric to illustrate both the AAVE and global English features
of the text, teachers can also note those features that have been mastered during the course of the term as well as those that require further work. Such a system of representation and interactive communication
can help students and teachers learn more about language while
improving writing skills.

"On The Corner" contains some further examples of ways of expressing ideas that are particularly common in the oral and written discourse
of AAVE speakers. When I discussed this text with my teaching colleague, she expressed particular concern because she felt that Jelani's
writing lacked sophistication in its organizational structure: "He simply presents a series of events—and then there was this . . . and then
there was this." She also felt that Jelani did not clearly express what
was going on inside his head so that she could share the same picture.
Finally, she had difficulty following Jelani's use of characters. Bugs, for
example, is never introduced. Because of my colleague's familiarity
with the syntactic, semantic, and phonological patterns of AAVE, she
was more concerned about the stylistic aspects of the student's text at
the discourse level that she did not fully understand. After several
readings of the text, we concluded that Jelani was combining a narrative about a specific event with a representational text—one that makes
a generalization about tendencies in two different social groups. The
text is presented in a style that closely resembles oral discourse: the non-
introduction of characters, false starts (e.g., "sometimes the Arabs call
this man says things that shouldn't be said"), and jumping from the
generalized "Arabs" to the specific Arab, "Bugs," are all more characteristic of oral discourse that had been written. In the global English
variety, this text may seem to lack an organizational pattern. In AAVE,
however, Jelani makes use of some patterns that are preferred by many
African American high school students.

An earlier research study that I conducted showed that, although
preferences for written organizational patterns do not differ substan-
tially among students in the lower grades, they differ significantly
among African American and non-African American high school students (Ball 1992). Although 73 percent of the non-African American
high school students in this study indicated preferences for using academic, literacy-based patterns for organizing written texts for school,
none of the African American students indicated this preference. In

Table 1

Explanations of Variations in Writing Forms Used by Jelani, the
AAVE-Speaking Author of "On The Corner"

Line #	Expression Used by Student	Characteristic Feature of AAVE that Explains the Expression	Reference for Further Reading
Line 4	"Bugs say"	Third-person singular	Lourie 1978
Line 5	"Doug be trying to tell"	Habitual *be*	Baugh 1980
Line 6	"dogging Doug out"	African American semantics	Smitherman 1977
Line 9	"that ain't cool"	Negation	Lourie 1978
Line 10	"don't do or say nothing"	Multiple negation	Lourie 1978
Line 11	"Thats all right"	Thematizing an indefinite noun phrase with a locative	Traugott and Pratt 1980
Line 12	"He willn't"	Hypercorrection	Wolfram and Whiteman 1971
Line 12	"nigga"	African American semantics [Note the distinction in the author's use of the word "Nigger" when he quotes the Arab and his use of "nigga" when he quotes a fellow AAVE speaker]	Smitherman 1977
Line 12	"He willn't call me a nigga. I'll whip his 'ass'"	Boasting and bragging	Kochman 1981
Line 14	"bout me"	Phonology	Lourie 1978
Line 14	"Back to the Black man"	Indicates topic shift or change in focus of the discourse	Michaels 1987
Line 14	"the Black man he"	Repetition of the noun	Lourie 1978
Line 15	"the Arab look"	Third-person singular	Lourie 1978
Line 15	"kinda big"	Phonology	Lourie 1978
Line 16	"Bugs wear his gear"	Third-person singular	Lourie 1978
Line 16	"wear his *gear*"	African American semantics	Smitherman 1977
Line 17	"look like you will *still*"	Phonology related spelling	Groff 1979
Line 18	"chilling on the corner"	African American semantics	Smitherman 1977
Line 19	"talk to your homies"	African American semantics	Smitherman 1977

fact, the African American high school students clearly indicated a preference for using oral-based patterns to organize their informal and academic texts. Jelani seems to prefer an oral-based style of communication as well.

In lines 1 to 17 of "On The Corner," Jelani talks about his experiences with Arabs, using strategies commonly found in AAVE. Frederick Erickson (1984) discusses coherence strategies used in conversations among African American adolescents—strategies they use to achieve underlying connectedness in representations of their knowledge of the world. He defines coherence as the "underlying organizing structure making the words and sentences into a unified discourse that has cultural significance for those who create or comprehend it" (xiv). His discussion makes it clear that in several story forms used in the African American speech community, adolescents use coherence devices that rely heavily on a shared understanding. In these story forms it is not necessary to state the underlying point explicitly—indeed, that would be inappropriate. Students also rely on strategies that include the presentation of explanation and argumentation through anecdotes and "rhapsodizing," that is, the stitching together of topics by drawing on a shared knowledge of the commonplace (91). Erickson notes that this shared knowledge of commonplaces between message sender and audience is an essential feature of persuasion in the African American speech community. The message sender must invoke symbolic solidarity with the audience in order to persuade. When Jelani talks about his experiences with the Arab, he is drawing on retellings of experiences involving commerce with proprietors of other ethnic groups that are assumed commonplace knowledge among many African Americans. Like the African American subjects in Erickson's research, Jelani uses an anecdote as a metaphorically concrete manifestation of an underlying abstract concept, in this case prejudice. For Jelani, the commonplace experience of having an Arab proprietor "calling me a nigga" is a metaphor for experiencing "prejudice."

The teacher's assignment was for Jelani to write a short story retelling an incident, in one or two pages, about a time when he experienced prejudice. Erickson's (1984) research and Heath's (1983) work point out that some AAVE-speaking students may respond to such assignments in the form of anecdotes, metaphors, and similes rather than in detailed descriptions. Heath notes that "Trackton children . . . never volunteered to list the attributes. . . . They seem, instead, to have a gestalt, a highly contextualized view, of objects which they compare without sorting out the particular single features of the object itself" (107). When my friend and colleague was pulling her hair out to get Jelani to give more details that appealed to the five senses by using nouns and verbs, I was reminded of the comment made by the Trackton grandmother:

> "We don't talk to our chil'rn like you folks do. We don't ask 'em 'bout colors, names, 'n things." AAVE speakers do not attend to bits and pieces of the world. Instead, they use among themselves, and direct to their children, analogy questions and requests for non-specific comparisons of time, events, and persons. (Heath 1983, 109)

Although the information provided in the analysis of "On The Corner" is by no means an exhaustive account of the complex linguistic system referred to as AAVE, it does serve to illustrate some obvious implications for writing instructors. This analysis provides a brief overview of some of the information composition teachers need to be aware of (concerning systematic differences in AAVE and global English patterns of expression) when they consider oral patterns that frequently occur in students' written texts. Such background information is needed in order for teachers to consider ways of expanding the range of discourse patterns students use in the classroom. Evaluation practices can improve as teachers become better able to distinguish random instances of poor writing from predictable, valid, and systematic patterns of expression that are culturally based. The information gained from our analysis of "On The Corner" helped my colleague and me in our efforts to interpret Jelani's text. It is important to note, however, that even after being prepared with this knowledge, my friend and I still found "On The Corner" to be a particularly challenging text to interpret. The complexities of gaining a full understanding of this student's text went beyond the boundaries of Jelani's use of AAVE oral-characteristic features in his writing. Other key principles also proved helpful in our efforts to accomplish this task.

Key Principles for Working with Students

Recognizing how the characteristic patterns of students' spoken language are reflected in their written texts is one key principle that underlies the successful evaluation of students' writing. Another key principle is the notion of expanding the role of writing conferences to include opportunities for teachers and students to better understand each others' intentions and visions for constructing a successful text. Using the writing conference to share basic assumptions and to develop common background knowledge is an important step when working with culturally and linguistically diverse students. Still other key principles that underlie the successful evaluation of students' writing can be gained by observing the strategies of professionals that work with students in non-school contexts, e.g., in community-based organizations.

Reconceptualizing the Writing Conference

A valuable source for gaining a better understanding of the AAVE features students use is through an expanded conceptualization of the writing conference. For teachers to gain the information they need about students' language, writing conferences must become centers for dynamic, free-flowing exchanges of ideas between students and teachers. Writing conferences should serve not only as places where skilled teachers provide students with guidance that is directed, encouraging, and validating, but also as places where social and cultural perspectives are shared. "Writing to" students about what they have done in their papers is not enough. AAVE-speaking students must be conferenced "with" and told about what they have done, what features are influencing their cultural patterns of communication, and what new features teachers want them to incorporate into their ever-broadening range of resources. Writing conferences must also become places where students can feel free to respond to teacher inquiries without censure; where they can express their intentions and purposes in creating a text; where they can absorb new knowledge through open-ended discussions; and where students can inform receptive adults. During student-teacher writing conferences, patterns once unconscious to the AAVE-speaking writer, foreign to the average writing instructor, and thus judged as incorrect can be understood in light of shared social, cultural, and linguistic experiences that enhance evaluation and pedagogy.

Working with students on their uses of style and discourse conventions has been a primary source of frustration for many writing teachers. This area of concern provides an excellent example of when information gained through literature reviews and an expanded conceptualization of the writing conference can be most useful. Familiarity with the research of Erickson (1984) (discussed earlier in the section on stylistic patterns) helps us understand how Jelani uses an anecdote as a metaphorically concrete manifestation of an underlying abstract concept, in this case, prejudice. For Jelani, the commonplace experience of having an Arab proprietor "calling me a nigga" is a metaphor for experiencing "prejudice." Within the context of a writing conference, this subtlety could be discussed and shared between the student and teacher. Then, together, they could investigate the relationships between Jelani's informal language patterns and the demands of academic discourse in schools by exploring ways to help Jelani use a wider variety of discourse patterns to express his ideas and experiences.

My research (Ball 1992, discussed earlier) on students' preferred patterns of organization helps us understand how Jelani seems to prefer an oral-based style of communication. "On The Corner" would be more comprehensible to global English speakers with the help of facial expressions, tonal emphasis, gestures, self-corrections, and pauses. The question remains, however, "How can teachers help students who are more comfortable with oral forms of discourse, whether AAVE speakers or not, to go from 'oral' to 'written' forms that are more restrictive codes of expression?" A writing conference in which the teacher asks the student a few probing questions would help the teacher arrive at a fuller understanding of the writer's intentions when using the oral code. The student could then be given strategies or tools that will assist him in producing a more detailed transcription of his message. For example, Jelani might be encouraged to use ellipses to indicate a pause, italics to indicate emphasis, and bolding to indicate loudness or intensity. This coaching could most efficiently take place within the context of a writing conference, but by all means, it must take place on an individual basis because we realize that, although this student is an AAVE speaker, he is first and foremost a unique individual.

Principles that Should Guide Our Evaluations

Erickson, Heath, and Ball's analyses of the coherence strategies, styles, and preferred organization patterns demonstrate that in African American adolescents' discourse styles, writing instructors are confronted with a fully developed, internally coherent, and entirely effective rhetorical system when used in in-group communications. But the question remains, "So what? What can writing instructors do with the texts they receive from these students? What principles should guide evaluation?" Several concrete suggestions come to mind. First, we can begin by heeding the advice of Baugh (1981) to develop attitudes of ethnosensitivity—viewing social topics and practices from the cultural perspectives of students who come from cohesive social groups. Next we can recognize that the development of new assessment forms will not, in and of themselves, improve the evaluation process. Such an improvement requires a new multicultural awareness among writing instructors in general. In particular, it requires that teachers learn about the linguistic practices of their students. Such knowledge would allow teachers to situate or contextualize student assessments (García and Pearson 1991, 254). I have discussed some ways to improve teachers' knowledge: through a review of the literature diligently developed over the decades to provide a more complex, more complete linguistic profile of African American linguistic behavior and through analyses of students' writing to become aware of the systematic differences in AAVE and global English patterns present in their texts. Once this expanded knowledge base is established, teachers can situate or contextualize student assessments using information gained from their expanded conceptualization of writing conferences.

Prepared with this information, teachers are empowered to accept, and even celebrate, the texts produced by their AAVE-speaking students that strongly reflect the oral characteristic features of their cultural language. This is especially appropriate in the early stages of the writing course and whenever the use of global or academic English is not a part of the particular assignment. As the course progresses, teachers should expect, and again celebrate, the presence of a mixture of AAVE and academic features in students' texts since this variation is an indication that students are experimenting with what they are learning.

At this stage of the course it is best that teachers refrain from focusing too heavily on word choice and surface-level features of students' writing, but rather on larger strategies for improving students' writing abilities and broadening their range of writing experiences. Teachers should specify a limited number of goals or skills they are focusing on for each assignment and should evaluate students' ability to demonstrate mastery of those specific goals. At the more advanced levels of the writing course, teachers should hold students responsible for using a wide range of writing styles that have been taught and practiced in response to an array of specific, authentic assignments. Finally, it is important that three significant points remain foremost in teachers' minds when evaluating the writing of diverse students. First, many variations in students' writing patterns are not random, but are influenced by the patterns of the students' spoken language. Second, students, although members of culturally and linguistically diverse communities, are individuals, and their individuality will also be reflected in their writing patterns. Third, some of the variation in students' writing can be attributed to cultural influences while others cannot—it will be the teacher's responsibility to distinguish between these two on the basis of the teacher's knowledge of the students' cultural and linguistic practices.

Some Additional Keys to Supporting the Writing of
AAVE-Speaking Students

As we critically consider our role in facilitating, supporting, and evaluating the writing of culturally and linguistically diverse students, we realize that once we understand the features of AAVE, we understand that good teaching for African American students can be much the same as good teaching for any group of students. One part of my research involves systematic observations of several classroom and nonclassroom instructors as they provide students with opportunities to develop discourse behaviors that are appropriate in a variety of contexts— behaviors that empower students as they attempt to cross borders between new and different learning and work environments. Through my observations of these instructors, I have found five key principles that underlie the creation of successful writing and assessment contexts for all students:

1. Give students numerous opportunities for talk, learning, and skills development.

2. Ensure students' access to adult role models who support them with high expectations and opportunities to experiment with language-interaction models. These high expectations should reflect not only standards of the dominant society, but also standards of the students' subcultures as they attempt to interpret appropriate communicative behaviors in different contexts and create successful contexts for learning.

3. Provide structured environments in which exchanges of interactive discourse take place along with a wide variety of activities to motivate talking, writing, and communication in other modes.

4. Stress collaboration, negotiation, responsibility, and commitment.

5. Model appropriate language use in and for a wide variety of learning, work-related, and social contexts that encourage students to develop and practice discourse behaviors that work for them as they explore new horizons.

My most recent research involves conducting investigations into the worlds of community-based organizations and analyzing the interactive, transitioning uses of discourse that go on among AAVE-speaking participants and group leaders in four different community-based classrooms (Ball 1993, 1995a). This research investigates language and literacy skills and resources that often go unrecognized in mainstream institutions because of cultural differences in language-use patterns or styles of interaction individuals use to demonstrate their knowledge. Tentative findings reveal some key principles modeled in successful community-based organizations that might be useful to writing instructors who work with diverse populations. Successful learning environments allow participants to see themselves as responsible contributors in a dynamic language environment that allows them to question the status quo, give answers in areas where they feel a sense of accomplishment and achievement, respond without censure, absorb new knowledge through experience, and disseminate knowledge among accepting adults and peers. In one successful environment after another, I have observed dynamic, free-flowing exchanges of ideas: ongoing dialogues that go along with skilled guidance that is directed, encouraging, and validating. I have observed group leaders giving students the words they need to hear: "Look what you have done here! Here are the things that are influenced by your own cultural patterns. Here are the things you did well, and here are some new features that I'd like to see you incorporate into your ever-broadening range of resources." In the successful writing classrooms I observed, these exchanges often took place within the context of writing conferences.

Although community-based organizations remain largely invisible and unacknowledged as positive environments for learning in our society, this research illustrates how organizations like community-based job-training programs, rites-of-passage programs, and neighborhood youth dance programs provide structured, predictable, and challenging environments in which important activities take place that help prepare youths for more successful transitions in our society. These community-based programs provide opportunities for inner-city participants to see themselves as responsible, capable, and contributing members of a community-valued environment that allows them to question the limits of their present realities in ways their families and schools often do not.

Taken together, the key principles that underlie the successful work of classroom and non-classroom instructors can be summarized within three domains: principles that should be applied before encountering students, during interactions with students, and when we are responding to or evaluating texts. Principles that should be applied before our encounters with students include acknowledging students' individuality, developing attitudes of ethnosensitivity, recognizing a broad region of validity when considering linguistic styles, and developing a better knowledge base about diverse language patterns. Principles that should be applied during interactions with students include giving students opportunities for talk, ensuring models of diverse language patterns, providing structured—yet supportive—learning environments, stressing collaboration, and making available shifting types of communicative activities. Principles that should be applied when responding to or evaluating students' texts include remembering that many variations are not "errors," encouraging students to experiment early in the composing process, and holding them accountable for using a wide range of styles in their linguistic representations. These tasks may appear overwhelming at first glance, but they will become more manageable as we realize that all of the responsibility does not rest on the classroom teacher. Responsibility is shared as teachers allow themselves to learn from their fellow colleagues, community members, and from the students themselves.

Conclusions

The past three decades have been active ones for educators and scholars who have devoted their work to the goals of educational parity in a pluralistic society. Because of their accomplishments, the writing profession is undergoing a period of change and reform. In the spirit of that reform, this chapter raises some important questions about how we can best support the writing of diverse students. Although we should be cautious about seeking to provide definitive answers to questions about the *one* best way to evaluate the writing performance of diverse students, I have highlighted some useful principles for change that can help writing instructors who seek to evaluate and support students in their writing experiences.

Many of today's writing instructors are seeking ways to improve their evaluation and instructional practices. Examples provided by exemplary writing classrooms and community-based organizations demonstrate that teachers can, indeed, support students by stressing important socialization skills like collaboration, negotiation, responsibility, and high expectations, and by indicating a recognition of and respect for their culturally influenced patterns. This support begins with teachers making their everyday instructional and evaluation practices conform to what is known about language learning, language structure, and language variation, and by throwing out old practices that have been based on questionable results. Support for the writing of culturally and linguistically diverse students can best be initiated, first, by recognizing that students' oral cultural experiences will affect their writing patterns. Once acknowledged, then, second, teachers must make overt and aggressive efforts to learn more about students' language varieties. As teachers learn more about students' language varieties as well as their individual patterns and needs, they can, third, begin to accept students' language variation in writing as evidence that students are experimenting with what they are learning. Fourth, teachers must focus not on word choice and surface-level features of students' writing, as much as on larger strategies for improving students' writing abilities and broadening their range of writing experiences. Finally, in addition to analyzing students' texts to discover oral features of students' cultural expressions that influence the written text, teachers can learn to broaden the region of validity for student text productions through an expanded conceptualization of the writing conference. Here, the writing conference becomes a dynamic, free-flowing exchange of ideas where skilled teachers provide guidance that is directed, encouraging, and validating and where students unlock the power of their writing by sharing the "secrets" of their language. In doing so, both students and teachers gain an understanding of their language, empowering both to cross new bridges in the educational experience.

Recommended Reading

A more exhaustive understanding of the characteristic features of AAVE can be gained through a study of the works of Roger Abrahams (1970, 1976), Ball (1992), Baugh (1983a, 1883b), Joey Dillard (1972), Erickson (1984), Ralph Fasold and Walt Wolfram (1970), Shirley Brice Heath (1983), Thomas Kochman (1981), William Labov (1972), and Smitherman (1977). Margaret Lourie (1978) and Traugott and Pratt (1980, 325–34) provide useful summaries of many of the characteristic features of AAVE as well.

Note

1. I am indebted to Keith Denning, Jennifer Massen, and Caroline Taylor Clark for their collaboration, support, and encouragement in the development of this chapter. I am also especially grateful to the community-based organizations' participants and group leaders, classroom teachers, participating students, and especially Jelani (pseudonym). Without their cooperation and support, this chapter could not have been completed.

Works Cited

Abrahams, Roger. 1970. *Deep Down in the Jungle: Negro Narrative Folklore from the Streets of Philadelphia.* Hatboro, PA: Folklore Associates.

———. 1976. *Talking Black.* Rowley, MA: Newbury House.

Applebee, Arthur, and Judith Langer. 1983. "Instructional Scaffolding: Reading and Writing as Natural Language Activities." *Language Arts* 60 (2): 168–75.

Ball, Arnetha F. 1992. "Cultural Preference and the Expository Writing of African-American Adolescents." *Written Communication* 9 (4): 501–32.

———. 1993. "Community-based Discourse, Neighborhood-based Organizations, and African American Adolescents' Transitions to the Workplace: What Writing Professionals Can Learn." Paper presented April, 1993 at the Annual Conference of the Conference on College Composition and Communication. San Diego, CA.

———. 1995a. "Community-based Learning in Urban Settings as a Model for Educational Reform." *Applied Behavioral Science Review* 3 (2): 127–46.

———. 1995b. "Language, Learning, and Linguistic Competence of African-American Children: Torrey Revisited." *Linguistics and Education* 7 (1): 23–46.

Baugh, John. 1980. "A Re-examination of the Black English Copula." In *Locating Language in Time and Space,* ed. William Labov, 83–106. New York: Academic Press.

———. 1981. "Design and Implementation of Writing Instruction for Speakers of Non-Standard English: Perspectives for a National Neighborhood Literacy Program." In *The Writing Needs of Linguistically Different Students,* ed. Bruce Cronnell, 17–44. Los Alamitos, CA: Southwest Regional Laboratory Education Research and Development.

———. 1983a. *Black Street Speech: Its History, Structure, and Survival.* Austin: University of Texas Press.

———. 1983b. "A Survey of Afro-American English." *Annual Review of Anthropology* 12: 335–54.

Cronnell, Bruce A. 1973. "Black English and the Spelling of Final Consonant Clusters." *Dissertation Abstracts International* 34: 3015A–16A.

Delpit, Lisa D. 1992. "Education in a Multicultural Society: Our Future's Greatest Challenge." *Journal of Negro Education* 61 (3): 237–49.

Dillard, Joey L. 1972. *Black English: Its History and Usage in the United States.* New York: Random House.

Erickson, Frederick. 1984. "Rhetoric, Anecdote, and Rhapsody: Coherence Strategies in a Conversation among Black American Adolescents." In *Coherence in Spoken and Written Discourse,* ed. Deborah Tannen, 81–154. Norwood, NJ: Ablex.

Fasold, Ralph, W., and Walt A. Wolfram. 1970. "Some Linguistic Features of Negro Dialect." In *Teaching Standard English in the Inner-City,* ed. Ralph W. Fasold and Roger W. Shuy. Washington, DC: Center for Applied Linguistics.

García, Georgia E., and P. David Pearson. 1991. "The Role of Assessment in a Diverse Society." In *Literacy for a Diverse Society,* ed. Elfrieda H. Hiebert, 253–78. New York: Teachers College Press.

Groff, Patrick. 1979. "Black English and the Teaching of Spelling." In *Teaching the Linguistically Diverse,* ed. Judy I. Schwartz, 64–75. New York State English Council Monograph. New York: New York State English Council.

Heath, Shirley B. 1983. *Ways with Words: Language, Life, and Work in Communities and Classrooms.* New York: Cambridge University Press.

Kochman, Thomas. 1981. *Black and White Styles in Conflict.* Chicago: University of Chicago Press.

Labov, William. 1969. "The Logic of Non-Standard English." In *Report of the 21st Annual Round Table on Linguistics and Language Studies,* Monograph Series on Language and Linguistics 23, ed. J. E. Altis. Washington, DC: Georgetown University Press.

————. 1972. *Language in the Inner-City: Studies in the Black English Vernacular.* Philadelphia: University of Pennsylvania Press.

Lourie, Margaret A. 1978. "Black English." In *A Pluralistic Nation: The Language Issue in the United States,* ed. Margaret A. Lourie and Nancy F. Conklin, 78–92. Rowley, MA: Newbury House.

Michaels, Sarah. 1987. "'Sharing Time': Children's Narrative Styles and Differential Access to Literacy." *Language in Society,* 10: 423–42.

Robinson, Jay L. 1990. "The Wall of Babel; or, Up Against the Language Barrier." In *Conversations on the Written Word: Essays on Language and Literacy,* ed. Jay L. Robinson, 53–91. Portsmouth, NH: Boynton/Cook-Heinemann.

Smitherman, Geneva. 1977. *Talkin' and Testifyin': The Language of Black America.* Boston: Houghton Mifflin.

Traugott, Elizabeth C., and Mary L. Pratt. 1980. *Linguistics for Students of Literature.* New York: Harcourt Brace Jovanovich.

Whiteman, Marcia F. 1970. *Dialect Influence and the Writing of Black Working-Class Americans.* Ph.D. Diss., Georgetown University.

Wolfram, Walt A., and Marcia F. Whiteman. 1971. "The Role of Dialect Interference in Composition." *Florida FL Reporter* 9 (1/2): 34–38, 59.

Wright, Richard. 1941. *12 Million Black Voices.* New York: Thunder's Mouth Press.

12 Latino ESL Students and the Development of Writing Abilities

Guadalupe Valdés
Stanford University

Patricia Anloff Sanders
Jane Lathrop Stanford Middle School, Palo Alto, California

ESL Students in American High Schools

Elisa and Bernardo, the students whose texts we will present in this paper, are young people of Latino background who arrived in this country speaking only Spanish. They enrolled in a middle school in California in the greater San Franciso Bay Area, and they bravely began their struggle to learn English to acquire an education. Both of these children, however, were and are at risk. Indeed, as is the case in countries worldwide, children who do not speak the language in which schooling is conducted face grave difficulties in obtaining an education.

Currently, newly arrived, immigrant Latino students who enter American schools at the middle school and secondary levels face particularly difficult circumstances (LaFontaine 1987; Davis and McDaid 1992; Minicucci and Olsen 1992; Chamot 1992; Rumbaut 1990; Chamot 1992a; Portes and Gran 1991). Schools, especially those that until recently served mainstream English-speaking populations, are unprepared to work with large numbers of very different students who often have had little access to quality education in their own countries.

For the most part, schools have dealt with "the problem" in similar ways. They have expanded their ESL programs; they have instituted "sheltered" instruction[1] in some subjects; and, in some cases, they have even provided instruction in non-English languages in a limited number of subject areas. New teachers (ESL specialists, language-development

249

specialists) are being hired to teach these "different" students, while established, existing faculty concentrate on the often dwindling number of "mainstream" students.

The dilemma facing schools is a difficult one. In many schools, for example, there are currently two separate worlds: the world of ESL and the mainstream world in which "real" American schooling takes place. In the best of cases, even when they are "mainstreamed" in other subject-matter classes, few nonnative, English-language-background students ever manage to enroll in what has become the most permanent barrier to college preparatory study for immigrant students: the *regular* (non-ESL) English class.

Indeed, while viewed by many as a positive step forward, the current national focus on writing and on the development of writing skills has led to what may be an untenable situation for those students in American schools whose first language is not English. Because of the emphasis on writing and on the development of writing abilities, English teachers often see themselves as incapable of working with students who are not native-like in their English-language abilities. Their training has not prepared them to "teach" those students who, although they may have learned everything that ESL classes in the school had to teach them, are still in the process of acquiring the language fully.

The purpose of this paper is to offer a guide for "regular" teachers of English composition who come into contact with nonnative, ESL-background students and who have many questions about what these students are like, what abilities they bring with them, and what kinds of practices make sense. The paper presents results of a study carried out in three middle schools during a two-year period and provides a description of the writing instruction currently available for non-English-background students. Especially, we will focus on two middle school students who arrived in this country with what we term "zero" English. Through a description of the instruction they received and of the stages of development through which they went as writers of English, we hope to present a vivid picture of both the needs and competencies of ESL students in general and to suggest how "mainstream" non-ESL teachers of composition can work successfully with these apparently "different" students.

The Study

The study[2] from which data will be presented here was designed to fill a gap in the existing literature on the writing of non-English-background students and at the same time to contribute directly to describing the levels that can generally be attained after two years by newly arrived, immigrant students who enroll in secondary school programs. It focused on a total of eight newly arrived, immigrant middle school students who enrolled in English-medium schools for the first time. In the tradition of other scholars who have investigated writing and the development of writing in schools (e.g., Dyson 1989, 1993; Edelsky, 1986), the study followed these students across a two-year period and sought to describe the stages of growth and development of their English-language proficiency within the academic context.[3] Specifically, the study focused on the growth of these students' English language and writing abilities in fine detail.

Writing Development and Developmental Levels

For this paper, we have selected two of the eight students we followed in the larger study in order to describe the development of their writing abilities We have selected Bernardo, a serious and dedicated student who made little progress in English-language growth, and Elisa, a successful, well-liked student who made impressive progress in her English-language abilities. We believe that the contrast between these two very different students illustrates both the problems faced by these youngsters as well as the promise and rewards that teachers can discover in working with non-English-background students.

The writing abilities of the focal students discussed here developed in both interesting and unexpected ways. In order to depict this development more precisely, we have elaborated a set of descriptions of the abilities revealed by students at different stages. This set of descriptions is included in Table 1.

It is important to point out that these descriptive statements focus on what students are able to do and *not* do. Moreover, these descriptions consider students' performance in the areas of communication, organization, and mechanics. They are less concerned with the type of text (cards, lists, letters) produced by students than with the communicative functions students were able to carry out in writing. More important, perhaps, these descriptions attempt to offer more detail about the kinds of functions that students were able carry out in attempting to respond to the writing demands made in the school setting.

In presenting this set of descriptions, it is our purpose to try to capture some of the many features present in the writing of our focal students as well as the abilities and proficiencies reflected in their writing. We must emphasize the fact, however, that these descriptions are based on a study of writing abilities that students developed in instructional

Table 1

Description of Levels of Developing Writing Abilities
in L2 Students

Levels	Communicative Tasks Performed	Organization	Mechanics
Level 1	Displays familiarity with English words.	Writes lists of familiar English words.	Spells some words correctly. Uses Spanish spelling conventions to spell English words.
Level 2	Attempts to display information.	Writes simple unconnected sentences that he/she can produce orally. May attempt to write by translating from L1.	Sentences reflect transfer from student's L1. Spelling errors are frequent. Uses Spanish spelling conventions to spell English words. Does not attend to capitalization and punctuation.
Level 3	Provides limited personal information. Recounts personal experiences with little detail.	Can write very short connected discourse (two or three sentences) on topics about which he or she can produce conected oral discourse (e.g., family, self, school). Can imitate some elements of models of written language presented to him or her.	Sentences continue to reflect transfer from student's L1. Does not attend to capitalization and punctuation. Spelling errors are frequent. May still use Spanish spelling conventions to spell English words. Writing may reflect oral language pronunciation resulting in both spelling errors and non-native like features.

Continued on next page

Table 1 continued

Levels	Communicative Tasks Performed	Organization	Mechanics
Level 4	Displays limited amounts of personal and general information. Explains at a very basic level. Summarizes at a very basic level. Recounts personal experience with more detail.	Can write short connected discourse (a paragraph) on a limited number of academic topics about which he/she can produce connected oral discourse.	Sentences continue to reflect transfer from student's L1. Begins to attend to capitalization and/or punctuation. Spelling errors are frequent. Writing may still reflect oral language pronunciation, resulting in both spelling errors and nonnative like features.
Level 5	Displays larger amounts of information. Explains giving more detail. Summarizes giving more detail. Recounts personal experience with greater detail. Expresses personal perspective to a limited degree. Attempts to give reasons for personal perspective.	Can write longer segments of connected discourse. Writes single, very long paragraphs. Includes many unrelated ideas in the same paragraph.	Sentences continue to reflect transfer from student's L1. Some basic syntactic patterns are still not mastered. Begins to write compound sentences. Capitalization and punctuation are still not mastered. Uses an exclusively oral style.

Continued on next page

Table 1 continued

Levels	Communicative Tasks Performed	Organization	Mechanics
Level 6	Displays information to show that she knows to show that she read. Explains giving more detail. Summarizes giving more detail. Recounts personal experience with greater detail. Expresses personal perspective clearly. Gives some reasons for personal perspective.	Demonstrates little or no audience awareness. Has little notion of text organization but begins to use several "paragraphs." Continues to include unrelated ideas in the same paragraph. Uses idiosyncratic, unconventional criteria for selection of supporting details.	Sentences continue to reflect transfer from student's L1, but basic syntactic patterns have been mastered. Punctuation may still not be mastered. Uses an exclusively oral style.
Level 7	Displays information to show that she knows to show that she read. Explains more fully. Summarizes more fully. Recounts personal experience with greater detail. Narrates with some skill. Expresses personal opinion clearly and confidently. Justifies position. Expresses feelings in writing.	Sense of audience begins to develop. Growing sense of text organization emerges.	Growing ability to choose language for its precise meanings begins to emerge. Awareness of variety of styles used in writing for different purposes emerges.

programs that were often less than ideal and that were not directly concerned with writing.

What we can say by using the descriptors in Table 1 is that our two students (Bernardo and Elisa) initially began as Level 1 writers. In the educational settings we have described in this report, one of our students (Bernardo) developed limited writing abilities characteristic of Level 3 by the end of the two-year period. The other student, Elisa, reached Level 7.

Opportunity to Learn: Writing Instruction in the ESL Classroom

The two students whose writings we will present here began their study of English in a traditional ESL classroom taught by Mrs. Gordon.[4] Bernardo remained in this classroom during the two years of our observations and acquired a limited amount of English proficiency during that period. Elisa, although she also remained in the same school, used every opportunity to interact with English-speaking peers and pushed to be moved into regular classes. Her control of oral English developed quite rapidly.

In examining both the development of English-language proficiency as well as the development of writing abilities, it is important to examine the school context and the opportunities afforded to students both to acquire English and to develop writing abilities in this language. If students have little access to English, they will not learn either to speak or to understand the language. Similarly, if students rarely write for genuine reasons, we cannot expect that they will develop the ability to carry out communicative tasks in writing.

Summarizing broadly, Eliza and Bernado had little opportunity to develop writing abilities in their ESL classroom. This was not because Mrs. Gordon was not an excellent teacher. She was, in fact, a well-intentioned teacher who had much to offer to her students and who had strong beliefs about the ways in which language was learned and should be taught. Very specifically, she followed a grammar syllabus and believed strongly in error correction. Free composition concerned her because she feared that students would produce many more errors than she could correct, given their limited knowledge of English. She, therefore, tried to guide her students into producing sentences that were grammatically correct. In order to do so, she involved students in a very controlled composition process in which she wrote sentences on the board and asked students to fill in blanks in sentences with their "own" information. For such "composition" activities, Mrs. Gordon generally offered a frame such as

Capuchin monkeys _____.

She also provided a set of elements that could be placed in the blank. For the capuchin monkey piece, for example, the following elements were written on the board:

breaking nuts on branches

live in the jungle in trees

live in South America

medium size monkeys

can jump from one tree to another

black and white monkeys

As will be apparent from the above example, students who could manipulate these basic structures by adding needed elements actually produced grammatically correct sentences. Low-level students, however, simply copied the structures and produced sentences such as

Capuchin monkeys breaking nuts on branches.

Capuchin monkeys black and white monkeys

In general, when students had little interest in the topic on which they were "writing," activities such as this produced little frustration. Students simply did as they were told and copied sentences from the board. These activities resulted in almost identical papers written by different members of the class.

From the beginning—as our detailed description will make clear—Bernardo and Elisa differed in their response to these writing tasks. Bernardo slavishly followed the model and greatly pleased his teacher. Elisa, on the other hand, constantly tried to add "real" information and her own interpretation of the writing task. Consistently, Elisa's efforts met with disapproval from Mrs. Gordon. She did not view Elisa's original writing attempts as progress in finding her own voice. Rather, in commenting on Elisa's compositions, she focused on the large number of "errors" present in the text and stated that Elisa needed to control English structure better before she became carried away with content.

Bernardo

Bernardo's writing abilities in English developed slowly. At the time of the first assessment in May 1992[5] (after he had been in the United

> pele have friends   played soccer
> pele he played for the New York   Pele
> played his first   Pele He became a
> millionaire   He was the most famous

Figure 1. Bernardo: Sample 1 (5/92).

> fader eat the beibi have pencil sister

Figure 2. Bernardo: Sample 2 (5/92).

States for five months), Bernardo produced the two pieces of writing shown in Figures 1 and 2.

The first sample was produced in response to our request that he write about a reading in English that he read as a part of the language assessment administered to all focal students. Bernardo was allowed to refer to the reading as he wrote. As will be noted, Bernardo appeared to be copying directly from the text, and in one instance, it is possible that he did not understand exactly what he was copying. This is suggested by the fact that he left the sentence "Pelé played his first" unfinished.

Bernardo's limitations were far more evident, however, in the second example, when he was asked to write about his school or his family. At this point in his English language development, Bernardo was only able to write a list of words across the page. The list includes two verbs (*eat, have*) and several nouns (*fader, beibi, pencil, sister*) as well as an article (*the*). Bernardo made no attempt, however, to construct complete sentences. Bernardo used Spanish spelling conventions to spell English words. He wrote *fader* and *beibi* for *father* and *baby*. However, he also used conventional English spelling.

During the second year of the study, Bernardo spent his time filling in worksheets that accompanied the New Horizons series used in the traditional teachers' classes. Frequently, however, he wrote assignments such as that in Figure 3.

What is interesting here is that Bernardo was conjugating English verbs incorrectly. Moreover, he was inconsistent in his use of sentence-final punctuation as well as capitalization. Moreover, as was the case when the teacher provided stimulus sentences for controlled composition activities, some of the sentences produced by Bernardo were ungrammatical.

```
30
30
60 sentences                          Bernardo Salas
                                       Date Sept,28, 1992

I write a book.                        I write a letter.
you write a book.                      you write a letter.
He write a book.                       He write a letter
She write a book.                      She write a letter
They write a book                      They write a letter

I write a music                        I eat a banana.
you write a music                      you eat a banana.
He write a music                       He eat a banana.
She write a music                      She eat a banana.
They write a music                     They eat a banana.

I eat a sandwich?                      I eat a ice cream cone
you eat a sandwich?                    you eat a ice cream cone
He eat a sandwich?                     He eat a ice cream cone
She eat a sandwich?                    She eat a ice cream cone
They eat a sandwich?                   They eat a ice cream cone
```

Figure 3. Bernardo: Sample 3 (9/92).

For Assessment III (the second assessment carried out of Bernardo's English-language proficiency), Bernardo wrote the piece in Figure 4.

Here, Bernardo displays some ability to construct sentences in English and to produce these sentences in writing. He is able to communicate four ideas about himself, which in standard English would read

My name is Bernardo Salas

I am 13. (Bernardo's *have 13* is a literal translation of the Spanish *tengo 13* [años].)

I like to play soccer.

I love my father, mother, sisters, cousin and uncle.

After approximately one year of schooling in the United States, Bernardo could provide limited information about himself in English in written form. The information, however, might not be comprehensible to persons who are not familiar with the writing of nonnative speakers of English.

Dec. ,1992

Bernardo
Mi name is Bernardo Salas have
13 I'm lake play soccer.
Mi love fathe, mothe, sisters
counsin and uncle.

Figure 4. Bernardo: Sample 7 (12/92).

It is important to point out that instruction in Bernardo's ESL class was not directed at helping students to develop specific functional abilities such as requesting information, providing information, recounting an event, summarizing material read, etc. During the same period that Bernardo wrote sample 7 for our assessment, in class he was normally writing material such as that in Figure 5.

By the second semester of the second year (January to May of 1993), however, the teacher began work on a "long" autobiographical piece. For this autobiographical piece, the teacher had introduced a prewriting activity involving semantic mapping. She handed out blank maps to all students and then proceeded to help them fill out the various categories. Bernardo's map is included in Figure 6.

Again, the teacher wrote vocabulary words on the board that students could copy to fill in their various categories. As will be apparent, some

Bernardo Salas   Today is Monday
                                Date 12-14-92

1. This is my hair.
2. These are my eyes.
3. This is my nose.
4. This is my mouth.
5. This is my foot.
6. This is my school.
7. This is my room.
8. This is my teacher.
9. These are my friends

Figure 5. Bernardo: Sample 8 (12/92).

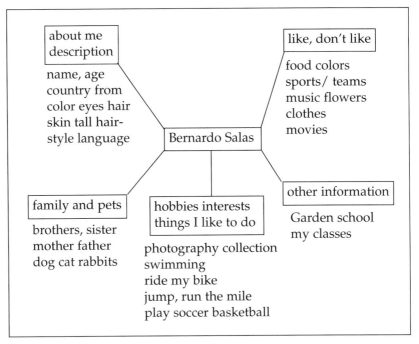

about me
description

name, age
country from
color eyes hair
skin tall hair-
style language

Bernardo Salas

like, don't like

food colors
sports/ teams
music flowers
clothes
movies

family and pets

brothers, sister
mother father
dog cat rabbits

hobbies interests
things I like to do

photography collection
swimming
ride my bike
jump, run the mile
play soccer basketball

other information

Garden school
my classes

Figure 6. Bernardo's semantic map.

of the suggested subcategories made assumptions about the students' lives that were somewhat questionable and revealed the teacher's lack of familiarity with the lives of her students. In our experience, new immigrant students who live in poverty do not have either pets or hobbies.

Once again, even when using a process approach to writing, the teacher did not trust her students to create or communicate their own meanings. As will be evident from the final draft of the piece produced by Bernardo (Figure 7), she still controlled the content of the students' papers to a very large degree.

At this point in Bernardo's development, he was able to talk about a variety of the categories included on his semantic map. It is evident, however, that he was not writing entirely independently. Nevertheless, he was indeed able to include genuine information about himself, his activities, and his friends. Even though he was confused about the format of the assignment, and even though he included some letter-like elements, it was Bernardo's first attempt to say something real in writing. With a bit of effort, the reader of this piece (Figure 7) is able to learn that Bernardo is a sports enthusiast. He appears to be familiar with several teams, and he reports that he plays soccer with a group of friends, whom he lists.

My name is Bernardo Salas.
I am 14 year old my color
of my eyes are brown my leg is long
my skin is brown my hair is
black and white my favorite is
language I like play soccer my
favorite color is green, red, blue I like
the jump, run the mile my favorite
teams is raiders. Do you like sports
What team did you like on football.
Do you like raiders. I like chicago bulls
on basketball. In Garden middle school
we have 36 rooms. We don't cat
in the classes I like the movies universal
soulder, vethoven, and the movie Delta
force I have two I like swimming with
my ancles, my father, friends every day my play
soccer in the school Cedars with Daniel,
Jose.m., Juan. E. Jesus landa and Alfredo my
food favorite is pizza of chese I have
my bike of color black and white
the school garden is big have
cafeteria, library

          Sencerely
          Bernardo Salas

Figure 7. Bernardo: Sample 11.

The piece is clearly disorganized. Bernardo has little notion of paragraph development or paragraph unity. This is not surprising because neither Bernardo nor his classmates received instruction about these matters. Until this assignment was presented, the students had been writing lists of numbered sentences on a single topic.

Bernardo's Writing Development: A Summary

Overall, Bernardo's writing development moved slowly. At the end of a two-year period in which he had been enrolled primarily in ESL core classes (three periods) and in art, cooking, and PE, Bernardo had reached only a very beginning level of writing proficiency. He could, for example, (1) write simple, unconnected sentences that he could produce orally; (2) write very short connected discourse on topics about which he could produce connected oral discourse (e.g., family, self, school); and (3) imitate some elements of models of written language presented to him. He often failed, however, to attend to capitalization and punctuation and other details that were included in the models. At best, he reached only our developmental Level 3 in Table 1.

Elisa

As compared with Bernardo, Elisa made an impressive amount of progress in her ability to write in English during the two years of the study. As was the case with all focal students, Elisa began by writing what appeared to be a list of single words in English. However, as will be evident from a closer look at Figure 8, Elisa was really writing a series of sentences that read: *Thes tha paper; Thes tha father; Thes tha mother.* She is consistent in her use of ditto marks under the original sentence as far as the word *baby.* Elisa also includes another complete sentence: *My mother is Magda.*

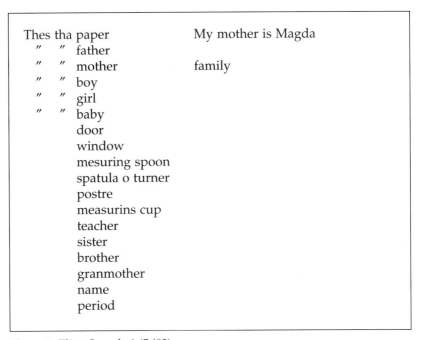

Figure 8. Elisa: Sample 1 (5/92).

As was the case with Bernardo, Elisa produced few writing samples during her first semester in the traditional ESL teacher's classroom. Most writing activities involved filling in worksheets or copying vocabulary and producing very controlled compositions. In the spring, Elisa wrote the piece in Figure 9 as part of a class project on national parks.

Compared with the other students' writing on national parks, Elisa's writing was quite superior. She was not following the teacher's controlled sentence structure, nor was she simply filling in blanks. In this piece, Elisa is displaying information, expressing a personal perspective, and giving a reason for her personal perspective.

It is important to note that by the time Elisa wrote her national parks project, she was able to produce connected discourse on a variety of familiar topics in English. Our assessment of her oral language made clear that, after nine months of schooling, Elisa was able to provide personal information, to role-play, and to read simple academic materials in English. She was able, for example, to provide an oral summary of what she read. In short, as compared with Bernardo, Elisa had made spectacular progress in her acquisition of listening comprehension and speaking abilities in English.

Elisa's progress in written English, while dramatic, was less spectacular. For example, her written summary of a reading on Barbra

---

Social Studies 1°3°   Elisa Lara
My favorite Park   5-3-92

I like Yellowstone National Park,
because in there is a beautiful
vision. Yellowstone Park is in three
state. They are Wyoming, Montana and
Idaho. There is a Interesting thing
like, boiling water, Old Faithful, water-
ful, the blue water in a pool and some
animals. The Old Faithful is very
Interesting for me because in every
hours shoot water. The Yellowstone
Park have a river and you can go
fishing. I think the Yellowstone
National Park was the first
Park in America or The United States.

Figure 9. Elisa: Sample 3 (5/92).

Streisand, produced during the second assessment of her English-language abilities, did not make evident that Elisa had understood what she read or even that she could discuss the reading orally. Seen by itself, Elisa's summary (Figure 10) seems even more problematic than her piece on Yellowstone National Park. In her summary, Elisa demonstrates *some* mastery of English structure, but she fails to communicate anything beyond the two sentences with which the reading itself began.

There is no evidence in this piece of writing that indicates that Elisa has the ability to display information, to react to it or evaluate it, or to justify such an evaluation. On the basis of this sample, one would be tempted to rate Elisa as a very beginning ESL writer. What needs to be taken into account, however, is that Elisa had had no experience in attempting to produce oral or written summaries. She did not know quite where to begin her summary of the content of what she had read about Barbra Streisand. Another possible factor influencing her performance was the timed nature of the assessment itself. Students were given approximately ten minutes to write summaries of what they had read.

The second writing sample produced as part of the second assessment revealed much more about Elisa's English-language proficiency. Here Elisa responded to the our request that she write about herself. She wrote about school and about why she liked going to school (Figure 11). Again, in this piece, Elisa was successful in expressing an opinion and in supporting a justification for her position. In this sample, it is evident that Elisa was writing what she could already say. Moreover, her written English reflects the spoken language directly.

As was pointed out earlier, this particular text reflects Elisa's confusion between spoken and written English. The use of *a* for *I*, for example, in

a learn a lot of English

a do (esperimin)

April, 1992
Barbra was a very ugly girl and she wanted
to be a actress but her wanted to she need to be
a secretary; Barbra wanted to learn dance but
her ~~dat~~ don't like to her daughter dace because
she think the is going to break.

Figure 10. Elisa: Sample 4 (4/92).

I like to came to the school because a
learn a lot of English.
and I learn to do art home a run
the mile and a do (esperimin) and I learn. Math.
and I learn a lot of things. and I want then
when I be big I have a good job.
another thing they a like to come to the school is
because I have a lot of ~~freinds~~ friends.
And because the teaches are very good.

Figure 11. Elisa: Sample 5 (4/92).

reveals that she produces a schwa-like sound for the pronoun *I* in speaking. She then transcribes this sound both as *a* and *I*. Transfer of native-language syntax is also evident here. Elisa uses an English subjunctive

> and I want then when *I be* big

to translate the Spanish subjunctive *(cuando sea grande)*.

This text is also characterized by small "errors" that would have passed undetected were one listening to Elisa's rapid speech in English. For example, Elisa wrote:

> another thing *they* a like to do

> the *teaches* are very good

In rapid speech, these small irregularities in Elisa's English would have been insignificant. An interlocutor speaking to Elisa would probably have "heard"

> another thing *that* I like to do

> the *teachers* are very good

Given her growing control of the language and her ability to communicate meaning, elements such as these generally went unnoticed in Elisa's speech. However, when writing in response to a task such as that required by Assessment II, Elisa reflected her oral language patterns and simply transcribed what she could say. This resulted in a set of very unique "errors."

During the second year, Elisa's desire to write independently became more evident. In the same month that she produced the Koko text for her ESL teacher, Elisa wrote the text included here as Figure 12 and turned it in to her science teacher for extra credit. Here, Elisa recounts

Silicon Ghaprics it a big company this company has a lot of buildings, we went to two buildings first we went to building sis, and the people who works there, they take us to a room where the presidents of the company has they meatings. And then we divide us in two groups and then my group went to the second building that was building two. They call building two   Human
                                                                    Factors
                                                                      Lab
in building two they talk what the company made? The campany made computers, and they also talk about what they do in building two. What they do is to test people to see how they do in computers. And they ask if someone of us wanted to try to do the test. Then we went to a room and there was two big t.v.'s and we was watching at him doing the test. And then we went to building to again and then I have the chance to play with the computer and it's very easy to play in that computer it was a very nice expeirence to meat people, learnd about computers They tell us some of the activitis they do. Every year competitive of the best video of the year. They show us the video and there was very good. I like did we meat some workers, there was the person who made the aplications her name is Mimi Celis. The secretery's name is Clara Colon. The engineer name is Pablo Sanches. The manufacturing's name is Velia Rico. The security's name is Hank Sisneros. All they tall us something about ther life.
Dwayne Corneleas/Product Demo.
Hi talk's about the Iris Indigo, and then hi show us a video about Moviemaking Tirers
T.V   Safety
Medical   Video
There are made it with computers
Hi also talk about his life.

Hi give us a talk on staying in school

the field trip end at
2:02
9-28-92

Figure 12. Elisa: Sample 7 (9/92).

an experience and provides information about a company located in Silicon Valley.

From one perspective, this text shows Elisa's strong continuing development in written English. This is a far longer text than those she produced previously. There is significant evidence here of increasing fluency.

On the other hand, from the perspective of organization and mechanics, this text appears to be quite flawed. It contains spelling, punctuation, and capitalization errors, and the direct reflection of Elisa's spoken English is quite evident. Elisa is using a completely oral style to write this report. Her notion of a written sentence, as opposed to a spoken utterance, is still developing.

For a number of reasons, it could be said that Elisa is writing beyond her competence. She has not acquired either the structures or the vocabulary essential for writing about this particular subject. More important, perhaps, this text is quite unfocused. The emphasis shifts from a strictly chronological recounting of the field trip to a number of different details. As a single paragraph, this long segment of text is incoherent.

However, considering the fact that Elisa had received no instruction on text organization and that she had been in the United States only one year, this text is quite exceptional in what it reveals about Elisa's potential and about the ways that limited-English-speaking students begin to write using their growing oral language abilities.

Figure 13 displays Elisa's ability to use the same strategy (writing what she could say) to prepare a report for her mainstream prealgebra class. This texts illustrates the kind of writing that is increasingly being required in middle school mathematics. Here, Elisa responds to her teacher's prompt and attempts to explain, show, and demonstrate the relationship between 1/2 and 50 percent. At this point in the second school year, Elisa was quite confident of her ability to express herself in all her classes. Perhaps because her writing had not been responded to negatively by any of her teachers (except, perhaps, by her ESL teacher), Elisa saw herself as a writer of English. She did not view writing as difficult or problematic. For Elisa, writing was simply written down speech. She was totally unaware of most writing conventions (e.g., paragraph development) and the fear of violating them appeared never to enter her thoughts.

In this text (Figure 13), Elisa selects a practical, familiar situation (shopping at Target) to explain the relationship in question. Once again, the piece has a number of problems. However, it is evident that Elisa can indeed explain and demonstrate using written English. It is

Math 2°   Elisa Lara
                                          2/10/93

Explain, show or Demonstrate the Relationship
between 1/2 and 50%. Do this in as many different
ways as you can.

She draws 4 of these proportions

The relationship between 1/2 and 50% is that 50%
of 1 pizza is the same than 1/2 of one pizza.
50% is half something, 1/2 is half of something too.

"Problem"
I only have forty dollars and I want to
buy a pair of jeans and a T shirt.
If I go to Target and I see a pair of jeans
that cost forty dollars, but now is on sale
for 50% off. That means that the jeans
cost half of the forty dollars, because 50% means
half of something. I saw a T shirt over
there in the corner that cost fourty dollars, but
now is 1/2 off. That means the same thing as
50% did for the jeans. Now I got what I wanted,
I have a pair of jeans, a T shirt, and
I only spent forty dollars. cool!!

Figure 13. Elisa: Sample 8 (2/93).

also evident that even without instruction on English-language structure directed at correcting her grammar, Elisa is now producing fewer
noticeably nonnative errors. In this text, what is most salient is her use
of colloquial English.

Elisa's growing sense of herself as a writer of English became
especially evident when she fell in love for the first time. The object
of her affections was a monolingual English-speaking youngster
whom she had met at a church social. Because they lived in different parts of the Bay Area, most or their relationship was carried out
in writing.

Figure 14 includes two versions of a prose poem that Elisa prepared to send to her friend Joshua. She shared this writing with us because she wanted us to see how well she was beginning to write. We suspected that the text was not entirely original.

By the spring of the second year of the study, then, Elisa believed that she could write in English. She sought opportunities to do so, and she produced different kinds of texts for her different classes, including reports, recipes, and recountings of events.

As will be noted, at the end of her second year in this country, Elisa was able to carry out a number of speech acts in writing. She could display information, recount events, express opinions, justify opinions, and express feelings. From an ESL perspective, that is, if one compares Elisa with most Latino students who have been here for only two years, her performance is exceptional. Nevertheless, some ESL teachers would possibly be concerned about her lack of grammatical accuracy. Others, however, seeing the continued acquisition of English structure without direct instruction, would feel confident that many of her "errors" would disappear over time.

From a mainstream perspective, however, Elisa's writing is quite problematic. Many regular English teachers, especially those who are not used to reading the writing of incipient and developing bilinguals, would perhaps not appreciate what Elisa has accomplished and what she might accomplish with good instruction in writing itself.

---

friend is a big gift that life give to people
And here I got, one of the bigest pressents,
you has a friend

If you could see trough my heart you would see a
light shining every singale minute that I think about you
this light means our friendship our beautiful
friend ship. And my heart and me, have decidedo to keep it.
And you know way? ~~We have dicided to keep it? WELL~~ becouse
you have been very nice ~~to me and very kind~~ and cool. to me
~~has never someone haven do that before~~
I hope we can be best friends for our whole life
Please don't let this light inside of me go away.

Figure 14. Elisa: Sample 9 (3/93).

Fortunately for Elisa, her first encounter with a mainstream English teacher was a positive one. During the summer of 1993, she enrolled in two summer school sessions of remedial English for native-speaking high school students. The teacher, an experienced professional committed to developing students' writing proficiency, encouraged Elisa's sense of herself as a competent writer, while pointing out some patterns and features in her writing that could be improved. Under Mrs. Carson's direction, Elisa produced texts such as the one in Figure 15.

In this text, Elisa is concentrating on writing vivid descriptions. One can see a clear growth in her ability to choose descriptive adjectives.

Gorilla
Last weekend I went to the zoo, I went to see the snakes first, then I saw the Gorillas at the other side, I saw all this people trying to see the Gorillas suddenly a boy had fell down in the Gorilla's cave or place. The Gorilla was far away but as sooniest it saw the boy, it started walking with its bit dirty feet, its hairy storng legs, its bouncing stomach, its long arms, hiting its schest making a loud noice, its black teeth, eyes and hairy head. I don't think it was a good experience for that little kid.

Figure 15. Elisa: Sample 13.

7/1/93
Mexican Wedding Cookies
Ingredients: 1/4 cup better
                   2 table spoon sugar   "oven 325°"
                   1/2 teas spoon water
                   1/2 teas spoon vanilla
                   1/2 cup sifted flour
                   1/4 cup chopped nuts
Put the butter/sugar blend it for a little bit then add water/vanilla. Blend. Add flour/nuts/ Blend untill mix and kind of soft if not thats ok. Put it in the refregirater for four hour or next day. Make cookies. Put them in the oven for 20 mintutes.
               When hot ROLL them in powdered
                            sugar.
               AND YOUR DONE!

Figure 16. Elisa: Sample 14 (7/93).

For the first time, Elisa appears to be conscious of how to use English for specific effects.

The recipe text included in Figure 16 displays another of Elisa's developing abilities. Here, once again, she writes directions as she might give them when speaking. In spite of the fact that she had read and used many recipes in English, she did not choose to imitate "standard" recipe language. The text demonstrates that Elisa can indeed give directions in written English, but it also reflects the fact that she has not focused on peculiarities of style that will be essential to her becoming a near-native speaker and writer of English.

In Figure 17, Elisa attempts to summarize a movie seen by the class in order to respond to the teacher's prompt, which asked for a discussion of the importance of the relationship between Mrs. Treadgood and Evelyn for the story told in the movie. As do many native-English-speaking beginning writers, Elisa begins by recounting the events in the story and perhaps assumes that the recounting itself is the main point of the writing. She responds superficially to the

---

Essay-Fried Green Tomatos
First Copy
English   Fried Green
Essay   Tomatoes

    The relationship between Mrs. Treadgood and Evelyn started when Evelyn went to visit her husband's sister which didn't like Evelyn at all.

    On day Evelyn was waiting for her husband that was inside in some room visiting with his sister, outside in a couch. Mrs. Treadgood was walking around when she saw Evelyn seating there in that couch alone Mrs. Threagood started talking to Evelyn when suddenly she end up telling Evenlyn a story about a young girl named Ijie.

    Evelyn would visit Mrs. Threadgood more often. During all that time Mrs. Threadgood would kept on telling Evelyn the story of Ijie. Suddenly they both realize that they were becaming good friends. Every time Evelyn visited Mrs. Treadgood she had bring something with her for Mrs. Treadgood. Kind of like a present for " " "

    The reason why this relationship is so important to this movie, its because it Mrs. Treadgood wouldn't have met Evelyn, the story wouldn't had been told.

Figure 17. Elisa: Sample 17.

teacher's question. In Gentile's (1992, 22) terms, this paper would perhaps be rated as an *attempted discussion* as follows:

> Paper includes several pieces of information and some range of information. In part of the paper, an attempt is made to relate some of the information (in a sentence or two) but relationships are not clearly established because ideas are incomplete or underdeveloped (the amount of explanation and details is limited).

In spite of its limited discussion, however, from a speech-act perspective, Elisa demonstrates, in Figure 17, that she is able to recount a story with some detail.

The final sample, Figure 18, is a rough draft for a longer paper. Here, Elisa's growing ability to talk about herself and her family is quite evident. Compared with where she began, a mere two years before, Elisa displays, in this paper, a good control of English syntax and morphology. She also displays an increasing sense of organization. The three

---

7/8/93

Family Essay   ＼ Rough Draft

My family is made by four people, my sister whose name is Evelyn, my mom whose name is Magda and my dad whose name is Roberto and of course me. We all live in an apartment, my sister and I have ~~(are)~~ our (on) own room and my mom and dad have own their room too, we also have a little kitty for a pet. My mom and dad are always working so we go to school and most of the time we're busy doing work at home.

Not all the members of my family are from Honduras. My dad is from Guatemala and has lived here for five years already. My mom is from Honduras and she has live here for eight years already. My sister and I have lived here for two years already.

From the background of my dad, I don't know anything but from my mom backgrounds' I do know some. My (greatgram) great grandma's name is Maria Jesus, and her two son's names are Antonio and Alberto, her daughder's name is Herlinda. Herlinda is my mom's mom, which that means that she's my grandma. Nobody has the same names in the family They all have different names. I don't know why.

(and I can't ask because my mom is in the Hospital)

Figure 18. Sample 18 (7/93).

paragraphs in the text indicate that Elisa has now acquired a sense of the fact that different paragraphs focus on different topics. Her second paragraph, for example, is limited to discussing the place of origin of members of her family and the time that they have been in this country. In the final paragraph, she speaks exclusively about her family background and extended family.

Elisa's Writing Development: A Summary

Overall, Elisa's writing development throughout the two-year period was impressive. She began by listing English words, and she ended by being able to perform a variety of communicative acts in writing. Her English itself improved over time, even though she did not receive direct instruction in English grammar directed at this purpose. The ESL instruction she did receive was limited to teaching basic English structure and vocabulary.

The greatest difference between Elisa and Bernardo is that Elisa learned to speak and understand English quite well. She had access to English in her mainstream classes at school and outside the school at church, with family friends, and with her dad. She spoke English daily for real-life purposes, and she was motivated to communicate with many people that she liked who were monolingual speakers of English.

For Elisa, writing in English was writing what she could already say. She approached writing as communication in written form and, at least in the beginning, considered success in writing to mean that she had been able to say what she truly wanted to say. She was not concerned about form or organization because she had little awareness of the importance of these two factors in academic writing.

In many ways, Elisa offers a profile of a student whose English-language writing abilities emerged almost by themselves. For Elisa, what was important is that she was encouraged—not discouraged—by her teachers, that she began to see herself as a writer, and that she began to use writing to express her feelings.

Now that Elisa is in mainstream classes, the question is whether she can develop rapidly enough the near-native abilities required for writing in present-day classrooms, so that she will not be returned to the often-marginalizing ESL program.

The Next Steps: Advice to Teachers of Composition

The work carried out with Latino ESL students allowed us to begin to describe the levels and stages of development that these students experienced during a two-year period and to offer to the profession a point of departure for working with limited-English-speaking students. While our descriptions reveal what is possible in two years for *some* students, they also reveal that growth takes place slowly and often involves small steps. For example, for one of the two students described in this paper, going from listing unrelated words to being able to display personal information in one or two sentences involved a period of two years.

If these descriptions are useful, it is that they can suggest that within two years, even students who start at zero can reach the point where they can carry out speech acts—like explaining, describing, and narrating—in writing. For Latino students, this was possible when these youngsters were able to acquire the ability to carry out these same speech acts in oral language. When they could display information orally, they were then able to begin to display this information in writing as well. What this implies is that it is important for teachers to help students to develop functional oral abilities in English. Once these are in place, they may provide—as they did for the students in this study—an important point of departure from which the teaching of writing can proceed.

For ESL teachers, the set of descriptions (Table 2) can serve as an indication of what is possible. For mainstream English teachers, these descriptions can suggest that, in spite of shortcomings in organization and in mechanics, students at Levels 6 and 7 can indeed communicate quite effectively in the written language. In a very direct way, the set of descriptions is also intended to suggest that for ESL students—as is the case with mainstream students—organization and mechanics are quite separate. Students can learn how to structure paragraphs even if they have not yet mastered the niceties of punctuation. More important, however, it appears that over time and even without direct instruction, many mechanical "errors" tend to work themselves out.

The following guidelines—used successfully by the second author of this paper—can serve as a point of departure for evaluating the writing of students whose English is still very much in the process of development. In assigning a grade to a paper, for example, teachers may want to take the following factors into account:

1. Did the student turn in the assignment?

    Initially, in beginning to work with ESL students, a teacher may want to "evaluate" their writing by focusing on the following basic questions: Did the student turn in the paper? Did the student complete the assignment? In responding to ESL students' papers, it is important to appreciate the very fact that the work was turned in.

For students who feel inadequate and insecure, doing the assignment and turning it in is a major first step. At the beginning of the year, for example, grades can be given simply on that basis. Students receive an S for turning in the assignment. The teacher may also respond to the paper as a sympathetic and interested reader.

2. Is the paper neat, and does it appear that the student carefully carried out the assignment?

    Teachers can also respond to assignments by focusing on appearance. Does the paper look neat? Does it look like the student cared about what she was turning in? Many students who have just arrived in this country need to be taught that in American schools, the appearance of papers turned in is very important. In grading, focusing on this one factor can do much to socialize students to this type of expectation.

3. Did the student follow directions?

    Grading can also reflect the degree to which students followed instructions about both the content and the organization of the assignment. Did the student write about trees if she was asked to do so? Did she write two paragraphs, or nine sentences, or whatever? Students—even at the point where they produce little English—can be expected to turn in writing assignments in which they attempted to say something about the topic assigned and to do so as instructed.

4. Is the student aware of basic patterns of organization?

    Very early in their ESL classes, students can be taught that writing in this country involves the linear presentation of information—that is, a topic is introduced, aspects of it are supported or elaborated, and ideas are brought together in some form of a conclusion. ESL students must be helped to see how texts work in English. It cannot be taken for granted that without explicit instruction, such students will come to understand that, in English, good texts have, for example, an introduction, a body, and a conclusion. After students have been taught basic patterns of organization, the evaluation of their writing can focus also on the degree to which they attempted to produce these patterns in writing their assignment.

5. Did the student communicate?

    When students begin to write in English, it is important to remember that they are trying to communicate meaning. Even in almost indecipherable passages, it is possible to see these attempts and to give students credit for communicating ideas. For example, in both Elisa and Bernardo's early attempts to write in English, a reader not used to the writing of beginning ESL students would possibly struggle to make sense of their passages. But a number of complete ideas were certainly present. For example, when Elisa wrote about Koko the gorilla and said that "She leard how to signs words and she know what is birthday mean," she was communicating important information about Koko. In spite of its imperfections, Elisa's writing clearly communicated that she had learned a great deal about this very famous gorilla.

6. Does the student's voice come through?

It is important to remember that even students who don't write well and who have an imperfect command of the language can still manage to produce writing that can "grab" at a teacher's heart. Listening for voice at these initial stages involves seeing whether the student attempts to let the reader know how she feels. Does he really love the dog that died? Does she really miss the grandmother who stayed behind? Again, attempts at expressing such feelings will be imperfect, but if the teacher is looking for voice, he or she can frequently find it in the writing of students who are still struggling with the language. What is needed is for the teacher to expect that the voice will be there and to read beyond the surface imperfections.

7. Is the student improving in his or her control of mechanics?

One approach to the evaluation of mechanics is to look for change and improvement over time. This approach takes the position that students will begin to apply rules of punctuation, capitalization, and the like as they are taught, but that it will take time for such aspects to be mastered entirely. Grades can reflect improvement or lack of improvement in this area.

8. Is the student improving in his or her control of the complexities of language?

Since native-like control of English develops slowly, it is frequently unproductive for teachers to mark all or most of students' morphological, syntactic, and idiomatic errors. However, the expectation that they will attempt to improve one or two aspects of English usage at a time (e.g., consistent use of *-ed* in past tenses) is a reasonable one. Grades can reflect improvement or lack of improvement on selected errors identified by the teacher for each student or for the entire class.

Evaluation of ESL student writing, then, can focus on what all students should be able to do (e.g., turn in neat assignments on time) as well as on those aspects of writing that are present even in the early attempts of nonnative writers. These aspects include the communication of ideas and the expression of feelings in writing.

Evaluation can, of course, also focus on language itself, on usage, and on mechanics. It is important, however, that a concentration on bits and pieces of language does not interfere with students' growing desire and ability to share meaningful information with their readers.

ESL students face many challenges. Even after two years, the most motivated and best students in our study were not quite native-like in their writing. There was much that they did not know; there was much that they had never been exposed to. As opposed to English monolingual students, who have been surrounded by texts of different kinds all of their lives, the ESL students had limited exposure to the traditions of written edited English. What is clear, however, is that with the right response from their teachers, such students can begin to believe that they have something important to say and that they can learn how to express what they want to say *in writing*.

Notes

1. Sheltered content courses are classes in which teachers—who may or may not speak the non-English language(s) spoken by their students—present subject-matter instruction using special strategies. They modify their use of English, and they provide many illustrations of the concepts they are presenting. Research conducted in California on such classes (Minicucci and Olson 1992) has found that in comparison to mainstream classes, sheltered classes provide very sparse coverage of the subject-area content.

2. The research project was supported under the Educational Reseach and Development Center Program (Grant No. R117G10036 for the National Center for the Study of Writing).

3. There are many terms in use in schools today that refer to students whose home language is not English and who are not yet speakers of English. In this paper, we have chosen to use the term *ESL students* to refer to those students who receive ESL (English as a Second Language) instruction and are in the process of acquiring English. We are concerned exclusively with two ESL students who are representative of youngsters who arrive in the United States at the middle school level, who have received very little schooling in their home countries, who spend most of their school day in the ESL classroom, and whose "regular" instruction is limited to physical education and cooking.

4. All names used for teachers are pseudonyms.

5. During the entire length of the project, students' language abilities were assessed periodically. Initial assessments were made of Spanish-language reading and writing. Continued assessments focused on English and evaluated students' ability to speak, understand, read, and write English.

Works Cited

Chamot, Anna Uhl. 1992. "Changing Instructional Needs of Language Minority Students." In *Proceedings of the Third National Research Symposium on Limited English Proficient Student Issues: Focus on Middle School and High School Issues.* Washington, DC: Office of Bilingual Education and Minority Language Affairs. http://www.ncbe.gwu.edu/ncbepubs/symposia/chamot.htm

————. 1992a. "What Have We Learned from Research on Successful Secondary Programs for LEP students? A Synthesis of Findings from Three Studies." In *Proceedings of the Third National Research Symposium on Limited English Proficient Student Issues: Focus on Middle School and High School Issues.* Washington, DC: Office of Bilingual Education and Minority Language Affairs. http://www.ncbe.gwu.edu/ncbepubs/symposia/lucas.htm

Davis, D., and J. McDaid. 1992. "Identifying Second-Language Students' Needs: A Survey of Vietnamese High School Students." *Urban Education* 27: 32–40.

Dyson, Anne Haas. 1989. *Multiple Worlds of Child Writers: Friends Learning to Write.* New York: Teachers College Press.

————. 1993. *Social Worlds of Children Learning to Write in an Urban Primary School.* New York: Teachers College Press.

Edelsky, Carole. 1986. *Había una vez: Writing in a Bilingual Program.* Norwood, NJ: Ablex.

Gentile, Claudia. 1992. *Exploring New Methods for Collecting Students' School-Based Writing: NAEP's 1990 Portfolio Study.* Washington, DC: National Center for Education Statistics.

LaFontaine, Herman. 1987. "At-Risk Children and Youth—The Extra Educational Challenges of Limited English Proficient Students." In *Council of Chief State School Officers, 1987 Summer Institute in Washington, D.C.* 2–16. Washington, DC: Council of Chief State School Officers.

Minicucci, Catherine, and Laurie Olsen. 1992. *Programs for Secondary Limited-English Proficient Students: A California Study.* Washington, DC: National Clearinghouse for Bilingual Education.

Portes, A., and D. Gran. 1991. *Characteristics and Performance of High School Students in Dade County (Miami SMSA).* Baltimore, MD: Johns Hopkins University.

Rumbaut, Ruben. 1990. *Immigrant students in California Public Schools: A Summary of Current Knowledge.* Technical Report # 11. Baltimore, MD: Center for Research on Effective Schooling for Disadvantaged Students.

13 Texts in Contexts: Understanding Chinese Students' English Compositions

Guanjun Cai
University of Arizona

When some English teachers see the writing of students who are native speakers of Chinese, they tend to focus on sentence-level problems, especially the absence of the "-ed" tense marker, the misuse or overuse of the definite article "the," and the frequent employment of the "although . . . but . . ." construction. Such problems are attributable to deep linguistic differences between English and Chinese. For example, while tense in an English sentence is often, though not always, revealed by the different forms its verb takes, such as the "-ed" form, past experience in Chinese is not marked by the verb itself, but indicated by an appended aspect article like *ge* or *liao*. Chinese, unlike English, does not have definite and indefinite articles, and a complex Chinese sentence in which the linked clauses speak contradictory statements requires the combined use of "although" and "but," instead of just one of them as in English. These problems and others like them are bound to arise in the English writing of Chinese students who have not yet fully understood the differences between Chinese and English.

Chinese students have to wrestle with even more substantial differences in writing to an American audience, however, as the following anecdote by Mark Salzman illustrates. In *Iron and Silk*, Salzman (1986) tells a story about helping a Chinese English instructor correct an English translation of a Chinese text. The text is a letter of application for a World Bank loan for the Chinese college where they both work. Salzman thinks the grammar is fine, but he points out to the Chinese teacher that, from a Western point of view, the content is weak and thus unacceptable as an official application for a loan. To his surprise, the Chinese teacher replies, "But this is a translation of the text written by the officials of our college. This is the

Chinese way of writing this sort of thing. I am only an English teacher; I cannot presume to change it" (21). Clearly, the difference that Salzman speaks of is well beyond sentence and grammar levels in an application letter.

More important, Salzman's story indicates that some distinct features of English texts written by Chinese students may not be *violations* as they are currently marked, but at most *differences* unfamiliar to composition teachers who are native speakers of English. These features are evident at all levels of discourse, ranging from lexical choice to overall organization and rhetorical stance. "Violations" in these areas, such as "indirectness," "digressions," and "lack of transitional signals," are perceived as violations because native speakers of English make judgments within rhetorical contexts quite different from those in which the Chinese students do their writing. Within the Chinese contexts, the perceived violations may not be violations at all; they may correctly fulfill the expectations of a Chinese audience.

Teachers of English composition may better understand and analyze texts by Chinese students and, consequently, more effectively teach English rhetorical conventions to these students if the teachers themselves are familiar with the typical rhetorical strategies of Chinese academic writing, the underlying rhetorical ideologies, and the sociocultural contexts in which these strategies and ideologies are embedded. My purpose in this chapter[1] is to develop a cross-cultural perspective on writing by explaining the Chinese rhetorical contexts and then applying this perspective to the work of a Chinese student, a high school graduate in China who recently entered an American university.

A Cross-cultural Perspective on Writing

From a social constructionist standpoint, writing is a social act and takes place within a specific sociocultural context (Bruffee 1986; LeFevre 1987). The process of writing is also a process of sociocultural ideology formation (Berlin 1988; Eagleton 1991), in which the rules for a certain type of writing are set, such as what can and must be said and who gets to say it. Further, changes in political power and the associated ideologies cause drastic changes in rhetorical norms and language use (Saville-Troike 1989). Therefore, writing and rhetoric are inherently sociopolitical and ideological constructs.

In Chinese as well as in English contexts, rhetoric and academic writing have always been bound up with sociopolitical beliefs. In Chinese culture, they serve the ideological claims of the Chinese society, which greatly values social harmony and group orientation. These values are different from those in American culture, which prizes an individualism that is deeply "entrenched as a privilege and a characteristic of American society" (Hoffman 1965, 113). In China, harmony, derived from Confucianism, is still cherished. The individual is conceived as a communal being rather than an independent being in the American sense; the individual is, to borrow Regamey's term, a "harmonized collection of universals" (1968, 517). The concept of individuality may even have negative connotations, taken to mean egoism or selfishness. The sense of self is realized, not through self-fulfillment, but only when group values are recognized and accepted.

Further, in contrast to the American belief that self-expression helps minimize conflict (Van Niekerk 1987), Chinese social ideology discourages free expression of personal views. The Chinese believe that knowledge resides in collective wisdom and social norms; no ordinary individual can claim the authority of knowledge. As Fan Shen laments, "[In China] both political pressure and literary tradition require that 'I' be somewhat hidden or buried in writings and speeches; presenting the 'self' too obviously would give people the impression of being disrespectful of the Communist Party in political writings and boastful in scholarly writings" (1989, 460). In fact, personal views are often associated with wrong ways of thinking, and free self-expression is believed to cause conflict and disrupt social harmony.

For the same reasons, creative language use is discouraged. In ancient times, Confucius remarked that "artful speech and ingratiating demeanor rarely accompany virtue" (Soothill 1968, 3). Laotzu warned his disciples that "truthful words are not beautiful, beautiful words are not truthful" (1963, 79). These sages' words still influence academic writing in China. In effect, the Chinese language is planned and developed to include a large number of prescribed expressions. Classic books like *Li Ji* or *The Book of Etiquette* (Oliver 1971, 149) and more recent pamphlets like *San Jiang Si Mei Wu Re Ai* or *Three-Do's, Four-Beauties, and Five-Loves* are written to inform people of what to say and how to say it in every normally encountered situation.

Under these guiding ideologies, academic writing in China has become an appendage to politics. Discourse features, such as overall organization, topic choice, paragraph organization, sentence structure and lexical choice, self-expression and language use, and purpose for writing, are direct products of changing Chinese sociopolitical contexts. This can be seen in the practices of the eight-legged essay, the four-part essay, and the three-part essay.

The Eight-legged Essay

The eight-legged essay, known in Chinese as *ba gu wen*, was a part of the Chinese civil service examinations,[2] which were used by the Chinese ruling class to recruit local officials. It thus constituted the basic framework of expository and persuasive writing in classical Chinese and has since influenced academic writing in Taiwan, Hong Kong, Singapore, and modern China. An eight-legged essay must have the designated eight parts: (1) *po-ti*; (2) *cheng-ti*; (3) *qi-jiang*; (4) *qi-gu*; (5) *xu-gu*; (6) *zhong-gu*; (7) *hou-gu*; and (8) *da-jie* (Wang 1950), literally meaning opening up, amplification, preliminary exposition, first argument, second argument, third argument, final argument, and conclusion. The most important part was *cheng-ti*, usually consisting of two or three sentences, in which the writer introduced the chosen topic and expressed the intended thesis of the essay. In the next five parts, the writer elaborated on the topic for ten to twenty sentences by drawing from some Chinese classics. Then, the writer concluded the essay in two to four sentences. In addition, every part had to be carefully balanced by rhymed words, paired phrases, and matched length of sentences.

The structure of the eight-legged essay was reformed twice because of changes in the dominant sociopolitical ideologies. The first reform took place during the New Cultural Movement in 1919. As a result, expository and persuasive writing came to follow the *qi-cheng-jun-he* four-part organizational pattern (Zhang 1938): the introduction, the elaboration on the topic, the transition to another seemingly unrelated point, and the summing up. The second reform occurred in the 1960s when Mao Tsetung criticized the *qi-cheng-jun-he* pattern and regarded it as the "Party eight-legged essay." Mao felt that such a writing format failed to "convey the revolutionary ideologies to the people" (1967, 63).

In response, students were taught to organize their expository and persuasive essays in a somewhat *fan lun-yi lun-jie lun* three-unit progression. In the *fan-lun* or "generalization," a writer made use of a standardized statement addressing the then-ongoing political propaganda, regardless of the topic under consideration. Then, the writer proceeded to the *yi-lun* or "discussion"; in this section, the writer took up the topic and elaborated on it by giving one or two examples for brief analysis. Finally, the writer went into the *jie-lun* or "conclusion." But instead of concluding the essay, the writer actually anticipated the possible future discussion of the topic, shifting to a point seemingly irrelevant to the topic examined in the *yi-lun*.

Topic choice was also subject to the changing sociopolitical ideologies. For example, all topics for eight-legged essays were derived exclusively from such Chinese classics as the *Four Books* and the Five Classics, which convey the philosophical teachings of Confucius, setting forth the moral and ethical basis of society. During the New Cultural Movement (1919), the most-written-on topics for the four-part essays in both classrooms and professional publications came to be patriotism, the fate of the nation, and the pursuit of national awakening. The same was true during the Great Cultural Revolution (1966–1976), when school education was exclusively directed to serve the interests of the proletariat class and "the people's democratic dictatorship." As a result, academic writing focused explicitly on topics of moral and ideological education, such as self-criticism, new Party policies, and so on (Cheng 1987).

The broad rhetorical differences between Chinese and English that I have sketched are also evident in the paragraph organization of the eight-legged, the four-part, and the three-part essays. Robert Kaplan (1966) claims that most native-English-speaking writers favor a direct approach to a chosen topic. In the sense of paragraph organization, this means that English writers tend to arrange a paragraph in a hierarchical order (Fagan and Cheong 1987) in which a topic sentence is supported by other sentences. By contrast, Chinese writers tend to construct a paragraph using the *qi-cheng-jun-he* pattern (Mo 1982), the same structure for organizing an essay. In *qi*, the writer prepares the reader for the topic, and in *cheng*, he elaborates on it; after wandering into a *jun*, a seemingly unrelated point, the writer comes back and wraps up everything in a *he*. Shen describes this type of paragraph organization as peeling an onion, layer by layer, moving "from surface to the core" (1989, 462).

And finally, rhetorical differences between Chinese and English are embedded even in sentence structure and word choice. While most English writers write with "forthright, straightforward, simple expressions" and are "generally free of sentimental expressions, exaggerations, and reference to the past" (Fagan and Cheong 1987, 25), Chinese writers tend to avoid expressing personal thoughts, a tendency characteristic of the eight-legged, the four-part, and the three-part essays. The avoidance of self-expression is usually accomplished by, for example, "use of quotations and reference to the past" (25). In fact, in Chinese writing, *pang zheng bo yin and yin jing ju dian*, or quoting the classics and referring to the past, are not only considered "the height of culture" and "the mark of good breeding" (Tsao 1990, 109), but also regarded as a willingness to respect authorities and to accept traditional values, social norms, and group ideologies, and as a desire to be polite.

Moreover, English-speaking writers are trained to write with direct and explicit assertions in every part of an essay: "Tell 'em what you're going to tell 'em, tell 'em, and tell 'em what you've told 'em" (Reid 1984, 449), whereas Chinese writers are inclined to prefer "suggesting" (Leki 1992, 95) or "indirectness" (Jensen 1987, 135). That is, instead of directly "imposing" their ideas on the reader, Chinese writers tend to use rhetorical questions, metaphor and simile, analogy, and illustrative anecdotes (Gregg 1986, 356) to imply their propositions. In doing so, the writers expect the readers to "supply some significant portion of the propositional structure" (Kaplan 1988, 292), and "to work to glean meaning [on their own]" (Leki 1992, 97) from a text.

The use of all these strategies reveals the essential purpose and function of rhetoric and academic writing in the Chinese language. The primary function of Chinese rhetoric "is not to enhance the welfare of the individual speaker or listener but to promote [social] harmony" and collectivity (Oliver 1971, 261). The ultimate purpose of Chinese writing is not to argue for differences and uniqueness but to maintain the norms and traditions. Within Chinese contexts, students' writing practices are taken as a fundamental means of making a connection between classrooms and social reality, promoting harmony and collectivity, preserving social norms and traditions, and showing respect to authorities past and present (Matalene 1985, 795).

Text Analysis: A Case Study

The texts selected for the following analysis are from Fang Li's writing portfolio for English 306 at the University of Arizona. Fang (not the student's real name) is representative of millions of high school graduates in China. She started learning how to write basic academic essays in the fourth grade, under the strong influences of the eight-legged, the four-part, and the three-part essays. Like her peers, she started learning English in the seventh grade. Since English is primarily learned not for any instrumental purpose, but for such technical reasons as translating literary works and exchanging scientific information, and since English composition is not a part of the school curricula, students are not exposed to English rhetoric and academic writing. As a result, Fang is among the thousands of new Chinese students who walk into American secondary schools or universities thinking and writing English essays in the Chinese way.

Fang, now in her early twenties, has been in the United States for three and a half years, during which time she has taken five college-level writing classes, including English 306. Previously, she had taken

English 106, 107, and 108, which are specially designed as a sequence of composition classes for first-year international students, and also English 308, a course emphasizing technical writing that is usually reserved for scientific or technical juniors and seniors. English 306 is intended to improve students' expository and persuasive writing skills and is open to all interested students after their first-year composition sequence (Applen, McNenny, and Ransdell 1992, 7). Fang took this course in the spring semester of 1993.

Despite her extensive contact with the English language and considerable experience with English composition, Fang's perspective on English rhetoric and composition is still significantly more Chinese than American. Most of her schematic knowledge about rhetoric and writing remains as a solid construct of the Chinese sociocultural and political contexts and her experience with Chinese academic writing, which is yet to be influenced by the English contexts. All Fang's six essays consistently show the following characteristic features of Chinese rhetoric and academic writing. Her topic choice tends to be more reliant on the given reading material than on her own imagination. As a result, her essays' content appears more a restatement of the readings than personal argument. Furthermore, the overall organization of Fang's essays seems to be more identifiable with the eight-legged or four-part pattern in Chinese writing than with the English introduction-body-conclusion linear progression, and her paragraphs demonstrate the *qi-cheng-jun-he* structure and disinterest in English cohesion. Finally, instead of directly asserting her personal views, Fang tends to develop her points by frequently employing questions, quotations, abstract wording, and word-by-word translation into English of Chinese prescribed phrasings or sayings. The detailed analysis that follows may suffice to illustrate the above features, which are not what Fang's instructor expected to see in her essays. I hope that, unlike Fang's instructor, other native-English-speaking instructors will not see these differences as violations, but recognize these features for what they are. Of course, native English speakers who have little experience with academic writing also have problems with, for instance, making their paragraphs cohesive in conventional ways and with "getting to the point." In this analysis, however, I want to compare the qualities of Fang's writing only with those of competent, native English speakers' prose.

The sociocultural ideology and political register of Chinese rhetoric are clearly evident in Fang's topic choice for all six essays. Fang and her classmates were not given any specific assignment instructions or prompts for writing these essays; rather, they were asked to read chapters from their multicultural reader, *Our Times,* by Robert Atwan (1993), and develop six arguments on any topics they felt comfortable with. However, Fang seemingly did not want to take any risk or write on subjects of her own, but decided to comment on subjects others had defined; that is, she chose topics either similar to or the same as those raised in the chapters she read. For example, after reading chapters on "Television Broadcasting: Does it Distort the News?" and "Television and Sex Roles: Is TV Defying the Stereotypes?" Fang wrote Essay #1, "For a Better Future," in which she posed exactly the same questions about mass media. Fang entitled Essay #2 "Cultural Diversity: Is It a Good Thing?" using almost the same wording as the chapter title she read: "America's Cultural Diversity: Is It a Good Thing?" In the same way, Fang's Essay #3—"Racism on Campus: Why Does It Happen?"—derived from her reading of chapters on "Racism on Campus: How Can We Explain It?"

Further, all Fang's essays address the issues of diversity, racism, and equality, which are dealt with by Atwan's book. I asked Fang why she chose to write about those topics. She explained that she was exposed to these issues when she was still in China, and the readings in English 306 reminded her of those issues. What Fang said is true. In fact, topics on problems of cultural diversity, racism, and equality are the most often used in recent Chinese political writing that criticizes Western cultures, and they are inevitably popular themes in school composition and ideology education, which warns young generations that the West is not as ideal a place as expected, and so "Going West" may not be the best choice in life. In light of her experience in China, Fang's topic selection also had clear political and moral-thematic foundations.

Moreover, Fang's topic choice is quite consistent with her perception of the function and purpose for writing, which is also reflective of Chinese rhetoric and sociocultural ideologies. Instead of intending to convince her reader of her own perspectives on the chosen topics, Fang and her writing make it clear that she has the following three common purposes in mind for all her essays. First, Fang thinks of writing in terms of demonstrating her understanding of the assigned readings to her instructor, that is, paraphrasing or repeating the authorities. Second, she intends to draw moral lessons on the chosen issues through her essays, such as in her statement: "We should try our best to eliminate racism." Finally, she sees writing as an important means for achieving or preserving social harmony. She makes this purpose clear when she claims, on the cover page to Essay #1, that "We do not want increased social conflicts and we want a peaceful future."

Fang's essays reveal some topic development strategies typical of Chinese rhetoric and sociocultural and political contexts. The overall formats or "superstructures" (Connor and Lauer 1988, 142) of Fang's six essays have a clear commonality of topic development, which is identifiable with the traditional eight-legged or four-part pattern in Chinese writing. Essay #4, below, in which Fang writes about how to achieve equality, illustrates these topic development tactics and, as my analysis will show, other rhetorical strategies characteristic of Chinese academic writing (I have numbered the paragraphs to aid in discussion).

On Equality

[1] Equality, a notion which was posed in the French Revolution two hundred years ago, has been a primary concern in most of the political movements in the last two centuries. Generations and generations of people all over the world have striven for this political ideal. However, no nation in the world has succeeded in realizing equality in their society. This failure leads people to ponder the implication of the notion itself. The debate on equality becomes a hot topic in the 1990s.

[2] In the French Revolution in the 19th century, the revolutionaries claimed that every citizen has the right to participate in the nation's politics; this is not a privilege only belonging to the nobility. In the turbulent days of revolution, various social groups—the nobility, the bourgeoisie, the urban working class and the peasants fought with each other violently for their political power, since everybody seems to believe that you are either the winner or the loser in society, and the only way to make yourself the winner is to make others the loser. However, the result of French Revolution as a whole suffered the turbulent violence of group rivalry and the old problem of inequality in the country's political, economical life had not been solved.

[3] The failure of the revolution which aims at the goal of the equality leads people to ponder what is going to be an effective way to pursue this ideal. Since human beings are born differently, some with more intelligence, some with more material wealth, some with more physical strength, the distinction among them determines that they will not achieve success in the same degree, and they will have different needs to in order to realize their goals. Because of this distinction among individuals, how the society can provide the opportunities to its members based on their different needs should be the primary concern in the process based on their divergent economic, intellectual and social conditions.

[4] Since the distribution of wealth is not equal in our society, every individual has a different economic ability to achieve their goals. A person born with several million dollars will certainly have the opportunity to receive a good education and

to pursue whatever he/she decides to do in his/her life. However, people with a poor economic background will have a hard time, struggling for economic stability while they are trying their other personal goals. However, like President Kennedy said thirty years ago, "If a country cannot help the poor, it will not save a few rich." The practice of equality is to relieve the nightmare of poverty for every member of the society. It means that the poor and the economically unwell-to-do should be guaranteed the basic necessities for living, such as social security and health care, and the essential opportunity to pursue success, such as the access to a good education. Under these conditions, every individual in the society can concentrate on their career and will be more likely to succeed. At the same time, the society as a whole will benefit because the success of individuals will naturally contribute to the wealth and civilization of the society.

[5] Another crucial aspect of equality to be considered is intellectual equality. It is a matter of fact that some people are born as intellectual geniuses, and some are not. Geniuses only count a small percentage of the population; the vast majority are ordinary people like you and me. How to create opportunities so that everyone can give play to their wisdom to the highest degree is an essential factor in achieving the intellectual progress of the whole society.

[6] I feel the American higher education system has more advantages than the Chinese one because it offers more opportunities for students to pursue their education. In the Chinese system, the admission to colleges and universities totally depends on the student's score on the College Entrance Examination which is highly competitive, for only 10–30 percent of students will be accepted. A student may have been an "A" student in six years in middle school, and get sick on the day of the test, and cannot get into college for several points lower than the admission standard. One shortcoming of the Chinese higher education system is that it is not open to a large population of students, only the "perfect" students can squeeze into the door of college. In contrast, U.S. colleges have a much higher admission rate. Therefore, not only the smartest, but also the intellectually ordinary students are able to get in. In addition, after getting college, students can switch majors, which allows them to choose a field they are good at and most interested in to work on. The outcome of the flexibility of the education system and the recognition of the distinction among individual students allow more members of the society to become well-educated individuals and the society as a whole will enjoy higher level of intellectual wealth. This point can be proved by the fact that the United States is in the lead in the world's scientific and cultural fields.

[7] Social equality involves the issue of diversity. Although ethnically and culturally divergent, every citizen in the society has the right to voice their opinions. At the same time, every one has to listen to people with backgrounds different from one's own, to understand their perspectives. It is human nature that we tend to like people that are the same as us and mistrust people different from us. However, if everyone sticks to this point, the whole society will become the battle ground of various social groups. The dialogue with other members in society will allow us to examine and reexamine our notions about people different from us and gradually eliminate various kinds of social stereotypes which are the stumbling blocks to social equality.

[8] My own experience shows how important it is to listen to the divergent point of view instead of only listening one side of the argument. When I had just arrived at the University of Arizona, I used to hear some Chinese students talking about blacks in a despising tone. Not having had any contact with blacks before, that was the first impression that I got about blacks. However, after living here for two years, because of the everyday contact with black students, I found out that black people are remarkable individuals, and what I have heard about them are just racial stereotypes.

[9] The search for equality is a formidable path, because we have to deal with economic, intellectual, and social diversities which are complicated issues. However, there is hope if we recognize the difference among individuals and respect people unlike ourselves. In this way, we will not necessarily be rivals of each other, but there is the possibility that everybody can become a winner on his/her life. That is the real implication of equality and it is what we should strive for.

In Paragraph #1, Fang appears to define the notion of equality. But because the paragraph is so abstract and general, it falls short of explaining what equality is and seemingly has little to do with the thesis implied in Paragraphs #2 and #3, which is, in her own words: "The failure of the revolution which aims at the goal of equality leads people to ponder what is going to be an effective way to pursue this ideal." As a result, Paragraph #1 appears to be the *po-ti* in the eight-legged pattern, the *qi* in the four-part format, and the *fan-lun* in the three-unit pattern, which all offer a grand opening up to an essay.

Fang proceeds to the part of *cheng-ti* (the amplification) or *cheng* (the elaboration) in the next four paragraphs by taking up the proposed thesis in Paragraphs #2 and #3 and offering general solutions to the problem in economic, intellectual, and sociopolitical contexts. Then, in Paragraph #8, she suddenly turns to a short discussion of her own experience with "racial stereotypes," which seems to have little relevance to the subject under consideration: "I found out that black people are remarkable individuals." Finally, she ends the essay by tying everything together, not "logically" in a Western sense, but simply by repeating her main point in general terms: "The search for equality is a formidable path . . . and it is what we should strive for."

The apparent irrelevance of Paragraph #1 to the rest of the essay, the abrupt transitions from topic to topic, and the brief mention of her own experience also come to the notice of Fang's instructor. In his endnote to the final draft of this essay, Fang's instructor remarks: "Ultimately, the paper is not very cohesive. The topic you <u>start</u> discussing isn't very well connected to the topic at the <u>end</u> of the essay." He characterizes this disconnection, not as a *difference*, but as a clear *violation* of English's rhetorical norms. He underlines both "start" and "end" to bring what he considers the incoherence of her ideas to Fang's attention, and he repeated this view to me when I asked him about it. More important, without knowledge of alternate rhetorical traditions, he does not point out to Fang in his endnote why he considers the incohesive topics as something absolutely wrong and not merely different from the rules Fang follows.

At the intersentential level, Fang tends to structure her paragraphs in the *qi-cheng-jun-he* progression that Mo and Tsao speak of rather than the more straightforward topic-support structure of English paragraphs. Paragraph #4 provides examples. Fang introduces her reader to the paragraph with the statement that "every individual has a different economic ability to achieve their goals." This statement, which is the *qi* part, does not necessarily have the same function as a topic sentence in English does because, unlike an assertive topic sentence, the *qi* statement is, rather, a general comment on the *implied* theme of the paragraph.

Then, Fang proceeds to the *cheng* part and comments in the next two sentences on the implied theme that inequality in wealth hinders many individuals' pursuit of personal goals. Before ending the paragraph with *he* in the last sentence, Fang leaves the theme with the *jun*, turning to government responsibility and welfare, topics only loosely related to the general theme. Fang offers a brief "However" warning of this turn, but it is not enough to keep her native English-speaking readers on the track. Her instructor, who again does not see the *difference*, writes his frustration on the margin: "I don't understand the significance of the quote."

In addition to their typical topic-support structure, English paragraphs also display coordinate or subordinate relationships between sentences. These relationships are often enhanced by the use of external cohesion devices. Fang's paragraphs, by contrast, illustrate the Chinese perception of cohesion and coherence. In Chinese writing, the semantic chain of each sentence to the other is more important than the syntactic and lexical cohesion to the concerned topic, in part because the Chinese language is more "tolerant" of lexical absence (Tsao 1990, 101–5). This can be seen in Paragraph #5, in which Fang does not use any lexical cohesive device (e.g., "but" or "however") to help shift from Sentence #2 to Sentence #3 in the way that an English writer might. The semantic relation between these two sentences is, however, strong and clear to Fang and her Chinese readers, who are instilled with the ideology that geniuses are rare and that the only way to succeed is to "work hard and make progress everyday."

As regards topic development at the sentence level, features of Fang's self-expression and language use are worth noting. Fang's self-expression tends to be general, impersonal, and less direct than what American academic writing expects. First, instead of direct assertions, Fang often employs questions to imply her points. The following example is from Paragraph #2 of Fang's Essay #2:

> Facing this situation, some people begin to doubt: Is cultural diversity a good thing? Is it a mistake of the founders of this country to allow every race and nationality to move into America? Is separation of different groups and encouraging them to live in their own community a way to reduce ethic conflicts?

On the surface, there seems nothing inappropriate about the use of these questions. But these questions are not just rhetorical gestures. Placed in the introduction, and clearly intended as the thesis statement for the whole essay, these sentences are a way of stating a thesis without direct imposition of an opinion.

Second, Fang frequently uses quotations and references to other sources in order to avoid expressing personal views, but without "citing references" in the Western style. In Paragraph #2 of Essay #4 above, for example, Fang makes substantial reference to the French Revolution, suggesting the origin and history of the concept of equality. Also, Fang does not credit the source of the information—the assigned readings in Atwan's book. This is permissible in Chinese academic writing because *pang zheng po yin* or *yin jing ju dian* does not necessarily require the writer to provide full citation information. Similarly, in Essay #2, Fang writes that:

> As a major instrument to propagate the dominant ideology for the society, the mass media always picks upon the minority groups because they usually do not have enough strength to fight back and therefore are the perfect target. Stereotypes against various groups, such as Blacks, Indians, Asians, and other unpopular groups are

all of the same nature: the crucification of these groups as the scapegoat of social pathology.

In addition to taking phrases such as "social pathology," "unpopular groups," and "to propagate the dominant ideology" directly from the assigned readings, Fang also paraphrases several passages from them in writing this segment. This causes her instructor to be concerned, for he is not sure why Fang does what she does. When I asked about this, he explained that Fang "got more help than she should," suggesting that she used others' ideas without properly crediting them. But instead of explaining this to Fang, he writes next to the segment in an almost sarcastic tone: "This sounds like very <u>sophisticated</u> language."

Finally, Fang tends to address her topics in general, abstract, and impersonal terms. For example, in defining equality in Essay #4, Fang uses such abstract terms as "primary concern," "political ideal," "privilege," "goal," "opportunities," "distribution of wealth," "economic stability," and "intellectual geniuses" vs. "ordinary people," and so on. Without knowing her intention, Fang's instructor runs out of patience during his reading of Paragraph #3 and literally begs: "As a reader, I am <u>desperate for details</u> at this point of your essay." Again, he underlines his concern and request.

Other aspects of Fang's language reflect her view of language not as a vehicle of individual expression, but as part of a communal store of accepted notions. For example, Fang's language use tends to be both impersonal (in the sense of being not "individualized") and prescribed (rather than "original"). Even though Fang uses the personal pronoun "I" in every one of her essays—especially in personal anecdotes—impersonal pronouns, such as "we" or "us," "you," "one person," "everyone," "everybody," "people," "our society," "they" or "their," and "every individual," are usually among her first choices when taking a stand. In addition, many of Fang's sentences are direct translations of prescribed sayings in *si xiang jiao yu* ("ideology education") pamphlets in China, for example;

1. Generations and generations of people all over the world have strived for this political ideal.

2. You are either the winner or the loser in society, and the only way to make yourself the winner is to make others the loser.

3. Since human beings are born differently. . . .

4. That is the real implication of equality, and that is what we should strive for. (numbers added)

Sometimes Fang's translation relies too much on Chinese wording, word order, and sentence structure to be understood by her instructor. Once again, considering what Fang does as being absolutely unacceptable, he marks the following sentences with phrases like "awkward expression," "What do you mean?" and in one place, simply a question mark:

1. *The search for equality is a formidable path.*

2. The society as whole will benefit because the success of individuals will naturally contribute to *the wealth and civilization of the society.*

3. Its negative portrayal of minority groups efficiently promotes social stereotype and turns out to be *a public health hazard.* (numbers and emphasis added)

While these sentences make little sense to Fang's instructor, they ring with meaning for Chinese speakers. The first sentence is a direct translation of a popular Chinese saying: *xun zao ping den shi yi tiao jian kou de dao lou.* The phrases of "the wealth and civilization of society" in the second sentence and "a public health hazard" in the third render *shi hui de chai fu yu wen ming* and *da zhong wei sheng de yin huan* in Chinese.

Conclusion: Implications for Composition Teachers

The foregoing theoretical discussion and textual analysis suggest the following two principal implications for understanding English compositions by Chinese students. First, ESL composition teachers need to realize that rhetoric and writing are direct products of sociocultural and political contexts; they are schematic representations of the writer's experience and interactions within the given sociocultural context. Therefore, English composition teachers should be aware that Chinese students may write in accordance with a set of rhetorical norms that differ from those of English. The ultimate goal of such awareness is acknowledgment of and respect for rhetorical traditions outside of the West. As Jensen (1987) states,

> We have exhausted ourselves probing the Western rhetorical heritage, which honors verbal expression, reason, cause and effect linear linkages, directions, clear organization, unadorned style, and the debating of opposing views so that truth will emerge more purely from the clash. We have overlooked the rhetorical heritage of the East, which honors non-expression, silence, the nonverbal, the softness and subtlety of ambiguity and indirectness, the insights of intuition, and the avoidance of clash of opinion in order to preserve harmony. We have not

> fully appreciated communication which highly values reasoning
> from authority and example, which relies heavily on analogy
> and metaphor. With our devotion to individualism we have not
> fully appreciated communicative behavior which puts groups
> above the individual, which greatly respects relationships with
> others based on age, relative status, and tradition. (135)

Teachers should examine Chinese students' English compositions by first considering the Chinese contexts. In doing so, teachers will be able to find out why students compose a text as they do, identify those schemata typical of Chinese ideology, and eventually better understand the students' writing. More important, teachers will be able to acknowledge students' strengths as writers and then help them modify and make the Chinese rhetorical schemata in their English compositions more in tune with those of English.

The second primary implication of my discussion is that, being aware of rhetoric and writing as sociocultural constructs, teachers need to help Chinese students get to know English contexts and audience expectations for English compositions. That is, Chinese students should not be taught isolated composition skills (e.g., establishing a thesis up front, being straightforward or original); rather, they need to be taught English rhetorical norms and the broader sociocultural contexts in which these norms are embedded. If teachers want Chinese ESL students to organize their English compositions along the "Introduction-Body-Conclusion" three-part pattern, the students should be explicitly taught that this pattern represents an implicit agreement between the writer and the reader in the English language; that the writer uses this pattern to fulfill the reader's expectations; and that English culture and academic writing value linearity over other thought patterns. Similarly, if teachers want Chinese ESL students to "Be original" or "Be yourself" in their writing, these students should be taught that individuality is encouraged and appreciated in English culture and that free expression of personal views and thinking is essential in English academic writing. By the same token, Chinese ESL students should be reassured that although a direct, straightforward approach to a topic may give their readers the impression of "imposing," it will eventually promote intellectual understanding between themselves and their English-speaking audience. Only such explicit teaching of English discourse ideologies can produce changes in the discourse strategies in ESL students' writing, because change in language use comes from change in guiding ideologies and expectations. In other words, only when Chinese ESL students understand the underlying discourse schemata shared by American academics are they able to compose properly and acceptably in English.

Further Sources

Teachers can turn to recent research in contrastive rhetoric and second-language writing to learn more about the English writing of Chinese students and, most important, about strategies for helping those students with their writing. These include several of the studies that I mentioned earlier, particularly those done by Kaplan, Matalene, and Shen. Kaplan's "Cultural Thought Patterns in Inter-cultural Education" (1966) and other numerous writings will help familiarize teachers with the notion of contrastive rhetoric. Kaplan argues that rhetoric is a culturally coded phenomenon and that different languages embody different rhetorical norms and conventions for writing. He suggests that teachers take note that writing in a second language will be influenced by the rhetorical preferences in the first language.

In "Contrastive Rhetoric: An American Writing Teacher in China," Matalene reminds teachers that Chinese students may not only write, but also think the Chinese way in their English classes. She indicates that teachers may need to take the initiative to explain their comments, such as "Use new language," because "Chinese students are too puzzled and too polite to point this out—and they are certainly not in the habit of questioning teachers" (1985, 92). On the other hand, Shen's "The Classroom and the Wider Culture: Identity as a Key to Learning English Composition" offers other ways of helping Chinese students with their writing. Shen explains that, in his English essays, he was using the Chinese approach of *yi-jing*, creating a mental picture that went along with the abstract meaning he was trying to argue. He suggests that, in order for him to write good English essays, his English professors had to help him "get rid of" this approach and, instead, use "Western logical critical approaches" (1989, 460). Finally, teachers may find Ulla Connor and Robert B. Kaplan's *Writing Across Languages: Analysis of L2 Text* (1987), Donna M. Johnson and Duane H. Roen's *Richness in Writing: Empowering ESL Students* (1989), and Ilona Leki's *Understanding ESL Writers: A Guide for Teachers* (1992) very helpful.

Notes

1. I wish to thank my fellow graduate student Clyde Moneyhun, who offered me guidance throughout the writing process; this chapter would not have been possible without his generous help. I would also like to express my gratitude to my professors, Clair Bernhardt Brohaugh, Muriel Saville-Troike, Rudolph Troike, and Tilly Warnock; my editors, Charles Cooper and Lee Odell; and my wife, Jie Liang, for their insightful comments and suggestions for improvement.

2. This civil system was invented in the Warring States Period (475 B.C.E.–221 B.C.E.), officially implemented in the Tang Dynasty (618–907 C.E.), and fully developed during the Ming (1368–1644) and Qing (1645–1911) dynasties. It consisted of three basic parts: the examination, the appointment, and the evaluation. It was the examination part that required the eight-legged writing since the Ming dynasty. For more information on this system, consult Jinfan Zhang's (1990) "A Comprehensive Discussion of China's Ancient Civil Service System," *Social Sciences in China* 2: 35–58.

Works Cited

Applen, J. D., Gerri McNenny, and D. R. Ransdell, eds. 1992. *A Teacher's Guide to Composition,* 1992–93 Edition. Tucson: The University of Arizona, Composition Program. [Photocopy.]

Atwan, Robert. 1993. *Our Times/3: Reading from Recent Periodicals.* Boston: St. Martin's Press.

Berlin, James. 1988. "Rhetoric and Ideology in the Writing Class." *College English* 50: 477–94.

Bruffee, Kenneth A. 1986. "Social Construction, Language, and the Authority of Knowledge: A Bibliographical Essay." *College English* 48 (8): 773–90.

Cheng, Bixiang. 1987. *Xian Dai Hanyu Yuyan Jiaoyu Fa Zhan Shi* (A Dynamic History of Modern Chinese Language Education). Kunming, PRC: Yunnan Educational.

Connor, Ulla, and Robert B. Kaplan. 1987. *Writing Across Languages: Analysis of L2 Text.* Reading, MA: Addison-Wesley.

Connor, Ulla, and Janice Lauer. 1988. "Cross-Cultural Variation in Persuasive Student Writing." In *Writing Across Languages and Cultures: Issues in Contrastive Rhetoric,* ed. Alan C. Purves, 138–59. Newbury Park, CA: Sage.

Eagleton, Terry. 1991. *Ideology: An Introduction.* New York: Verso.

Fagan, Edward R., and Peggy Cheong. 1987. "Contrastive Rhetoric: Pedagogical Implications for the ESL Teacher in Singapore." *RELC: A Journal of Language Teaching and Research in Southeast Asia* 18 (1): 19–31.

Gregg, Joan. 1986. Comments on "Academic Writing and Chinese Students: Transfer and Developmental Factors." *TESOL Quarterly* 20 (2): 354–58.

Hoffman, Frederick J. 1965. "Dogmatic Innocence: Self-Assertion in Modern American Literature." In *Innocence and Power: Individualism in Twentieth-Century America,* ed. Gorden Mills, 112–25. Austin: University of Texas Press.

Jensen, Vernon J. 1987. "Teaching East Asian Rhetoric." *Rhetoric Society Quarterly* 17 (2): 135–49.

Johnson, Donna M., and Duane H. Roen. 1989. *Richness in Writing: Empowering ESL Students.* New York: Longman.

Kaplan, Robert B. 1988. "Contrastive Rhetoric and Second Language Learning: Notes Toward a Theory of Contrastive Rhetoric." In *Writing Across Languages and Cultures: Issues in Contrastive Rhetoric,* ed. Allan C. Purves, 275–304. Newbury Park, CA: Sage.

———. 1966. "Cultural Thought Patterns in Inter-cultural Education." *Language Learning* 17 (1/2): 1–20.

Laotzu. 1963. *Dao De Jing.* Trans. D. C. Lau. Harmondworth, England: Penguin.

LeFevre, Karen. 1987. *Invention as a Social Act.* Urbana, IL: National Council of Teachers of English.

Leki, Ilona. 1992. *Understanding ESL Writers: A Guide for Teachers.* Portsmouth, NH: Boynton/Cook.

Mao, Tsetung. 1967. "Oppose Stereotyped Party Writing." In *Selected Works of Mao Tsetung,* Trans. and ed., 53–68 Foreign Languages Press. Beijing, PRC: People's.

Matalene, Carolyn. 1985. "Contrastive Rhetoric: An American Writing Teacher in China." *College English* 47 (8): 789–808.

Mo, J. C. 1982. "A Study of English Reading Comprehension from the Point of View of Discourse Function." *English Teaching and Learning* 6 (3): 39–48.

Oliver, Robert T. 1971. *Communication and Culture in Ancient India and China.* Syracuse, NY: Syracuse University Press.

Regamey, Constantin. 1968. "The Individual and the Universal in East and West." In *The Status of the Individual in East and West,* ed. Charles A. Moore, 503–18. Honolulu: University of Hawaii Press.

Reid, Joy M. 1984. "ESL Composition: The Linear Product of American Thought." *College Composition and Communication* 35 (4): 449–52.

Salzman, Mark. 1986. *Iron and Silk.* New York: Vintage.

Saville-Troike, Muriel. 1989. *The Ethnography of Communication: An Introduction.* 2nd ed. New York: Blackwell.

Shen, Fan. 1989. "The Classroom and the Wider Culture: Identity as a Key to Learning English Composition." *College Composition and Communication* 40 (4): 459–66.

Soothill, William E., trans. 1968. *The Analects of Confucius.* New York: Paragon.

Tsao, Feng-fu. 1990. "Linguistics and Written Discourse in Particular Languages: Contrastive Studies: English and Chinese (Mandarin)." *Annual Review of Applied Linguistics* 11: 99–117.

Wang, Chun. 1950. *Zuo Wen Zha Ji* (A Miscellany on Composition). Beijing, PRC: The Worker.

Van Niekerk, Barend. 1987. *The Cloistered Virtue: Freedom of Speech and the Administration of Justice in the Western World.* New York: Praeger.

Zhang, Jinfan. 1990. "A Comprehensive Discussion of China's Ancient Civil Services." *Social Sciences in China* 2: 35–58.

Zhang, Yiping. 1938. *Zuo Wen Jiang Ping* (Lectures on Composition). Shanghai, PRC: Beixian.

IV Issues in Assessment

As much as we have learned during the past thirty years, and as much as we may learn from the chapters in Parts I through III of this book, we must remain nonetheless critical, inquiring students of writing, its teaching and learning, and its evaluation. Many fundamental issues still need to be explored and researched in our classrooms.

In Part IV, five authors raise important questions and identify significant problems:

> —How can we resolve the discrepancies between our personal goals for evaluating writing and our actual practices?

> —How might a classroom portfolio-evaluation system change students' and teachers' roles in assessing students' achievements as writers?

> —How can we integrate the evaluation of reading and writing achievement in large-scale assessments?

> —How can we accommodate experimental and vernacular writing in large-scale assessments?

Chris Anson, in Chapter 14, reminds us that many issues in evaluating writing remain unresolved and that, in fact, the major questions have hardly been considered in any systematic, shared way. Anson takes up the issue of widely divergent instructor responses to a single student text. He is not dismayed by the variety of responses to the text he presents, finding them perhaps inevitable. Instead, he is concerned that writing instructors become more reflective about *how* they respond. Anson uses these divergent responses to speculate about why we respond as we do on different occasions. Among these are reading a text as a draft, revision, or candidate for an end-of-course portfolio; applying or resisting institutional standards; relying on personal beliefs; and attending to rhetorical or situational goals. These thought-provoking speculations lead to six specific suggestions for improving "reflective practice" in evaluating student writing—from teacher workshops to classroom research. Reflective practice, Anson believes, should lead, if we can achieve it, to greater "thoughtfulness, balance, and clarity of method" in evaluating student writing.

Sandra Murphy and Mary Ann Smith, in Chapter 15, address the problem of finding the "delicate balance between guiding and prescribing" students' work with writing portfolios. Although widely advocated, portfolios remain a challenge to implement in crowded classrooms. Published reports from many teachers have taught us how to set up and manage a portfolio system, consider alternative portfolio designs, and involve students in various ways. Yet we do not know how widely portfolios are being used, and we do not know how the teachers who use them are translating reported practice. Acknowledging that there are "no guarantees" if we decide to involve students in designing and evaluating their own portfolios, Murphy and Smith nonetheless advocate a major role for students. They discuss this role as one of negotiation, interaction, reflection, and ownership. They offer many classroom examples of students and teachers negotiating portfolio designs and interacting to choose writing samples and evaluate portfolios, and they also describe ways in which teachers have attempted to guide students in reflecting on what they have achieved as writers. This chapter suggests many questions that we must continue to think about if we and our students are to evaluate portfolios in a way that leads to higher achievement in writing:

- What kinds of learning should we expect to see demonstrated in a collection of writing?
- How can portfolios help us communicate more clearly to students and their parents what is to be learned?
- How does evaluating individual pieces and collections differ?
- How do we negotiate portfolio designs and evaluative criteria with students to ensure that they reach our course goals?
- How can portfolios help us raise our expectations of students as readers and writers?
- What special kinds of thinking are required for students to reflect on their learning in English classes?
- How can we best guide students to reflect on this learning?
- How might students' work with portfolios help us to better define our subject English?

Fran Claggett, in Chapter 16, asks why we evaluate reading and writing separately even though we now recognize that "we comprehend as we compose, and compose as we read." Claggett argues that while we need to understand even better the relationship of reading and writing, we know enough to design large-scale state and national assessments that do not foster the separation of reading and writing in our classrooms. Avoiding abstraction and exhortation, Claggett presents a concrete example of one statewide assessment that integrates reading and writing into a three-day exercise in which reading achievement is assessed through brief writing activities; discussion deepens reading and prepares for extended writing; and writing achievement is evaluated in part by what the reading and discussion contribute to writing. With Claggett coordinating, classroom teachers developed this sophisticated assessment, which has become the model for New Standards' *English Language Arts Reference Exam*. Claggett presents one complete prompt, which begins with a selection from Alice Walker's *In Search of Our Mother's Gardens* and concludes with a reflective essay assignment. To preclude rosy scenarios, Claggett reports how political conservatives' opposition to some of the reading selections and writing activities halted administration of the assessment after one year. Even in politically more moderate times, authentic or performance assessments like CLAS and New Standards require further development and refinement. In addition, scoring costs are formidable, and scoring problems remain (mainly the problem of obtaining reliable scores for individual students).

Roxanne Mountford, in Chapter 17, also addresses a problem of large-scale writing assessment—whether current tests are fair to women and African American students. She argues that they are not and proposes four specific changes that would make them so. She recognizes, however, that before large-scale writing assessments can meet her standards of fairness, the dominance of the "speaking and writing habits of educated Northern European immigrants and their descendants" in schools and colleges must be reformed. She advocates writing courses that encourage experimental writing, especially writing "that could begin to articulate and reflect women's values and experiences," but also writing that respects the discourse patterns of African American Vernacular English (see Ball's chapter in this book for a description of this dialect).

14 Reflective Reading: Developing Thoughtful Ways to Respond to Students' Writing

Chris M. Anson
University of Minnesota

Writers improve by *being read*. Hearing other people's response to their work helps writers to develop a kind of internal monitor, a "reading self," that informs their decisions as they enter new and more sophisticated worlds of writing. By experiencing a range of responses to their work—from teachers, peers, and others—young writers gain a sense of their own authorship, learn how their composing choices affect their readers, and become more able to assess the effectiveness of their syntax, diction, and organization.

Early research and scholarship on response to student writing aimed to develop principles and methods that teachers could use more or less uniformly to help students improve their writing in different settings. However, more recent scholarship, which is well demonstrated in the contributions to this collection, has been exploring response and evaluation in complex and multifaceted ways that take into account issues of gender, culture, and personality (see also Elbow 1993; Hake 1986; Sperling 1993; Straub and Lunsford 1995; McCracken 1993). In practice, as much of this work suggests, response to writing is richly complex, highly context-dependent, and widely varied in method, style, and focus both within and across classrooms. Our stated beliefs about teaching and our descriptions of our response styles are not always reflected in what we write on students' papers, which may vary depending on our mood, context, or knowledge of specific students and their writing. In many cases, such variation takes place so tacitly that we may not be aware of the differences between our beliefs and the different roles we play as readers (see Purves 1984). The self-confessed grammarian, for example, finds himself so thoroughly engaged in a paper that he stops reading with, as Mina Shaughnessy put it, "a lawyer's eyes, searching for flaws" (1977, 7). He unconsciously overlooks several errors that he would have identified for a student with less engag-

ing material. The response or evaluation then displays a greater enthu-
siasm for the captivating material, and the proportion of identified
errors goes down. Similarly, a teacher who claims that she always tries
to render her comments as questions for revision might become so
frustrated with a student who changes very little between drafts that
she starts writing specific, controlling directions. Her response might
look authoritative (and certainly inconsistent) next to her stated practices, but she is using her best intuitions as a teacher to guide this
particular student.

Faced with discrepancies in our response practices, many teachers become frustrated or anxious, as if we have been made aware of
some small but annoying hypocrisy. We don't like to think of ourselves reading students' writing subjectively, messily. The hope for
uniformity and consensus becomes a way to remove such feelings of
instability or inconsistency. In the practice of response to student
writing, we like to think that if we can discover some key method,
informed by theory and predictable in outcome, its application will
lessen some of the bewildering complexity that reading students'
work inevitably calls into play.

But given the influence of context on our responses, we need to
reconsider this prevailing attitude toward inconsistency. As Straub and
Lunsford (1995) have shown in their study of the differences in response
styles among twelve "expert" composition scholar-teachers, it seems
problematic to develop a unified set of practices for responding to students' writing. Response is so rooted in context and human tempera-
ment that accepting diverse and even contradictory approaches or
rhetorical styles may be more useful than searching for a single method
supported by empirical research. It may be entirely appropriate, in
other words, to use quite different response strategies as long as we
know how to choose and apply them constructively. This is not to suggest that we don't bring to our responses an overarching disposition
or educational theory that guides our choices and sometimes makes us
do similar things with different pieces of writing. But it allows us to
admit some flexibility with which we can make informed choices about
the strategies to employ for a specific piece of writing.

Such a shift in priorities mirrors new theories of teaching effectiveness
which place the locus of teachers' improvement not on the accumulation
of research findings but on developing a higher consciousness, a kind of
"thoughtfulness," often captured in the phrase "reflective practice" (Schön
1983, 1987). In the area of response to writing, such an approach assumes
that developing a greater awareness of how our context influences the way
we read students' writing can help us to make more informed decisions—
and to become more able to adapt our responses to specific situations.

This chapter looks first at an interesting and troubling student essay in order to describe some of the contextual factors that influence our response practices in classroom settings. What external conditions shape our responses? How might situations change the way we look at a piece of student writing? The chapter then turns to some practical ways in which we can become more thoughtful readers of students' writing, developing the strategic knowledge that allows us to adapt our response methods to various students, classrooms, and institutions in educationally productive ways.

Some Varieties of Response and their Possible Sources

As an illustration of how we might begin to explore the ways in which our responses may be contextually influenced, consider an unusual, essay, written by Leang, a young Cambodian refugee who was a first-year college student enrolled in a regular section of an introductory composition course.[1]

My Message

Thanks God for let me have my life still, also thanks for let me have my little brother too, plus my older one and sisters. But I still can't forget my others. My parents and the people of Cambodia. What a past! I miss my family so very much and my country too. I wished I had my family back. The family of ten brothers and sisters stood side by side with my parents plus my nieces, nephews and grand nephews running all over the house. What had happened to my family and every family in the whole country? Who had created that problem???

April, 17, 1975, It was the day that Cambodia had collapsed into communism. In that day every thing in my country had changed. It was the disastrous day for my people. All school, hospitals, shops and markets and any business were closed. A lot of city people were killed by communist sodiers. And the rest were force to leave the cities to the country side. The jungle where no one live before. There was no more freedom. It was "THE COMMUNISM." The regime that all the properties were belong to the government alone. That was under the leader of Pol Pot. Imagine, Phenom Phen, the capital city of Cambodia used to be noisy with the sound of cars, trucks, radio, T.V., school children and everything, had been turned

---

1. Leang graciously allowed me to use his essay in faculty workshops as well as to reproduce and comment on it here. Because his essay is so much a part of this chapter, I offered him an honorarium for his contribution and invited him to write a response to be included in the chapter, but he declined both, simply glad, he said, that his essay was being put to use.

into the city of graveyard. The new rules and regulation had been set to people by the communist. It said "There are no more rich, no more people. We are all equal. No more religion, and no more believe in anything, but there is one to believe in "FARMING". My family the same as the rest of the city people were forced to leave the city with bare hands to work in the farm. Over there, there were no buildings, no houses, no street-shops or market, but there were trees, forest far away in the country side. At first, my dad had started with to cut the trees branches and leaves to make hut our-selve. We ran out of food, medicine clothing and lack of others con-sumer goods that we needed. Because the fierce Goverment would not let us so. The communists starved to give people very little of food, almost nothing day by day. But, they forced us to work so damn hard, at list 12 to 16 hours every day. We worked like slave. We worked without enough food. When we got sick, the fierce com-munists ignored us and gave us no medicine. They used the forces on people. They said all kind of bad words and even killed some-one just to show the rest not to do the same. "You'll must work in the farm! You'll must obey the communist's Rules! And must do whatever the communists have said, other wise, you people are known as the enemy of the communist Goverment! The enemy must dead!!!" The rule had set.

Three years and eight months living in communism was a trash. Life was really a tragic. In my family alone, first one of my sisters was dead, six months later, one of my brother was dead. Then my Aunts, uncles, nieces, nephews, my other brothers plus sister-in-laws. And at last when the communist ground our peo-ple so bad, my parents passed away. My parents died only one week apart. My family, my people, the whole couple millions of cambodian died one after others because of the starvation and the killing. I still rememberd how my dad died. He died because he was sick. He could not go to work for them (communist Gover-ment) and they starved him for weeks to die. My mom too, if they kindly gave my mom only a tea spoon of sugar to make home made medicine, probably she still suvive till today. I had seen every movement of my parents before they died because I was living with them.

In communism, actually we lived seperatly in the group of age. Children must lived differented from adults, adults lived differently from older adults and elderly. The reason that I could live with my parents and my four years old brother because I took a risk of my own life. I ran away from my group. There was nothing hurt more than seeing family, parents and a little brother laying sick side by side on a dirty mat at home with out food, medicine and water and had not a thing around. At that time I was about 12 years old, I myself was so weak too because I had malaria for months. I was so skinny with all my body turned pale; my eyes was kind of blue and yellow. But I had no more thinking of myself. I had tried all my best to find out the things that my family needed. I was became a thif. I stole foods from people. I disobeyed the rules of the com-munism and running around to find helps. I even prayed to God

to take my life or killed me first before he took my parents and my
little brother. But that was impossible, not very long later my parents died. God did not accepted my pray neither. Any way. I still
have my mom's last words before she died. Her word remind me
all the time I think of them. She said in a very weak sound that she
wanted me to stay alive; do not give up no matter what. She
wanted me grown up to be a man with mercy. A man that knew
right and wrong. A man that knew clearly between war-killing and
peace. A man that knew the difference between communism and
freedom. And before she met the end of her life she called me in
name, wispered and looked at me in the eyes and turned to look
at my ennicent brother sitting quietly on the dirty clothe near the
fire wood that I had made. My mom's eyes were full of tear. It seem
like she had million of words to say. Then she passed away and
left us behind in the middle of no where.

   When I think of "The War" I alway think of my country, my family and my people. I think the way they were destroyed . . . .
then, I turned to get angry, sad and even more frustrate. I still miss
my family and country so much. I love them always. I used to live
with comfortable when they're around.

After reading this essay, many teachers have strong feelings. The
content moves some to tears. Others are shocked to think the student
is enrolled in a standard first-year college composition course. Still
others become immersed in the underlying politics of Leang's "message," and reflect on their attitudes toward communism, human
rights, the Vietnam War, or whether Leang should be more radical
and proactive than his essay suggests. The variety of readings
prompted by this essay whenever it is presented without any
context—and the even greater range of suggestions about what we
might say to Leang about his writing—illustrate some of the many
sources of our response practices.

The Influence of Curricular Timing

Our choice of what to say to a student about his or her writing is heavily influenced by the point at which we read the writing in its development. Before the process movement began to pressure more
traditional teaching practices, response was heavily evaluative; it was
almost entirely summative, measuring the student's text against some
established standards. Comments aimed at improving the writing (or
the writer) looked toward the next occasion for practice; but comments
on the next paper were again judgmental, coming from sometimes new
and different sets of standards.

   In the contemporary, process-oriented classroom, response may vary
depending on when it is given in the development of a piece of writ-

ing. In such classes, response typically serves to motivate revisions (and encourage learning and further writing practice). A common response to Leang's essay, for example, locates the paper early in the process and treats it as a draft:

> Leang's story is *so* dramatic that it would be a great piece of writing if he could reorganize it, cut some material, expand some material, and clean up all the errors. I'd put him to work identifying as much of this as he could so that he could end up with a really first-rate paper.

Implied in this response is a vision of the classroom as a workshop, but one still very much focused on finished products. For both teacher and student, success is measured by the number of good papers produced, and the very best quality control (instruction, response, and evaluation) yields papers that can even be circulated or entered into contests. Although revision may play an important role in the course, it is directed toward the improvement of specific papers, without being generalized as a set of strategies for other and perhaps quite different tasks.

Some newer curricular approaches offer interesting and complicated varieties of this focus on the production of polished texts, requiring an even greater repertoire of response strategies. In some courses, a greater focus on the student shifts attention away from products alone and toward their writers, who will eventually move from site to site (into, say, a biology class or, later, a corporation or small business). In other courses in which students create portfolios of their work (see Belanoff and Dickson 1991), teachers may comment on students' in-process writing by playing the role of a (later) evaluator. This strategy involves first reading from the perspective of some institutionalized standards for the portfolio assessment, and then translating this reading into comments that recognize the progress of the student's work and its improvement. Some teachers who use a portfolio method, for example, would advise Leang that his narrative comes nowhere near the portfolio standards already established. The result may be a comment that invokes both the evaluator's and the teacher's different roles:

> I think as this essay stands that it won't be judged as ready for entry into Leang's portfolio. But I find it a really moving and interesting narrative, one that with some more revision and editing might just get there. I would say so to Leang, and then suggest that we sit down together so I can explain in more detail what he needs to do to get this ready for the portfolio assessment.

Some teachers may also be mindful of the entire process a student goes through in readying a piece for an external assessment; the response given on one occasion, then, plays a role in a later assessment of the student's overall performance on a writing project or in a course.

These potentially complicated readings of student writing suggest the need to identify and refine response strategies that are sensitive to issues of *timing and purpose.* While it may seem obvious that a response to a draft-in-progress will not look like a response to a final, graded paper, we must become more aware of how our choice of comments affects students at various points during this process. A teacher who "reads for meaning, not for errors," might not see the need to switch strategies between an in-progress draft and a final text submitted for a grade. But unless we are subverting an institutional grading system, differences must exist between these two occasions—differences in our roles as guides and coaches vs. gatekeepers and evaluators. Knowing what these differences are, and how they govern our choice of strategies, offers us the kind of higher-level knowledge that leads to more principled practice.

The Influence of Institutional Standards

As Mina Shaughnessy suggested in her discussion of the reaction to open admissions policies in the late 1960s at CUNY (1977), one response to students who don't seem to exhibit the appropriate skills necessary to survive in an academic setting is to quietly eliminate those students through failure. This strategy almost always involves a sorting and ranking process. Typically, a teacher will make expert decisions about a student's ability relative to the available program of instruction:

> It's clear that Leang is misplaced. Something went wrong in the diagnostic or advising system. He belongs in an ESL class, where he would get the kind of help he needs as a non-native speaker, especially with the surface mechanics and grammar.

This has traditionally been called text-based response because it measures the student's writing against a preexisting, often institutionalized standard. Such response strategies involve at least some gatekeeping: The student's paper is "owned" by the system, rather than by the student (*cf.* Knoblauch and Brannon 1982). The teacher's role—often requiring considerable training, expertise, and knowledge of alternative curricula available in the system—is to accurately assess ability against the standards set at the gate.

Standards for judging the quality of writing come to us from many sources at many levels—cultural, institutional, disciplinary, departmental, and personal (Anson and Brown 1991, 257–66). At the highest level, a "cultural ideology" of writing often influences how we think about and respond to students' work. Schools, while maintaining their autonomy and academic freedom within the larger culture, often reflect and amplify "larger sets of social and cultural values in the emphases they give to kinds and ways of knowing" (Piché 1977, 17). Nationally sponsored "writing report cards," speeches by the secretary of education or other high-ranking officials, reportage and editorials in newspapers and periodicals, and other commentaries on the state of education all subtly influence our values. Some teachers confess to using response practices that invoke much tougher standards in the wake of such commentaries, which may leave some students confused or frustrated as they try to figure out why there has been a sudden shift in the language or focus of the response.

In the case of recommending Leang to a different curriculum, the ranking takes place at an *institutional* level that focuses on the necessary skills and preparation of a college student, ignoring the kind of intellectual and emotional "preparation" that Leang brings into that setting from a regime in which he experienced atrocities that many American students can hardly imagine. Teachers comfortable with such an institutionalized ranking system will not feel as conflicted in their responses as those who may be opposed to it; but it is the very relationship between the two systems—institution and classroom—that guides our responses (see, for example, Mary Traschel's [1992] study of the role of college entrance examinations in the teaching of English).

Discipline-specific norms and standards may also influence our response to students' writing. When students enter an academic discipline as novices or outsiders, they may not be familiar with these norms. In such contexts, it is important for teachers to learn how to respond both as a representative of the discipline (gatekeeper) and as one who helps students to learn the information and strategies needed to pass through the gate. A response from the former position alone may be entirely unhelpful in enculturating students into the field.

Occasionally an individual *department* may have collective practices that are somewhat different from those expected professionally. Teachers in technical or scientific fields who tolerate or even encourage students to write from a highly subjective position may respond in ways antithetical to the goals of more traditional colleagues. In such situations, response to writing might come entwined with commentary about the discipline's received paradigm: "I really like the way you've placed yourself at the center of your case study, Peter. You know, of course, that many scientists would insist on a kind of clinical objectivity that your paper resists."

Some teachers may entirely avoid imposing institutional standards on students in a particular class, perhaps because they have more context-specific goals for their instruction than those that are generally expected across the campus. For example, in dislodging the emphasis on error hunting or pushing student writing into the synthetic mold of the five-paragraph theme, reader-response advocates have for several decades championed a less criterion-based way of responding to students' writing that deliberately avoids the didactic effluence of the red pen. This practice, in its further extension, may downplay the role of response and evaluation; the writing is produced in what Peter Elbow calls an "evaluation-free zone" (1993). The following often-heard reaction to Leang's essay illustrates this approach to the issue of standards:

> I'm incredibly moved by this account. In fact, the story is so authentic that cleaning up the errors makes it too Anglo, too fake. There is something compelling about the voice, the voice of a real refugee. I want to react in all my original horror, to be moved, because the story is moving and Leang should know it.

The strategy implied by such a response is to help Leang develop by focusing on function and meaning—a strategy strongly and elegantly advocated in much of the work of Russell Hunt (see Hunt 1986 and 1989 for representative accounts). Theoretically, literate activities are by nature purposeful, meaning-rich, and contextual (Bleich 1989; Brandt 1991). It follows that literacy improves mainly through meaningful literate experiences, not the practice of isolated skills or the production of artificial, readerless texts.

Yet approaches that deliberately avoid error hunts or red-ink corrections may seem puzzling to students who are already socialized into a system where their lived experience is subjugated to the goal of perfecting the linguistic features of their writing. From the student's perspective, this strategic withholding of response often appears deliberately, sometimes playfully, sometimes even unfairly evasive—the teacher's attempt to push the relativism of multiple rhetorical choices (see Perry 1970; Anson, 1989a). After working so hard to acquire English, Leang may be fully expecting to have his errors identified even in the context of so moving a personal account. An important strategy is knowing in advance when a student is ready for what may be an unfamiliar kind of response.

An extension of this meaning-focused response relates readerly reactions more closely to the process of revision:

> I wouldn't grade Leang's paper or invoke any kind of textual standards whatsoever. What he doesn't need right now are criteria; he needs a real, natural, reader-based response, one that can connect with him on the basis of his meaning. I'd say how moved I was. I'd

also indicate some places where I was confused or wanted more information, or where I stumbled over his expression. But I'd keep the focus pretty much on Leang's experience and my experience, and hope that my reaction would lead him to identify places he could improve.

Here, the goal is to use the reading process (usually characterized as "natural") to encourage the student to explore other options. It relies, in other words, on the social construction of meaning to create the dissonance that will lead to revision.

While reader-based response supports a purposeful, meaning-centered curriculum, it is wrong to assume that such reading is any more "natural" than hunting for errors. It is, after all, a kind of pedagogical strategy. Our position as educators is already inscribed by our context. Behind the apparently simple donning of an armchair-reader's perspective lies an elaborate set of theories about what might help students to develop their writing in just a few weeks. That development is not purely rhetorical and linguistic; it involves creating in students' own thinking the same underlying beliefs about writing being modeled in our response. (Much of the literature on peer groups suggests that students can learn to respond to each other's writing as we do, even though the conditions of their response are altogether different from ours.)

The Influence of Personal Belief

What specific beliefs do we bring to our reading, relative to its content, that might influence our response? Teachers reading Leang's essay sometimes respond in ways apparently designed to pressure him into thinking about the underlying political implications of his autobiographical account. When they take the form of typical academic consciousness-raising, such responses may place the teacher in a fairly neutral position, perhaps by invoking a reader who might not agree with the writer. When they take the form of a more direct challenge, however, such comments demonstrate a political critique designed to make the student intellectually uncomfortable. At its strongest, "contestatory" response admits that all texts (and all reactions to them) must be political and ideological. Instead of veiling this fact beneath the discourse of feigned neutrality, contestatory response tries to pressure students into becoming more aware of their political and personal conditions and how their writing and the writing of their culture can either reveal or hide such realities. As illustrated in the following paraphrase, the teacher can use this strategy to reflect a particular bias or position, very strongly deciding for the writer what intellectual journey he or she should travel:

> I don't think Leang goes far enough in trying to understand what
> Communism is, so he ends up simply endorsing (by default) an
> American system that has its own share of atrocities both national
> and international. He is almost blind to the ways in which he has
> been oppressed twice, and the second case is in some ways more
> insidious than the first because the oppression is less visible. I'd
> want to tell him so, and get him to critique his material conditions
> now, to examine what has really changed, and who is really in con-
> trol in the midst of his newfound freedom.

Because it is sometimes emotionally charged, such a response strategy can be very difficult to apply. Unconsciously, we may praise some
students for making assertions with which we agree, but then engage
our strategy of contestation for students whose thinking we want to
reform. The former students remain complacent in their views while
the latter are challenged.

At a time when many teachers are actively challenging students' atti-
tudinal complacencies, understanding the relationship between
response, personal belief, and the development of writing abilities has
never been more important. Many tensions now arising between teachers and students owe to mismatches of political and cultural attitudes
expressed in student writing and teachers' own often strongly held
beliefs. Better awareness of the sometimes tacit ways in which belief
systems influence response can help us to develop strategies that do
not condemn while they contest, strategies that are sensitive to the
goals of particular courses, as well as the backgrounds and dispositions
of particular students and their own intentions for their papers. We can
then more ably translate personal reactions into the kinds of comments
that help students to see multiple perspectives and not feel as if they
are being forced to accept particular views.

The Influence of Rhetorical and Situational Goals

Knowledge of the complicated relationships between the rhetorical
goals of an assignment and the student's interpretation of those goals
in her own rhetorical plans can strongly influence our response. Typically, response is shaped by the extent to which a paper (as a text) con-
forms to the implicit rhetorical standards of the assignment. Yet
students' own goals and plans offer a rich source of information about
a piece of writing that can completely change a teacher's response strategy. Jeffrey Sommers (1989), for example, has described a technique in
which students write a memo about their paper to help their teacher
decide how to respond. The response is shaped by the student's own
expressed needs. Similar strategies involve short, tape-recorded narrative commentaries from the student describing his or her goals for a

paper and calling attention to things the student wants to work on. In collections of students' work, the reflective "cover statement" accomplishes a similar objective—to provide teachers with the student's own "review and consideration and narration and analysis and exploration of what learning is occurring in writing" (Yancey 1992, 16). Response that expects students to articulate their own intentions, as illustrated in the following paraphrase, also helps to move students beyond what Sharon Crowley calls the "distressing fact that students' intentions may amount to little more than getting a passing grade on an assignment, or pleasing us by demonstrating their ability to observe the formal strictures we have laid down in class" (1989, 108):

> My response would be a set of questions to Leang. I want to know what he wants to do with this paper, who he's talking to, what his purpose is in sharing this piece. Does he want us to think differently about refugees or Cambodians? Does he want us to feel the tension between his love of his country and people and his hatred of the oppressive regime under which he suffered? Or is this therapeutic, a venting of his life woes, a completely self-directed text shared with us only through his educational circumstances?

Here the teacher is simply unable to talk to Leang without more complete knowledge of his purposes. Extended a bit further, this response can become a nonresponse, not in the sense of an "evaluation-free zone" (Elbow 1993), but an inability to respond until the student himself has helped the teacher to choose the most useful strategy for the student's needs.

Sometimes response may be influenced by imagined situational goals that extend beyond students' expressed needs, as shown in the following comment which has surfaced in discussions of Leang's paper at several schools:

> I've seen this sort of paper before. Such papers are all too common to people who work in writing labs. While I don't doubt the authenticity of Leang's account, many students who have had shocking experiences in other countries try to use these to get an emotional response from a teacher, softening the grammatical blow. Sometimes they'll use the same paper or experience several times because they know it works. It's a kind of unsinister ploy. I wouldn't play into it.

This response practice tries to take into account the student's subsidiary motives for choice of topic, writing style, or use of detail. It may come from thinking about the circumstances of the student's writing beyond the classroom (that the student is on an athletic team, or is trying to get into law school, or is the daughter of the department chair) or from imagining more general aspects of student "underlife" to which most of us have little direct access (see Brooke 1987; Anderson et al. 1990). Attitudes toward students in general or toward the particular kinds of students that attend our school can profoundly influence our response. In this case, the teacher simply guesses, perhaps in a less than charitable way, what nonnative speakers like Leang try to do with their writing.

In the absence of information from students about their intentions, we usually invoke instructional goals often deeply embedded in our teaching, such as the need to avoid generalizations, entertain a reader, or give evidence for assertions:

> I assume that in this kind of writing it is always important to use details and images to embellish and support more general claims. Under these circumstances, I would want Leang to go back over the piece and identify places where he could add detail or sharpen our image of the events.

This response practice comes from a more highly goal-driven pedagogy; specific papers are occasions to learn specific skills, sometimes in isolation. Narratives, for example, are used to work on "showing versus telling"; or five-paragraph themes are used to practice logical and argumentative structures. Such practices often owe to what Peter Mosenthal calls a "utilitarian ideology" that stresses the nature of tasks and the passing on of knowledge necessary to survive in real-world settings (1983, 40). Tasks are often organized in increasing complexity, using writing for their practice and acquisition. Assuming that Leang's assignment is designed to help students practice effective paragraphing techniques, the teacher might focus on various moments in his essay where such technique is lacking.

Bringing students' needs together with implied and expressed goals of particular assignments can lead to a more strategic, tailored response. The decision to focus on a particular rhetorical issue such as paragraph development, for example, can also be informed by a higher sense of what is appropriate given the content of the text, as well as Leang's personality, his interaction in class and in small groups, his office visits, the nature of his previous writing, and the amount of time already spent in class working on the skills being applied. Without knowledge of these often intricate details, we have no basis on which to cast a negative judgment on a response that puts aside Leang's meaning in favor, for this moment, of calling attention to errors.

The Influence of Readers' Circumstances

Most of the time, we respond to writing without reflecting consciously on the influence of our personal circumstances. We may be aware that we read four (of twenty-five) student papers early in the morning on a train or bus, ten more later in our office (with coffee), three during the evening news, and the final eight late at night after a long day. While such considerations may seem trivial, developing strategies for response in quite different circumstances can help us to avoid trying to use the wrong strategy at the wrong time. Some teachers aware of this issue split their response process into different readings. "First reading" can be done anywhere—it is an occasion to get a holistic impression of an entire text. "Second reading," however, is accompanied by careful response and must be done without distraction and in time blocks conducive to reflection.

Another external circumstance is the order in which papers are read. Most of us have experienced the curious phenomenon of searching for the paper of a "good" student when we are tired and want to respond just to one or two more pieces of writing. In such cases, we may be choosing a different strategy for response, one that acknowledges our readings of students' past work or class performance. The reading may seem easier because we expect fewer errors, organizational problems, or weaknesses in content. Our focus shifts to other, more meaning-centered issues, issues that may require less translation of our reactions into directed commentary for revision or assessment. Similarly, one paper in a group of essays may influence our subsequent judgments. Six papers all displaying the same lack of paragraph development may have a profound effect on the reading of the seventh, which is judged to be very strong when it might have been judged problematic if preceded by six superb essays. In Leang's case, the content of the essay may be so rich and culturally interesting on the heels of half a dozen bland accounts of minor car accidents and summer jobs that its quality improves by virtue of its location in a string of essays.

The "pace" or "tempo" of reading students' work can also influence the nature and focus of the response (see Himley 1989). Reading students' writing first requires a complicated, rich internal response, much of it never shared with the writer. Of this response, we then select relevant ideas and translate them into an external commentary, using appropriate, student-centered language. In most cases, the internal response is more elaborate and less strictly pedagogical than external response. Good teaching requires a highly complex process as we read, collect impressions, formulate an internal response, choose which of the many impressions and ideas the student should receive, and then decide what form the commentary should take, how long it should be, and what language and style it should be rendered in.

Developing expertise in response relies on a higher awareness of the "tempo" of this translation. Novice teachers sometimes experience little lag time between an internal reaction and an external written comment, time when a more experienced teacher might pause to reflect on the internal reaction and translate it into a comment that will carry more weight or be more instructive. Unable to slow their reading to the molasses-like pace that could yield a really full response for each of fifty (or 150) student papers, expert teachers learn to trade off external response time (marginal comments) against time to reflect internally, knowing that a single well-chosen and articulated comment can ripple through an entire paper and, for the right student, harvest a major and fortuitous revision. In other words, the teacher writes less but says more.

There are several reasons for disparities in the amount of reflection between internal and external response. Newer teachers often feel that quantity shows diligence: The more they can say or write, the more their students will improve. Some teachers may also suffer from conditions that work against reflection—150 papers begging for response, or large classes of blurred faces in a mechanical curriculum. Under these less-than-ideal circumstances, however, a changed tempo and a more reflective response may actually lessen a teacher's burden and offer students more useful feedback. Furthermore, some kinds of writing may require less time for reflection and translation of internal response than others. If a teacher is modeling the process of reading, then writing down internal responses as they occur may be more appropriate than reading the entire text, reflecting on it, and translating and distilling many impressions into a carefully worded summary.

Many other dimensions of our situations as educators affect our response to students' writing. The few I have touched on here represent some useful starting points for discussions of what we do when we respond and, given the great variety in our focus and styles, how we can make the best use of these in particular circumstances. Doing so, as I have argued, is helped by reflection—by sharing strategies and by developing as much consciousness of our practices as we can. The next section considers some of the ways in which, as teachers, we can practice such reflection, both individually and collectively.

Toward Reflective Practice in Response and Evaluation

As a kind of discourse, response to students' writing is carried out in an often-personal domain between teacher and student—necessarily personal, we might argue, because of the expert-novice relationship that ensues in most educational settings. Yet this privacy not only blocks the chance for collaborative inquiry into our practices, but, perhaps as a result, relegates response to a more tacit domain of instruction, unexamined and undiscussed. Unlike the course syllabus, which teachers develop with conscious attention to various educational principles and which is often seen and even responded to by other colleagues, response remains curiously shielded from collective view (Anson 1989b). Clearly, we need more effective approaches for drawing to the surface, in both personally meaningful and collectively useful ways, the complexities involved in reading, responding to, and evaluating students' writing. Several such approaches—including "authentic" faculty-development workshops, teaching portfolios, and deep cases—are promising ways to begin such individual and collaborative reflections on response.

Authentic Workshops on Response

In spite of the ultimately personal nature of response, the most productive methods for improving this area of teaching take place, not surprisingly, in collaborative settings involving sustained dialogue and exchanges among trusting peers. While any such group activities must adjust to local circumstances, they offer participants the chance to share and study the complex interactions between teachers and individual students.

Samples of students' work, such as the essay written by Leang, can help us to talk about and analyze our methods for response and evaluation. While the resulting discussion can be enlightening, most of the time it is set in motion by generalized "response schemas" based on typical educational settings. The discussion may also lead to remarks *about* the essay, not comments directed to the student who wrote it.

More useful for developing response strategies are workshops that invite participants to bring in actual samples of students' writing from their own classes, on which they have made either formative or summative evaluative comments. In such "authentic" workshops, teachers can take turns describing the context of the paper(s) they have brought, which inevitably calls into play descriptions of the student, assignment, curriculum, preceding classroom work, school, and other important information. Once the context of the writing is clear, the group can discuss the teacher's commentary in detail, focusing on the appropriateness of the remarks, their style, focus, length, and effectiveness. Reflection can be prompted by comparisons of the teacher's and other participants' internal responses; by careful analyses of the language the teacher chose, relative to his or her purposes in the context described; by discussions of the participants' impressions of specific comments, especially their attempts to understand the teacher's underlying purpose or rationale for the comment and its placement; and by conclusions about the relationship between the teacher's system of beliefs and the response he or she made. Sharing such reflections not only exposes us to different response strategies (perhaps ones we have never used or seen used), but also helps us to formulate theoretical and practical justifications for the decisions we make. What results from such discussions is at once a larger repertoire of response strategies and a clearer, more informed understanding of how to use such strategies in the classroom.

Teacher Portfolios as a Context for Reflection

Workshops that bring teachers together to share their ideas, observations, and practices provide a social context for faculty development, but individual teachers need time to reflect on their instruction and then try out new methods in their classrooms. As Centra (1993) points out, teachers "become experts in part by the lessons they learn through their own inquiries and insights" (111). The "teaching portfolio," a widely heralded method for instructional development, is ideally suited for encouraging such reflective inquiry.

Teaching portfolios have gained national attention, especially in higher education, as useful tools both for improving teaching through greater reflection and for evaluating teaching effectiveness through richer forms of documentation than student evaluations or peer-review notes (see Anson 1994; Edgerton, Hutchings, and Quinlan 1991; Seldin 1991). As repositories of documents that demonstrate sustained reflection on important teaching issues, portfolios give us a space in which to examine critically our own response practices and develop new strategies.

Portfolio entries to be shared in draft form during inservice meetings or faculty workshops could reflect on specific features of response, such as the balance of positive, negative, and constructive commentary, or even on the definition of such terms as "positive," "negative," and "constructive." In development programs for preservice teachers or teaching assistants, participants might work through several such features of response, each in a different portfolio entry (choice of language; choice of focus; clarity of explanations; amount of annotation; percentage of questions vs. command statements; balance of comments on surface features vs. matters of meaning; and so on). Teachers with more background in rhetoric or composition research could supplement their discussions with references to the theories that inform their practices. Over time, teachers could revisit samples of writing to which they responded years before and chart the course of their own development as readers of students' writing, along the lines of various developmental schema of teaching (e.g., Shaughnessy 1976; Anson 1989b).

"Deep Cases" of Response

In the absence of real samples of students' writing, "deep cases" may give enough context to enrich group discussions of student writing. Deep cases are real or highly realistic scenarios that invite readers to imagine themselves in the situation and often pose some problem or set of problems to solve. Such cases often take the form of narratives with various characters—teacher, students, supervisors, colleagues— and involve complicated, unresolved conflicts that lead teachers into long, involved conversations about the issues, problems, and potential solutions or courses of action in the case. Cases of student writing, for example, could offer rich, detailed background information about many of the factors that we have already examined in this chapter. Participants could then respond to the writing (in its draft or final form) and discuss, analyze, or rationalize their commentary in light of the deep background information provided. Cases could be created to highlight certain aspects of the response process or the teaching situation (see Anson et al. 1993; Hutchings 1993).

Collaborative Teaching

As teachers we should be actively experimenting with response methodology and sharing the results with colleagues. Portfolio programs for student writing, for example, have led to creative new teaching situations involving multiple readings of students' work (see Elbow and Belanoff 1986). Several experiments in which teachers team up to offer the same version of a course, but read and anonymously grade the work of each other's students, have offered interesting anecdotal information about the interpersonal dynamics of response (in one case, for example, students felt hopelessly cheated because their evaluator was not privy to their visible hard work and earnestness in the classroom—aspects of response and evaluation that beg for much more exploration).

Various institutionally sponsored initiatives can encourage teachers to pair or team up in ways that directly affect the way they respond to students' writing. Linked courses, for example, can bring teachers of English or writing together with teachers in discipline-specific courses such as psychology, history, or science to create joint-enrollment courses.

Teachers linked in such ways can design writing assignments together and then work out creative ways to read and respond to them. Constantly comparing their impressions and judgments can help them to reflect on the relationship between the students' work and the many other contextual issues influencing their decisions.

New Media for Response

In light of the electronic revolutions taking place in education at all levels, we must begin to explore more fully various alternative media for response. Although tape-recorded responses have been discussed in the literature sporadically for decades, few scholars or teachers have looked carefully into this alternative to handwritten marginalia (see Anson 1997). Computer programs are now available that allow teachers to deposit icons in the margins of their students' on-screen work; these icons turn on a computer tape recorder to record the teacher's verbal comments. A second click of the icon turns off the recording device until the next comment is desired. The student, opening her paper on her own computer screen later on, can click on the marginal icons and hear her teacher's voice commenting on her text. Such programs were once thought futuristic, but now they are being supplemented by video boxes that appear in the corner of the screen to give the verbal message a visual accompaniment.

Interactive computer technology, e-mail response, chat lines, virtual writing labs with tutors who telecommute, programs that pretend to read and analyze texts—all such systems and more will characterize the response environment of the next few decades. While many such alternatives seem exciting and novel, we must also be prepared to assess them from the perspective of the new awareness encouraged by deeper thought about our more conventional, traditional methods.

Response in Classroom-based Research

Most of us have little occasion to study the effects of our response and evaluative practices on our students or to test out new strategies. Such information usually comes to us in the form of successful or unsuccessful revisions of drafts on which we have commented, or when students are puzzled or upset by what we write or say about their work. A more systematic investigation of response and evaluation, however, can lead to many new insights about the teaching and learning processes. Questions teachers can explore without the need for much sophisticated apparatus or complicated research designs might include these:

1. What sorts of responses do students like and dislike the most, and why?

2. Which forms of response do they find most helpful? How are they judging what is "helpful"? What kinds of revision are prompted by the response?

3. How do the conditions of our response affect us?

4. What do we typically do with student writing when we respond to it?

5. How do we respond to different kinds of writing (short or long, basic or advanced) or by different kinds of students (men or women, native or nonnative speakers, majors or nonmajors, upper- or working-class)?

6. How do we vary our responses in light of our knowledge about the writer or the circumstances of the writing?

7. How do we change our response between in-progress work and final texts?

8. How do institutional or departmental standards affect our practices?

Studying such questions in the context of our own teaching not only forms higher-level awareness of our practices but also encourages improvement by giving us at least some quasi-empirical basis for our understandings and beliefs.

In this chapter I have claimed that multiple strategies for response may be more instructionally useful to us than aiming for a single, unified method. My belief is supported by my faith in the power of reflection to help us understand and justify our diverse practices, so that we do not fall into the trap that Richard Fulkerson (1979) documented in his analysis of unprincipled shifts in response styles. To adapt our practices to meet our increasingly diverse educational settings, we must become more reflective of the many complicated influences on our behavior. Those reflections, finally, will lead us to educational practices that are informed by thoughtfulness, balance,and clarity of method.

Yet, clearly, much more inquiry is needed into the relationship between teacher reflection and the practice of responding to students' writing. We do not know, for example, what effects a strong focus on reflective practice could have on the success of teachers' responses. Furthermore, the focus of reflective practice has remained steadily on teachers, largely ignoring the ways in which students' own reflections might provide information that facilitates both learning and teaching in specific classrooms. We need much more inquiry into what students bring to the response process—how they read our comments, and how, in turn, they develop new ways of reading their own and others' writing. In an interesting analysis of students reading and commenting on each other's writing, Lee Odell (1989) asks a number of questions about how students develop the ability to respond to other people's texts and to interpret the responses they receive. In addition to developing strategies for responding to students' writing based on fuller analyses of our situations, we need to be investigating and reflecting on how students interpret and act on these responses.

With the knew knowledge such investigations yield, and with more attention to the ways in which we can think about and develop our teaching and responding methods, we will be in a better position to play out our roles as expert readers in a context where many people are growing in different ways.

Works Cited

Anderson, Worth, Cynthia Best, Alycia Black, John Hurst, Brandt Miller, and Susan Miller. 1990. "Cross-Curricular Underlife: A Collaborative Report on Ways with Academic Words." *College Composition and Communication* 41: 11–36.

Anson, Chris M. 1989a. "Response Styles and Ways of Knowing." In *Writing and Response: Theory, Practice, and Research,* ed. Chris M. Anson, 332–66. Urbana, IL: National Council of Teachers of English.

———. 1989b. "Response to Writing and the Paradox of Uncertainty." In *Writing and Response: Theory, Practice, and Research,* ed. Chris M. Anson, 1–11. Urbana, IL: National Council of Teachers of English.

———. 1994. "Portfolios for Teachers: Writing Our Way to Reflective Practice." In *New Directions in Portfolio Assessment: Reflective Practice, Critical Theory, and Large-Scale Scoring,* ed. Laurel Black, Donald Daiker, Jeffrey Sommers, and Gail Stygall, 185–210. Portsmouth, NH: Boynton/Cook-Heinemann.

———. 1997. "In Our Own Voices: Using Tape-Recorded Commentary to Respond to Student Writing." In *Assigning and Responding to Writing in the Disciplines,* ed. Peter Elbow and Mary Deane Sorcinelli, 105–13. San Francisco: Jossey-Bass.

Anson, Chris M., and Robert L. Brown, Jr. 1991. "Large-Scale Portfolio Assessment: Ideological Sensitivity and Institutional Change." In *Portfolios: Process and Product,* ed. Pat Belanoff and Marcia Dickson, 248–69. Portsmouth, NH: Boynton/Cook-Heinemann.

Anson, Chris M., Joan Graham, David A. Jolliffe, Nancy Shapiro, and Carolyn Smith. 1993. *Scenarios for Teaching Writing: Contexts for Discussion and Reflective Practice.* Urbana, IL: National Council of Teachers of English.

Belanoff, Pat, and Marcia Dickson, eds. 1991. *Portfolios: Process and Product.* Portsmouth, NH: Boynton/Cook-Heinemann.

Bleich, David. 1989. "Reconceiving Literacy: Language Use and Social Relations." In *Writing and Response: Theory, Practice, and Research,* ed. Chris M. Anson, 15–36. Urbana, IL: National Council of Teachers of English.

Brandt, Deborah. 1991. *Literacy as Involvement: The Acts of Readers, Writers, and Texts.* Carbondale: Southern Illinois University Press.

Brooke, Robert. 1987. "Underlife and Writing Instruction." *College Composition and Communication* 38: 141–53.

Centra, John A. 1993. *Reflective Faculty Evaluation: Enhancing Teaching and Determining Faculty Effectiveness.* San Francisco: Jossey-Bass.

Cooper, Charles R. 1977. "Holistic Evaluation of Writing." In *Evaluating Writing: Describing, Measuring, Judging,* ed. Charles R. Cooper and Lee Odell, 3–32. Urbana, IL: National Council of Teachers of English.

Crowley, Sharon. 1989. "On Intention in Student Texts." In *Encountering Student Texts: Interpretive Issues in Reading Student Writing,* ed. Bruce Lawson, Susan Sterr Ryan, and W. Ross Winterowd, 99–110. Urbana, IL: National Council of Teachers of English.

Edgerton, Russell, Patricia Hutchings, and Kathleen Quinlan. 1991. *The Teaching Portfolio: Capturing the Scholarship in Teaching.* Washington, DC: American Association for Higher Education.

Elbow, Peter. 1993. "Ranking, Evaluating, and Liking." *College English* 55: 187–206.

Elbow, Peter, and Pat Belanoff. 1986. "Portfolios as a Substitute for Proficiency Examinations." *College Composition and Communication* 37: 336–39.

Fulkerson, Richard P. 1979. "Four Philosophies of Composition." *College Composition and Communication* 30: 43–56.

Hake, Rosemary. 1986. "How Do We Judge What They Write?" "In *Writing Assessment: Issues and Strategies,* ed. Karen L. Greenberg, Harvey S. Wiener, and Richard A. Donovan, 153–67. White Plains, NY: Longman.

Himley, Margaret. 1989. "A Reflective Conversation: 'Tempos of Meaning.'" In *Encountering Student Texts: Interpretive Issues in Reading Student Writing,* ed. Bruce Lawson, Susan Sterr Ryan, and W. Ross Winterowd, 5–19. Urbana, IL: National Council of Teachers of English.

Hunt, Russell A. 1986. "Could You Put In a Lot of Holes? Modes of Response to Writing." *Language Arts* 64: 229–32.

———. 1989. "A Horse Named Hans, a Boy Named Shawn: The Herr von Osten Theory of Response to Writing." In *Writing and Response: Theory, Practice, and Research,* ed. Chris M. Anson, 80–110. Urbana, IL: National Council of Teachers of English.

Hutchings, Pat. 1993. *Using Cases to Improve College Teaching: A Guide to More Reflective Practice.* Washington, DC: American Association of Higher Education.

Knoblauch, Cy, and Lil Brannon. 1982. "On Students' Rights to Their Own Texts: A Model of Teacher Response." *College Composition and Communication* 33: 157–66.

Lees, E. O. 1979. "Evaluating Student Writing." *College Composition and Communication* 30: 370–74.

McCracken, Nancy. 1993 (November). "Toward a Conversational Theory of Response." Paper presented at the Annual Convention of the National Council of Teachers of English, Pittsburgh, PA.

Mosenthal, Peter. 1983. "On Defining Writing and Classroom Writing Competence." In *Research on Writing: Principles and Methods*, ed. Peter Mosenthal, Lynne Tamor, and Sean S. Walmsley, 26–71. New York: Longman.

Murray, Patricia Y. 1989. "Teachers as Readers, Readers as Teachers." In *Encountering Student Texts: Interpretive Issues in Reading Student Writing*, ed. Bruce Lawson, Susan Sterr Ryan, and W. Ross Winterowd, 73–85. Urbana, IL: National Council of Teachers of English.

Odell, Lee. 1989. "Responding to Responses: Good News, Bad News, and Unanswered Questions." In *Encountering Student Texts: Interpretive Issues in Reading Student Writing*, ed. Bruce Lawson, Susan Sterr Ryan, and W. Ross Winterowd, 221–34. Urbana, IL: National Council of Teachers of English.

Perry, William G., Jr. 1970. *Forms of Intellectual and Ethical Development in the College Years: A Scheme.* New York: Holt, Rinehart & Winston.

Piché, Gene L. 1977. "Class and Culture in the Development of the High School Curriculum, 1880–1900." *Research in the Teaching of English* 11: 17–27.

Polanyi, Michael. 1966. *The Tacit Dimension.* Garden City, NY: Doubleday.

Purves, Alan C. 1984. "The Teacher as Reader: An Anatomy." *College English* 46: 259–65.

Schön, Donald A. 1983. *The Reflective Practitioner: How Professionals Think in Action.* New York: Basic.

———. 1987. *Educating the Reflective Practitioner.* San Francisco: Jossey–Bass.

Seldin, Peter. 1991. *The Teaching Portfolio.* Boston: Ankara.

Shaughnessy, Mina P. 1976. "Diving In: An Introduction to Basic Writing." *College Composition and Communication* 27: 234–39.

———. 1977. *Errors and Expectations: A Guide for the Teacher of Basic Writing.* New York: Oxford University Press.

Sommers, Jeffrey. 1989. "The Writer's Memo: Collaboration, Response, and Development." In *Writing and Response: Theory, Practice, and Research*, ed. Chris M. Anson, 174–86. Urbana, IL: National Council of Teachers of English.

Sperling, Melanie. 1993 (November). "Response to Writing Multiply Construed." Paper presented at the Annual Convention of the National Council of Teachers of English, Pittsburgh, PA.

Straub, Richard, and Ronald F. Lunsford. 1995. *Twelve Readers Reading.* Cresskill, NJ: Hampton Press.

Traschel, Mary. 1992. *Institutionalizing Literacy: The Historical Role of College Entrance Examinations in English.* Carbondale: Southern Illinois University Press.

Yancey, Kathleen Blake. 1992. "Teachers' Stories: Notes Toward a Portfolio Pedagogy." In *Portfolios in the Writing Classroom*, ed. Kathleen Blake Yancey, 12–19. Urbana, IL: National Council of Teachers of English.

15 Creating a Climate for Portfolios

Sandra Murphy
University of California–Davis

Mary Ann Smith
California Writing Project,
National Writing Project,
University of California–Berkeley

Several years ago, when we visited San Francisco's Newcomer High School, we noticed a sign posted outside a classroom door: "Math is not a spectator sport." The sign conjured up images of the stereotypical sports watcher, reclining in a chair, second-guessing the game—a far cry from individuals and team members in a contact sport in which performances are for keeps, and players are responsible for what happens.

The sign also signaled that teachers are increasingly concerned about and looking for strategies to help students have meaningful, substantial contact with their learning. Portfolios are one way to encourage that kind of contact, because they offer students practice at calling the shots and opportunities to shape and assess their own learning.

On the surface, portfolios may seem simply a receptacle for collecting student work. We want to argue, however, that portfolios are far more. They are a means for teachers to reposition students from the sidelines to the center of their schooling: to intensify students' efforts, ownership, and experimentation. Consequently, portfolios have the potential to change the student's and, therefore, the teacher's role in education. When students own their work, teachers act less as conduits for externally prescribed content, and more as expert guides for students who have a personal investment in their education.

Although there is no single approach to portfolios, we can nonetheless define them through commonly recognized activities. When students construct portfolios, they select, at various points during the year, demonstrations of their learning, sometimes including the drafts and notes that contributed to each selection. They reflect on their work samples, on occasion comparing one with another. Eventually, they may present their selections to an audience for a particular purpose. In this process, they are building new understandings of the craft of writing and of their own progress.

In terms of classrooms, this definition of portfolios suggests that students are players. Students make their ideas and experiences count by demonstrating and analyzing their learning. In other words, as players, they are also strategists, commentators, and owners.

The teacher is the key to helping students take on these roles. Rather than simply making choices for the student, for example, the teacher teaches how to make choices. Rather than being the sole commentator on a piece of student work, the teacher teaches how to reflect and analyze. In other words, the teacher explicitly creates a teaching and learning situation in which the central features are negotiation, interaction, reflection, and student ownership.

Negotiation

As teachers we face a dilemma. On the one hand, we know that learning proceeds best when students assume active roles as planners and decision makers, when they have opportunities to pursue their own interests and needs. On the other hand, we know that student learning has to accommodate the visions and expectations of administrators, parents, and the teachers themselves. In any classroom, then, there is a chorus of ideas about what and how students should learn. In many portfolio classrooms, teachers look to portfolios as one way to turn up the volume on the student's voice.

Negotiating Portfolio Design

Several years ago we joined a group of English teachers at Mt. Diablo High School who were experimenting with portfolios. Together, the twelve of us designed a seemingly attractive and rigorous framework for what should go into the student writing portfolios. All of us were pleased that we could be so forward-looking as to include different types of writing and indicators of growth and process. That first year, we asked students to include memory, opinion, and descriptive writings, learning logs or daily journal entries, and entries which included notes and drafts. The students complied but complained: "There's no place for my poetry." "I can't include my very favorite piece." "My best one won't fit. It's not what you want."

In succeeding years, we turned more and more to the students. What had begun as an exercise in what *we* thought was important ended in our consideration of what *they* thought was important. They wanted categories that were more open-ended. For example, instead of naming particular genres, they suggested categories such as "most imaginative" and "most challenging." It didn't take us long to recognize the learning potential in mutually negotiating a portfolio design.

Nationwide, teachers and students have hammered out a number of possibilities for portfolios that satisfy all the learners in the classroom:

- Having students include, along with more specified entries, whatever other pieces are important to them.

- Defining portfolio contents via broad guidelines for performances, processes or genres so that students have real running room in making choices.

- Designating the portfolio as a showcase for the students' best pieces.

In each of these instances, students are constructing a portfolio that demonstrates their writing abilities. Part of the building process may include rethinking the structure or shoring it up where it seems to sag—all invaluable learning experiences.

Designing a portfolio is analogous to creating a subject for writing. There is seldom a quarrel about the learning that happens when students are encouraged to find their own topics or when they make their own revisions. Indeed, if the teacher made all these decisions for the student, most of us would agree that the student might never learn how to initiate writing ideas or improve on drafts. The same is true for portfolios. If students have no opportunity to negotiate the contents of the portfolio, much of the learning evaporates.

The teacher's role in the portfolio decision-making process is not unlike her role in teaching students how to select writing topics. For example, teachers often brainstorm with students a lengthy set of options and possibilities for writing topics, or in the case of portfolios, for contents. Next, teachers teach students various strategies for selecting a promising option—from personal preference (which topics or contents students care most about) to more objective criteria. A criterion for selecting a paper topic, for instance, might be to find a topic that allows the writer to conduct interviews, make observations, and collect data. Criteria for selecting the contents of a portfolio might be to choose papers that demonstrate instances of the process of writing, such as editing and revision, or demonstrates a range of genres. In other words, the teacher's role is to show students—through models, examples, discussions, individual and group practice—how people make intelligent choices.

In some circumstances, teachers and students are not free to build the portfolio from scratch. For instance, external portfolios often bring with them a set of requirements and therefore, a defined starting point for negotiations. Notice that the students in this California classroom are asking the teacher how they can accommodate the rules of a particular external portfolio:

> What about music? Music is a huge part of my life. Can you include something in there—and how?
>
> Can you still do other things? I have different ideas.
>
> Can I include a copy of a speech?
>
> Is it OK to use group projects?
>
> Do we have to have a letter to introduce the portfolio? Can it be a poem?
>
> What do they mean by document? Just one document?

In this exchange, teacher and students are exploring the boundaries, but also the flexibility of external requirements. The role of the teacher is still to teach students about options, although in a more limited context. Here, teachers help students learn to interpret predetermined requirements. The New Standards portfolio design, for example, specifies portfolio entries such as a persuasive essay, a response to literature, a narrative account, a reflective essay (1995). In other words, even in more constrained circumstances, someone has to make the choices and cite the most important learnings. To the extent that teachers allow and provide for that someone to be the student, they are recognizing that the ability to evaluate one's own writing is a critical component of one's development as a writer.

Negotiating Curriculum

Portfolios are not an appendix, something tacked onto the tail end of classroom curriculum. They mirror, and in the best instances, they help to determine what happens in a classroom. Although teachers and students may need to accommodate a district or school curriculum, for portfolio negotiation to have any meaning beyond the design of a folder, students need to have some say-so about the curriculum itself.

Adapting curriculum to spotlight the learners is not new, of course. In many classrooms, teachers create opportunities for students to exercise some decision-making power. For instance, teachers might ask students to read something in common, and then, as described above, teach them to develop their own writing topics. In so doing, teachers are recognizing what Moffett and Wagner call

> the essence of the school's job [that is] to show learners what there is to choose from and to give them every opportunity to understand

how wise decisions are in fact made. Personal choice is at the center, not only so that the learner cares about what she is doing, but so that good judgment will develop. . . . (1983, 27)

Not only are student choice and rigorous curriculum possible at the same time, but to argue otherwise is to create a false dichotomy. The trick, as Linda Darling-Hammond explains, is "to develop settings that are both learning-centered—that is, focused on challenging curriculum goals for all students—and learner-centered—that is, attentive to the needs and interests of individual learners" (1996). Darling-Hammond has identified common features in the practice of teachers who are successful at developing "real understanding of challenging subjects" and who do so for "an array of students who include those traditionally thought to be at risk":

- They develop engaging tasks that give students meaningful work to do, projects and performances that use the methods of a field of study and represent a whole piece of work within that field: doing historical research, writing and "publishing" a short book, developing a computer simulation or scale model.

- They design these to allow students to build on their strengths and interests as they reach for new and more difficult performances.

- They develop what I call "two-way pedagogies" to find out what students are thinking, puzzling over, feeling, and struggling with. The tools of these pedagogies include student presentations, skillful discussions, journals and learning logs, debriefings, interviews, and conferences. Teachers consciously develop pedagogical knowledge about the specific learners in their classroom while relying on knowledge about learning generally.

- They constantly assess students to identify their strengths and learning approaches as well as their needs and to examine the effects of different instructional efforts. They understand assessment as a measure of their teaching as well as a measure of student learning. They publicly point to students' different strengths and accomplishments, creating a platform for legitimation and growth for each student in the classroom.

- They painstakingly scaffold a process of successive conversations, steps, and learning experiences that take students from their very different starting points to a proficient performance—including a great many opportunities for approximation and practice, debriefing and conversing, sharing work-in-progress, and continual revision.

- They pay attention to developing student confidence, motivation, and effort and to making students feel connected and capable in

school. They teach from the heart as well as the head. Strong relationships with students and with parents become especially
important because the world is harder and riskier. Successful
teachers' strategies for supporting learning extended beyond technical teaching techniques. They practice what John Dewey called
"manner" as method: Their voiced and enacted commitment to
student learning and success supports students in the risky quest
for knowledge. (Darling-Hammond 1996, 11–12)

One concrete instance of the kind of teaching Darling-Hammond
describes comes from Amanda Branscombe's ninth-grade classroom in
Georgia. Branscombe and her co-researcher, Shirley Brice Heath, created projects that addressed their goals of having students practice
ethnographic approaches and gather data, yet met the interests and
concerns of individual students. According to Branscombe and Thomas
"After we designed them [the projects], the students discussed all of
them, modified some, omitted others, and added their own" (1992, 8).
The following list of inquiry projects shows the influence of both students and teachers:

> (1) a study of baseball language and its rule structure, (2) a study
> of the ways people read to young children, (3) a comparative study
> of rap music and Elizabethan poetry and prose, (4) a comparative
> study of rules and strategies for video games and English gram-
> mar, (5) an autobiography of each student and a videotaped pre-
> sentation . . . (6) a class newspaper, (7) a study of poetry . . .
> (Branscombe and Thomas 1992, 8)

The point is not in the particulars of these projects. Rather, we offer them
as examples of the challenging content and creative activities that students and teachers can design together, beginning with a set of ideas
from any source, so long as it is open to authentic negotiation. Negotiated curriculum invites labor sharing and co-researching—a classroom
climate in which teachers and students collaborate to generate ideas.

Another example of negotiated curriculum comes from Terry
Underwood and Sandra Murphy's research study at Rutter Junior
High School in Sacramento, California. Underwood and Murphy
found that in classrooms where seventh and eighth graders were
completely free to select titles for their independent reading (reading
outside of class), students did not read more challenging books, nor
did their reading achievement scores improve during the school year.
On the other hand, when students were guided by their teachers—
when they picked books after some kind of negotiation—their selections were more challenging and their scores improved. "The teachers
conferenced individually with students," Underwood and Murphy

explain, "and negotiated learning goals with them which led students to titles and authors that they might not have ordinarily considered" (1996, 6). While Underwood and Murphy do not claim that reading selections and scores necessarily go hand-in-hand, they do demonstrate another benefit of negotiation. It can actually elevate the level of student work. The teacher does not have to impose or mandate, and yet her authority makes all the difference in moving the student beyond the status quo.

It is precisely to expand thinking that teachers invite students to consider what is important to learn, how to go about learning it, and how to capture that learning and represent it to others. Negotiating curriculum does not give away rigor; it depends on rigorous thinking.

Negotiating Criteria

In classrooms where students are learning to make choices and judgments, teachers can guide students in constructing criteria for assessing their work. One such teacher is Kathryn Howard, who has her eighth-grade Pittsburgh, Pennsylvania, class create wall charts that contain lists of qualities students believe essential to a good piece of writing. Howard teaches students to constantly revisit their lists and notes how criteria change over the course of the year:

> Early in the year students place an emphasis on form, grammar, and spelling when formulating class lists. In time, as the emerging writers gradually come to place more emphasis on the *ideas* that drive their writing—after discussion, modeling, and making the reading-writing connection—the quality of these lists rises significantly. Often, then, these same students voluntarily move form-related criteria to positions of lesser importance on their lists. (1993, 91)

Howard's observation is confirmed by researchers from the PACE Project in the Harvard Graduate School of Education:

> Once when we walked into Kathy Howard's eighth-grade class in Pittsburgh, students were reading their work aloud. Posted on the wall behind them was a list of their criteria for good writing. Smack in the middle of the list was "Long." A student read a very short piece about learning that his grandfather was seriously ill. So short that he had to read it over again for everyone to catch it. The room went still. Quietly, Kathy walked over to "Long" and asked, "What do you think?" A voice from the back of the room said, "What we meant was long enough." (Wolf, Greer, and Lieberman 1995, 5)

In contrast to this example of building knowledge are situations of prescribed criteria. The quality of such criteria is not the issue here. They may or may not merit a standing ovation, and they may or may not be of use to the writing teacher. At issue is the ultimate reason for introducing criteria at all: so that students can use them in any number of writing situations. We want to argue that merely supplying students with criteria does not help them make criteria their own.

The alternative is the Howard approach, that is, to invite students to grapple with all kinds of published and unpublished pieces of writing, and in the process, to try out different ways of describing them. In this way, students work from the inside out, extending not only what they know about particular features of writing, but also what they know about the complexities of defining a good piece of work.

Throughout this process, the teacher acts as both resource and expert guide and contributor. For example, it is the teacher's job to point out what she, too, sees in model papers, the use of specific details or the effectiveness of flashback as an organizational strategy. In this way, the teacher "catches" what students may be missing and at the same time models different ways to recognize and talk about specific characteristics of writing.

The teacher is, in fact, the absolute key to negotiation. As Davis High School's Linda Holte illustrates, the teacher must carefully craft student learning about criteria. Holte begins the year by asking each student to develop a personal, rank-ordered list of the "Five Commandments of Effective Writing." In whole-class settings, she periodically asks students to share their commandments and to examine the similarities among them. Examples of the most common critiera are writing should be purposeful; writing should engage the reader; writing should be carefully organized; and writing should exhibit strong control of mechanics.

Also during this whole-class sharing, Holte teaches students to reflect on and revise their lists—in response to what they are learning or to the demands of certain kinds of writing. At the end of each quarter, Holte asks students to explain their number one commandment of effective writing and then to relate it to their work. In individual conferences, she reviews commandments and teaches the student more about constructing significant criteria.

A final thought about the kinds of support teachers can provide while students are learning to write: guidance, or "scaffolding," to use the construction metaphor, is temporary:

> Students do not need scaffolds forever. They are adjustable; they can be raised, lowered, or moved depending upon [the teacher's] goals. And they are facilitative; they allow students to strive for goals they might not be able to achieve entirely on their own. (Underwood, Murphy, and Pearson 1995, 77)

Interaction

The idea that children learn by interacting with their world has a long history. Piaget's theory, for example, describes the child as an active constructor of knowledge. It is Vygotsky, however, who most clearly locates that child in a social world, where learners socially construct meaning. The idea is that an individual reshapes and extends internal understanding by collaborating and learning, "not from another, but through another" (Tomasello, Kruger, and Ratner 1993, 496). In the best of all worlds, portfolios will reside in the kind of classroom where students are actively engaged in interacting—with each other, with their teacher, and with their own reading, writing, and learning.

Interacting in the Classroom

Most of us would agree that it is useful for students to interact with other people, testing their assumptions and getting other perspectives on their writing. Students also benefit from opportunities to discuss the content and quality of their portfolios. The usefulness of these discussions, however, depends on what has preceded them—the kinds of practice students have had in working together.

Learning happens in the interaction between students and between teachers and students. In interactive classrooms, teachers do not cart in chunks of knowledge to be distributed equally among the students. Rather, they create structures that allow students to author new knowledge. For example, they plan occasions for students to work collaboratively and to respond to each other's writing. They confer with students in one-on-one settings, not to deliver directives to be followed, but to help students discover possible alternatives and to develop shared values. They model roles students can take, showing them how to function effectively as a reader and listener to other readers.

When students read and respond to each other's writing, they see their work through the eyes of another. When students work together on projects, they share the resources of another. When students and teachers confer over drafts of writing or thinking, everyone learns in the exchange, teachers and students alike. Indeed, mutual learning establishes the climate in which portfolios will thrive.

In her article "Making the Writing Portfolio Real," Kathryn Howard affirms the importance of acclimation, of a "warmup" for portfolios. For example, her students practice reflecting on their own writing:

> For my eighth-grade students, thinking of themselves as writers and thinking of writing as a continuing process were at first abstract and foreign concepts. Barriers began to come down,

> however, as students learned to share their written pieces
> aloud—with a partner, a small group, or the entire class.
> (Howard 1990, 4)

Howard recommends interactive processes such as modeling, collaborating, questioning, and reflecting as the rites of passage to portfolios. These processes also characterize constructivist classrooms often referred to as "communities of learners." Elizabeth Lee and Mary Lamon describe these communities as ones in which both students and teachers are actively engaged in learning, where the body of knowledge is not fixed but rather a growing organism, where critical questioning is highly valued, an environment in which motivation is intrinsic. (1995, 2)

An example of this kind of community comes from California teacher Joni Chancer, whose fourth and fifth graders talk passionately about their reading. "I stumbled into what has become a favorite part of our portfolio classroom," Chancer explains, "book clubs. I told a teacher friend that I wanted to capture the elements of my adult book club: the sharing, excitement, and anticipation of discovering really good books. I know how powerfully influenced I am by someone else's enthusiastic endorsement of a particular book or author" (Chancer 1993, 37).

Chancer groups the students in heterogeneous clubs that meet weekly. Students attend the meetings with a "Lit Letter" about a self-selected book, letters that may reflect on the reasons for choosing the book, personalities and changes in the characters, favorite parts or lines, and so forth. While Chancer poses questions for the students—"What will you remember the most about this book?" and "Was this book easy? Difficult? Challenging? Just about right? Why?"—she does not expect students to answer any or all of her questions (37). She does expect, however, that her students will get more out of their reading if they are personally involved as learners and teachers of each other:

> Children clearly address their letters to each other, not to the
> teacher. The other club members then jump off from the letter
> to a lively conversation. Frequently students jot down the titles
> of books that interest them, and I often ask the children to come
> prepared with a favorite excerpt to read aloud. . . . The book club
> meeting becomes the context for authentic assessments, providing
> me with rich opportunities for observation and informal
> note taking. (38–39)

Chancer, with her book clubs, and fellow teacher Howard, with her forums for sharing student writing, illustrate the teacher's role in building processes and structures that lead to portfolios.

Interacting with Portfolios

As a tool for learning, portfolios work best when students confer with their teacher or with each other, just as they would in revising a draft. How else, except by consultation, would students become aware of more than one possibility? And when the possibilities include every piece of writing a student has done, to be sifted and winnowed for the portfolio, teachers can help students learn to assess their own work.

For example, Linda Rief asks her New Hampshire middle school students to "arrange their writing from most effective to least effective and to evaluate it." To guide their self-assessment, she asks them questions such as "What makes this your best piece? How did you go about writing it? What makes your most effective piece different from your least effective piece?" (Rief 1990, 28). Teachers might also ask students, after they have ranked and analyzed their rankings, to trade portfolios with another student and ask for that student's independent rankings and reflections. By comparing the rankings, students could learn how their judgments compare with those of an outside reader. They could reconsider their selections and the reasons for those selections from another point of view. In this way, the views of other students and of the teacher can open up new perspectives for the student.

At schools like Walden in Racine, Wisconsin, and Central Park East Secondary School in East Harlem, New York, portfolio interaction includes a student's formal presentation or defense to a committee. Members may be other students, teachers, parents, or professionals from the community, all of whom listen to the presentation and ask questions. In the case of Central Park East, "If a presentation or a portfolio item is deemed not ready, it does not die; instead it goes back to the drawing board with specific suggestions for improvement" (Darling-Hammon and Ancess 1994, 34).

The significance of this kind of interaction is clear. All important stakeholders come together in a mutual endeavor to learn and evaluate. In particular, students can claim the power that is generally unavailable to young people: the right to explain and defend their work, knowing that they can revise it even after the evaluation. Without promoting this particular kind of portfolio interaction, we want to cite it as an example of student-led conversation and of dramatizing or giving meaning to student work and the standards it intends to represent. Further, we see a distinction between a "final exam" and a culminating moment that is introspective for the entire learning community:

It is in these committee meetings that all the members of the CPESS community can see the fruits of their labors. It is a sort of moment of truth for all involved in the teaching and learning process. There is no escaping what worked, what has not worked, and what needs more work. (Darling-Hammond and Ancess 1994, 36)

Reflection

The portfolio interaction that often captures the most attention is student reflection. Like other kinds of thinking, reflection is learned through interaction with others. As Elizabeth Lee and Mary Lamon explain,

> If reflection is the mental process of carrying out an internal dia-log with oneself, then students can only learn this through engag-ing in a dialogue with the teacher and other students. It is learned socially in the interpersonal zone before it is internalized and becomes intrapersonal. (1995, 6)

Reflection is also the result of interacting with criteria for writing, preferably as we explained earlier, criteria that students have internalized. Consider this eighth grader's introductory letter to her portfolio:

> Dear Reader:
>   My favorite writing piece I chose was "My First Kiss." I like this piece because it showed good dialogue, with enough descrip-tion to show how I was feeling. It also had some humor in it, which is good.
>   "My First Kiss" is an example of what I'm good at. I'm consid-erably good at using dialogue and using description for my emo-tions. I figure I'm good at this because I have a broad range of emotions to choose from. My weakness in writing is writing rough drafts because I don't see the point in it. I'm also weak at rewrit-ing long drafts, because I get really restless. When I get restless I watch T.V. and I may never stop. That's bad.
>   The method that I use for writing is I go to my living room, turn on the radio, and get cracking. The music helps me write. I don't know why, but the faster the music, the faster I write. I hate it when people are around me when I write. I don't know why, I guess I'm independent.
>   The type of writing I do best is narrative writing. I guess I like to write this way because I like telling stories and am good at mak-ing people understand how I feel.
>
>   Sincerely,
>   Francie Choy

Francie names several features that she is convinced contribute to good writing—dialogue, description, and humor. She is less convinced about the value of multiple drafts, possibly because she has not yet learned how to revise, but only to recopy. She seems to value a speedy pen, another example that her criteria for effective products and processes are still developing and she is still testing them out.

Another student, Larry, can pinpoint his criteria, particularly criteria for organizational devices and sentence structure:

> Although there are many strengths in my writing, there are weaknesses as well. My main goal for the second semester is to become consistent with transitions. Some are excellent and well thought out, while others need to be stronger. I am confident that I will be able to correct this error, based on the evident changes that have taken place in my writing so far this year. These changes have greatly improved my writing. I have eliminated such silly mistakes as weak or run-on sentences, word usage problems, and repetition. Because of these improvements I have grown in my ability to write and will undoubtedly continue to do so in this next semester and in the future.

For the student, reflection is a sizing up of progress, strengths and weaknesses, new directions or goals, and qualitative changes. Using the trail of evidence (the portfolio), the student can also make explicit those writing strategies that are in place (however wobbly) and those that need revisiting. The fact of recognizing and naming the evidence makes that evidence potentially available on other writing occasions. At the least, reflection dispels the notion of "doneness," that writing and learning screech to a halt at some arbitrary stop sign.

For the teacher, reflection has other benefits. Student papers come framed in a context: the student's intent, judgment, affections, and often, doubts. Writing is no longer an exchange of paper between relatives who live on opposite continents. Rather, the teacher has a collage, overlapping pictures of how a particular piece of writing came together or how the portfolio itself took shape, along with student frowns, blushes, and sighs of relief. Reflections also bring informative surprises. As Mississippi teacher Tamsie West explains,

> Any time you haul in a fishing net or a portfolio, you are going to get lots of unidentifiable wiggly sea creatures that you didn't expect to find. And sometimes those strange and curious creatures, upon closer examination, are just as valuable as what you set out to catch. (West 1993, 105)

What's more, teachers can investigate their own teaching through students' reflections. Edith Kusnic and Mary Finley, writing instructors at Antioch University in Seattle, Washington, explain that student self-evaluation creates new opportunities for productive exchanges between teachers and students:

> We learn what keeps students motivated, engaged, and interested and what they experience as important learning. What we hear may raise important questions about teaching and learning in the classroom: What we think we are teaching is not what students are learning; what we think is clear and simple is, instead, complex and troubling; what we say is heard differently by different students. A mechanism that gives us access to students' ideas about their own learning allows us to provide sounder and more effective educational experiences. (1993, 7)

Reflection is not simply a culmination. It can take the form of a reading or writing log, a writer's notebook, or an ongoing classroom conversation about how we learn what we learn. It can happen in moments, or it can happen from stacking up experiences, comparing one with another. Portfolios provide a home not only for retrospective reflections, but for the current state of affairs.

Reflection is not automatic, however natural it may seem at first glance. Many students have not had opportunities in their school careers to take stock. From her classroom research, Roberta Camp (1992) recommends easing students into reflection, beginning with reflections on a single piece and moving to reflections on a body of work. For example, teachers first ask students questions such as "What did you like best about this piece?" or "Which of your writing skills or ideas are you least satisfied with in this piece? Why?" In practicing reflection, students can also think about the processes involved in writing. Teachers sometimes ask students questions such as "How did you work on this piece?" or "What kinds of changes did you make?" or "What part of the process was hardest for you?"

Only later do teachers begin to ask students to reflect on a body of work. As a first step, they ask students to select one or two pieces to compare with work done on other occasions. Ultimately, teachers ask students to reflect on how they have changed as writers and to decide on their next steps. They ask questions like, "What do you notice when you look at your earlier work?" and "How do you think your writing has changed?"and "After looking at these pieces, what do you think you might want to work on next in your writing?"

Certainly, reflection can enhance learning. However, Brian Johnston (1987) explains that too often we do the reflecting for our students. In other words, we rush to mark their papers or to give them our ideas about how they can improve. "As teachers responding to student work or as outside evaluators," Roberta Camp says, "we have traditionally told students what *we* see and what *we* value—very often at precisely the point in their learning where they should be discovering what *they* see and what they value" (1992, 61).

Student Ownership

What Camp and Johnston, among others, seem to be telling us is that we, as teachers, need to allow students to own their work, not just rent it. Owners tend to care about their property and invest more in upgrades than do renters. Owners tend to examine the cracks in the walls with an eye to doing something about them. Renters, on the other hand, leave the fix up to the real owners.

Robert Tierney uses the analogy of owner/renter to describe the extent to which he expects students to have free rein with their portfolio choices. In Tierney's view, the teacher is the renter; the student is the owner. For that reason, Tierney, as teacher, asks a student if he can "rent a space" in the student's portfolio, when he wants to add a piece to the portfolio from the student's body of work (Tierney 1994).

In effect, Tierney is paying respect to the student's capacity to be an owner. His image of owner and renter may or may not work for every teacher or teaching situation. However, the idea that student ownership can advance the cause of learning is central to this discussion of portfolios. So, too, is the teacher's role in promoting responsible, productive ownership. At every step in the portfolio process, from design and preparation to presentation of the portfolio, the teacher is carefully crafting with students a range of choices and the basis for making those choices. At every step, the teacher is examining with students the ways that writers and portfolio makers take into account the needs of readers. At every step, the teacher is setting up authentic exercises and practice sessions for students so that they can audition their choices in front of real audiences and then revise those choices.

Elliot Eisner (1985) describes the connection between ownership and learning in this way:

> For experience to be educational, students must have some investment in it—must have some hand in its development—and without actual participation or the availability of real choices within the curriculum, schooling is likely to be little more than a series of meaningless routines, tasks undertaken to please someone else's conception of what is important. (69)

Conclusion

Teaching is a delicate balance between guiding and prescribing. Probably all of us have had the experience, at least once, of providing a structure—say, a discussion of a particular book or short story—and then stepping zealously over the line, telling the students exactly what to make of that literary work. The same temptation is there with port- folios. We often teeter between teaching students how to design, decide, and demand of themselves and doing all this for them. The latter is so much more neat and efficient! The former has no guarantees.

But unless students have practice in owning and being responsible, they may be unable to set their individual courses, let alone put their learning to work to help others. The teacher's role, according to Freire, is not to merely transmit knowledge, but to enable students to bring issues and experiences from their own lives into the classroom, so that reading and writing become personally relevant and connected to the larger world.

Recreating student and teacher roles through portfolios does not have to be an anarchical tornado of folders and paper, anymore than it has to be a factory-model assembly line. These are the two extremes. In between is another element of negotiation, interaction, and own- ership: setting up the system. Students and teachers might address questions such as "Where are we going to store our work samples?" "How are we going to keep track of works-in-progress?" "Should we pick up our work folders as we come into the classroom each day?" Every class endeavor requires a system. We have never met a teacher who has not established some procedures for managing student work and classroom activity.

Setting up procedures can give both teachers and students confi- dence that portfolios will not overpower them. Procedures may be the best starting point for some. But portfolios have to go beyond the pro- cedural level if they are to transform teaching and learning.

Frequently, a new approach in the classroom, like portfolios, seems awkward, like a new shoe that needs breaking in. It takes the very char- acteristics of the learning community that we have examined in this chapter to move that change beyond the procedural level and make it work to everyone's benefit:

- *negotiation:* giving students ample practice in weighing and mak- ing informed choices about their learning and the demonstration of that learning;

- *interaction:* engaging students in tasks in which the students, not the teachers, are the main performers; that is, tasks that put stu- dents in contact with each other, with the teacher and other adults, with works-in-progress and in publication;

- *reflection:* asking students to size up learning, using the portfolio to make the trail of evidence explicit;

- *ownership:* inviting students to put their learning on a par with their most valuable possessions and activities.

We began this chapter by comparing spectator and contact sports. In the name of contact, we want to offer a final note of encouragement: When students and teachers risk making contact with change, they may find the field muddy at times. But whatever the terrain, the fact that they are working together to improve their teaching and learning practices gives new meaning to the idea of winning the game.

Questions to Consider

Question: Can teachers try out portfolios in small doses?

Answer: Yes. Many of the teachers we know who are very successful with portfolios began with modest experiments: portfolios with limited contents, three or four pieces of writing, or limited timespans, a quarter vs. an entire year. By not taking on a huge portfolio project, these teachers made it safer for themselves and their students to assume new roles. Even when teachers are suddenly immersed in large, required portfolio projects, they can take it one piece of writing at a time.

Question: Will negotiation take up a lot of precious time? Is it the most efficient way to go about teaching our students?

Answer: The issue here is clearly what we value in terms of student learning. Yes, it is more efficient to simply teach "thinking appreciation," as Dan Kirby and Carol Kuykendall (1988) call it, and less efficient to allow students to wade into thinking itself. Grant High School teacher Edna Shoemaker values thinking: She sets the direction and goals for her twelfth graders, but she allows them to take different paths to the destination.

Question: To what extent do student-centered portfolios as described in this article match current curriculum and performance standards?

Answer: The issue here is about rigor, and the hidden question is "Are we becoming soft if we let students have a little say-so?" Standards for the assessment of reading and writing, developed by the International Reading Association and the National Council of Teachers of English now say that

"First and foremost, assessment must encourage students to reflect on their own reading and writing in productive ways, to evaluate their own intellectual growth, and to set goals" (IRA and NCTE 1994, 13). This vision of assessment assumes that students will be challenged in classrooms to take responsibility for their learning.

Works Cited

Branscombe, N. Amanda, and Charlene Thomas. 1992. "Student and Teacher Co-Researchers: Ten Years Later." In *Students Teaching, Teachers Learning,* ed. N. Amanda Branscombe, Dixie Goswami, and Jeffrey Schwartz, 3–21. Portsmouth, NH: Boynton/Cook-Heinemann.

Camp, Roberta. 1992. "Portfolio Reflections in Middle and Secondary School Classrooms." In *Portfolios in the Writing Classroom: An Introduction,* ed. Kathleen Blake Yancey, 61–79. Urbana, IL: National Council of Teachers of English.

Chancer, Joni. 1993. "The Teacher's Role in Portfolio Assessment." In *Teachers' Voices: Portfolios in the Classroom,* ed. Mary Ann Smith and Miriam Ylvisaker, 25–48. Berkeley, CA: National Writing Project.

Cope, Bill, and Mary Kalantzis, 1993. *The Powers of Literacy: A Genre Approach to Teaching Writing.* Pittsburgh: University of Pittsburgh Press.

Darling-Hammond, Linda. 1996. "The Right to Learn and the Advancement of Teaching: Research, Policy, and Practice for Democratic Education." *Educational Researcher* 25 (6): 5–18.

Darling-Hammond, Linda, and Jacqueline Ancess. 1994. *Graduation by Portfolio at Central Park East Secondary School.* Columbia University: National Center for Restructuring Education, Schools, and Teaching.

Eisner, Elliot. 1985. *The Educational Imagination: On the Design and Evaluation of School Programs.* New York: Macmillan.

Fox, Pat. 1995. "Writers' Reflections: The Rest of the Story." Unpublished manuscript. Savannah, GA: Georgia Writing Project.

Howard, Kathryn. 1990. "Making the Portfolio Real." *The Quarterly of the National Writing Project and the Center for the Study of Writing* 12: 4–7, 27.

———. 1993. "Portfolio Culture in Pittsburgh." In *Fire in the Eyes of Youth: The Humanities in American Education,* ed. Randolph Jennings, 89–102. St. Paul: Occasional Press.

International Reading Association and National Council of Teachers of English. 1994. *Standards for the Assessment of Reading and Writing.* Urbana, IL: National Council of Teachers of English.

Johnston, Brian. 1987. *Assessing English: Helping Students to Reflect on Their Work.* 2nd ed. Philadelphia: Open University Press.

Juska, Jane. 1993. "No More One–Shots." In *Teachers' Voices: Portfolios in the Classroom,* ed. Mary Ann Smith and Miriam Ylvisaker, 61–73. Berkeley, CA: National Writing Project.

Kirby, Dan, and Carol Kuykendall. 1988. *Mind Matters: Teaching for Thinking.* Portsmouth, NH: Boynton/Cook-Heinemann.

Kusnic, Edith, and Mary Lou Finley. 1993. "Student Self-Evaluation: An Introduction and Rationale." In *Student Self-Evaluation: Fostering Reflective Learning,* ed. Jean MacGregor, 5–15. San Francisco: Jossey–Bass.

Lee, Elizabeth, and Mary Lamon. 1995. "Thinking about Learning." Unpublished manuscript. Ontario Institute for Studies in Education.

LeMahieu, Paul, Drew Gitomer, and JoAnne Eresh. 1995. *Portfolios Beyond the Classroom: Data Quality and Qualities.* Research Report no. 94–101. Princeton, NJ: Educational Testing Service.

Moffett, James. 1981. *Active Voice: A Writing Program across the Curriculum.* Montclair, NJ: Boynton/Cook.

Moffett, James, and Betty Jane Wagner. 1983. *Student-Centered Language Arts and Reading, K–13: A Handbook for Teachers.* Boston: Houghton Mifflin.

Murray, Donald M. 1982. *Learning by Teaching: Selected Articles on Writing and Teaching.* Portsmouth, NH: Boynton/Cook.

Piaget, Jean. 1954. *The Construction of Reality in the Child.* New York: Basic Books.

Rief, Linda. 1990. Finding the Value in Evaluation: Self-Assessment in a Middle School Classroom. *Educational Leadership* 46: 24–29.

Tierney, Robert. 1974. "Coming to Grips with Alternative Assessment." Paper presented at the Elementary Education Association Conference, San Francisco, CA. 22 March.

Tomasello, Michael, Ann Cale Kruger, and Hilary Horn Ratner. 1993. "Cultural Learning." *Behavioral and Brain Sciences* 16: 495–511.

Underwood, Terry, and Sandra Murphy. 1996. "Using Portfolios to Monitor, Assess, and Motivate Voluntary Reading in a Northern California Middle School." Unpublished manuscript. University of California–Davis, Center for Cooperative Research and Extension Services for Schools.

Underwood, Terry, Sandra Murphy, and P. David Pearson. 1995. "The Paradox of Portfolio Assessment." *Iowa English Bulletin* 43: 72–86.

West, Tamsie. 1993. "The Teacher's Role in Portfolio Assessment." In *Teachers' Voices: Portfolios in the Classroom,* ed. Mary Ann Smith and Miriam Ylvisaker, 93–106. Berkeley, CA: National Writing Project.

Wolf, Dennie Palmer, Eunice Greer, and Joanna Lieberman. 1995. "Portfolio Cultures: Literate Cultures." *Voices from the Middle* 2: 4–6.

Wood, D. J., Jerome S. Bruner, and G. Ross 1976. The Role of Tutoring in Problem Solving. *Journal of Child Psychology and Psychiatry* 17: 89–100.

Vygotsky, Lev S. 1978. *Mind in Society: The Development of Higher Psychological Processes,* ed. Michael Cole, Vera John-Steiner, Sylvia Scribner, and Ellen Souberman, Cambridge, MA: Harvard University Press.

16 Integrating Reading and Writing in Large-Scale Assessment

Fran Claggett
Consultant for New Standards through the
National Center on Education and the Economy

The last ten to fifteen years have brought about major conceptual changes in how we teach writing. We now know how purpose shapes the composing process. We understand the recursive nature of composing. We know the value of teaching many different strategies so that students will be able to use those that fit their purposes in writing history or biology or calculus or, later, in whatever writing situations arise in their work and their lives. We value authentic voice and styles of writing that reflect the individual life experience, ethnicity, and gender out of which we forge our language. With the increasing use of writing assessments in many districts and states, we have also learned a great deal about how to assess student writing.

The same story cannot be told about reading. Although, as a profession, we have made significant advances in how we teach the reading of literature, too often we rely on our assessment of writing to gauge student understanding of a poem, an essay, or a novel. How can we measure how well students are reading? This is a question we need to address as we move toward a new understanding of how reading and writing inform each other and of how a new kind of assessment can play an important part in our teaching of both.

In this chapter, I will present one model for an integrated reading and writing assessment task and offer guidelines for constructing and scoring such a task. While I will draw primarily from work undertaken during my tenure as director of the development team for the California performance assessment program, I will also draw on my experience in designing and evaluating tasks for New Standards, a partnership of states and urban school districts that has developed national education standards and a multifaceted assessment system directly correlated with these standards.

Authentic assessment in California began in 1985, with a focus on assessing writing at grades 8 and 12. Very early, the assessment advisory group[1] made a decision that has had far-reaching implications not only for assessment but for classroom teaching in California: It endorsed the notion of placing primary responsibility for the development of assessment with classroom teachers. During the next two years, the teacher assessment-development team, under the direction of Charles Cooper, gave shape and substance to Cooper's vision of a writing achievement test based on writing types delineated primarily by writer purpose. Rather than conceiving of writing in a singular way, teachers used *purpose* as the primary differentiating feature underlying eight types of writing to be tested at each grade level (see Figure 1).

California initiated its statewide writing performance assessment program in 1986–87, with its primary objective that of obtaining school and district scores for achievement in writing. This goal was realized through a matrix sampling format in which each student wrote one essay, randomly selected from a bank of eighty prompts at each grade

Writing Type	Grade 4	Grade 8	Grade 10
Expressive	x		
Firsthand Biographical			
Sketch	x		
Reflection	x		
Narrative	x		
Story			x
Autobiographical			
Incident	x	x	
Persuasive	x		
Problem-Solution		x	
Evaluation		x	x
Speculation about			
Causes or Effects	x	x	
Interpretation			x
Controversial Issues			x
Informative	x		
Report of Information	x	x	
Observational Writing	x	x	

Figure 1. Types of writing to be tested at various grade levels.

level. Not only was there a range of writing types in this matrix design, there were ten different prompts for each writing type.

The first year of testing was revolutionary for teachers in California: Teachers statewide took part in state-sponsored staff development workshops conducted by the teachers who had written the prompts, designed scoring guides for each type of writing tested, and written handbooks which were distributed to every middle and high school in California. The writing handbooks were crucial elements in this statewide reform effort. Each writing type was defined and illustrated by classroom activities and professional essays. Extensive suggestions for teaching the various types of writing were accompanied by specific examples of annotated student writing. Teacher involvement in the process continued in the summer with forty to fifty classroom teachers, trained and led by a "chief reader" from the development team, scoring the assessment papers at eight different sites statewide. This massive teacher participation in the writing achievement test had an immediate and pervasive impact on the teaching of writing throughout the state. According to a survey conducted by Charles Cooper and Sandra Murphy, 90 percent of the eighth-grade teachers in the state had experienced some direct involvement in staff development related to teaching the kinds of writing tested by the end of the second year of the test.

As the writing assessment moved into its third year, members of the advisory committee and the development team turned their attention toward the next logical step, an integrated reading and writing assessment. Since we wanted our language arts assessment to incorporate current theory and exemplary teaching practices, we wanted to design a test that would show both the separate natures of reading and writing and also the ways that the two activities interrelate. Our older ways of perceiving of reading and writing allotted *comprehending* to reading and *composing* to writing. As the profession grew in its awareness of the role of *process* in both reading and writing, we came to see that we *comprehend* as we compose, and *compose* as we read. The nature of literacy encompasses both in reading, writing, and speaking and listening as well. We went beyond the traditional four elements of the English language arts, however, to include the comprehension and composing of graphic elements, an aspect of English language arts now embodied in the NCTE Standards.

When we began to design an integrated assessment, we were experienced in conducting a statewide writing assessment, using teachers in regional scoring sites to assess writing for both rhetorical effectiveness and conventions. How to incorporate our ideas about the processes of reading, however, was a more problematic affair. We had no models. We began by tapping all the resources we could find, exploring and expanding our understanding of what reading is. The advisory team met with such professional leaders as Judith Langer, Alan Purves, and James Moffett. The teacher assessment-development team read and discussed Langer's theory of "reading as an act of envisionment building" (Langer 1989). They studied Louise Rosenblatt's ([1938] 1978) definitions of aesthetic and efferent reading. They compiled an enviable collection of articles written by many other teachers and researchers. The teachers on the assessment-development team were committed to the task of constructing an integrated assessment built on the assumption that both reading and writing require negotiation between reader or writer and text. We found that we used writing as evidence of reading achievement, and used texts that students read as a basis for writing prompts. During many months of discussion and the development and field testing of various reading and writing tasks, we found that we had made great strides toward learning what questions and activities would allow us to get a look inside actively reading minds. The challenge then became how to design a scorable assessment task that credits students' margin notes, graphics, double-entry journals, short and extended written explorations, and reflections—in short, written and drawn evidence of a student's developing interpretation of a text.

An integrated reading and writing assessment task should incorporate familiar classroom strategies that enable students to demonstrate how well they can read a particular text or kind of text and how well they can use writing for a particular purpose. An on-demand reading and writing assessment task reflects, but does not replicate, a classroom assignment. Important differences stem from distinct underlying purposes: While the goals of a classroom assignment incorporate assessment, the primary goal is to help students learn; in contrast, the goals of an on-demand, large-scale assessment are largely to compare student achievement in schools and districts. Some states, including California, now give or are planning to give individual scores for on-demand assessments; such scores, however, must always be placed within the context of the student's total classroom performance. By themselves, they provide only a narrow window into the larger, more variable picture of a student's performance in diverse classroom situations.

Constructing an integrated task actually begins with the selection of a text, a process that touches on critical issues such as level of difficulty, accessibility, and possible bias or stereotyping reflected by the subject or its treatment. Once a text has been identified as a strong possibility, classroom teachers on the assessment team draft questions for the reading section, moving from them to writing possibilities, then finally to group activities. Beyond the initial drafting, the process becomes recursive as prompt writers move back and forth among the three parts of the test—reading, group work, and writing. In the course of writing a single prompt, many different groups of teachers respond and suggest revisions. The advisors work constantly with the prompt writing groups, bringing the process of collaborative writing and revision to a high art.

Before explaining the rationale for constructing each part of this kind of integrated assessment, let me illustrate a model task. This high school level prompt (see Figure 2), based on Alice Walker's essay "Beauty: When the Other Dancer Is the Self," was designed specifically for use with teachers in staff development workshops. In this very personal essay, from Walker's (1983) collection of essays *In Search of Our Mother's Gardens,* Walker explores her changing concept of *beauty* through a series of vignettes that take place both before and after an accident that left her blind in one eye.

An Example of an Integrated Assessment for Grade 10

Although I have retained the format of the test (see Figure 2), I have omitted the spaces for student responses. Where it seems necessary, I have included comments in brackets to clarify the format.

Constructing an Integrated Assessment Task

In this section, I will provide guidelines for constructing each section of the prompt separately, even though the creation of an integrated task is not a linear process.

Selecting Texts

Texts for the reading section of the prompt are selected from the kinds of reading typically found in an English/language arts curriculum. Task writers search for texts that represent a range of purposes—from stories or poems that we read primarily for literary purposes to articles and essays we select for informational as well as literary reasons, recognizing, of course, that readers usually have more than a single purpose in reading most texts.

Texts selected for assessment must have a high level of complexity and richness. After analyzing hundreds of student responses, our teachers on

Beauty: When the Other Dancer is the Self

SECTION ONE
READING

Before You Read

You are going to read an essay by Alice Walker entitled "Beauty: When the Other Dancer Is the Self." Walker, most famous for her novel *The Color Purple,* has been a strong advocate for racial and sexual equality. The essay you will read for this assessment is from her 1983 collection of essays, *In Search of Our Mother's Gardens.* As you read, you may underline or make notes in the margin to indicate ideas you find interesting, have questions about, or think are important. While it is not necessary for you to write margin notes, any notations that you do make will become part of the total picture of your understanding of this essay.

Reading Selection

[Text of the essay is printed here in a wide,   **MARGIN NOTES**
column leaving room for margin notes.]

After You Read

[Each question is followed by lines or boxes of appropriate length or size.]
In your responses to these questions, use references to the essay as well as the knowledge and experience that you brought to the reading.

1. What are your initial ideas about the meaning of this essay?
2. Walker describes a number of specific scenes both before and after the "accident." Think about which scenes are most vivid or important to you as you think about the meaning of the essay. In Column One of the double-entry journal below, copy or summarize key passages from two or three scenes that you find important or especially vivid. In Column Two, give each of these scenes a descriptive title.

Continued on next page

Figure 2. High school level prompt.

Figure 2 continued

In Column Three, explain what each scene contributes to the essay.

Column One   **Column Two**   **Column Three**

Important Scenes	Scene Titles	What Scenes Contribute to Essay
[expand space to a whole page]		

3. People often use images and symbols as well as words to express ideas. In the box below, use images, symbols, and words to represent what Alice Walker might be thinking and feeling as she reflects on the significance of the accident in her life.

4. Write an explanation of the meaning of the symbols and images which you included in your open mind diagram and explain why you chose them.

[box should take up a half page; within the box is an outline of a human head, front view]

5. Choose two of the quotations listed below (or you may use one of these and select one of your own) and tell what they mean to you in the context of the Walker essay.

Quotations:

(1) "'Eye's are sympathetic,' he says. 'If one is blind, the other will likely become blind too.'" (paragraphs 12 & 44)

(2) "Mommy, there's a *world* in your eye." (paragraph 47)

Continued on next page

Figure 2 continued

(3)   "The other dancer has obviously come through all right, as I have done. She is beautiful, whole and free. And she is also me." (paragraph 49)

(4)   Insert quotation of your choice:

Response to quotation number____:

Response to quotation number____:

[A half page is given for each quotation.]

6.   Comment on the title of this essay. You might address such questions as these:

   • What expectations did it create as you began to read?

   • How did its meaning change as you read the essay?

[A half page is given for this response.]

7.   What else can you say about the meaning of this essay? This is your opportunity to explore any aspect of the essay that you have not yet addressed. You may include questions that you want to bring up in your group discussion later.

This is the end of Section One.

SECTION TWO
WORKING WITH YOUR GROUP

Guidelines for Working with Your Group

During this part of the test, your group will discuss ideas stemming from Alice Walker's essay "Beauty: When the Other Dancer Is the Self" and do some prewriting for the writing assessment. It is important that everyone in the group has a chance to share ideas.

   Activities and suggestions for discussion:

1.   Begin your discussion by talking about the essay. Some starter questions:

Continued on next page

Figure 2 continued

- What did you think of it?
- What questions do you have about it?
- Was it easy to read or difficult? If difficult, can you say why?

2. Imagine that Alice Walker, now grown, is talking with her family. What might they say to each other? With each person in your group taking the part of one member of her family, role-play the conversation that might take place.

   After the conversation, talk about how each of you saw the other members of the family. Jot down key aspects of your discussion.

3. Discuss Walker's ideas about the word *beauty*. Then talk about what each of you means by the word *beauty*. What images and ideas are common to the group? Which are unique to one person?

   Draw a box that shows both the inside and the outside. (Or draw two boxes, one for each view.) Draw and write words on the outside of the box that show how your *group* defines or exemplifies *beauty*. For the inside of the box, draw or write words that show how *you* define or exemplify it.

4. Choose an idea or concept that is important to you, as the concept of *beauty* is important to Alice Walker. Write the name of the idea or concept in the box below:

   Idea or Concept Important to Me

   Think about how the meaning of this concept has changed for you over the years. Use the space below to cluster memories of at least three specific incidents that have contributed to your ideas about this concept.

Continued on next page

Figure 2 continued

Tell the group what concept you have chosen and share one or more of the incidents from your cluster with your group. Be sure each person has a chance to contribute to the discussion.

This is the end of Section Two.

SECTION THREE
WRITING

Writing Situation

You have read how Alice Walker's concept of *beauty* evolved through a series of incidents in her life. You have talked with your group about memories relating to an idea or concept that is important to you. Now your teacher has decided to have your class compile a collection or anthology of reflective essays about ideas and concepts that are important to members of your class. You will each write about a concept that is important in your life.

Directions for Writing

Write an essay for your class anthology reflecting on the concept you have chosen. Show how incidents in your life reveal your ideas about this concept. You may also wish to draw on experiences of people you know, of Alice Walker and other writers whose work you have read, and of people in general. Explore your ideas thoughtfully, showing how your ideas have come from your experiences, reading, and observations.

This is the end of Section Three.

---

the assessment team concluded that prompts based on texts in which the content is too familiar yield questionable evidence of reading ability. When students bring too much information and/or bias with them to the reading, it is difficult to determine to what extent responses are based on actual reading, prior knowledge, or preconceived opinion. It is important to have a sample of students write an initial response to the text in order to gauge its complexity, accessibility, and interest. These student responses help the teachers to determine whether a text actually goes to an outside, government-appointed review committee, the last step before becoming the basis for prompt development.

In some prompts, two texts are paired. Usually, a pairing is made on the basis of different treatments of the same theme, perhaps in different forms. A poem on loneliness or isolation, for example, might be paired with a prose passage depicting childhood loneliness in Maxine Hong Kingston's *Woman Warrior.* Such pairings provide opportunities for students to compare, contrast, and perhaps evaluate the effectiveness of the two pieces.

Composing Reading Questions and Activities

Once a text has been approved for development, two or three teachers on the assessment team begin to draft questions and activities that are likely to elicit thoughtful readings from students. Since this kind of assessment is based on a constructivist definition of reading, we design tasks that allow for a wide range of variations in how a reader reads. According to this definition of reading, the individual reader assumes responsibility for producing an interpretation of a text guided not only by the language of the text, but also by the reader's experience, cultural background, and prior knowledge. Directions and activities encourage students to develop understandings of their own rather than lead them into predetermined interpretations. Even experienced assessment-team teachers continually guard against composing questions that assume a single, central meaning.

The introduction to the reading selection is dependent upon the nature of the text. This section should not lead students into mind-sets that will color their interpretations, but rather orient them toward reading a specific text. It should name the title and author and give additional details about the author, the historical period, or other background information that would help students move quickly into the text. One difference between a large-scale assessment task and a typical classroom assignment is that extensive prereading activities such as those commonly used in the classroom are excluded to allow the reading selection itself to activate student involvement. The introduction, then, should avoid any gesture of interpretation, even a phrase such as "You are going to read a poem *about. . . .* " By avoiding comments that predispose students to a particular interpretation, we can more effectively assess direct transactions between students and texts and get a glimpse of their minds at work constructing meaning.

Questions and activities following the reading of the text itself are designed to elicit written and graphic responses that give scorable evidence of reading. Teachers on the assessment team constantly remind themselves of this seemingly obvious statement that points up differences between an assessment prompt, which must be clearly focused toward this goal, and a classroom activity, which may serve a number of diverse purposes simultaneously. In contrast to the typical "questions at the end of the chapter," which have a range of purposes—from simple comprehension of factual material, to provocative but often tangential discussion topics, to extended writing assignments—questions intended to assess reading must constantly invite readers to analyze, speculate, reflect, deepen, and revise their interpretations.

All reading tasks offer students the invitation to make notations in the margins as they read. The notations may take any form—questions, sketches, initial interpretative comments, or personal connections. Students are not required to write margin notes, but the opportunity is presented; a wide margin provides space for those who think with a pen. The section "After You Read" begins with an open-ended response invitation. Several additional questions and activities are written specifically for each text. There is no formula for designing these questions and activities; there are, however, some general kinds of questions and activities that assessment-team teachers have found particularly useful in helping students move beyond their initial response to a deeper construction and exploration of meaning. These questions and activities include such strategies as the dialectical or double-entry journal; diagrams to be filled in with symbols, images, and words; extended-response sections providing opportunities to predict, speculate, evaluate, and reflect; and charts or directions to compare characters or trace various kinds of changes that occur during the text.

In addition to questions that lead to written responses, we also include at least one opportunity for a graphic—a chance for students to use images, symbols, or drawing to show their understanding of a text. There is a great deal of evidence that visual thinking offers powerful insights into reading. As exemplified in *Drawing Your Own Conclusions: Graphic Strategies for Reading, Writing, and Thinking* (Claggett and Brown 1992), second-language students, whose reading ability often precedes fluency in writing, often find their way to language through the actual drawing of images and symbols depicting the students' understanding of a text. For students whose visual and spatial intelligence is more dominant than their verbal intelligence, the opportunity to portray understanding partially through the use of graphics may be vital, while for the verbally gifted, the shift to spatial thinking has a definite impact on the quality of subsequent writing. The graphic opportunity in the assessment is always followed by a question inviting students to explain why they chose the symbols or images they drew and how these drawings show their understanding of the text. In student responses to these questions, readers can actually see how the act of drawing images and symbols generates thinking in language.

Questions and activities constantly lead students back to the text, encouraging them to reread the selection as they explore its meaning. Each reading section closes with an open-ended question, an opportunity for students to write about any insights, issues, or concerns that may have developed during the reading process, responses that might not have been elicited by previous questions.

Assessment-team teachers are deeply aware of the needs of diverse groups—not only the many different ethnic groups in our population, but also the students who have not been successful learning in traditional ways. The integrated assessment, providing as it does multiple opportunities for students to grapple with both reading and writing, goes a long way toward accommodating different learning styles. By providing opportunities to draw as well as write, to discuss as well as listen, the new assessment design increases the chances that all students will be able to show what they can do. Teachers' experience in California is that nearly all students are able to respond with confidence to at least some segment of the assessment.

Creating Small-group Activities

Activities for small-group work serve two purposes: to extend students' understanding of the texts and to provide prewriting activities that lead directly to the writing prompt. In prompts that use paired texts, the group work also serves to initiate thinking and discussion about why the texts were paired. So that there will be a close fit between the group work and the writing that follows, activities for this section are designed concurrently with or after the writing prompt has been written.

In designing group activities, teachers on the team draw on their experience in the classroom: They try out the texts with their students to discover what kinds of small-group activities lead students to enriched understanding.

The group work begins with an opportunity for the four or five students to talk about what they read. The short, initial discussion is followed by a group activity such as constructing a chart, role-playing characters, designing a graphic to illustrate character motivation or plot line, or planning a poster to persuade people to a particular point of view.

In a prompt with paired texts, activities are designed to help students explore how ideas in the two texts parallel or contrast with each other.

Constructing a Writing Prompt for an Integrated Task

The writing prompt in the integrated reading/writing assessment is constructed to help students move beyond their often-tentative initial transactions with the text to write longer, more fully developed papers which are to be scored for rhetorical effectiveness and mastery of conventions. These prompts are either text-dependent or text-independent. The text-dependent prompts rely on and build on student understanding of the reading selection and lead to such writing types as interpretation, evaluation, or speculation at grade 10; problem-solution, speculation and evaluation at grade 8; and persuasive or informational at grade 4. The text-independent prompts use the reading as a springboard to types such as autobiographical incident and reflection at grades 8 and 10, and narrative or expressive at grade 4. It may be useful to include here (see Figure 1) a look at the full range of writing types tested at the three grade levels. The grade 4 categories are broadly based divisions developmentally appropriate for nine-year-olds, while the middle and high school categories reflect the finer distinctions among types appropriate in a writing curriculum for these age groups.

The writing prompt follows naturally from the student's previous work in the reading and group-work sections of the test. While not duplicating questions in these sections, the writing prompt builds on them, asking the student to go further in exploring an interpretation or in reflecting on ideas generated by the text. Once teachers have selected the writing type appropriate for the prompt, they follow guidelines for writing that particular kind of prompt. The format for writing prompts includes two sections: "The Writing Situation" and "Directions for Writing." "The Writing Situation" establishes the connection between the work students have already done in the reading and group-work sections and establishes the context and audience for the writing prompt. The second section, "Directions for Writing," states the writing assignment explicitly and cogently. Although students have already been prepared for the topic in the group-work section, directions here establish a finer focus and more specific instructions. One caution that prompt writers must observe is not to lead too directly—not to provide any semblance of an outline or framework for the essay—while at the same time providing enough information for students to write an appropriately focused, supported, substantive essay within the specified genre.

Each kind of writing has specific prompt-writing guidelines as well as a scoring guide. Particularly useful to the classroom teacher interested in understanding the rhetorical features of the different kinds of writing are the writing handbooks for middle and high school teachers published by the California Department of Education. These handbooks, written by classroom teachers on the team that developed the California assessment, detail how to teach, assess, and score all the kinds of writing that have been tested at grades 8 and 10. They also include guidelines for constructing writing prompts, scoring guides, and samples of student writing.

Scoring an Integrated Reading/Writing Assesment

The powerful effects of the California Learning Assessment System (CLAS) assessment on instruction stem largely from the involvement of so many teachers in the scoring process. In 1994, over 3,000 teachers participated in the summer scoring sessions. Before the reading, chief readers and table leaders—assessment-team teachers and other classroom teachers who had undergone training in scoring procedures—met to select anchor papers and "rounds" of student papers to be used in training teachers for scoring. Teachers who applied to be scorers met in one of the thirty-four locations in the state for a five-day scoring session. Nearly one whole day was given to intensive training in the prompt, the scoring guide, and representative papers. At each location, one reading prompt or one writing type was scored. For example, fifty or sixty teachers at one site would score a single reading prompt for grade 8, while at another site, a different group would be scoring persuasive writing prompts for grade 4. Table leaders had to prequalify for accuracy and consistency in scoring; readers qualified during training before actually scoring "live" papers. Those who did not qualify on the first try received additional training before taking another "calibration" round. Table leaders constantly monitored readers at their tables for consistency and accuracy. In addition to time spent during the training in discussing student papers and scoring guides, chief readers provided opportunities for teachers to explore and share ideas about the classroom implications of what they learned not only about scoring student work, but about teaching an integrated reading and writing program as well.

The Reading Scoring Guide

The reading scoring guide, first used on a statewide level in 1993 with close to a million students (grades 4, 8, and 10), was designed by assessment-team teachers, who read and analyzed hundreds of student papers in the process of constructing the guide. Recognizing that large parts of the reading process are internal and therefore inaccessible, teachers approached student papers with an eye toward identifying specific observable performances or behaviors that characterize exemplary readings. These performances, listed below, let us use writing and drawing to assess students' interpretations. A distinctive feature of this guide is that it reflects performances that transcend age groups or development. As the three grade-specific groups of teachers worked to design an appropriate measure of student achievement in reading, they discovered that fourth graders exhibit the same reading performances as eighth and tenth graders. Some performances appear infrequently in fourth-grade responses, but all are clearly present in the responses of some young readers. Working together, across grade-level groups, the teachers developed a single reading scoring guide that is appropriate for all grade levels. Each grade level, however, anchors the scoring guide to the appropriate grade level by selecting grade-specific sample papers for each score point. Separate anchor papers are selected for each reading prompt. (See the "Notes" section of this chapter for information about the California assessment grade-level samplers,[2] which contain not only the scoring guide but representative student papers at different score points.)

The following list of performances from California's reading scoring guide shows the range of behaviors that we have been able to identify from students' written and drawn responses to the questions and activities in reading prompts. Readers are not expected to exhibit all these behaviors, but more effective readers are likely to exhibit a wider range. In general, readers also demonstrate more advanced levels of achievement by the degree to which they attend to increasingly more complex structures of meaning.

As readers demonstrate the quality, range, and comprehensiveness of their transactions with texts through written and graphic representations, they

1. Demonstrate intellectual engagement with the text: experiment with ideas; think divergently; take risks; express opinions; speculate, hypothesize, visualize characters or scenes, explore alternative scenarios; raise questions; make predictions; think metaphorically.

2. Explore multiple possibilities of meaning; consider cultural and/or psychological nuances and complexities in the text.

3. Fill in gaps; use clues and evidence in the passage to draw con-
    clusions; make warranted and plausible interpretations of ideas,
    facts, concepts, and/or arguments.

4. Recognize and deal with ambiguities in the text.

5. Revise, reshape, and/or deepen early interpretations.

6. Evaluate; examine the degree of fit between the author's ideas or
    information and the reader's prior knowledge or experience.

7. Challenge and reflect critically on the text by agreeing or dis-
    agreeing, arguing, endorsing, questioning, and/or wondering.

8. Demonstrate understanding of the work as a whole.

9. Attend to the structure of the text: show how the parts work
    together; how characters and/or other elements of the work are
    related and change.

10. Show aesthetic appreciation of the text; consider linguistic and
    structural complexities.

11. Allude to and/or retell specific passages to validate and expand
    ideas.

12. Make connections between the text and their own ideas, experi-
    ence, and knowledge.

13. Demonstrate emotional engagement with the text.

14. Retell, summarize, and/or paraphrase with purpose.

15. Reflect on the meaning(s) of the text, including larger or more uni-
    versal significances; express a new understanding or insight.

Following the reading performances in the reading scoring guide is
a description of achievement at each score point. These score-point
descriptors incorporate a range of reading performances that teachers
found to be central to reading at all three grade levels. Score point 6 is
reprinted here; the entire reading scoring guide is available in the samplers listed in the "Notes" section of this chapter:

Score Point 6: Exemplary Reading Performance

An exemplary reading performance is insightful, discerning, and
perceptive as the reader constructs and reflects on meaning in a
text. Readers at this level are sensitive to linguistic, structural, cultural, and psychological nuances and complexities. They fill in
gaps in a text, making warranted and responsible assumptions
about unstated causes or motivations, for example, or drawing
meaning from subtle cues. They differentiate between literal and
figurative meanings. They recognize real or seeming contradic-

tions, exploring possibilities for their resolution or tolerating ambiguities. They demonstrate their understanding of the whole work as well as an awareness of how the parts work together to create the whole.

Readers achieving score point 6 develop connections with and among texts. They connect their understanding of the text not only to their own ideas, experience, and knowledge, but to their history as participants in a culture or larger community, often making connections to other texts or other works of art. Exceptional readers draw on evidence from the text to generate, validate, expand, and reflect on their own ideas.

These readers take risks. They entertain challenging ideas and explore multiple possibilities of meaning as they read, grounding these meanings in their acute perceptions of textual and cultural complexities. They often revise their understanding of a text as they reread and as additional information or insight becomes available to them. They sometimes articulate a newly developed level of understanding.

Readers performing at level 6 challenge the text. They carry on a dialogue with the writer, raising questions, taking exception, agreeing, disagreeing, appreciating or criticizing text features. They may test the validity of the author's ideas or information by considering the authority of the author and the nature and quality of evidence presented. They may speculate about the ideology or cultural or historical biases that seem to inform a text, sometimes recognizing and embracing and sometimes resisting the position that a text seems to construct for its reader.

The Writing Scoring Guides

Writing scoring guides indicate levels of achievement in rhetorical effectiveness for each of the types of writing tested by CLAS at all three grade levels (See Figure 1). A separate conventions scoring guide, which is the same for all types of writing, defines levels of achievement in mechanics, usage, and spelling. The rhetorical effectiveness scoring guides were constructed by assessment-team teachers who read, sorted, and analyzed large numbers of student field-test papers before developing a guide. A six-point scale for each writing type describes the salient features of achievement at each level. The writing scoring guides, published in the California *Writing Assessment Handbooks* (see "Notes" section for ordering information) have proved to be reliable instruments for large-scale testing. Teachers have found them useful in instruction as well. As an example, excerpts from the grade 10 rhetorical-effectiveness scoring guide for "Reflection," the type of writing specified in the sample prompt, follow:

Rhetorical Effectiveness Scoring Guide, Grade 10, Reflective Essay

Score Point 6: Exemplary Writing Performance

Occasion for Reflection. The writer of a score point 6 essay presents the occasion for reflection (a thing seen, read, or experienced) richly and memorably, often with the fine detail of the naturalist or auto-biographer. Though the occasion does not dominate the essay at the expense of reflection, it is often presented in extended, concrete detail. Whether an anecdote or an observation of nature or a literary text, the occasion grounds the entire essay.

Reflection. The reflection about the idea suggested by the occasion is exceptionally thoughtful and perceptive. The reflection tends to be extended and serious, sometimes tenacious, probing and exploring. There is movement in the essay: It does not become mired down in repetition of ideas without expansion or different angles subtly changing the force of the exploration.

The reflection may include generalizations about the subject relevant to the writer's own experience, but must include consideration of the larger social implications as well. Most score point 6 essays will have some explicit, insightful general reflection. In some notable papers, however, the writer's presentation of the occasion is couched in such a way that the reader sees that the occasion clearly stands for an entire class of events characteristic of human nature or of social interaction. In these papers the general reflection is implicit, embedded in phrases or clauses that cue the reader to move beyond the specific occasion to the abstraction that underlies it. The tone, established by a distancing of self from occasion, clearly conveys the reflective nature of such essays.

The reflection of a score point 6 paper often reveals discovery or deepening insight and may end without a sense of conclusiveness about the subject. The paper itself, however, will have an appropriate sense of conclusion.

Coherence and Style. The score point 6 essay is coherent, each section flowing naturally and logically from the previous one. The writer achieves emphasis, organization, logic, and repetition through recurrences of language, syntax, and ideas. Because of the nature of reflection, there may be abrupt shifts of focus, but the careful reader will see that these shifts are warranted by associational leaps of mind. The effective paper will eventually account for the full range of shifts, however, either explicitly or implicitly.

The writer uses language with imagination, precision, and appropriateness. The writer exhibits an exceptional control of sentence structures.

Placing the On-demand Assessment in Perspective

The concept of an integrated reading/writing assessment, while still problematic for many people, is far beyond the hypothetical stage.

Teacher involvement in the annual scoring of the integrated assessments of nearly a million students in California is testimony to classroom teachers' commitment to authentic assessment of student achievement. While teachers, state department assessment personnel, politicians, and statisticians are still coping with the logistics of administering and scoring such a complex instrument, the work to date shows that large-scale authentic assessment—from design to construction to scoring—can be accomplished by teachers working with administrative support.

The evolution of the CLAS test has not been as smooth as it may sound in this history. With its roots in a highly successful direct writing assessment, it expanded into a more complicated instrument. The legislative requirement for assigning individual scores in addition to school and district scores led to a public controversy regarding censorship, family rights of privacy, and racial and ethnic equity. Questions arose, too, concerning the validity of matrix sampling in a test that changed midstream to assign individual scores. The entire California assessment program became so highly politicized that it became the focus for scores of media stories and editorials and highly controversial school board gatherings. The CLAS test became the target of attack in major political campaigns, from that of the state superintendent of education to that of governor. In a complete overhaul of the state assessment department, the entire assessment program in all disciplines was completely discontinued.

In what turned out to be a futile effort to resolve some of these issues, the advisory committee proposed many changes, including an alternative model for an integrated reading and writing assessment. As yet untested in large-scale assessment, it has been used successfully at school and district levels. This model (see Figure 3) preserves successful elements of the CLAS test while offering some important additional dimensions. Although the format looks very similar to that of the model presented earlier, this test design would be scored differently. Responses to each text would receive a separate reading score. The writing prompt, limited to types of writing that require knowledge of the text (interpretation, for example), would be scored both for rhetorical effectiveness and for an additional reading score. This test would be supported by two additional tests: a stand-alone direct writing assessment, which has already been tested successfully for a number of years; and a multiple-choice reading and editing test. Together, the package would result in a vastly increased number of scores for each individual, giving each student an opportunity to demonstrate achievement in a variety of reading and writing modes. The student's ultimate score would be based on statewide standards for reading and writing.

Reading: Text 1	Reading: Text 2	Group Work	Reading/ Writing
Questions and activities	Questions and activities	Integrating questions; preparation for writing	Text-dependent writing prompt to be scored for both reading and writing
45 minutes	20 minutes	20 minutes	45 minutes

Figure 3. Model #2 for integrated reading/writing assessment.

Any on-demand test model, to place this kind of assessment in perspective, represents only one aspect of a larger vision of assessment. The most complete assessment materials available are those designed by New Standards; the total program includes not only an on-demand test similar to that described in this chapter, but a comprehensive portfolio program as well. Some teachers who were involved in the development of the California test have worked with New Standards leadership and teachers from many other states to develop the model for an on-demand performance test and portfolio assessment. The New Standards Reference Exam for English/Language Arts, an on-demand integrated reading and writing test that references the standards, is a one-period test which provides open-ended questions pertaining to a reading selection. The final question of the test is a text-based essay question, scored for both reading and writing, as a truly integrated test should be. In addition to this integrated assessment, the New Standards Reference Exam includes a full-period writing assessment.

As legislators and constituencies become more sophisticated in their understanding of the rich, varied processes involved in performance assessment tied to rigorous standards, it is likely that other large-scale assessments will move in this direction. Serving as one aspect of such comprehensive assessment programs and placed within the framework of state or national standards, a large-scale, on-demand assessment can provide teachers and students with a critical checkpoint—a snapshot revealing the performance of a particular student on a particular day, reading and writing specific texts for given purposes. Because the design of the test and the scoring guides are based on teacher expertise supported by theory and research, this kind of assessment model makes a contribution not only to the data so coveted by administrators and politicians of districts and states, but to teachers, parents, and students, where even a large-scale assessment can provide insight into an overall picture of a student's achievement over time and across a broad range of reading and writing experiences.

Notes

1. The advisory group included Dale Carson, Department of Education assessment director; James Gray and Mary Ann Smith from the California Writing Project; Mary Barr and Mel Grubb from the California Literature Project; and a number of additional educational leaders. The Educational Testing Service, in Emeryville, California, was the first statewide contractor for the development and implementation of the California writing assessment and provided invaluable assistance with the logistical aspects of testing some three-hundred thousand students at each grade level.

2. The following materials are available from Publication Sales, California Department of Education, P.O. Box 271, Sacramento, CA 95802-0271. Tel: 1-800-995-4099.

The *Writing Assessment Handbook, Grade 8,* (item # 0887, $8.50 plus tax, S & H) and the *Writing Assessment Handbook: High School* (item # 1073 $9.50 plus tax, S & H) include characteristics of eight writing types at each level, suggestions for teaching, annotated student papers, sample prompts, guidelines for writing prompts, published pieces representative of each type, and scoring guides.

English Language Arts Samplers available for elementary, middle, and high school contain annotated student responses to reading and writing assessments illustrating representative score points: Grade 4, 1994, item #1099; Grade 8, 1992, item # 1061; Grade 8, 1994, #1120; Grade 10, 1992, item #1062; Grade 10, 1994, item #1121. Prices range from $6.00 to $9.00.

For information about New Standards, contact *New Standards* at 700 Eleventh Street, NW, Suite 750, Washington, DC 20001. Tel.: 202-783-3668; fax: 202-783-3672.

Works Cited

Claggett, Fran, and Joan Brown. 1992. *Drawing Your Own Conclusions: Graphic Strategies for Reading, Writing, and Thinking.* Portsmouth, NH: Boynton/Cook-Heinemann.

Langer, Judith A. 1989 (April). *The Process of Understanding Literature.* Report Series 2.1. Albany: State University of New York, Center for the Learning and Teaching of Literature.

Rosenblatt, Louise. [1938] 1978. *The Reader, the Text, The Poem: The Transactional Theory of the Literary Work.* Carbondale: Southern Illinois University Press.

Walker, Alice. 1983. "Beauty: When the Other Dancer Is the Self." In *In Search of Our Mother's Gardens,* 384–93. *Womanist Prose.* New York: Harcourt Brace Jovanovich.

17 Let Them Experiment: Accommodating Diverse Discourse Practices in Large-Scale Writing Assessment

Roxanne Mountford
University of Arizona

> Our language and our written text represent our visions of our culture, and we need new processes and forms if we are to express ways of thinking that have been outside the dominant culture.
>
> —Lillian Bridwell-Bowles (1992, 349)

> No hegemony stays automatically in place or unproblematically retains its appearance as common sense.
>
> —Richard Ohmann (1992/3, 57)

As teachers and evaluators, we increasingly find ourselves working with students from diverse backgrounds, students whose writing and speaking don't fit our conventional notions of good academic writing. Instead of announcing a topic or a point, some students seem to beat around the bush. Other students present their ideas not through evidence and reasoning, but by telling stories that don't seem all that clearly connected to their point. In short, their writing just doesn't look like what we have expected of an academic essay. At such moments we all ask ourselves, "How do I respond to this writing?" More specifically, "How do I evaluate it?"[1]

I suspect that most of us have responded by suggesting that all students must learn to write an academic essay, a form of writing in which they learn to "display knowledge and argue a single point or hypothesis" (Heath 1993, 105). If we ask them to write a narrative or personal essay, we expect the "point" of the story to be suggested by the end. If the story is told in a linear fashion—that is, without tangents—so much the better. This perspective is surprisingly interdisciplinary. While scoring midcareer placement essays recently with a group of faculty from the sciences, engineering, and humanities, I was struck by the general agreement about "good academic writing." The faculty were unanimous in their belief that student essays should come to a point quickly and should be supported by a series of arguments and supporting examples arranged hierarchically. When pressed to explain why students should learn to write this way, their answer was that that is "what is expected in the academic world."

But there are some problems with these assumptions. First, as Chris Anson and Robert Brown point out, "schools and departments" in universities are "complex institutions engaged in *varieties of production*" (1991, 267). That is, what scholars write in one part of the university would not necessarily be considered academic writing in another. Even within disciplines there are disputes about proper "formats" for scholarly publication. Peter Elbow counts ten different "traditions" of academic writing in English studies alone (1991, 138–39). Second, if you look at academic writing in foreign journals, what counts as an academic essay may have much in common with what some of our nontraditional students produce. For instance, in Brazil a scholar would want to "beat around the bush," since making a "point" in Portuguese is considered a crude way to argue. In other words, the way our nontraditional students are writing and speaking may not be wrong from another cultural perspective. "Academic writing" differs markedly across cultures. Third, some American academic writers, especially those who have been influenced by French philosophers and feminism, are publishing writing that does not look like anything being taught in composition texts, even at the college level. Nonlinear and multivoiced, this "experimental" writing is often produced to challenge the notion that writing and thinking can and should be hierarchical, unified, and objective. So there may be some good reasons to encourage our nontraditional writers to keep writing differently. In fact, it would seem that the reasons are no longer simply cultural—increasingly, they are also ideological.

So why aren't we recognizing a wider variety of ways to write well when we teach and assess writing? The problem may lie in our strong belief that writing that is linearly arranged and focused around a point constitutes successful college writing. Leading textbooks in the field and major first-year college writing programs operate on this tacit belief. It has been my own assumption throughout twelve years of teaching and continues to dog my own attempts to recognize alternative ways to teach and evaluate writing. These assumptions or norms for writing caused one editor to seek me out after a conference presentation I gave on this subject. Her question was this: If our journals will print alternative forms of academic prose (e.g., Brodkey 1994; Dixon 1995; Bishop 1995), and if many scholars now find such writing exciting (e.g., Bridwell-Bowles 1992, 1995), then why aren't textbook authors submitting manuscripts that reflect this change in what can be counted as academic writing?[2]

As I will argue in this essay, the problem is not that we are incapable of conceiving experimental writing assignments and corresponding assessment prompts for our students. Rather, the problem is that we think of our composition courses as preparing "students for what they will do in other academic courses." At the high school level, we think of our writing courses as preparation for college. And we are reminded of this fact, often, from faculty in other departments. But what often accompanies this expectation is a rather narrow vision of what counts as good academic writing. There has been good discussion on how we might broaden this vision by studying what kinds of writing scholars actually do (see especially MacDonald 1994). But what I want to consider here are the arguments made for broadening our vision on behalf of the diversity of persons who enter our classrooms. To do that I will work with arguments that are made against academic prose as defined in college textbooks and in much of our teaching, including my own—those voices in our heads that say, "Where is the point?" As I work through these arguments, I will be using this narrow vision of academic prose as a foil, for the examples of accomplished multivocal and nonlinear essays I cite below are themselves now the new examples of academic prose. What I want to get to are reasons to discard a narrow vision of what our students should/could be doing in the classroom and to offer ways this broadened vision might affect our assessment practices.

There are always two parts to changing our vision of what our students should be writing. The first part involves conceiving of exciting writing assignments that have the effect of drawing in more of our students. This involves our vision of what students writing *could* be. For this reason I will offer many more examples of published experimental writing than student examples. The second part involves learning how to evaluate those writing assignments in a way that honors a diversity of approaches to all the assignments we offer our students. Ultimately, changing our ways of thinking about the norms for writing will have an effect on the way we evaluate writing.

The research that I present below asks us all to remember, over and over, that composition courses are founded upon the speaking and writing habits of educated Northern European immigrants and their descendants, a group that includes me and my extended family. These habits of speaking and writing are not going on in the homes of an increasingly large number of students. We must learn to appreciate the norms for writing that arise from these different cultural expectations, and this learning often involves adjusting our world view. It involves asking questions of our shared professionalization, a professionalization that brings us to write "Where is your thesis?" and "What is the point?" in the margins of essays that confound our comfortable notions of clarity and coherence. What is clear and what is coherent can come in a variety of packages. But that writing may require more work of us as teachers and evaluators.

Acknowledging and supporting diverse discourse practices can have unexpected political implications, as an Oakland, California, school board discovered when it voted, in 1996, to recognize "ebonics" (or Black English Vernacular) as the second language of the majority of its students. In commenting on the ebonics controversy, Baron (1997) argues that a potential problem with accommodating diverse discourse practices in the classroom is that we could in fact be charged with glamorizing difference without liberating those who are different. bell hooks puts it this way: "Within commodity [mass] culture, ethnicity becomes spice, seasoning that can liven up the dull dish that is mainstream white culture" (1992, 21). What I hope to be articulating here is not a mere invitation for the discourse practices or marginalized students to season the "dull dish" of writing assignments we offer them, nor to accommodate their styles without teaching them other ways to write. Rather, I hope to be arguing for a more interesting reform in which styles of argumentation and organization characteristic of a diversity of cultures (and "experimental" writers) are taught—and then tested—in school, for the benefit of all students.

Why Teach a Broader Definition of "Academic Prose"?

> Education may well be, as of right, the instrument whereby every individual, in a society like our own, can gain access to any kind of discourse. But we well know that in its distribution, in what it permits and in what it prevents, it follows the well-trodden battlelines of social conflict. Every educational system is a political means of maintaining or of modifying the appropriation of discourse, with the knowledge and the power it carries with it.
>
> —Michel Foucault (1972, 227)

Whether we know it or not, when we assess students' writing, we are engaging in a silent political act. We are imposing our expectations over the inevitable pluralism we find in student texts, expectations that reflect our cultural values. What we think of as the traditional academic essay reflects a particular set of cultural values not shared by all cultures. As John Clifford argues,

> [T]he conventions of the typical academic, deductive essay as it appears in countless handbooks can be seen . . . as ideologically committed: the confident thesis statement and the logical arrangement of concrete evidence is, in fact, a specific way of asserting that the world is best understood this way, that knowledge can be demonstrated in this unproblematic form, that the self can be authentic within these set confines. (Clifford, qtd. in Wall and Coles 1991, 238)

In other words, when we ask students to write an essay that begins with a confident statement of the thesis and proceeds to prove the thesis through a series of points, we are asking them to adopt a world view and a specific way of relating to others. The world view involves believing that a specific idea (a "focus") can be easily and unproblematically deduced from all the ideas that might influence it and then elevated to the level of "truth" through evidence and reason. In addition, this approach to academic writing suggests to individual students that they can and should take a position of authority in their writing. Olivia Frey (1990) has argued that this world view is "Darwinistic": Information is arranged carefully so that only one person (the author) survives the struggle for truth. The most extreme form of this world view is represented by textbooks that teach the "two sided argument," organized so that the author names his or her opponents and picks apart their arguments before expressing the "best" perspective.[3]

But what if our students hold another world view, such as the idea that knowledge is like an intricate spider web to which they can contribute only a small strand? In "The Anthropology of the Academy," Brazilian anthropologist Roberto Kant de Lima (1992) observes that writing an academic essay "in English" is a fundamentally different process from writing an academic essay in his country. Kant de Lima took two semesters of undergraduate composition at an American university where he was a Ph.D. student. Afterward he realized that in order to write "in English" he had to change his own world view. Echoing Clifford, he observes that English instructors like to see "points" presented hierarchically, points that are clearly announced and developed with a thesis statement, an idea in each paragraph, two to three paragraphs per page, and a formal beginning and ending that have the same function (announcing "the point") (1992,

204–6). He found the insistence on "clarity" bizarre; he writes: "The clarity made me 'simpler' but is also simplified the object about which I was writing" (205). When he reverted to a more Brazilian form of writing because he "did not think [his subject] could be broken up by the analytical operations demanded by the [English] style books," an American colleague told him his writing was "unclear" (205). "Clarity," Kant de Lima (1992) writes, occurs when a writer meets the culturally inscribed expectations of a reader. In Brazil, his writing is "clear."

Kant de Lima suggests his experience in an American composition class and with his colleagues in anthropology is not an isolated case by discussing how American translators treat the rhetorical traditions of international scholars. To American translators and their editors, "French sociology is very 'limp' . . . , 'metaphysical,' 'general,' and 'repetitive'; German very 'dense' and 'complex' with its 'interminable paragraphs'; and Latin American 'not very objective'" (1992, 206). When a scholar comes from a culture that values indirectness and an American translator makes the writing more direct in English, Kant de Lima argues that the foreign author "*suffer[s] an implicit uniform distortion of their thought*" (1992, 206; my emphasis). Specialists in cross-cultural communication have studied this problem among international students. Muriel Saville-Troike and Donna Johnson (1994) report that "our Japanese and Chinese students . . . adopt and use the negative terms that Americans have used to describe 'what's wrong' with their rhetorical styles from the viewpoint of the American audience and analyst: 'nonlinear,' 'circular,' 'slow to get to the point,' 'indirect,' 'lacking cohesive ties,' 'digressive,' etc." But when asked to use their own cultural perspectives to describe what they think of American patterns of argumentation, Japanese and Chinese students indicate that they prefer to write in their own rhetorical styles. In their discussions with these students, Saville-Troike and Johnson discovered that "the Japanese term which characterizes 'direct' American style can best be translated as 'rude'" (239). Saville-Troike and Johnson (1994) and Kant de Lima (1992) suggest that when using traditional norms for assessment, American composition teachers may be overlooking other valuable ways of knowing—and writing about—the world.[4]

Until recently, the standard response to nontraditional student writing has been to accept the idea that evaluation will exclude some valuable ways of writing, but that these exclusions are inevitable in all institutions (Farr and Daniels 1986: Bartholomae 1987; Patterson 1987). In other words, when in Rome, do as the Romans do. For instance, David Bartholomae argues that

> If we take the problem of writing to be the problem of appropri-
> ating the power and authority of a particular way of speaking, then
> the relationship of the writer to the institutions within which
> he[/she] writes becomes central (the key feature in the stylistic
> struggle on the page) rather than peripheral (a social or political
> problem external to writing and therefore something to be politely
> ignored). (1987, 70)

In this essay, Bartholomae sidesteps the question of transforming academic writing, arguing that we must teach students to "move into that
discourse" that already exists (1987, 72). Teaching writing, for Bartholomae, is teaching students how to appropriate—to "move into"—
American academic prose. He argues that equality never exists in
language: "[W]riting except, perhaps, in rare cases) defines a center that
puts some on the margins. It is impossible to speak like an expert without pushing against ways of speaking that are taken to be naive" (72).

However, some composition scholars and practitioners are beginning to explore what Saville-Troike and Johnson call "culturally biased
value judgments" in the teaching of writing (1994, 239) and have begun
to question Bartholomae's (1987) assumptions. Shirley Brice Heath,
citing the philosopher Michel Foucault, writes: "People know what
they do; frequently they know why they do what they do; but what
they don't know is what what they do does'" (1993, 122). That is, as
teachers and evaluators we often act without considering how our
actions affect those we evaluate. Heath suggests that American academic writing excludes many interesting ways to construct meaning,
such as collaborative dialogues, arguments that explore options, narratives, riddles, and other forms of writing that seem more like conversation than talk but nevertheless are effective in exploring and
communicating meaning (1993, 112–13). In excluding these forms,
Heath (1993) suggests, we have the effect of excluding many of our
students—intelligent, potentially excellent students—from academic
success.[5] In a recent essay, Bartholomae (1993) admits that he has
begun to question his earlier assumptions about teaching only traditional academic prose in basic writing, citing Mary Louise Pratt's concept of the classroom as a "contract zone" among students' cultural
differences as a significant challenge to his earlier work. Classrooms,
he suggests, should mediate between the dominant university culture
and the students' home cultures. He laments: "[B]asic writers may be
ready for a different curriculum [that promotes alternative forms of
writing], but the institution is not" (1993, 15).

What do we lose by refusing to broaden our standards? When we
turn to the literatures on nontraditional speakers and writers within
the United States, especially on women and African American stu-

dents, we can see the cost. Like Kant de Lima, but without the education and privilege, many students experience patterns of misunderstanding and underappreciation. In fact, some of the same criticisms leveled at foreign academic prose styles have been leveled at the language and prose styles of some European American women and African Americans. Although cultural anthropology has again and again shown that cultural difference underlies schisms between European American and African American patterns of speech and writing, and between men's and women's speech patterns in many American subcultures, our academic policies—particularly on writing—have largely worked to ignore or erase such differences. As I will explain below, some feminist and African American scholars have responded to this pattern of exclusion by proposing experimental forms of writing and pluralistic notions of good writing.

Women's Discourse

When delineating differences in styles between men's and women's—or between European American and African American—forms of writing, it is important to make clear that in no way does "difference" imply "disability." Mastery over European American academic discourse is not dependent on one's heritage or gender; anyone can, with practice, write in ways valued by schools. Alternatively, one does not have to be part of a historically disadvantaged group to write in a way that is resistant to traditional norms of academic writing. Otherwise, it would be hard to explain the presence of a William Faulkner or a James Joyce.

At the level of everyday discourse, studies show that women, whose experiences are shaped in most American subcultures by the reality of male dominance, may learn patterns of thought and habits of expression that differ from those exhibited by men. Anthropologists who have observed this phenomenon worldwide note that the differences represented by women's speech and writing in patriarchal cultures "are not simply 'ways of speaking'"; the differences in content or perspective that they construct deserve equal attention. Indeed, it is in the conjunction of form, content, and context of performance that women's consciousness emerges" (Gal 1991, 192). Within the feminist community, that struggle had led to explorations of, and calls for, experimental writing, writing that could begin to articulate and reflect women's values and experiences (Yaeger 1988; Tompkins 1989; Frey 1990).

What do we know about women's writing? First of all according to the muted-group theory (Ardener 1978), without special educational opportunities, like that offered by feminist consciousness-raising, many women students may not only speak and write regularly from prevailing norms while in the classroom, they may not even be aware that other alternatives exits.[6] However, psychological, linguistic, and reading studies demonstrate that before putting pen to paper, or fingers to keyboard, women may *experience* the world differently from men overall, suggesting that some women may bring different values to writing tasks. In studies by Carol Gilligan (1982), Belenky et al. (1986), and Deborah Tannen (1990), European American women's perspective and conversation styles may be summarized as follows:

1. Women tend to value interdependence, men independence;
2. Women often communicate to build coalitions, men to share information;
3. Women often reason from context, men from set principles.

Anthropologists who disagree with the research of Tannen and Gilligan note that in fact there is a great range of communication practices among women just as there are among men. Gal, in an essay summarizing research on women's communication patterns in many cultures, validates the perspective that women's "genres" of writing and oral performance exist worldwide, but "can best be read as commentary that shows a range of response—acceptance, resistance, subversion, and opposition—to dominant, often male discourse" (1991, 192–93).

The studies on gender in composition classrooms suggest that while there is no essentially "feminine" or masculine" writing, there may be a difference in the way women and men feel about engaging in traditional academic writing. Perhaps the central observation is that some men students may prefer to use writing to distance themselves from others and their own experience, and to value writing that exhibits their own power and expertise (Flynn 1988; Kraemer 1992; Tobin 1996). Some women students, on the other hand, may prefer to use writing to focus on connection with others and to the experience of reading, and often are reluctant to draw conclusions, instead immersing themselves in details and multiple perspectives (Flynn 1988; Gannett 1992). Feminist rhetoricians note that our dominant discursive practices are handed down through a rhetorical tradition that systematically excluded women's participation from public affairs until well into the twentieth century. Writing that requires distance between an author and her audience, or requires the author to isolate one idea as superior to all others, is based on a system of cultural values that many students—but especially many women students—find alien. Kris Ratcliffe (1996) calls this problem "Bathsheba's dilemma": having the words, cultural conventions, and discourse of men but having the thoughts and feelings of a women. Feminists since Virginia Woolf have worked to write out of an/other perspective and to develop an/other tradition.[7]

Consider, for example, an essay by Jane Tompkins (1989), "Me and My Shadow." In this essay, Tompkins writes a review of Ellen Messer-Davidow's "The Philosophical Bases of Feminist Literary Criticisms," a task normally accomplished with a traditional academic essay that asserts mastery over the text under review. However, this stance of mastery strikes Tompkins as inappropriate for how she has responded to the essay (she feels a sense of connection with the author that will seem violated by writing in this way, even though she wants to point out a problem in her essay). So instead of writing the traditional review essay, Tompkins writes a dialogic essay—that is, an essay written in two very different voices, styles, and world views that resist one another. Introducing the essays, Tompkins writes,

> There are two voices inside me answering, answering to, Ellen's essay. One is the voice of the critic who wants to correct a mistake in the essay's view of epistemology. The other is the voice of a person who wants to write about her feelings (I have wanted to do this for a long time but have felt too embarrassed). This person feels it is wrong to criticize the essay philosophically, and even beside the point: because a critique of the kind the critic has in mind only insulates academic discourse further from the issues that make feminism matter. That make *her* matter. The critic, meanwhile, believes such feelings, and the attitudes that inform them, are soft-minded, self-indulgent, and unprofessional. (1989, 122)

Tompkins goes on to write that these voices are "gendered," since men are "culturally conditioned to repress" feelings, while "women in our culture are not simply encouraged but *required* to be the bearers of emotion" (1989, 123). Of recognizing this dilemma for the first time, Tompkins writes, "No wonder I felt so uncomfortable in the postures academic prose forced me to assume; it was like wearing men's jeans" (1989, 124).

Tompkins's essay is organized as follows: I. Introduction; II. Traditional review; III. Interlude (introducing the next section); and IV. Nontraditional review. By far the longest section is the nontraditional review. Three things strike me about the nontraditional sections: (1) It "rambles" while holding my attention completely; (2) it is personal while being rigorous; and (3) it demonstrates the complexity of the issue without drawing conclusions.

Because the traditional review is familiar territory to most of us, let me give some examples of the language of the nontraditional review:

Just me and my shadow, walkin' down the avenue.
   It is a beautiful day here in North Carolina. The first day that is
both cool and sunny all summer. . . (This is what I want you to see.
A person sitting in stockinged feet looking out of her window—a
floor to ceiling rectangle filled with green, with one red leaf . . .)
(1989, 128)

> Sometimes I think the world contains no women.
>   Why am I so angry?
>   My anger is partly the result of having been an only child who
> caved in to authority very early on. As a result I've built up a huge
> storehouse of hatred and resentment against people in authority
> over me (mostly male). Hatred and resentment and attraction . . .
>   A therapist once suggested to me that I blamed on sexism a lot
> of stuff that really had to do with my own childhood . . .
>   Maybe it would, but that wouldn't touch the issue of female
> oppression. (1989, 136–37)

Notice in the second quoted passage how Tompkins introduces an emotional response but then stops to explore where it comes from, taking
her on another "tangent." The result of this section is to demonstrate
that emotional responses come from experiences that deserve exploration. Tompkins presents herself as perhaps unsure of the origins of her
anger—a position that strengthens the reader's belief that the exploration
is worthwhile. Through this nontraditional format (and voice), Tompkins adopts a different world view, one that does not posit a set of
answers, does not see the possibility of separating emotion from reason,
experience from abstract thinking. She sees this experimental form of
writing as a way to enter the academic world "as a woman."

   Some take exception to Tompkins's (1989) association of writing
that is personal, nonlinear, and narrative with women. For instance,
Heather Brodie Graves (1993) worries that much research based on
gender differences in the writing classroom serves to reinforce stereotypes about men and women. In fact, feminists such as Linda Alcoff
(1988), Judith Butler (1990), and Teresa de Lauretis (1990) deny the
possibility that we can lump all "women" into the same category as
if they shared the same identity. Women may write with or against
gender stereotypes in our own classrooms (Rubin and Greene 1992;
Haswell and Haswell 1995).

   There need be no trap here. As Rubin and Greene (1992) put it, "Curriculum decisions are ultimately decisions about ideology, and require
a commitment to what *ought to be* as well as knowledge of what *is*"
(34). Institutional change may come about for many reasons, not only
because current practice may "put women students at a disadvantage."
The rhetorical strategies of what researchers suggest is occurring in
some women's writing, e.g., the tendency to forestall conclusions, may

suggest a valuable alternative to current intellectual practices in American composition classrooms—for women *and men*. When I first became a professor, many women graduate students came to see me complaining that in an effort to encourage all students to write "publishable" essays, our program had discouraged risktaking and exploratory writing. They asked me if I would consider offering them the opportunity to write in exploratory formats such as Tompkins's review. So in addition to a required semester-long exploratory journal, I began to offer students the choice between writing two kinds of essays: the traditional research paper and the experimental essay. I asked students who take the latter track to read the work of academics who experiment with writing for political and/or theoretical reasons. Until recently, only women have opted for the experimental essay, and all have used this paper as a place to bring out complexities in their topics without drawing conclusions and to weave nonacademic voices into their writing. In one paper I received, a woman student used italicized paragraphs to signal disruptions of the argument and indented dialogues from taped conversations to serve as alternative perspectives. As a result of the experience, she wrote a paper for another teacher on how the experience of writing this paper freed her to think more creatively about her academic work. This same student has now introduced the dialogic essay into the first-year composition program at the small college where she teaches. As Fuss (1989) puts it, this graduate student was "energized" by the thought—and therefore the experience—that writing experimentally *included* her more than writing the traditional academic essay. Since then this assignment has been used by women *and* men students in my classes to step beyond—and resist—traditional forms of academic writing.[8] In doing so, they gain confidence in their writing and take a step toward becoming authors (Penrose and Geisler 1994).

African American Discourse

The "difference" offered by African American discourse is rarely challenged by scholars. On the contrary—perceptions of difference have been the cause for efforts at remediation throughout the twentieth century. Most teachers of writing have at one time been introduced to linguistic studies on Black English Vernacular (BEV), but few know the anthropology of New World African culture. While sociolinguistics has established the grammatical logic of BEV, anthropologists since the 1920s have been establishing the distinctly African nature of New World African subcultures in places as disparate as Bahia, Brazil, and South Carolina. By the end of World War II, anthropologists agreed that the astonishing similarity in folklore and rhetorical practices in these communities warranted a new belief about New World African cultures: that the languages and culture of New World Africans is viable, coherent, and consistent with African languages and culture worldwide (Parsons 1923; Hurston 1938; Herskovits [1941] 1990; Landes 1947). As Smitherman-Donaldson (1988) notes, this research did not gain a sympathetic audience until well into the 1970s. However, the research is significant because it suggests that *rhetorical* practices in African American cultures have a coherence and integrity and deserve to be treated as such. Smitherman-Donaldson (1988) suggests that for reasons of racial stereotyping and bias, American scholars did not take up this suggestion in earnest until after the civil rights movements created a place for African American studies.

Scholars in African American studies have worked quickly to fill the gap. For instance, Henry Louis Gates, Jr. (1988) offers the cultural concept and rhetorical practice of "signifyin'" as an example of a uniquely African rhetorical practice. The Signifying Monkey is a trickster character in African American folklore. In the folk tales the Monkey tricks the Lion by making him think that other characters, e.g., the Elephant, are putting him down. When the Lion attacks the Elephant and is, in turn, flattened, the Monkey has won. The game turns on literalism. If the Lion is silly enough to take the Monkey seriously, he deserves what he gets. A wonderful example of signifyin' occurs in Zora Neale Hurston's ([1938] 1978) folklore study *Mules and Men*. Rather than suggesting that her book is "objective" and "true" (in fact, the work is partly a fiction), Hurston concludes with an odd little twist:

> Once Sis Cat got hongry and caught herself a rat and set herself down to eat 'im. Rat tried and tried to git loose but Sis Cat was too fast and strong. So jus' as de cat started to eat 'im he says "Hol' on dere, Sis Cat! Ain't you got no manners atall? You going to set up to de table and eat 'thought washing yo' face and hands?"
>
> Sis Cat was might hongry but she hate for de rat to think she ain't got no manners, so she went to de water and washed her face and hands and when she got back de rat was gone.
>
> So de cat caught herself a rat again and set down to eat. So de Rat said, "Where's yo' manners at, Sis Cat? You going to eat 'thought washing yo' face and hands?"
>
> "Oh, Ah got plenty manners," de cat told 'im. "But Ah eats mah dinner and washes mah face and uses mah manners afterwards." So she et right on 'im and washed her face and hands. And cat's been washin' after eatin' ever since.
>
> *I'm sitting here like Sis Cat, washing my face and usin' my manners.* ([1938] 1978, 251–52; my emphasis)

What is significant about this act of "signifyin'" is that it comes through a folk tale, one of the most common places "signifyin'" occurs. Another place is on the street corner. Kermit Campbell (1992) reports the following example of "signifyin'" on the street"

> *First Speaker:* Man, when you gon pay me my five dollars?
>
> *Second Speaker:* Soon as I get it.
>
> *First:* (to audience) Anybody want to buy a five dollar nigger? I got one to sell.
>
> *Second:* Man, if I gave you your five dollars, you wouldn't have nothing to signify about.
>
> *First:* Nigger, long as you don't change, I'll always have me a subject. (Mitchell-Kernan, qtd. in Campbell 1992, 99)

As Campbell puts it, the point of "signifyin'" is to "shift the balance of power through demonstration of oneself as a verbal virtuoso" (1992, 99). The form is punning and joking, and the practice is shared among African American subcultures across the United States.

We would expect with such different discourse practices in their home cultures that some African American children would find themselves in a very odd world when coming to school. The work of Arnetha Ball (1992) and Orlando L. Taylor and Maryon M. Matsuda (1988) confirm this insight. In her review of the literature on African American discourse, Arnetha Ball (1992) demonstrates that African American communication patterns are significantly different from European American communication patterns—and that those patterns are culturally consistent, whether the communicative event involves the oral or the written word. Echoing Kant de Lima (1992), Ball (1992) argues that African American rhetoric involves different ways of thinking, and therefore, different organizational patterns in expository writing situations. On the basis of her research of African American high school student writers, Ball (1992) suggests that there are two different organizational patterns that show up in African American students' writing: circumlocation and narrative interspersion.

Circumlocation involves thematic development through narrative in which anecdotes are linked through implicit associations (1992, 509). African American students in her study used this organizational approach for a variety of writing assignments. To illustrate, Ball reproduces the following letter:

> I can still remember when we were freshmen and we planned to take a trip to Mexico. As soon as either one of us learned to drive

we were gonna take off south of the border. I've been looking forward to it for three years and that's why I'm so disappointed that
we can't go. It's just that I know that we're gonna have to be
shelling out the big bucks for our senior (year). I mean, with the
prom, grad-night, pictures, etc.
    Speaking of learning to drive, when are we going to get our
licenses. I thought I was bad because I took safety ed and drivers
training in November 1988. But you're worse. If I'm not mistaken,
you took them both in June, '88. So I'm jammin' compared to you.
I guess we're both just too lazy to go down to the DMV.
    Speaking of lazy, I don't want to work mornings. I hate hav-
ing to get up early just to feed cinnamon rolls to grouchy, half-
awake, old people. I'd rather keep working afternoons and
evenings when all the gorgeous guys drop in on their lunch
breaks. . . . (1992, 510)[9]

In this letter, the author begins by explaining that she is disappointed
that she and the woman to whom she is writing cannot take a drive
into Mexico during their senior year because of the expense. In the
next paragraph she moves to the subject of learning to drive and getting a driver's license. The third paragraph is about the writer's summer job. The letter is held together around the topic "summer"—that
is, all the paragraphs address the issue of what the writer is doing in
the summer. To a reader accustomed to authors who announce the
theme or topic of their writing, such writing appears to be incongru-
ent "lists" of subjects, associatively (implicitly) linked. The author's
"meaning" or "message" must be inferred. It seems very indirect by
traditional standards.

According to Ball, "Narrative interspersion is a pattern, or a sub-
pattern embedded within other patterns, in which the speaker or writer
intersperses a narrative within expository text," but in a manner different from the "use of a narrative as an example or as a kind of evidence in the academically accepted mainstream pattern" (1992, 511). In
this pattern, the African American student blurs the traditional distinctions between narratives used as evidence with narratives that are
themselves the main point. This practice has much in common with the
writing produced by some women students who write with narratives
that themselves carry a significant message that is never announced or
explained. It is another form of indirectness.

In a survey of high school students' preferences for the above organizational forms and traditional academic forms, Ball found that
African American students differed from students of other ethnicities
in their preference for the above narrative forms for academic writing tasks. Rather than seeing these expository writing practices as
"deficient," Ball argues for upgrading African American forms to

viable options alongside more traditional academic forms. As one of the editors of this volume suggested, there is some precedence for viewing circumlocation as a viable option at the national level: the prose of syndicated columnist Andy Rooney.

Like Ball, Orlando L. Taylor and Maryon M. Matsuda (1988) argue that "narrative competence" as defined by American schools has more to do with the ways European and some Asian American schoolchildren tell stories that with the ways children of other cultures do. Because storytelling involves narrative structure, structure that is built on cultural expectations, children must learn from their families how to tell a story. However, the "surface structure" of a story varies from culture to culture. For example, "among Hawaiian and some African cultures, the listener(s) is important in the storytelling so that 'good' storytelling necessarily involves audience participation," whereas "among children of European cultural backgrounds and among Japanese children [the trend] is toward less involvement of [the] listener(s) in the telling of the stories" (1988, 209). Other differences involve the framework of the stories. Citing Michaels, Taylor and Matsuda (1988) distinguish between "topic-centered" and "topic-associated" narratives (also called "literate-strategy narratives" and "oral-strategy narratives"). Children who use a "topic-centered" narrative strategy focus on a single topic; use explicit lexical markers indicating "referential, temporal, and spatial relationships"; have a "high degree of thematic coherence and a clear thematic progression"; finish "with a punch-line sort of resolution, signaled by a markedly lower pitch or falling tone"; and keep their stories "short and concise" (Michaels, qtd. in Taylor and Matsuda 1988, 214). Children who use a "topic-associating" narrative strategy associate narrative fragments "that may seem anecdotal in character, linked implicitly to a particular topical event or theme, but with no explicit statement of an overall theme or point"; shift foci often; leave relationships between foci unexplained; offer no recognizable "end" and thus do not seem to have a point; and seem to go longer and to not be concise (Michaels, qtd. in Taylor and Matsuda 1988, 214). Here is an example:

> I went to the beach Sunday/and to McDonald's/and to the park/and I got this for my birthday/(holds up purse) my mother bought it for me/and I had two dollars for my birthday/and I put it in here/and I went to where my friend/named GiGi/I went over to my grandmother's house with her/and she was on my back/and I/and we was walkin' around my house/and she was HEA:VY//(Michaels and Cazden, qtd. in Taylor and Matsuda 1988, 215)

Not surprisingly, topic-centered narrative strategies have been associated with European American students, whereas topic-associated narrative strategies are associated with African American children (Taylor and Matsuda 1988, 217). In addition, teachers and students respond to topic-associating strategies positively or negatively on the basis of their own cultural background. In one study, European American and African American graduate students at Harvard were presented with the same topic-centered and topic-associating narratives. The European American graduate students commented negatively on the topic-associating narratives, whereas the African American graduate students responded positively to the topic-associating narratives (Taylor and Matsuda 1988, 217). On the basis of the studies they reviewed for their article, Taylor and Matsuda write that

> [T]he argument can be made that many minority children come to the classroom with narrative schema different from those of their teachers. It becomes the teachers' responsibility to be culturally sensitive and to recognize the difference in storytelling style for what it is: a cultural difference and not an error or deficiency. If teachers fail to accept this responsibility, they could be rightfully accused of making minority children the object of discrimination by denying these children equal access to learning. (1988, 218)

There are three very good reasons to reconsider the norms we use when teaching and evaluating academic writing. First, while the majority of essays we see published are written like the essays in this volume (hierarchical, unified, point-driven), a growing number of scholars and professional writers are experimenting with the format of the academic essay in order allow other cultural values to be represented on the page. Second, there are students whose habits of writing and speaking in their home culture do not conform to our expectations. But upon closer inspection, the values upon which these styles are based, e.g., subtlety vs. directness, associative vs. hierarchical thinking, are legitimate and interesting ways of presenting information that could inspire new writing assignments and evaluative practices. Third, when we require all students to write within narrow conceptions of writing, our nontraditional students may miss the opportunity to see their own ways of speaking and writing legitimized. As Taylor and Matsuda (1988) note, if we continue to disqualify these ways with words, we could rightfully be considered discriminatory.

Teaching and Evaluating in the Multicultural Classroom

> Arguments that any currently privileged set of stylistic conventions of academic discourse are inherently better—even that any cur-

rently privileged set of intellectual practices are better for scholarship or for thinking or for arguing or for rooting out self-deception—seem problematic now.

—Peter Elbow (1991, 153)

Research on world culture, women's discourse, and African American students' discourse has influenced some composition teachers and scholars to ask the question that has begun the process of reform: How then, are we to change the teaching and assessment of writing to accommodate cultural differences? The most creative responses to this question occur among some feminists and African Americans who work to create a place for "difference" in the classroom as a political goal. Even theorists such as Judith Butler, who are most opposed to arguments that turn on assumptions of "difference," end their books with a call for institutional practices that "proliferate" differences (1990, 149). In other words, although men are now more likely to avoid experimentation in my classroom, advancing multiple forms of acceptable academic writing may encourage them to experiment with academic writing as well. The objective is to give students a way to merge their home culture and school culture and a place to practice alternative rhetorics. However, to make such a break with traditional views of academic writing, American teachers must model new forms of writing in their classrooms.

While feminist approaches to composition have been a relatively late development in the interdisciplinary feminist movement, they share some of the larger movement's goals: to critique sexism (and, increasingly, racism) and to honor alternative ways of knowing, speaking, and writing. Feminist pedagogies assume that to see the world through the eyes of a person not in power requires education, since all our sanctioned institutions tend to operate through a privileged view of the world. Seeing and hearing difference in positive ways is extremely difficult without special training.

To effect such training, feminist composition experts recommend reorienting assignments to render women's voices audible. Terry Myers Zawacki, in an essay exploring "alternatives to traditional academic discourse [that offer] other ways of knowing and writing about what we know" (1992, 35), suggests that we challenge "the traditional academic hierarchy which privileges expository prose by rejecting the distinction between personal writing and expository writing" (1992, 37). In addition, Zawacki (1992) encourages both women and men students to explore devalued essay forms for the rhetorical opportunities they offer. By presenting students with research on women and men's discourse patterns and upgrading women's patterns to a rhetorical option, such a course offers a way to validate such rhetorical patterns without suggesting to students that "all" women write one way or the other.[10]

In addition to offering students the opportunity to write in different forms, feminist composition experts suggest introducing students to the politics that cause one form of writing to be valued over another. For instance, the contributors to "A Symposium on Feminist Experiences in the Composition Classroom" suggest that students be introduced to literatures such as the ones I briefly describe above and asked to analyze their worlds for evidence of the power of language to inscribe difference (Eichhorn et al. 1992, 317). In particular, Jarrat suggests that students write essays that are grounded in details about the particular social, historical, and material conditions of their lives (Eichhorn et al. 1992, 317), a political act she elaborates elsewhere as a way for women and other disadvantaged groups to resist the dominant narratives of our culture (Jarratt 1991a, 1991b). In all the narratives in the "Symposium," teachers challenge the racism, sexism, and, with less success, classism in their students, creating not a maternal, "safe" environment, but rather one in which students are encouraged to bring their differences to the table. Jarratt argues that the best way for students to see their discursive options is to ask them to analyze and practice a wide range of styles, finally encouraging them to find a "public voice" (1991a, 121).

Feminist and poststructuralist scholars in literary and composition studies are themselves experimenting with alternative forms to the traditional academic essay. In general, their efforts range from the punning and unstructured prose of Victor Vitanza (1987), to the dialogic (personal/academic) prose in Jane Tompkins's (1989) essay. However, perhaps the most far-ranging challenges to traditional forms of writing come not from feminists and poststructuralists, many of whom are themselves European American, but rather from the work of novelists and scholars of color. With their creative, groundbreaking play with language, these scholars—especially those whose identity is self-consciously African American—present the best case for embracing difference. The African American oral traditions embedded in the prose of novelist and anthropologist Zora Neale Hurston ([1938] 1978), for example, provide an excellent example of accomplished experimental writing (Mountford 1996). Joyce Middleton has applied her work on Toni Morrison's prose style to the classroom (1993b), showing how writing students can learn about difference through an analysis of Morrison's fiction (1993a). Geneva Smitherman (1992) employs African American idioms in her academic essays. Consider, for example, these lines from her essay "White English in Blackface, or Who Do I Be?":

> Bin nothin in a long time lit up the English teaching profession like the current hassle over Black English. . . . School bees debating whether: (1) blacks should learn and use only standard white English (hereafter referred to as WE); (2) blacks should command both dialects, i.e., be bidialectal (hereafter BD); (3) blacks should be allowed (??????) to use standard Black English (hereafter BE or BI). The appropriate choice having everything to do with American political reality, which is usually ignored, and nothing to do with the educational process, which is usually claimed. I say without qualification what we cannot talk about the Black Idiom apart from Black Culture and the Black Experience. Nor can we specify educational goals for blacks apart from considerations about the structure of (white) American society.
>
> And we black folks is not gon take all that weight, for no one has empirically demonstrated that linguistic/stylistic features of BE impede educational progress in communication skills, or any other area of cognitive learning. . . . (1992, 101–1)[11]

Gloria Anzaldúa (1987) pushes the envelope even further by incorporating common phrases in Spanish into her creative nonfiction and not translating them into English, implicitly arguing that perhaps we should all consider learning this increasingly common American language.[12]

All these examples point to the possibility of new directions for student writing, writing that may be full of manners of speaking/seeing that represent one's culture/gender—genre-bending, richly narrative, indirect, explorative, suggestive but not explicit, and focused on nontraditional subjects. These new directions for our teaching suggest new directions for large-scale writing assessment.

Implications for Large-scale Writing Assessment

Undoubtedly, the search for instruments capable of assessing—and not discriminating against—nontraditional forms of writing is imperative if schools and universities are to expand narrow definitions of academic writing. The pedagogical work of Smitherman (1992), Jarratt (1991a), Zawacki (1992), and others will be of limited use if students must continue to pass through writing assessment tests that measure only their ability to write traditional, point-driven academic writing.

Within institutional constraints, there are ways to move toward more inclusive large-scale writing assessment procedures. Some procedures delineated in this volume and others to promote fairness and reliability for all students will aid in the prevention of bias. For instance, in timed placement tests, it is imperative that prompts draw on knowledge with which all students, regardless of cultural background or nationality, have had experience. Good prompts will pass what I call the "cultural anthropology" test—that is, they will draw on some aspect of experience that any introductory anthropology textbook suggests all human cultures have in common. Other useful tips for creating good prompts include specifying the purpose and audience, avoiding topics that require high prior knowledge of the dominant culture, and offering clues to guide students in selecting appropriate content and organizational forms (Ruth and Murphy 1988, 236–90). In addition to these general guidelines, I offer the following special procedures for addressing the needs for nontraditional students.

(1) *Develop multimodal assessment procedures that resist "traditional" genre boundaries.* One of the outcomes of the 1987 English Coalition Conference was a call for portfolio assessment of student writing (Lloyd-Jones and Lunsford 1989, 6–7; Elbow 1990, 166–71). Portfolio assessment has the benefit of rewarding students for the whole of their efforts in a course, or, in the case of college placement testing, to reward students for their efforts in several courses. However, portfolio assessment, while allowing for pluralistic standards of "good writing," is only as flexible and inclusive as the administrative procedure which govern it. For instance, at the State University of New York at Stony Brook, the portfolio system used as an achievement test at the end of the first-year composition course asks students to submit three revised essays as well as an in-class piece of writing. The revised pieces include (1) an informal piece of writing ("narrative, descriptive, or expressive") that is derived from the student's experience; (2) an academic essay "organized around a main point"; and (3) an academic essay that analyzes another piece of writing (Elbow and Belanoff 1991, 7). While asking students for all these traditional forms of academic prose is superior to assessing them on the basis of just one essay writing under time restrictions, these essays, as described, do not appear to offer ways to assess nontraditional forms of writing. Even the narrative essay, which, on the surface seems to invite students to write from their own heritage, may be misleading if the evaluators expect the European American storytelling form or the significant ("epic") experience. For instance, African American students, following the storytelling formats described by Taylor and Matsuda (1988), would be rated poorly by European American readers.

However, constructed imaginatively, a portfolio does offer the opportunity to add writing assignments that encourage and reward nontraditional thinking and writing. Letters, journal writing, and explorations of a topic that draw no conclusions could be added to the list of types of writing requested in a portfolio.[13] Instead of looking for unified "points" or a controlling argument, these essays could be evaluated structurally for their subtlety and indirectness, depth of insight, overall interest and understanding of a subject and/or an audience, and the use of details and examples.[14] Since code switching and home dialect are required in letters to some audiences, evaluators should reward students' use of these sociolinguistic markers when they occur. Another category of writing that might be added to the portfolio assessment is experimental writing. Experimental writing might include observations that do not draw conclusions, academic writing interspersed with personal writing (that is, writing that includes two voices), and/or academic prose written playfully or ironically (for instance, an essay imitating and satirizing an especially formal professional language, such as legalese).

(2) *Educate evaluators on the organizational features of some African American and American women's writing.* Throughout this essay I have distinguished between "the traditional academic essay" and "experimental" or "nontraditional writing." Some may argue that, especially in the case of K–12 instruction, students are already encouraged to write in a variety of genres, including autobiographies and other forms of personal writing, and that in some of the best school systems, teachers and administrators encourage such writing and even test for it. However, the research I have presented thus far suggests that indeed, when it comes to the problem/opportunity of teaching and testing for cultural difference, the devil is in the details. Teachers and administrators who broaden the types of writing required of students may still choose to evaluate that writing according to traditional norms. One innovative state recognized this problem and decided to invite twelfth-grade students to write both traditional and nontraditional writing in a statewide assessment. Students wrote eight different kinds of essays, including (1) an autobiographical incident; (2) interpretation of a piece of literature; (3) a reflective essay; and (4) speculation about causes or effects—four essays that involve students in writing from personal experience or reflection. But what is truly innovative about this state's assessment system is the scoring guide (*Writing Assessment Handbook* 1993). The guide asks evaluators to reward highly reflective essays that include "probing and exploring," "implicit" point making or generalizing "embedded in clauses or phrases"; lack of "conclusiveness" about the reflections; and "abrupt shifts of focus . . . warranted by associational leaps of mind." As Matsuda and Taylor (1988) note above, often it is not in the *type* of genre that cultural differences are embraced or erased—rather, is it in the *standards set* for the genre. Scoring guides that specifically credit essays for nontraditional responses send a message that these essays forms must be valued.

In addition to planning for nontraditional responses, assessment planners and/or writing program administrators (WPAs) should train evaluators in recognizing features of student writing associated with some women and African American students. Nontraditional students essays could be mixed into the batch of practice or anchor essays, and the WPA could lead a discussion of how to score this writing. While we tolerate indirect or inexplicit writing in professional writing, we tend not to respond well to such writing in student tests. However, evaluators who are aware of this bias and the existence of other cultural patterns of organization will not equate the use of such patterns with poor writing skills. Instead, such writing should be judged for the presence of detailed and/or colorful examples and strong discussion of the topic (that is, when the writer discusses, but does not seem to address, the topic). Even in evaluation situations in which an assessment prompt includes explicit instructions on the rhetorical situation, students may perceive indirectness as the best way to address the audience. When assessing narrative or autobiographical essays, evaluators should be prompted not to rate topic-centered over topic-associated narratives, and not to prefer "mastery" over "relational" narratives.[15]

(3) *If only one writing sample will be evaluated, avoid assessing students on their ability to write autobiographical essays.* Gender and cultural difference is perhaps nowhere more marked than in the autobiographical or "personal" essay. In articulating a self, persons rely upon cultural assumptions about themselves as gendered, raced, and classed. *Faced with a pile of autobiographic writing, evaluators inevitably find themselves evaluating the writers' cultural values* (Faigley 1989). For an entire summer, one writing program for which I served as a holistic scorer used the following prompt: "We have all had relationships that are important to us. In an essay, tell us about one relationship that was/is important to you." The prompt evoked religious themes, sentimental language, psychological anguish (in the case of those who were lonely or who had broken relationships), confusion (in the case of nonnative speakers who did not have a cultural understanding of the term "relationship"), and ways of viewing self and other that were offensive to me and to the other evaluators, e.g., sexual conquest narratives. Such a topic poses a special problem for gay, lesbian, and bisexual students, who may feel the need to hide their sexual orientation in order to be rated fairly. In general, it is best to follow the advise of Ruth and Murphy, who assert that the test maker cannot assume students have the same view of themselves as the test maker (1988, 260). The worst prompt evoke a wide gulf between how the students see themselves and how the test maker and evaluators see them. The more autobio-

graphically oriented the prompts, the more dangerous the cultural misunderstandings. It is better to ask students to use their personal knowledge and experience to solve a problem or comment on an issue.

(4) *If only one writing sample will be evaluated, prompts should be designed to evoke information available to any person, regardless of cultural background.* All human cultures share some broad traits, including language, ceremony, kinship system (e.g., rules governing family organization), a sense of religion and/or myth, political organization, and systems for production and distribution of goods (Rosman and Rubel 1989). However, even within a nation, there are significant cultural variations in the ways in which these broad categories of life are defined. Some of the worst prompts involve deep cultural knowledge, such as questions that involve a particular national event (e.g., the American public's response to the Vietnam War), a particular national event (e.g., going to the movies or playing in sports), or a particular cultural phenomena (e.g., teenage rebellion). For instance, in my extended family there are individuals who for religious reasons have never seen a movie or played cards. Women and members of some other cultures may be disadvantaged by "mastery" prompts such as the following: "Think of a time you were successful at doing something. Describe what it was you were doing and why you believe you were successful at it." Promoting one's own abilities may be associated more with advantaged groups in societies with a strong sense of individualism. Perhaps the most successful prompts I have seen involve students in writing about how to improve a community in which they have lived. Most human beings have lived in a community, however small, and most are aware of common problems and needs in that place. Another successful prompt I have seen involves students in evaluating a letter or brief essay that is in rough-draft form and offering advice about how the rough draft could be revised. This test offers students a wide variety of ways to respond successfully and rewards them for their overall knowledge of writing, the writing process, and peer-review techniques.

In general, test makers and administrators should maintain procedures that open the assessment of writing to the multiple communities who are served by their tests, but particularly women, African Americans, and other groups who are not well represented in the policy-making circle. Only through good-faith interaction, interaction preceded by multicultural education, can evaluation procedures become responsive to cultural and gender difference. However, a more important initiative—prior to the development of writing assessment procedures—

is to invite *all* our students to write within the varieties of genres that count for academic writing, from the subtle, Latino argument, to the multivocal, feminist experimental essay. Through inviting students to consider writing from many styles and cultural perspectives, many will see themselves invited to the table for the first time.

Looking Forward

Changing standards of evaluation is not an easy task. As I work with teaching assistants, composition boards of other colleges and high schools, and my own stubborn sense of what counts as "good writing," I am surprised at how difficult it is to broaden norms that have been part of our shared professionalization. As one of my teaching assistants put it recently, "But it is so easy to look for a thesis sentence!" Yes, it is easier than identifying what works in a multivocal student essay. Therefore, I am convinced that to embrace other standards of evaluation we must work for a different kind of professionalization. In the Prologue to *What Makes Writing Good?* William Coles says of a particularly wonderful student essay, "Try putting that paper . . . in one your prose analyzing machines!" (1985, v). That sense of finding what is wonderful in student writing needs to happen again and again, from one cultural perspective to another, from one style to another, so that we have in front of us the variety of ways that writing can be good. From this practice, and from the publication of experimental writing that particularly wow us, I believe we can begin to offer new standards that can make our large-scale writing assessment more inclusive.

As we learn to articulate what is good about, say, an essay written like the excerpt of Geneva Smitherman's above, we will, no doubt, encounter public opposition. Several years ago an old friend of mine from the Bay Area exclaimed in horror, "Our public schools are letting black kids write in street slang!" At the time, I responded with something inane like, "What do *you* know about teaching writing?" But recently, on an airplane, an anxious parent asked me if her child's teacher should be sending her child's stories home with misspelled words. This time I was thrilled to learn that her child's teacher knew what he was doing. Our challenge is to articulate to ourselves and to the public the relationship between standards and error, good writing and bad, in a way that disrupts these binaries and makes a place for cultural difference and experimentation in writing.[16] What counts as "bad writing" in a narrative written in the topic-associated style? What counts as "error" in an essay partially written in Black English Vernacular or Chicano Spanish? I am hopeful that as a field we will find persuasive answers to questions such as these and successful ways to articulate them to the public.

Notes

1. I am grateful to the editors and to Randi Browning, Diane Davis, and Tom Miller for helpful readings of this essay and to Lillian Bridwell-Bowles and Gary Tate for their support and encouragement.

2. The composition textbook she is publishing and the textbook proposals she is receiving include alternative writing assignments only at the prewriting level.

3. See Ramage and Bean (1995), for instance, who write: "When rebutting or refuting an argument, you attempt to convince your readers that an opposing view is logically flawed, erroneously supported, or in some other way much weaker that the opponent claims" (171). Among other advice, they offer seven ways to find weakness in an opponent's use of evidence.

4. For futher reading on international intercultural communication, see Hall and Hall (1987, 1990) and the *International Journal of Intercultural Relations*.

5. Charles Cooper asked me why we don't find examples of this kind of writing in Heath's own work. Perhaps the answer lies in Brodkey's statement: "One of the pleasures of writing that academics rarely give themselves is permission to experiment" (1994, 527). As more writers experiment, perhaps Heath and others will allow themselves the pleasures they would give their students.

6. In other words, women and men are equally capable of writing in the way a teacher requires. It is not a question of ability. For instance, Hillocks, reviewing the literature on syntactic structure among "American white children," concludes that "at least in syntactic development, boys and girls are more or less even or, if not, they become even" (1986, 71). Ardener (1978), Elshtain (1981), and Gal (1991) suggest that women may speak and write publicly one way (e.g., for the classroom or the boardroom, the newspaper or the academic journal) and privately another. Elshtain (1981) suggests that unfortunately, women, like men, are trained in school to dismiss the private in favor of the public, so that they may not value their own ways of speaking and writing to each other. For an insightful study (sponsored by the American Association of University Women) on the difficulties of overcoming this "hidden curriculum," see Peggy Orenstein (1994).

7. See Kris Ratcliffe's book *Anglo-American Feminist Challenges to the Rhetorical Traditions* (1996) for a full treatment of feminists' contributions to new rhetorical traditions.

8. One of these experimental essays was recently published in a major journal (Cushman 1996), a sign that experimental writing is becoming an acceptable form of academic prose.

9. Some may argue that letters and e-mail always tend toward a loose organizational style. However, while Ball (1992) uses a letter as an example here, she is suggesting that the circumlocution it illustrates is used by some African American students in essays and other writing tasks as well.

10.   See also Don J. Kraemer, Jr. (1992). In his composition course, Kraemer presents research on women and men's discourse patterns and then asks students to analyze their won personal essays, written earlier in the course, for evidence of these patterns. Kraemer reports that both the personal essays and students' analyses of them offered opportunities for students to examine why their "representation of conventional acts" tended to be gendered.

11.   I have presented this essay to my composition students to give them the sense of the politics behind favoring European American over African American speaking and writing.

12.   In an experimental paper for my class, Donna Phillips (1996) writes, "In reading Latina writers, I think I have discovered another [reason to write experimentally]. Experimental writing is also a way to make *personal* knowledge *external*, reclaiming the place of the story, restoring I/you/we amid the intellectualizing and depersonalizing that tend to accompany traditional academic writing. And perhaps is it nowhere more needed than in our (as in think-we're-in-the-majority people) efforts to fathom those who Gloria Anzaldúa calls Other. Here, if anywhere, is needed another kind of knowing, another kind of speaking, one that attempts to capture the thoughts, the feelings, the conversation that has been so long in coming."

13.   Although SUNY–Stony Brook adapted a more limited vision of the portfolio, Elbow (1990) has suggested "a placement test that builds in not just exploratory writing but also sharing drafts with peers and revising or a proficiency exam that helps students think about genre and audience by having them write . . . a letter, a story, and an essay all about the same material" (1990, 171).

14.   Evaluators should keep in mind that authentic letters often involve shared knowledge unavailable to other readers and thus less-apparent detail. Students should be alerted to the need for detail—if evaluators want the letters to be understood by more than one audience—in the directions for compiling their portfolio.

15.   "Mastery" narratives are narratives in which students describe how they triumphed over adversity or attained a significant goal. "Relational" narratives are those narratives in which students make the point of the story their relationship with others or their experiences within a group.

16.   As this essay goes to press, some teachers and scholars have begun to respond to the "ebonics" controversy in Oakland, California, mentioned earlier in this essay. See Barton (1996) for an especially good article that includes interviews with scholars in rhetoric and composition, linguistics, and literary theory, and Baron (1997) for an op-ed piece by a linguist.

Works Cited

Alcoff, Linda. 1988. "Cultural Feminism versus Poststructuralism: The Identity Crisis in Feminist Theory." *Signs: Journal of Women in Culture and Society* 13: 405–36.

Anson, Chris M., and Robert L. Brown, Jr. 1991. "Large-Scale Portfolio Assessment: Ideological Sensitivity and Institutional Change." In *Portfolio: Process and Product*, ed. Pat Belanoff and Marcia Dickson, 248–69. Porstmouth, NH: Boynton/Cook.

Anzaldúa, Gloria. 1987. *Borderlands/LaFrontera: The New Mestiza*. San Francisco: Aunt Lute.

Ardener, Edward. 1978. "Belief and the Problem of Women." In *Perceiving Women*, ed. Shirley Ardener, 3–21. New York: Halstad Press.

Ball, Arnetha F. 1992. "Cultural Preference and the Expository Writing of African-American Adolescents." *Written Communication* 9: 501–32.

Baron, Dennis. 1997. "Ebonics Is Not a Panacea for Students at Risk." *Chronicle of Higher Education* (Jan. 24): B4–5.

Bartholomae, David. 1987. "Writing on the Margins: The Concept of Literacy in Higher Education." In *A Sourcebook for Basic Writing Teachers*, ed. Theresa Enos, 66–83. New York: Random House.

———. 1993. "The Tidy House: Basic Writing in the American Curriculum." *Journal of Basic Writing* 12: 4–21.

Barton, David. 1996. "A World of Words." *The Sacramento Bee* (25 Dec.): 1C+.

Belenky, Mary Field, Blythe McVicker Clinchy, Nancy Rule Goldberger, and Jill Mattuck Tarule. 1986. *Women's Ways of Knowing: The Development of Self, Voice, and Mind*. New York: Basic Books.

Bishop, Wendy. 1995. "If Weathers, Winston Would Just Write To Me On E-Mail." *College Composition and Communication* 46: 97–103.

Bridwell-Bowles, Lillian. 1992. "Discourse and Diversity: Experimental Writing within the Academy." *College Composition and Communication* 43: 349–68.

———. 1995 "Freedom, Form, Function: Varieties of Academic Discourse." *College Composition and Communication* 46: 46–61.

Brodkey, Linda. 1994. "Writing on the Bias." *College English* 56: 527–47.

Butler, Judith. 1990. *Gender Trouble: Feminism and the Subversion of Identity*. New York: Routledge.

Campbell, Kermit. 1992. "Towards a Definition of Black English Vernacular Rhetoric." In *Rhetoric in the Vortex of Cultural Studies: Proceedings of the Fifth Biennial Conference*, ed. Arthur Walzer and Laurie Ward Gardner, 93–101. St. Paul: Rhetoric Society of America.

Coles, William. 1985. "Prologue." *What Makes Writing Good?: A Multiperspective*, v–vi. Lexington, MA: Heath.

Cushman, Ellen. 1996. "Rhetorician as Agent of Social Change." *College Composition and Communication* 47: 7–28.

de Lauretis, Teresa. 1990. "Upping the Anti (sic) in Feminist Theory." In *Conflicts in Academic Feminism*, ed. Marianne Hirsch and Evelyn Fox Keller, 255–70. New York: Routledge.

Dixon, Kathleen. 1995. "Gendering the 'Personal.'" *College Composition and Communication* 46: 255–75.

Eichhorn, Jill, Sara Farris, Karen Hayes, Adriana Hernández, Susan C. Jarratt, Karen Powers-Stubbs, and Marian M. Sciachitano. 1992. "A Symposium on Feminist Experiences in the Composition Classroom." *College Composition and Communication* 43: 297–321.

Elbow, Peter. 1990. *What Is English?* New York: Modern Language Association of America.

———. 1991. "Reflections on Academic Discourse: How It Relates to Freshmen and Colleagues." *College English* 53: 135–55.

Elbow, Peter, and Pat Belanoff. 1991. "State University of New York at Stony Brook Portfolio-based Evaluation Program." In *Portfolios: Process and Product*, ed. Pat Belanoff and Marcia Dickson, 3–16. Porstmouth, NH: Boynton/Cook.

Elshtain, Jean Bethke. 1981. *Public Man, Private Woman: Women in Social and Political Thought.* Prinston, NJ: Princeton University Press.

Faigley, Lester. 1989. "Judging Writing, Judging Selves." *College Composition and Communication* 40: 395–412.

Farr, Marcia, and Harvey Daniels. 1986. *Language Diversity and Writing Instruction.* New York: ERIC Clearinghouse on Urban Education.

Flynn, Elizabeth A. 1988. "Composing as a Woman." *College Composition and Communication* 39: 423–35.

Foucault, Michel. 1972. *The Archaeology of Knowledge and the Discourse on Language.* New York: Pantheon Books.

Frey, Olivia. 1990. "Beyond Literary Darwinism: Women's Voices and Critical Discourse." *College English* 52: 507–26.

Fuss, Diana. 1989. *Essentially Speaking: Feminism, Nature and Difference.* New York: Routledge.

Gal, Susan. 1991. "Between Speech and Silence: The Problematics of Research on Language and Gender." In *Gender at the Crossroads of Knowledge: Anthropology in the Postmodern Era*, ed. Micaela di Leonardo, 175–203. Berkely: University of California Press.

Gannett, Cinthia. 1992. *Gender and the Journal: Diaries and Academic Discourse.* Albany: State University of New York Press.

Gates, Henry Louis, Jr. 1988. *The Signifying Monkey: A Theory of Afro-American Literary Criticism.* New York: Oxford University Press.

Gilligan, Carol. 1982. *In a Different Voice: Psychological Theory and Women's Development.* Cambridge, MA: Harvard University Press.

Graves, Heather Brodie. 1993. "Regrinding the Lens of Gender: Problematizing 'Writing as a Woman.'" *Written Communication* 10: 139–63.

Hall, Edward T., and Mildred Reed Hall. 1987. *Hidden Differences.* Garden City, NY: Doubleday/Anchor.

———. 1990. *Understanding Cultural Differences.* Yarmouth, ME: Intercultural Press.

Haswell, Janis, and Richard H. Haswell. 1995. "Gendership and the Miswriting of Students." *College Composition and Communication* 46: 223–54.

Heath, Shirley Brice. 1993. "Rethinking the Sense of the Past: The Essay as Legacy of the Epigram. In *Theory and Practice in the Teaching of Writing: Rethinking the Discipline*, ed. Lee Odell, 105–31. Carbondale: Southern Illinois University Press.

Herskovits, Melville J. [1941] 1990. *The Myth of the Negro Past.* Boston: Beacon.

hooks, bell. 1992. *Blacks Looks: Race and Representation.* Boston: South End Press.

Hurston, Zora Neale. [1938] 1978. *Mules and Men.* Bloomington: Indiana University Press.

Jarratt, Susan C. 1991a. "Feminism and Composition: A Case for Conflict." In *Contending with Words: Composition and Rhetoric in a Postmodern Age*, ed. Patricia Harkin and John Schilb, 105–23. New York: Modern Language Association of America.

————. 1991b. *Rereading the Sophists: Classical Rhetoric Refigured.* Carbondale: Southern Illinois University Press.

Kant de Lima, Roberto. 1992. "The Anthropology of the Academy: When We Are the Indians." In *The Anthropology of Science and Technology Studies,* Knowledge and Society, Vol. 9, ed. David J. Hess and Linda L. Layne, 191–222. Greenwich, CT: JAI.

Kraemer, Don J. Jr. 1992. "Gender and the Autobiographical Essay: A Critical Extension of the Research." *College Composition and Communication* 43: 323–39.

Landes, Ruth. 1947. *The City of Women.* New York: Macmillan.

Lloyd-Jones, Richard, and Andrea A. Lunsford, eds. 1989. *The English Coalition Conference: Democracy through Language.* Urbana, IL: The National Council of Teachers of English.

MacDonald, Susan. 1994. *Professional Academic Writing in the Humanities and Social Sciences.* Carbondale: Southern Illinois University Press.

Middleton, Joyce Irene. 1993a. "Orality, Literacy, and Memory in Morrison's *Song of Solomon.*" *College English* 55: 64–75.

————. 1993b. Address given at the Annual Convention of the Conference on College Composition and Communication. San Diego, CA. 31 March.

Mountford, Roxanne D. 1996. "Engendering Ethnography: Insights from the Feminist Critique of Postmodern Anthropology." In *Ethics and Representation in Qualitative Studies of Literacy,* ed. Peter Mortensen and Gesa E. Kirsch, 205–27. Urbana, IL: National Council of Teachers of English.

Ohmann, Richard. 1992/3. "On PC and Related Matters." *The Minnesota Review* 39: 55–62.

Orenstein, Peggy. 1994. *School Girls: Young Women, Self-Esteem, and the Confidence Gap.* New York: Doubleday.

Parsons, Elsie Clews. 1923. *Folk-Lore of the Sea Islands, South Carolina.* Cambridge, MA: The American Folk-Lore Society.

Patterson, Orlando. 1987. "Language, Ethnicity, and Change. In *A Sourcebook for Basic Writing Teachers,* ed. Theresa Enos, 148–57. New York: Random House.

Penrose, Ann M., and Cheryl Geisler. 1994. "Reading and Writing without Authority." *College Composition and Communication* 45: 505–20.

Philips, Donna. 1996. "*Compañeras o desconocidas*/Companions or Strangers: An Experimental Encounter with Latina Writers." Unpublished manuscript. Rensselaer Polytechnic Institute, Spring 1996.

Ramage, John D., and John C. Bean. 1995. *Writing Arguments: A Rhetoric with Readings.* 3rd ed. Boston: Allyn & Bacon.

Ratcliffe, Krista. 1996. *Anglo-American Feminist Challenges to the Rhetorical Traditions: Virginia Woolf, Mary Daly, Adrienne Rich.* Carbondale: Southern Illinois University Press.

Rosman, Abraham, and Paula G. Rubel. 1989. *The Tapestry of Culture: An Introduction to Cultural Anthropology.* 3rd ed. New York: Random House.

Rubin, Donald L., and Kathryn Greene. 1992. "Gender-Typical Style in Written Communication." *Research in the Teaching of English* 26: 7–40.

Ruth, Leo, and Sandra Murphy. 1988. *Designing Writing Tasks for the Assessment of Writing.* Norwood, NJ: Ablex.

Saville-Troike, Muriel, and Donna M. Johnson. 1994. "Comparative Rhetoric: An Integration of Perspectives." *Pragmatics and Language Learning Monograph Series* 5: 231–46.

Smitherman, Geneva. 1992. "White English in Blackface, or Who Do I Be?" 1973. In *Exploring Language,* 6th ed., ed. Gary Goshgarian, 100–9. New York: HarperCollins.

Smitherman-Donaldson, Geneva. 1988. "Discriminatory Discourse on Afro-American Speech." In *Discourse and Discrimination,* ed. Geneva Smitherman-Donaldson and Teun A. van Dijk, 144–75. Detroit: Wayne State University Press.

Tannen, Deborah. 1990. *You Just Don't Understand: Women and Men in Conversation.* New York: Morrow.

Taylor, Orlando L., and Maryon M. Matsuda. 1988. "Storytelling and Classroom Discrimination." In *Discourse and Discrimination,* ed. Geneva Smitherman-Donaldson and Teun A. van Dijk, 206–20. Detroit: Wayne State University Press.

Tobin, Lad. 1996. "Car Wrecks, Baseball Caps, and Man-to-Man Defense: The Personal Narratives of Adolescent Males." *College English* 58: 158–75.

Tompkins, Jane. 1989. "Me and My Shadow." In *Gender and Theory: Dialogues on Feminist Criticism,* ed. Linda Kauffman, 121–39. New York: Blackwell.

Vitanza, Victor. 1987. "Critical Sub/Versions of the History of Philosophical Rhetoric." *Rhetoric Review* 6: 41–61.

Wall, Susan, and Nicholas Coles. 1991. "Reading Basic Writing: Alternatives to a Pedagogy of Accommodation." In *The Politics of Writing Instruction: Postsecondary,* ed. Richard Bullock and John Trimbur, 227–46. Portsmouth, NH: Boynton/Cook.

Writing Assessment Handbook: High School. 1993. Sacramento: California Department of Education.

Yaeger, Patricia. 1988. *Honey-Mad Women: Emancipatory Strategies in Women's Writing.* New York: Columbia University Press.

Zawacki, Terry Myers. 1992. "Recomposing as a Woman—An Essay in Different Voices." *College English* 43: 32–38.

Index

Editors

Charles R. Cooper began his career as a high school English teacher and is now professor emeritus in the Department of Literature, University of California–San Diego. Long active in NCTE, he has been a member of the Editorial Board and chaired the Committee on Research. His numerous publications include *Evaluating Writing: Describing, Measuring, Judging* and *Research on Composing* (both with Lee Odell), *Researching Response to Literature and the Teaching of Literature*, and *Studying Writing: Linguistic Approaches* (with Sidney Greenbaum), as well as two current textbooks, *The St. Martin's Guide to Writing* (with Rise Axelrod and *Writing the World* (with Susan Peck MacDonald).

Lee Odell is professor of composition theory and research at Rensselaer Polytechnic Institute. His current research interests include visual communication and the redefinition of literacy in ways that connect the literacy practices of inexperienced readers and writers with those of highly competent, sophisticated adults. For the past ten years, he has worked with teachers in grades K–12, helping to develop an approach to writing across the curriculum and, more recently, to establish a program that involves students from all disciplines in writing for communities outside their classrooms.

Contributors

Chris M. Anson is professor of English and director of composition at the University of Minnesota. His publications include *Writing in Context; Writing and Response: Theory, Practice, and Research; A Field Guide to Writing; Writing Across the Curriculum; Scenarios for Teaching Writing: Contexts for Discussion and Reflective Practice;* and *Using Journals in the Classroom: Writing to Learn.* His articles have appeared in numerous journals and edited collections. His research interests include writing-to-learn, response to writing, and the nature of literacy both within and outside of schools.

Arnetha F. Ball is assistant professor of education in the Language, Literacy, and Learning program of the School of Education at the University of Michigan. Her research focuses on an interdisciplinary investigation of oral and written literacies, particularly as they relate to culturally and linguistically diverse populations. Her program of research focuses on linking sociocultural and linguistic theory concerning the oral and written literacy patterns of marginalized, vernacular English speakers and the educational practices of teachers in urban and inner-city schools, community-based organizations, and cross-national contexts, both in the United States and South Africa.

Richard W. Beach is professor of English education at the University of Minnesota, where he teaches English education methods courses. His research interests include the areas of response to literature/media and reading/writing connections. His publications include *A Teacher's Introduction to Reader-Response Theories, Teaching Literature in the Secondary School* (with James Marshall), and *Journals in the Classroom: Writing to Learning.* He is the former president of the National Conference on Research in Language and Literacy.

Guanjun Cai, an Advisory Software Engineer at IBM, received his Ph.D. in rhetoric, composition, and the teaching of English at the University of Arizona, where he taught first-year composition, basic writing, advanced composition, and technical writing. He also taught English as a foreign language in China. He co-edited *A Student's Guide to First-Year Composition* and contributed to *Encyclopedia of Rhetoric and Composition, Keywords in Composition Studies,* and *Theorizing Composition: A Critical Sourcebook of Theory and Scholarship in Contemporary Composition Studies.* His dissertation studied what functions as rhetorical in the Chinese context and critiqued the theories of (Western) rhetoric, comparative rhetoric, and ESL writing.

Fran Claggett, an educational consultant for schools and districts nationwide, taught high school and college English and humanities for many years. She is a consultant to New Standards as well as a former director of the California teacher-assessment team. As department chair and mentor teacher at Alameda High School, she initiated and implemented a districtwide writing achievement and portfolio assessment program for the Alameda schools. She has also been a teacher-consultant to the Bay Area Writing Project for twenty years. Her publications include *Drawing Your Own Conclusions: Graphic Strategies for Reading, Writing, and Thinking; A Measure of Success: From Assignments to Assessment in English Language Arts; Daybooks of Critical Reading and Writing,* grades 6 through 12 (co-authored with Louann Reid and Ruth Vinz); and a book of poems, *Black Birds and Other Birds;* among others.

Martha Kolln recently retired as associate professor of English at Pennsylvania State University, where she taught composition, editing, and grammar for twenty-five years. Her publications include the textbooks *Understanding English Grammar* (4th ed.), widely used for classes in modern grammar, and *Rhetorical Grammar: Grammatical Choices,* which integrates grammar into the writing process. She is a founding member and president of NCTE's Assembly for the Teaching of Grammar, which is dedicated to reestablishing the study of language structure as part of the language arts.

Elizabeth Vander Lei received her Ph.D. from Arizona State University, where she taught first-year composition courses for both native-English speakers and ESL students and writing teacher training courses. Her dissertation investigated the intermediate audiences that influence academic writers in first-year composition. She has presented several papers on audience as well as ESL composition.

Denise Stavis Levine has taught at the elementary and middle school levels as well as the graduate level. Currently, she is an associate at the Institute for Learning at the University of Pittsburgh, where she spends six weeks a year working on ways to bring standards-based education to schools in Community School District Two in New York. She is a frequent presenter at national and international conferences and, when not reading cheap novels, loves writing about teaching and learning.

Kathleen Medina is a high school teacher credentialed in English and history. She is currently serving as director of the Area 3 History and Cultures Project, a professional development project for teachers, located on the Davis campus of the University of California, and one of the ten sites of the California History-Social Science Project, and ultimately, of the California Subject Matter Projects.

Richard S. Millman has taught mathematics (including a course about writing in mathematics) or electrical engineering at Southern Illinois University, Michigan Technological University, Wright State University, the University of Maryland, and California State University–San Marcos. He was program director in geometry at the National Science Foundation and is currently provost and dean of faculty at Whittier College. He has co-authored three books (about Euclidean geometry, differential geometry, and calculus) as well as co-editing others, and has published numerous articles in the areas of geometry and mathematics education.

Roxanne Mountford is assistant professor of rhetoric, composition, and the teaching of English at the University of Arizona, where she teaches courses in writing, contemporary rhetorical theory, and research methods. She has written numerous essays and chapters on teaching writing and rhetorical theory through an ethnographic perspective; her work has appeared in *Rhetoric Review* and *Journal of Advanced Composition*, among others. The focus of her own ethnographic and textual studies is feminist rhetoric within the context of professional discourse.

Sandra Murphy is professor and director of the Center for Cooperative Research and Extension Services for Schools (CRESS) in the Division of Education at the University of California–Davis, where she teaches graduate-level courses on the teaching of reading and writing. Formerly, she has taught high school English and freshman composition. Her publications include *Designing Writing Tasks for the Assessment of Writing* (with Leo Ruth) and *Writing Portfolios: A Bridge from Teaching to Assessment* (with Mary Ann Smith), as well as several articles on the acquisition of literacy and the assessment of writing.

Duane H. Roen is professor of English at Arizona State University, where he directs and teaches in the composition program as well as teaching courses in discourse analysis, linguistics, literature for young adults, and writing across the curriculum, among others. His research interests include gender and written language, collaboration, audience, and WAC. He has published three books—*A Sense of Audience in Written Communication* (with Gesa Kirsch), *Richness in Writing: Empowering ESL Students* (with Donna M. Johnson), and *Becoming Expert: Writing and Thinking in the Disciplines* (with Stuart Brown and Robert Mittan)—and has authored numerous book chapters, articles, and conference papers.

Phyllis Mentzell Ryder is a doctoral student in rhetoric and composition and the teaching of English at the University of Arizona, where

she has served as a graduate assistant to the director of the composition program. She has taught writing at community colleges in
Baltimore and Tucson, and for the past nine summers has taught
high school students at Johns Hopkins University's Center for
Talented Youth, where she served as the program's academic dean in
1994. Her research interests include critical composition pedagogy,
collaborative learning, and audience analysis. She has co-edited a
composition textbook—*A Student's Guide to First-Year Composition*—
and published or presented papers on gender and composition pedagogy as well as feminist rereadings of classical rhetoric.

Patricia Anloff Sanders teaches at Jane Lathrop Stanford Middle
School in Palo Alto, California. A teacher for thirty-six years, she has
taught primarily English and ESL at the elementary, middle school,
and adult school levels and has had everything from suckling babies
to eighty-year-old men in her classes. She is active in both local and
national professional organizations as well as in community activities and has been a frequent presenter at both CATE and CATESOL.

Mary Ann Smith is executive director of the California Writing
Project and co-director of the National Writing Project. She is co-
author (with Sandra Murphy) of *Writing Portfolios: A Bridge from
Teaching to Assessment* and co-editor (with Miriam Ylvisaker) of
Teachers' Voices: Portfolios in the Classroom. Her own writing portfolio is heavily weighted toward professional writing, which suggests that she should take her own advice and diversify.

William Strong directs the Utah Writing Project at Utah State
University, where he chairs the Department of Secondary
Education and teaches courses in English education. He has
received awards for excellence in teaching and has been honored
by the Utah Council of Teachers of English for service to the state.
His most recent publications include *Sentence Combining: A
Composing Book* (3rd ed.); *Rhythm, Rhyme, and Rap: Developmental
Sentence-Combining Exercises;* and *Writer's Toolbox: A Sentence-
Combining Workshop.* He is a frequent presenter at NCTE confer-
ences and at sites of the National Writing Project.

Guadalupe Valdés is professor of education and professor of Spanish
and Portugese at Stanford University. She works in the areas of
applied linguistics and sociolinguistics and focuses on how two languages are acquired, used, and maintained by individuals who
become bilingual in immigrant communities.

This book was set in Palatino and Helvetica by City Desktop Productions, Inc.
The typefaces used on the cover were Trajan and Gill Sans.
The book was printed on 60-lb. Starbright Opaque offset
by Versa Press, Inc., East Peoria, Illinois.